SEAFARING AND MOBILITY IN THE LATE ANTIQUE MEDITERRANEAN

SEAFARING AND MOBILITY IN THE LATE ANTIQUE MEDITERRANEAN

Edited by Antti Lampinen and Emilia Mataix Ferrándiz

BLOOMSBURY ACADEMIC
LONDON • NEW YORK • OXFORD • NEW DELHI • SYDNEY

BLOOMSBURY ACADEMIC
Bloomsbury Publishing Plc
50 Bedford Square, London, WC1B 3DP, UK
1385 Broadway, New York, NY 10018, USA
29 Earlsfort Terrace, Dublin 2, Ireland

BLOOMSBURY, BLOOMSBURY ACADEMIC and the Diana logo are
trademarks of Bloomsbury Publishing Plc

First published in Great Britain 2022
Paperback edition published 2024

Copyright © Antti Lampinen, Emilia Mataix Ferrándiz & Contributors, 2022

Antti Lampinen and Emilia Mataix Ferrándiz have asserted their right under the Copyright,
Designs and Patents Act, 1988, to be identified as Editors of this work.

For legal purposes the Acknowledgements on p. xiv constitute an extension of
this copyright page.

Cover design: Terry Woodley
Cover image © The sunken city of Kekova in the Bay of Uchagiz in Antalya province
of Turkey. Saida Nabiyeva / Alamy Stock Photo

All rights reserved. No part of this publication may be reproduced or transmitted
in any form or by any means, electronic or mechanical, including photocopying,
recording, or any information storage or retrieval system, without prior
permission in writing from the publishers.

Bloomsbury Publishing Plc does not have any control over, or responsibility for,
any third-party websites referred to or in this book. All internet addresses given in
this book were correct at the time of going to press. The author and publisher
regret any inconvenience caused if addresses have changed or sites have
ceased to exist, but can accept no responsibility for any such changes.

A catalogue record for this book is available from the British Library.

Library of Congress Cataloging-in-Publication Data

Names: Lampinen, Antti, editor. | Mataix Ferrándiz, Emilia, editor.
Title: Seafaring and mobility in the late antique Mediterranean /
Antti Lampinen, Emilia Mataix Ferrándiz.
Description: New York : Bloomsbury Academic, [2022] | Series: Ancient Environments
Identifiers: LCCN 2022004110 | ISBN 9781350201705 (Hardback) |
ISBN 9781350201743 (Paperback) | ISBN 9781350201712 (eBook) |
ISBN 9781350201729 (epub) | ISBN 9781350201736
Subjects: LCSH: Navigation–Mediterranean Region–History–To 1500. |
Seafaring life–Mediterranean Region–History–To 1500. |
Shipping–Mediterranean Region–History–To 1500. |
Mediterranean Sea–Navigation–History–To 1500. | Naval history, Ancient.
Classification: LCC VK55 .S43 2022 | DDC 387.509163/8—dc23/eng/20220504
LC record available at https://lccn.loc.gov/2022004110

ISBN: HB: 978-1-3502-0170-5
PB: 978-1-3502-0174-3
ePDF: 978-1-3502-0171-2
eBook: 978-1-3502-0172-9

Series: Ancient Environments

Typeset by RefineCatch Limited, Bungay, Suffolk

To find out more about our authors and books visit www.bloomsbury.com
and sign up for our newsletters.

Dedicated to the memory of Simon Keay

CONTENTS

List of Illustrations   ix
List of Abbreviations   xi
Notes on Contributors   xiii
Series Preface   xv
Acknowledgements   xvii
Note on Translations   xviii

Introduction: Approaches to the Later Imperial Mediterranean as an Environment *Emilia Mataix Ferrándiz and Antti Lampinen*   1

Part I Imagination and Domination: The Mediterranean as a Conceptual Environment

1 Knights, Kings and Dragons: The Symbolic Conquest of the Mediterranean Sea in Late Antiquity and Its Historical Background *Joanna Töyräänvuori*   13

2 Migrating Mosaics: Transforming Images of Oceanus and Marine Environments from the Imperial Period to Late Antiquity *Alexandra Grigorieva*   26

3 Mediterranean as a Contested Environment in Late Antiquity *Antti Lampinen*   49

Part II A Networked Environment

4 Connecting People in the Mediterranean: Mobility and Migration in Ostia and Portus *Arja Karivieri*   71

5 . . . διά νήσων πλέειν . . . Taking the Island Route: Trade and Exchange Along the Coast of Southern Naxos *Hallvard R. Indgjerd* 88

6 'Stepping across thresholds': Islands as Resilient Spaces of Connectivity in the Passage from Late Antiquity to the Early Middle Ages (c. 500–c. 700) *Luca Zavagno and Zeynep Olgun*   114

Part III Braving the Sea in the Later Empire

7 'Washed by the Waves': Fighting against Shipwrecking in the Later Roman Empire *Emilia Mataix Ferrándiz*   133

Contents

8	Upwind Sailing Capabilities of Square-Rigged Ships in Late Antiquity and the Ramifications for Trade Networks *Doug Forsyth*	149
9	On the Byzantine Tradition of *D.* 14.2.9 (Maec. *Ex Lege Rhodia*): A Note Concerning the Emperor as Ruler of the Sea *Valerio Massimo Minale*	167

Bibliography 181
Index 209

ILLUSTRATIONS

1.1	Cylinder seal impression of the theriomorphic Mediterranean Sea (left)	17
2.1	A second-century mosaic still-life with a realistic looking moray. Antiquarium of Ostia (Italy). Here and throughout the article drawings are by Lisa Plavinsky	28
2.2	A late third- or early fourth-century mosaic of Oceanus. Bardo National Museum (Tunisia)	30
2.3	A first-half-of-the-sixth-century Constantinople mosaic. Great Palace Mosaic Museum (Turkey)	32
2.4	An end of the second–early third-century mosaic of Oceanus (detail). The National Roman Museum, Palazzo Massimo alle Terme (Italy)	33
2.5	A second–third century mosaic of Oceanus. Antakya/Hatay Archaeological Museum (Turkey)	34
2.6	A 160–90 CE mosaic of Oceanus (possibly conflated with Celtic Cernunnos). Verulamium Museum (St Albans, UK)	34
2.7	A 234 CE mosaic of Oceanus (possibly conflated with Celtic Cernunnos). Bad Kreuznach, Germany (in situ)	35
2.8	A fourth-century mosaic of Oceanus. Eugène-Camoreyt Museum (Lectoure, France)	37
2.9	A mid-second-century mosaic of Oceanus with a moray. Sousse Archaeological Museum (Tunisia)	38
2.10	A 234 CE mosaic of Oceanus, marine fauna (detail). Bad Kreuznach, Germany (in situ)	39
2.11	A badly damaged end-of-the-second-century mosaic of a giant Oceanus mask. Found in Bad Vilbel, a reconstructed copy in situ. The original is in Hessisches Landesmuseum Darmstadt (Germany)	40
2.12	A late fifth–early sixth-century mosaic of baptism of Christ. The Arian Baptistery (Ravenna, Italy)	43
5.1	Survey projects included in the South-East Naxos Survey	89
5.2	Ad-hoc wooden structures used to ease the access to a sand beach on Kato Kouphonisi with the help of a few boulders fallen from the escarpment behind and the limestone rocks at the foot of Dhaskalio	91
5.3	Grammata Bay, Syros. Euploia by Eunomios, identifying as a Jewish sailor from Naxos (possibly first century BCE) and a fourth–fifth century Christian invocation by Eulimenios from Ephesus (Photo: Rebecca Sweetman.)	93

Illustrations

5.4	Aerial view of Panormos Bay and Irokastro and Aerial orthophoto of the ballast piles in shallow water in the bay of Panormos	94
5.5	Dressel 2-4 similis amphorae on the sea floor at Panormos reef	97
5.6	Travel time to reach Naxos in summer, based on ORBIS (http://orbis.stanford.edu)	103
5.7	Graphic rendition of the route descriptions in the *Stadiasmus of the Great Sea* for the South Aegean. Dark showing through routes, grey links to Delos	104
8.1	Wind Roses for April, July, and October. Used with permission of Rod Heikell, *Mediterranean Cruising Handbook*, Imray, pp. 110–11	151
8.2	Close hauled and close reach sailing angles	156
8.3	Diagram of sailing angles relative to wind direction	157

ABBREVIATIONS

The abbreviations used in this volume generally conform with the conventions of *Oxford Classical Dictionary* (fourth edition) and in the case of Byzantine sources and journals of Byzantinology, *Lexicon zur byzantinischen Gräzität*. Abbreviations for works not found in either, or those where we have decided to deviate from them, are given below.

AG	*Anno Graecorum* (Seleucid Era)
AJA	*American Journal of Archaeology*
a.m.	*anno mundi*
ARS	African Red Slip ware
AUPA	*Annali del seminario giuridico dell'Università di Palermo*
B.	*Libri Basilicorum*
BAR	*British Archaeological Reports*
BIDR	*Bullettino dell'Istituto di diritto romano*
Blockley	*Fragmentary Classicising Historians of the Later Roman Empire*
D.	*Digesta*
CI	*Codex Iustinianus*
CID	*Corpus des inscriptions de Delphes*
CTh	*Codex Theodosianus*
Cosm.	*Cosmographia Aethici Istriotae*
ED	*Enciclopedia del diritto*
EDCS	Epigraphik-Datenbank Clauss / Slaby
ETMG	*Expositio Totius Mundi et Gentium*
GGM	*Geographi Graeci Minores*
IGRRP	*Inscriptiones Graecae ad Res Romanas Pertinentes*
IJNA	*International Journal of Nautical Archaeology*
IMT	*Inschriften Mysia & Troas*
JJP	*Journal of Juristic Papyrology*
LIMC	*Lexicon Iconographicum Mythologiae Classicae*
LRA	Late Roman Amphora
LRC	Late Roman C ware
LRD	Late Roman D ware

Abbreviations

MNAT	Museu Nacional Arqueològic de Tarragona
Notit. Urb. Const.	*Notitia Urbis Constantinopolitanae*
NRN	*Nomos Rhodion Nautikos*
Pon.Nom.	*Ponema Nomikon*
PS	*Pauli Sententiae*
RDN	*Rivista del diritto della navigazione*
RGDA	*Res Gestae Divi Augusti*
RIDA	*Revue Internationale des Droits de l'Antiquité*
RIMA	*Royal Inscriptions of Mesopotamia, Assyrian Period*
REA	*Revue d'études anciennes*
RHD	*Revue d histoire du Droit (Tijdschrift voor Rechtsgeschiedenis)*
s.a.	*sub anno*
Scyth. Vind.	*Scythica Vindobonensia*
SDHI	*Studia Documenta Historiae et Iuris*
SGDI	*Sammlung der griechischen Dialekt-Inschriften*
Syn.Min.	*Synopsis Minor*

CONTRIBUTORS

Doug Forsyth completed his PhD in Ancient History at the University of St Andrews in 2020 with a thesis on the economic and social development in the Cyclades between 1000 and 480 BCE. He currently has an Associateship position with St Andrews and works on several archaeological projects in the central Cyclades. He has published on seafood processing, trade routes, and aspects of economic development, principally in the Greek sphere. Prior to returning to academia, Doug spent nearly 40 years working in the US seafood industry owning and managing at-sea processing ships operating mainly in Alaska.

Alexandra Grigorieva has a PhD in Classics from Moscow State University, Russia. She is a Classics and Food History scholar with a particular interest in the history of food words and food in art, a former research fellow of the Helsinki Collegium for Advanced Studies, now an independent researcher based in Helsinki, a Latin teacher and a mother of three.

Hallvard R. Indgjerd has degrees from the universities of Oslo (BA, MA) and Cambridge (MPhil), and received his doctoral degree with a thesis on the Late Roman and Early Medieval Cyclades from the University of St Andrews. Currently he is a research fellow in GIS and Spatial Archaeology at University College London. He has participated in fieldwork on the islands of Naxos, Keros-Dhaskalio and Kos, as well as in Morocco, Turkey, Italy and on Cyprus; his interests include island archaeology, ceramic studies, and connectivity and network theory through the implementation of GIS approaches.

Arja Karivieri is the Professor of Classical Archaeology and Ancient History at Stockholm University. She also worked as the Director of the Institutum Romanum Finlandiae in Rome from 2017 to 2021. Between 2015 and 2019, Karivieri led the research project 'Segregated or Integrated? Living and Dying in the Harbour City of Ostia, 300 BCE–700 CE', funded by the Academy of Finland and Tampere University, in which she and her team delved into the history of the ancient Roman port cities of Ostia and Portus. The project's results were published in *Life and Death in a Multicultural Harbour City* (Rome: Acta Instituti Romani Finlandiae 47), 2020.

Antti Lampinen holds the title of Docent in Classical Philology at the University of Turku; since 2018, he has worked as the Assistant Director at the Finnish Institute at Athens. His areas of special interest include ancient ethnographical and geographical writing, perceptions and portrayals of outgroups and subalterns, and the use of triumphalist rhetoric especially in Late Antiquity.

Emilia Mataix Ferrándiz is a Postdoctoral Researcher at the University of Helsinki and a research fellow at the Käte Hamburger kolleg from Münster (Germany). She has a PhD

Contributors

in Roman law (University of Alicante and Facoltà di Giurisprudenza di Palermo and a second PhD in archaeology (University of Southampton and Lyon 2 La Lumière). Her research interest lies on Roman law and archaeology, especially on its commercial and maritime focus.

Valerio Massimo Minale completed his PhD in Byzantine history at the Università degli Studi L'Orientale in Naples (2009). He has conducted research at the Freie Universität Berlin, the Max-Planck-Institute für Europäische Rechtsgeschichte in Frankfurt am Main and the Università Commerciale Luigi Bocconi in Milan. He is currently Associate Professor in Roman law at Università degli Studi Federico II in Naples, where he has the chair of Byzantine law. He has published three monographs, and many articles on the study of Byzantine legal sources.

Zeynep Olgun is an MA student at Central European University, Vienna, in the Department of Medieval Studies. She holds an MA degree from Koç University, Istanbul, Department of Archaeology and Art History with a specialization in Maritime Archaeology. Her research focuses on Byzantine maritime communities and culture, and how the relationship between the Mediterranean and the Byzantines is reflected in archaeological and textual records.

Joanna Töyräänvuori holds the title of Docent in Ancient Near Eastern Studies and a doctorate in Hebrew Bible Studies at the University of Helsinki. Töyräänvuori's expertise centres on the political mythologies of the Eastern Mediterranean. Currently, Töyräänvuori holds a postdoctoral fellowship in the Centre of Excellence of the Academy of Finland, Ancient Near Eastern Empires.

Luca Zavagno is the Assistant Professor of Byzantine Studies in the Department of History at Bilkent University. He is the author of many articles and books on the Early Medieval and Byzantine Mediterranean. His latest book is entitled *The Byzantine City from Heraclius to the Fourth Crusade, 610-1204: Urban Life after Antiquity;* he is currently working on the *Routledge Companion to the Byzantine City* (a volume co-edited with Nikolas Bakirtzis to appear in 2022).

SERIES PREFACE

While our intention in writing this preface was to provide a neutral introduction that could stand for the whole series, recent events are too dramatic and relevant to ignore. The Covid-19 pandemic and the climate emergency have increased awareness of human reliance and impact on the environments we occupy, dramatically emphasised human inability to control nature, and reinforced perceptions that the environment is the most pressing political and social issue of our time. It confirms our belief that the time is right to situate our current (abnormal?) relationship with nature within an examination of human interactions with the environment over the *longue durée* – a belief that has given rise to this series.

Ancient Environments sets out to explore (from a variety of perspectives) different constructions of the 'environment' and understandings of humankind's place within it, across and around the Mediterranean from 3500 BCE–750 CE. By 'environment' we mean the worlds of living and non-living things in which human societies and cultures exist and with which they interact. The series focuses on the *co-construction* of humans and the natural world. It examines not only human-led interactions with the environment (e.g. the implications of trade or diet), but also those that foreground earth systems and specific environmental phenomena; it investigates both physical entities and events and ancient, imagined environments and alternate realities. The initial and primary focus of this series is the ancient world, but by explicitly exploring, evaluating and contextualising past human societies and cultures in dialogue with their environments, it also aims to illuminate the development and reception of environmental ideas and concepts, and to provoke a deeper understanding of more long-term and widespread environmental dynamics.

The geographical remit of this series includes not only the cultures of the Mediterranean and Near East, but also those of Southern Europe, North Africa including Egypt, Northern Europe, the Balkans and the shores of the Black Sea. We believe that encompassing this broader geographical extent supports a more dynamic, cross-disciplinary and comparative approach – enabling the series to transcend traditional boundaries in scholarship. Its temporal range is also far-reaching: it begins with the Neolithic (a dynamic date range, depending on location in the Near East/Europe) because it marks a distinct change in the ways in which human beings interacted with their environment. We have chosen *c.* 750 CE as our end date because it captures the broadest understanding of the end of Late Antiquity in the Central Mediterranean area, marking the rise of the Carolingians in the West, and the fall of the Umayyad Caliphate in the East.

Our series coincides with, and is inspired by, a particular focus on 'the environmental turn' in studies of the ancient world, as well as across humanities more generally. This

Series Preface

focus is currently provoking a reassessment of approaches that have tended to focus solely on people and their actions, prompting scholars to reflect instead (or alongside) on the key role of the environments in which their historical subjects lived, and which shaped and were shaped by them. By extending beyond the chronological and geographical boundaries that often define — and limit — understanding of the meaning of 'antiquity', we intend that this series should encourage and enable broader participation from within and beyond relevant academic disciplines. This series will, we hope, not only advance the investigation of ancient ecological experiences, but also stimulate reflection on responses to contemporary ecological challenges.

The editors would like to express heartfelt thanks to everyone at Bloomsbury Press, especially Alice Wright who first conceived of the idea and suggested it to Esther, and who has done so much to develop it, and Georgina Leighton, for her work in launching the series and her continued support. We are extremely grateful to the members of the Series Board, who have provided such wonderful encouragement and support, and to our authors (current and future) who have entrusted their work to this 'home'. Thanks also to the Leverhulme Trust for crucial funds that made it possible to initiate the series. We have chosen the 'Mistress of Animals' or *Potnia Theron*, a figure found in Near Eastern, Minoan, Mycenean, Greek and Etruscan art over thousands of years, as the motif for the series.

Anna Collar
Esther Eidinow
Katharina Lorenz

ACKNOWLEDGEMENTS

As we all know, ancient long-distance shipping was a perilous venture and many such expeditions finished up at the bottom of the sea – but sharing the risks and finding support from third parties helped to overcome the hazards of seafaring. In that same fashion, this volume would not have been possible without the generous encouragement, support, and dedication of many people. Firstly, we are deeply thankful to the editors of Bloomsbury's fresh series Ancient Environments, Anna Collar, Esther Eidinow, and Katharina Lorenz, who contacted us early on and have been extremely supportive to the project in each of its stages. We are very grateful to the Academy of Finland's Centre of Excellence *Reason and Religious Recognition* (Faculty of Theology, University of Helsinki, headed by Risto Saarinen), the Academy of Finland research project *Segregated or Integrated? – Living and Dying in the Harbour City of Ostia, 300 BCE – 700 CE* (University of Tampere, headed by Arja Karivieri), and the ERC project *Law, Governance and Space: Questioning the Foundations of the Republican Tradition* (headed by Kaius Tuori) for their generous support in organizing the XXV Finnish Symposium on Late Antiquity 'Seafaring, Mobility, and the Mediterranean in Late Antiquity (c. 150–700 CE)' held in Tvärminne on 26–7 October 2018, where many of the papers included in this volume were first presented. The last of these projects also provided funding for the workshop 'Law, trade, and the sea' that took place in Helsinki in 2019, where some of the ideas presented in this volume were shaped and debated. We would also like to thank the Helsinki Collegium for Advanced Studies, the Finnish Institute at Athens, the Eurostorie Centre of Excellence in Law, Identity and the European narratives (funded by the Academy of Finland), and the Käte Hamburger Kolleg from Münster for supporting our research in a myriad of different ways. Maijastina Kahlos, Raimo Hakola and Ville Vuolanto provided much useful advice in sharing their experience of editorial work. The labour of editing would have been much harder for us without the kind help of Heta Björklund, Maria Erma, Sara Heinonen and Karla Schröter from the Centre of Excellence in Law, Identity and the European Narratives. We would like to offer our warmest thanks to Alice Wright, Georgina Leighton and Lily MacMahon at Bloomsbury for guiding us along the route of publishing this volume, as well as to the series editors and anonymous readers for their useful comments and advice. Last but not least, we would like to thank the illustrator Karin Eremia for providing two samples of her designs as potential book cover illustrations, and although unfortunately these were not used in the end, we remain very appreciative of her generosity and talent.

NOTE ON TRANSLATIONS

The contributions of this volume will mostly present translations of ancient texts for the reader, except in those cases where the discussion is focused on the language or vocabulary of the original: in these cases the original text is presented alongside the translation.

The translators of each passage are indicated in the appropriate endnote. If no translator is indicated, the passage has been translated by the contributor themselves.

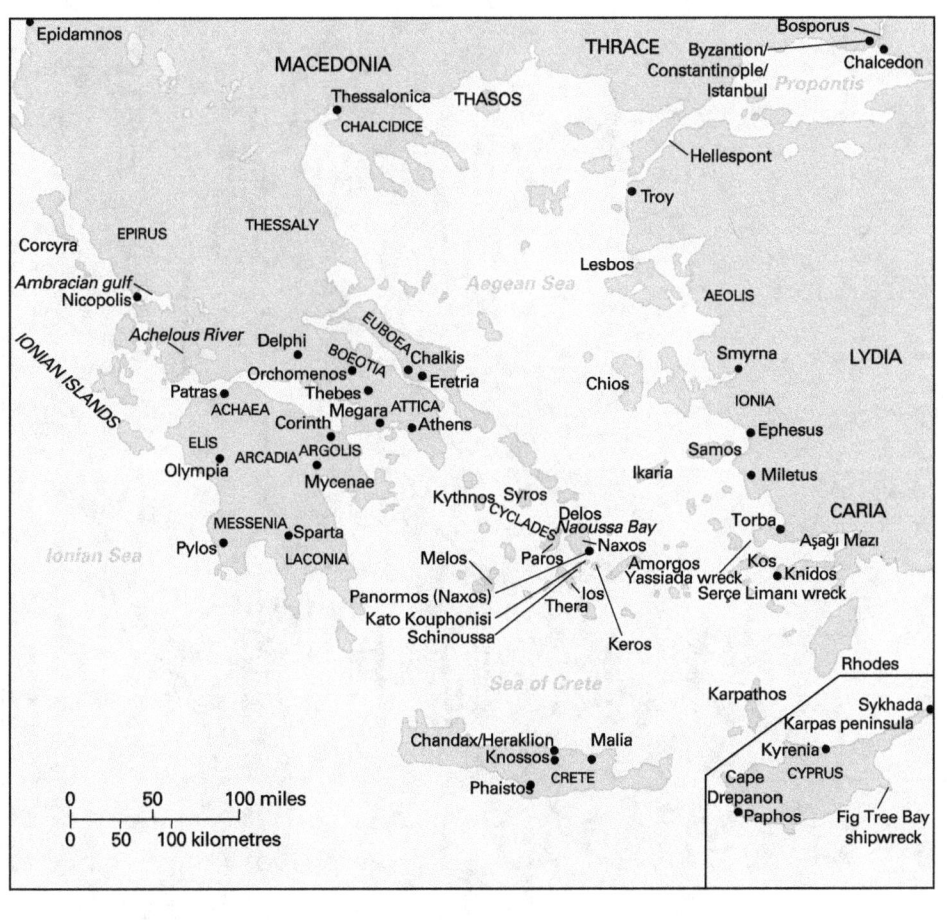

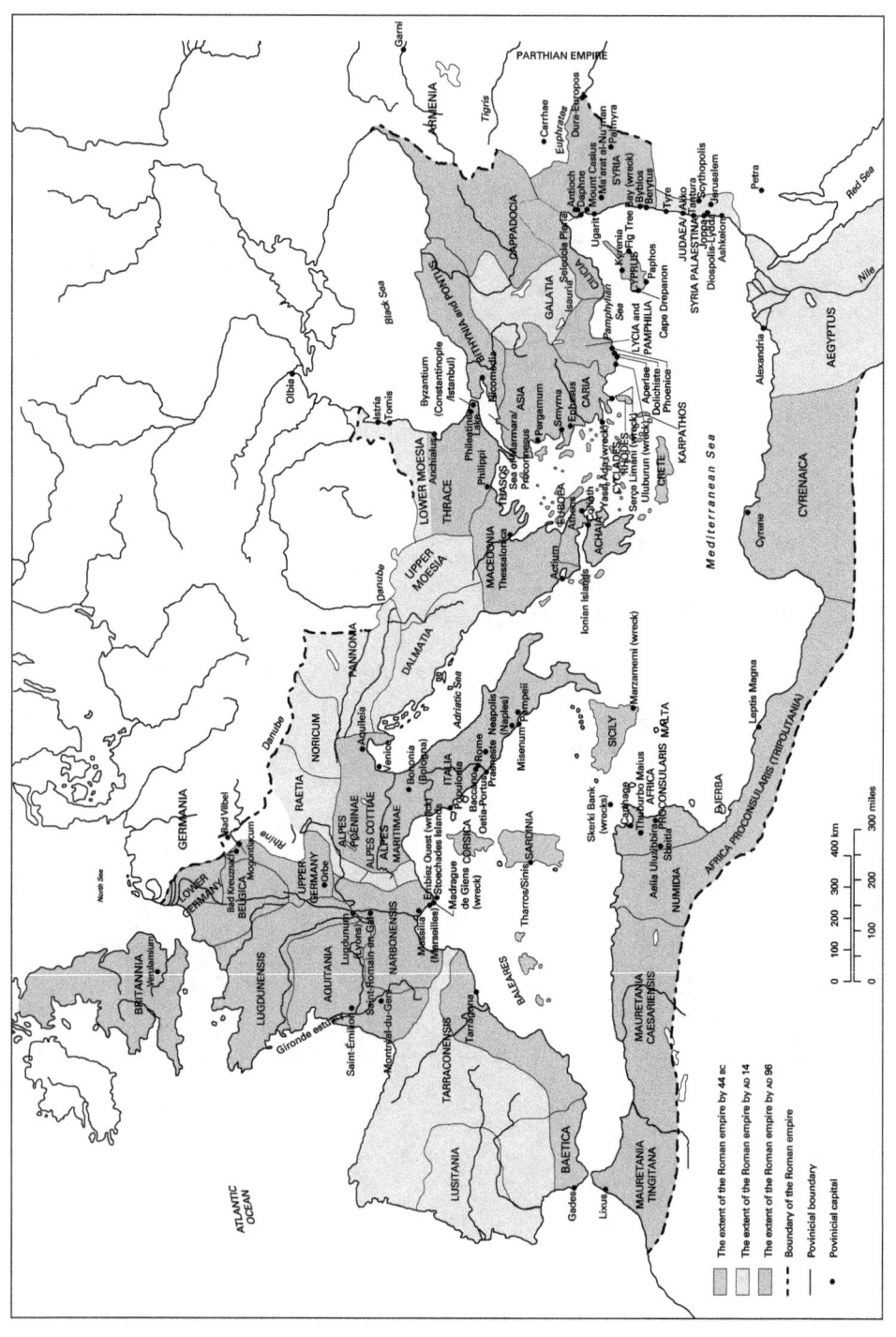

INTRODUCTION
APPROACHES TO THE LATER IMPERIAL MEDITERRANEAN AS AN ENVIRONMENT
Emilia Mataix Ferrándiz and Antti Lampinen

1 Imagining and Experiencing the Mediterranean Environment

One of the lesser-known feats of Alexander the Great was his brief stint as an underwater explorer. In the late additions to Alexander's purported letter to Olympias in the redactions β and γ of Pseudo-Callisthenes' *Alexander Romance*, the Macedonian conqueror tells how he set out to accomplish the ultimate act of domination by being lowered into the bottom of the ocean in a sort of diving bell made of glass, with the intention of bringing up a token of his conquest from the seafloor. He developed the urge to collect the riches of the depth after harvesting seven magnificent pearls from the shell of a monstrous crab he encountered and killed. Alexander enters the diving bell himself in order to 'attempt the impossible', and makes several dives. On his third descent, 'around 308 cubits' deep, an astonishingly huge fish grabs the diving bell in its maw and drags it – and the ship from which it is suspended – far away to the coast, spitting the gnawed hulk of the offending device out onto dry land. Badly shaken, Alexander admits he was 'scarcely breathing and frightened to death' and, falling to his knees, worshipped Providence for having saved him. The conqueror makes a promise to give up attempting the impossible, lest it would cost him his life.[1]

The sight of the immeasurably valuable pearls is the first element that kindles Alexander's interest in the seafloor. Secondly, it is perhaps a testament to his daring that even though the text frames already the surface of the sea as uncharted, he heads straight into its watery embrace. Another significant facet is the need to introduce a technical innovation to withstand hostile underwater conditions, as well as the drastic trial that the design is put to by the monstrous fish.[2] The greatest conqueror of humankind has met his match and is cast ashore trembling and gasping: the sea has meted out an unequivocal *memento mori* to him. The depths of the sea are frequently cited, even today, as an under-explored horizon – one which requires considerable technological sophistication. Similarly, almost as if he had been Jacques Cousteau's ancient predecessor, Alexander's bathyscaph is not merely an instrument of conquest, but also of enquiry.[3] This could well have been connected with the idea that Alexander's curiosity had been shaped and directed by his tutor, Aristotle.

This rich and gripping passage points out to several noteworthy aspects in the Late Imperial perception of the sea as an environment, and hence can serve as our first dip into the topic.[4] It points to the myriad interconnections in the perception of the sea, its interplay of riches and risk, of calm and danger, and the need to master the most appropriate technologies available to cope with it successfully and safely. Recent scholarship into past human societies' interactions with different environments (or, indeed the environment) has found much use for cross-disciplinary perspectives, where different datasets and frames are brought to bear on the wider set of questions, which themselves interlock.

Across the varied range of angles represented in its contributions, this volume is intended to emphasize the ancient experience of the Mediterranean as a lived, negotiated, symbolic and imagined environment. This includes equally the material, navigational, economical, propagandistic, ideological and legal approaches. The mobility of goods, ideas and people affected by all these approaches is the thread weaving its way through the volume. Another goal of this collection is to get over the lingering remnants of the culture/nature division that have for so long hindered the study of the environment from the direction of humanities.[5] Yet we must remain alert to those cases where our Late Imperial sources do, in fact, engage with said *topos*: these instances are valuable evidence of past societies' metaphoric and value-laden use of the associations evoked by parts of the environment. In that sense, through the different contributions of this volume, we will address the agency of the sea on human beings, as well as the attempts of various authors to conceptualize and create a framework of definition and management of that space.

2 Imagination and Domination: The Mediterranean as a Conceptual Environment

There is no reason to assume that the sea would not have been experienced already in antiquity in contradictory ways: as powerful but serene, beautiful but dangerous.[6] The chapters included in Parts I and III address these and related issues and, while engaging with the symbolic visions of the sea in the ancient mind and subsequent material and conceptual characterizations, they also benefit from the idea that the sea, as an environment, is in a state of continuous change and transformation.

Joanna Töyräänvuori's chapter portrays the origin and development of the symbolic conquest of the Mediterranean. In her chapter, Töyräänvuori reflects on the ancestry of the well-known legend of Saint George and the dragon and its connection with maritime symbolism. Here, the conquest of the sea is mirrored in the defeat of a monster by a powerful character, being either a god or an individual of political importance. In this light, the sea is an environment that promotes the establishment of political mythologies – something that connects her chapter with those of Antti Lampinen, Valerio Massimo Minale and Emilia Mataix Ferrándiz – in which the sea appears as a symbolic problem for conquering monarchs who nonetheless were limited by their own mortality. While the Hellenistic stories of Alexander the Great did not yet see him descend into the seafloor in a bathyscaph, unlike in Late Antiquity, Töyräänvuori notes that in Strabo's account of Alexander's march along the Pamphylian coast[7] there are some elements of triumphing over the sea. But in narratives like this, the question possibly was how to dominate a primordial element that gives such a visceral impression of permanence and resistance. In her case, the effects of sea conquest found expression in legends and iconography, while in other cases, studied in the later chapters of this book, it had an impact in the creation of legal tools to handle the dangers of such environment. Approaching the conquest of the sea through personification makes it easier to indicate a degree of finality for such a feat: the cosmogonic usefulness of this is obvious.

It is perhaps important how often the sea was first and foremost conceptualized not so much as governed by a deity, but as a deity itself. Alexandra Grigorieva's chapter explores the ideas and iconographies of Oceanus and his marine environments in mosaic imagery. The figurative representations in works of art – especially those which could be fairly publicly seen in some spaces of the Roman cities, such as bathhouses or *nymphaea* – can, in some ways, stand in for a host of other culturally shared representations about the characteristics of the sea. In this way, impressions about the sea would have spread far beyond actual coastal environments and harbour cities. Neither were these impressions limited to mythological characters, but also included species of fish and crustaceans, as well as boats and ships of diverse kinds. Travel, then, was not the only way of being transported to experience the sea. This everyday contact with sea-themed iconography formed an important part of the ways in which the sea was conceptualized by different individuals. The recurrence of some stylistic motives in diverse locations highlights the mobility of symbolic elements and their persistence in time and space. Looking at a sea-themed mosaic floor from its edge was, to those ancient viewers unused to the real thing, almost like marvelling at the wonders of the deep from a coastal cliff. Grigorieva's chapter notes that a strict delineation between an imaginary or fantastic type of sea elements and one that was more realistic should not be overemphasized: crossovers and mixtures seem frequent, which is something that could be indicative of the broader cultural perceptions about the sea and its denizens. It was, after all, a mysterious world where the limits of human knowledge appeared in stark relief. Much as in Arja Karivieri's contribution, Grigorieva also underlines the role of mobility and the recurrent flows of people and ideas that characterize the ancient Mediterranean.

Lampinen's chapter investigates how an environment that, despite its unpredictability, has become largely conceived as more or less knowable can, in changing conditions, become perceived as being a contested one, with familiarity giving way to caution and unease. In the case of the Mediterranean, it could even be argued that something of the inscrutable, dangerous qualities retained throughout the Imperial Era by the Ocean were seeping back into the perceptions of the Mediterranean during the Later Imperial centuries. Even if the analogy may be a bit of a stretch – and certainly a simplification – it could perhaps be said that, from a somewhat treacherous highway, in the Later Empire the Mediterranean turned into an environmental obstacle more comparable with mountains[8] and, much like these, it could throw enemies at the settled societies. With the environmental and geographical unity of the Mediterranean so easily portrayed as providential and predetermined, even a rupture in the safe and uncontested knowability of the sea could be symbolically potent and allow for the communication of widely differing claims and values. These uses of the sea as a conceptual environment may also have been somewhat transferable between cultures – much like the symbolic imagery of triumphalist rhetoric (see Töyräänvuori's and Grigorieva's chapters).

Even in times of peace, the sea had a certain reputation as a dangerous environment, and the stereotypes and *topoi* of the sea are something that need to be borne in mind. No doubt they influenced the perception of at least the members of the literary elite regarding the rigours of seafaring – though probably leaving many of the actual toilers of the sea comparatively less affected – but they may also give an inflated idea about the dangers of seafaring. Yet the literary emphasis on the imagery of turbulence, danger and unpredictability, despite its conventionality, depends on a constant repetition of the *topoi* which maintains their significance for its audience; the way in which certain elements have been judged as 'only a *topos*' is not a useful way of treating them.[9] In terms of intensity and emotional charge, the Later Imperial imagery of the sea as an environment may well have reflected the feeling – whether real or not – that more than the accustomed dangers coming from the seaward direction were a distinct possibility.

3 A Networked Environment

Seaborne connectivity is enabled by – and in turn engenders – particular geographical, cognitive and social parameters. The contributions in Part II of this volume also touch upon the question of how movement is studied in different disciplines. The chapters present a variety of approaches in studying connectivity, from transitional environments to port networks and beyond. There still exist substantial conceptual and technical barriers to the more holistic exploration of connectivity and interaction: these impediments range from asymmetrical fieldwork traditions and practices to narrow research specializations and methodological corollaries stemming from certain assumptions and unavoidably leaving something behind.[10]

In her chapter, Arja Karivieri explores the way in which the Mediterranean flows of mobility and migration shaped Ostia and Portus, a burgeoning double-node of the network of the Mediterranean maritime environment. Basing her analysis on a selection of recent studies about ancient mobility, such as Laurence Tacoma's typology of the kinds of movement that the Roman Empire fostered,[11] Karivieri emphasizes in her chapter the multiplicity of social and demographic pull factors that shaped the 'fluvio-coastal mobility' around the mouth of the Tiber. This followed the environmental ebb and flow of resources, sailing seasons and workforce needs. It was this strong seasonality that made the connectivities of the Mediterranean (or the sea more generally) unique among the environments of the Roman Empire.[12] The sea experienced a seasonal variation that created and strengthened the two parallel associations of both broad connectivities and almost complete isolation.[13] Indeed, one fundamental problem arises when mobility is defined merely on a single scale, instead of multiple ones. For example, mobility can all too easily come to be equated with macro-scale processes such as migration. However, as the contribution of Karivieri demonstrates, such movements were relatively intermittent, performed by concrete subjects who had particular reasons to move, and consequently making movement seem less frequent in the past than many scholarly works seem to indicate.[14] These works have sometimes ended up highlighting the importance of mobility in antiquity, a discourse that is often used to assert the modernity of the ancients, sometimes estimating its scale by using as comparison the trends present in the global era.[15]

The need to combine research approaches in order to furnish a fuller picture of the use of the sea environment in the Mediterranean also applies to archaeological data. The Cycladic area, in particular, has been a fruitful region for the study of island environments and archipelagic networks in various chronological contexts.[16] Hallvard Indgjerd uses his intimate knowledge of the underwater archaeology along the southern coast of Naxos to discuss the recent advances in our understanding of this rich and complex example of a coastal trading environment, while also providing a hitherto missing Late-Imperial angle for the discussion of Naxian maritime environments and, more generally, of small-island worlds.[17] This approach has great potential for the study of ancient environments and the small-scale engagement of ancient communities with them; it has also allowed the research teams to gain practical first-hand experience in navigating these coastal waters. Local knowledge, small-scale infrastructure and strict adherence to seasons all emerged as important considerations.

While the work of Indgjerd focuses more thoroughly on the relations and interactions of people moving in this Naxian context, the contribution of Luca Zavagno and Zeynep Olgun examines the nature of islands as ambiguous environments, being isolated centres and clear hubs of connectivity at the same time, from the 'long fourth century' onwards.[18] Combining historical and archaeological evidence, Zavagno and Olgun reflect on the role of islands and their strategic locations in an environmental canvas, tying their chapter to that of Lampinen. Their chapter is also highly complementary with that of Indgjerd, and reflects on the nature of islands as particular environments which enable the development of specific forms of interaction – something that has promoted the view that islands occupy their own particular subfield of archaeology.[19] In the case of Zavagno and Olgun, islands appear as 'resilient spaces' and threshold environments, while Indgjerd reflects on the connections enabled by a series of islands composing an archipelago, rather than on the role of particular islands within that environment. Zavagno and Olgun discuss the perception of islands as extensions of the sea – a conceptualization that is not only reflected in literary or historical sources, but also in legal texts.[20] In addition, islands are revealed as barriers that act as junctions in a network thoroughly characterized by the watery environment – at least for those who look at islands from across the sea: historically, on larger islands the locals themselves have sometimes been surprisingly independent of the sea.[21] For these existing contradictions, the intricate and diverse connections between land-based and marine culture should be considered from a perspective of 'viewing the world through the island'.[22]

4 Braving the Sea in the Later Empire

Part III of this volume aims to provide a more general assessment of the technical and conceptual interconnectivities required to successfully brave the sea. Its chapters will deal with the emergence of the structures of maritime navigation both as a logistical and a normative enterprise embedded within the spatial context of the sea environment and its challenges. The emphasis will be on the role of space and place for understanding history and of its relation with the environment.[23] Seas are historically and culturally constructed through narrative processes, legislation, mapping, navigation, shipping and commerce and, in that sense, they constitute vaults filled with information.[24] With that focus in mind, the last section will take as its starting point the suggestion that the sea as an environment is not merely a neutral concept and cannot be considered independent from that which it contains, nor can it be considered as immune to historical, political and aesthetic changes.[25]

Emilia Mataix Ferrándiz's chapter starts, accordingly, with a review of Roman approaches to the practice of plundering; she demonstrates that conceptions of shipwrecking were intimately interlinked with ancient ideas about the sea and its coasts, but also influenced by the states' projection of their own power in the Mediterranean Sea. The definition of plundering as unlawful conduct is in many ways at the centre of Mataix Ferrándiz' chapter, and it is also a very significant theme when we conceptualize the imagery and juridical thinking affecting Late Imperial portrayal of disturbances taking place in one part or another of the Mediterranean.[26] For the Romans who debated the matter, the main issue was not sovereignty of the sea, but rather the political implications that such an extraordinary command, and with it, unusual powers, would have. These discourses of power symbolized in law-making are also present in the contribution from Valerio Massimo Minale, making the two chapters complementary.

The Mediterranean was, in any case, becoming less of a Roman lake during the Late Imperial centuries, and it is thus not surprising that from the juridical sources one gets the impression that the imperial administration was anxious to disincentivize provincials from attempting to gain any profit from shipwrecks, or indeed to wreck them purposefully.[27] The chapters of both Lampinen and Mataix Ferrándiz note that the apparent state of Mediterranean peace under the High Empire may have been a partial illusion – principally conjured up in some modern scholarship. Piracy no doubt remained a part of the Mediterranean conditions, though smaller in scale and somewhat opportunistic in nature.[28] It was also kept alive in the ancient popular imagination due to its frequent use as a conventional element in novels and other narratives.[29]

Minale's chapter, taking the *Lex Rhodia de iactu* as its starting point, studies the Byzantine tradition of the Digest' fragment 14.2.9 (Vol. Maec. *Ex Lege Rhodia*). The tradition of the fragment 14.2.9 could be seen as quite emblematic of the Byzantine conception of law, finding identification in a structure coming from the past, but kept alive by a continuous evolution. In that way, the *imperator* represented the pivot between the Roman and Byzantine worlds, which kept each other in mind.[30] The judgement may very well have its origins in a setting where a group of professional seafarers such as sailors, captains or merchants had petitioned the emperor's protection in case of economic hardship deriving from a shipwreck. Minale focuses on the complicated issue of the text's mention of the emperor as the master of the world, but the *Lex Rhodia* as being the rule that controls the sea, and then uses the Byzantine tradition of the text to clarify the puzzling formulation. As the meanings attributed to some textual terms transform through time and space, so do the values and functions attributed to them. In that sense, the chapter provides a thorough study on key imperial themes such as the extent of the emperor's power and consequently, its limits in time and space. It is the stance of the Late Roman emperors, posing as the protectors of the sea, which ties this chapter in with those of Töyräänvuori, Mataix Ferrándiz and Lampinen. Interestingly, in the field of Late Roman law the figure of the emperor emerges as a kind of an island of his own: he represented a point of union between the marine and terrestrial worlds.

But if the other chapters of Part III discuss the Mediterranean as an environment in which legal conceptions apply to institutionally protect seafarers from the dangers of navigation, Doug Forsyth's chapter brings the discourse to the topic of know-how to overcome sea hazards. Forsyth discusses the environmental effects of the Mediterranean winds and their influence on the sailing conditions, and explores the ways in which the design of commercial trading vessels was adapted to suit the prevailing wind conditions, and the Late Antique innovations aimed at maximizing the efficiency of sailing. Forsyth's exploration provides very valuable observations about the concrete technological and skill sets on which the Later Imperial sailing would have relied. He also demonstrates how even fairly closely situated islands, such as Paros and Delos, would in certain seasons – summer, in particular – have seemed further apart than they actually were if one takes into account the sailing capabilities of the ships and the prevailing winds.[31] The latter mirrors the human environment of the Mediterranean, since human knowledge and tools are applied to manage the vagaries of the natural world: perhaps more so than any other type of environment, the sea is a 'landscape of technology'. This epistemic aspect forms the crucial link between Forsyth's chapter and the two other chapters in Part III, which consider how legal instruments also help define and cope with the dangers and uncertainties of the savage sea.

Planning a trip was the key to success.[32] It is also worth considering the limitations of maps, itineraries and *periploi* in antiquity because, despite the familiarity of sailors with wind roses and navigating across the open sea using the stars and an azimuth, none of this experience transmitted itself from practice to cartographic theory or multi-dimensional perception.[33] Therefore, the experience, knowledge and technology used by sailors appear as the fundamental elements which support maritime navigation. The latter connects Forsyth's chapter to Indgjerd's, as well as that of Zavagno and Olgun, addressing the human element behind the maritime networks discussed by these authors.

* * *

The Mediterranean environment shrank and expanded seasonally; this would almost certainly have had an impact on the coastal communities' perceptions of connectivity, insularity and the character of the sea.[34] This is an aspect that a modern observer, juddering along aboard a Greek inter-island ferry, could all too easily forget. Yet aspects of seasonality are still present in the way people divide their lives, professions and mobilities between the islands and the mainland. In antiquity, the almost regular occurrence of the 'halcyon days' in the midst of the Aegean winter, calming the stormy sea, confirmed to the ancient islanders that connectivities were a blessing and the safe passage of the sea a special boon during what seemed like a providentially ordained period of isolation.[35] Even landing on a non-native island in the ancient Mediterranean could have had a slight whiff of the *Odyssey* about it; if you were not familiar with its landforms, recognizing the identity of an island would have relied on an encounter with the locals – who could, in times of turmoil, have been suspicious of newcomers.[36] Reflecting on such encounters, one final aim of this book will be to provide a contribution for writing a human history of the seas, which act as environments bridging the gap between cultures and people and create narratives in their turn.

Notes

1. [Callisth.] *Hist. Alex. Magni* 2.38. See Ross 1967. Nawotka 2017: 188 considers the section inauthentic and leaves it out of his commentary (cf. ibid. 1, 30–2). Yet it was these embroidered later redactions that inspired the subsequent vernacular reception of the Alexander Matter, e.g. Stoneman 2012: 197–98.
2. See, e.g., Thommen 2012: 53 and Bosak-Schroeder 2020: 127–9 on the ancient perceptions of fish that eat humans.
3. Cf. Romm 1992: 112.
4. The dating of the *Alexander Romance* is a complex question, but the relevant added sections of the β recension must post-date the third century CE: Stoneman 2012: ix–x; Nawotka 2017: 3–5.
5. As very engagingly explored by Hartman 2017; on the long life of the nature-culture dichotomy, Braun 2004.
6. A very rich recent exploration of the conceptions of the sea – along with other forms of water – is Irby 2021.
7. Str. 14.3.9.
8. On which, see now the contributions in Hollis and König 2021.
9. See Zerjadtke 2020.
10. See the debate which started with the paper from Brughmans and Poblome 2016; later discussed by Van Oyen 2017, and finally concluded by the reply from Brughmans and Poblome 2017.
11. Tacoma 2016; cf. also Eckardt 2010.
12. There are several publications on the Mediterranean sailing seasons, of which we would like to highlight Tammuz 2006; Beresford 2012.
13. See El Safadi and Sturt 2019.
14. Horden and Purcell 2000; Moatti 2004; *ead.* 2006; *ead.* 2013. An exhaustive list is provided in Woolf 2016b.
15. Pitts and Versluys 2014.
16. Broodbank 2000: 207–10.
17. There are many publications associated with the Small Cyclades Islands Project, which can be consulted at https://smallcycladicislandsproject.org/.
18. Zavagno has already addressed some of these issues concerning islands of the Mediterranean in Çaykent and Zavagno 2014.

19. There are several publications on the field but see, e.g., Rainbird 2007.
20. See, e.g, *D.* 41.1.7.3 (Gaius 2 *Rer. Cott.*) (=I.2.1.22); *D.* 41.1.1.1 (Gaius 2 *Rer. Cott.*).
21. Pungetti 2012.
22. Ma 2020.
23. Then engaging with the broad discourses targeted in the field of environmental humanities. See, e.g., Luccarelli and Bergman 2015: 1–23.
24. Mawani 2018: 292–309.
25. As can be appreciated in key publications such as Horden and Purcell 2000 or Abulafia 2011.
26. Mataix Ferrándiz 2019.
27. *CI* 11.6.1; Solazzi 1939: 254–5.
28. De Souza 1999: 205–13; see also Arnaud 2016.
29. Ormerod 1997: 257; Braund 1993: 106–7; Noy 2000: 142.
30. See also the innovative approach on ethnicity in Byzantium and its relationship with Rome, in Kaldellis 2019.
31. Eur. *IA*, e.g. 80–110.
32. Cf. Warnking 2015.
33. Whittaker 2004: 65–76.
34. Leidwanger 2020: 65–7.
35. For the aetiology of the *halkyonides*, see Ov. *Met.* 11.410–591; Hygin. *Fab.* 65.
36. Hom. *Od.* 10.56–132 on the island of Laestrygonians, where Odysseus and his men were unwelcome.

PART I
IMAGINATION AND DOMINATION: THE MEDITERRANEAN AS A CONCEPTUAL ENVIRONMENT

CHAPTER 1
KNIGHTS, KINGS AND DRAGONS: THE SYMBOLIC CONQUEST OF THE MEDITERRANEAN SEA IN LATE ANTIQUITY AND ITS HISTORICAL BACKGROUND

Joanna Töyräänvuori

Introduction

Mesopotamian royal inscriptions feature recurrent references to the symbolic conquest of the Mediterranean Sea. This political mythology of the king conquering the sea was founded during the reign of the legendary King Sargon of Akkade (previously Agade), and it was likely at least partially based on his real-world military campaigns to the Mediterranean coast. A succession of texts refers to the subjugation of the divinized Mediterranean from Old Babylonian royal inscriptions down to texts recording the deeds of Alexander the Great, whose historiographers likely adopted this tradition from the Persian monarchs preceding him. The same tradition has also been connected to later rulers of the ancient world, such as the Carthaginian general Hamilcar Barca, the Roman Emperor Caligula, and the Sassanid ruler Khosrow. The stories connected to these rulers seem to mix mythological tropes with historical events. A review of the textual evidence shows that a version of this story was known in most of the cities of the Eastern Mediterranean, and while it found alteration in different historical periods up to and including Christianization in Late Antiquity, the legend of the conquest of the Mediterranean Sea was rewritten time and again for thousands of years in order to elevate historical kings.

The Christian legend of Saint George and the dragon is at least somewhat familiar to most modern Europeans, at least insofar as the symbolism goes.[1] The iconographic depictions of the motif have been a recurring theme in European art ever since the medieval period (c. 500–1500), and many are still found on paintings, statues, crests, and symbols throughout the world, most notably in England whose patron saint George is.[2] The motif may also have given rise to depictions of the archangel Michael slaying the Dragon in Judeo-Christian iconography.[3] Due to the strong association of Saint George with England and dragons in particular with Arthurian legends,[4] fewer people are aware that the legend of Saint George, along with the connected but independent narrative of a hero defeating the dragon, originated in the coastal cities of the Eastern Mediterranean.

The origin of the medieval legend of Saint George and the Dragon – and indeed it is a *legend* in a very literal sense of a hagiographical account of an event – is believed to be in Late Antiquity, although the historicity of the person of Saint George was questioned from early on. But whether Saint George ever was an historical person, on the Eastern

Mediterranean such stories of a hero's defeat of a monstrous foe predate the life and times of this Christian martyr by thousands of years. This chapter discusses the origin and background of the narrative of the hero battling a dragon and the real-world origin of the mythic story in the ideologically driven conquest of the Mediterranean Sea by Mesopotamian kings. In addition, it addresses how local traditional accounts of the story about the pacification of the sea as an environment were transformed into Christian legends in Late Antiquity.

Background

Saint Georgius of Lydda (modern Lod or al-Ludd), known as Diospolis in antiquity, on whose character the Christian legend is based, was supposedly a Roman military commander of Cappadocian Greek origin. Georgius was martyred under the Roman Emperor Diocletian in the third or early fourth century.[5] While the possibly historical person has been located in Late Antiquity, like the Arthurian legends, the story of Saint Georgius is also best known to modern scholars through a Medieval romance. While the story likely had a long oral history, it was written down in the thirteenth century by the Dominican friar and Prior of Lombardy, Jacobus de Varagine,[6] who used older hagiographies or biographies of saints in the writing of the legend, some of which date to Late Antiquity.[7]

In the so-called *Golden Legend* (*Legenda Aurea*), Jacobus de Varagine tells the story of how Georgius happens upon the daughter of the king of Ashkelon (modern al-Majdal Asqalan) weeping on the shore of the sea, to be delivered as tribute to the dragon that lived in a lake or a pool ('a stagne or a pond lyke a see') by a city in 'the provynce of Lybya to a cyte whyche is sayd Sylene,' likely referring to Leptis Magna on the African coast. After defeating the dragon, Georgius binds its neck with the girdle of the king's daughter, who then leads the bound dragon into the city to be slain and its corpse scattered in the surrounding fields.[8] The story of the defeat of the dragon is not a part of the earliest hagiographic records of Saint George and seems to have been added to his character at a later date. The person of Saint George is, however, connected with the Levantine coast from the very beginning.

The origin of the story of the hero's defeat of the dragon is interesting. There seems to exist a localized version of this narrative that is found in most of the coastal cities on the Levantine littoral, from ancient Ugarit on the Syrian coast down to Gaza and even onto Memphis in Egypt, most of them written down by Hellenistic or Roman historiographers.[9] However, the oldest extant versions of the narrative seem to go back all the way to the Bronze Age, second millennium BCE.[10] The story of the champion defeating the monster was a living tradition in these Levantine cities for millennia. One of the better-preserved iterations of this mythological story is the Baal-Cycle from ancient Ugarit (modern Ras Šamra), an epic myth in which the Storm-god of Mount Casius (Jebel al-'Aqra) defeats his enemy, the personified Mediterranean Sea.[11]

In the story, the two gods battle over the kingship of the gods and a seat at the head of their assembly, which the Storm-god ultimately wins by the help of weapons forged by a

Smith-god. In the second part of the myth, the new king of the gods is challenged by Death, loses and is taken to the underworld, and both him and the languishing, suffering nature must be rescued by the maiden goddess, Anat. The personified Sea (Yamm) plays a central role in the first part of the narrative cycle, and the Ugaritic text written in the local cuneiform alphabetic script remains the best source of how ancient inhabitants of the Mediterranean coast conceived of the sea in the Bronze Age.[12] The monstrous creature that must be vanquished by the Syrian Storm-god in these stories is the very Mediterranean Sea itself.[13]

While the cast of characters (Hero, Monster, Maiden) in these regional myths seems to have been inherited from Bronze Age mythology, the Levantine regional stories were mostly recorded by later Roman mythographers such as (Pseudo-)Hyginus (*Poet. astr.* 2.30, *Fab.* 197),[14] Ovid (*Fast.* 2.458, *Met.* 5.319), and Diodorus Siculus (2.4.2) in the first century BCE, all of which retell the rescue of a goddess from a monster by a hero. It has also been suggested that the final battle between Zeus and Typhon in Hesiod's Theogony (*Theog.* 820–822) recalled the struggle between a god and 'a kind of dragon' in the literatures of the ancient Near East, referring to this mythic combat. In fact, according to Felix-Marie Abel, all the Hellenistic Typhon traditions belie a Syrian – and more specifically, an Amorite – origin.[15] And there seems to have been a rationale for the continued transmission of this story in the area of the Levantine littoral in the legitimation of ancient kingship by the conquest of the Mediterranean Sea. These conquest narratives seem to have had a specific historical precedent.

Conquest of the Sea: Legitimation of Ancient Kingship

Mythologizing stories of conquering the Mediterranean Sea have been connected to several historical rulers in the ancient Near East.[16] It seems that stories of the hero's combat against a monstrous sea creature were connected to the legitimation of kingship in the Eastern Mediterranean as a foundational story that supported monarchic claims, drawing both on mythology and the authority of foregone rulers and ancestral kings. To this end, Mesopotamian royal inscriptions – being written cuneiform records of the lives and times of Babylonian and Assyrian rulers – contain references to the symbolic conquest of the Mediterranean Sea by various kings.[17] This political mythology was established during the reign of the legendary usurper king Sargon the Akkadian (*c.* 2334–2279 BCE), and it was likely at least partially based on his real-world military campaigns up along the river Euphrates to the Mediterranean coast, which Sargon had accomplished. According to the court ideologues of the Akkadian dynasty, he had managed this feat of power with the help of the Syrian Storm-god whose central cultic shrine was at the city of Aleppo.[18] According to the texts,[19] on the completion of his campaign Sargon had plunged his spear into the Mediterranean Sea in front of his formally arrayed army as a symbolic act. Centuries after his death, Sargon was still regarded one of only two kings to have seen the ends of the earth (in addition to the Hittite King Nur-Dagan), a king so great that he and his legend served as a prototype for later rulers across the Mesopotamian area for centuries.[20] There are no written narratives about the conquest of the (Mediterranean) sea that predate Sargon.[21]

There is a succession of texts referring to the subjugation of the divinized Mediterranean Sea from the Old Babylonian royal inscriptions down to texts written about the life of Babylon's Macedonian conqueror, Alexander the Great, whose historiographers likely adopted this tradition from the Persian monarchs preceding him.[22] These rulers reported not only conquering the Mediterranean Sea, but often plunging their weapons into the very sea in imitation of their predecessors.[23] Alexander's historiographers seem to have made use of the motif in order to make him appear as the legitimate king of Babylon, establishing Alexander as completing feats in their writings that the Persians rulers that came before him had boasted of in their royal inscriptions.[24] The boasts of the Persian rulers seem likewise to have been based on earlier precedent.

In Arrian's *Anabasis* (6.19), Alexander is reported to have made a sacrifice of several bulls to the Hellenistic Sea-god Poseidon,[25] which he cast into the sea with a golden libation cup and bowls as 'thanks-offerings' for safe passage through the sea. Arrian's description of the sacrifices may offer a rare glimpse into what exactly transpired during such rituals performed by earlier Mesopotamian kings: a libation was poured on the living bulls, the bulls were slaughtered, and then both bulls and vessels were given to the sea in concerted staging by the king to show his abilities to expand his sway even beyond the limits of the physical world (and the terrestrial environment). Strabo (14.3.9) also recorded Alexander's conquering of the sea not as a symbolic gesture but in actuality: 'Alexander came [to the Pamphylian Sea (Gulf of Antalya)] when there was a storm, and trusting generally to fortune, set out before the sea had receded, and the soldiers marched during the whole day up to the middle of the body in water'. The very sea bending to Alexander's will seems to collapse the mythological and historical narratives into one and the same. But in addition to this long succession of both mythological and historical textual records of this story, there are also iconographic depictions of the narrative that display a concurrent visual evolution of the motif.

Syrian Iconography of the God of the Mediterranean Sea: A Precursor to Dragon Imagery

The sea was depicted in Bronze Age Syrian iconography as a winged anthropomorphic and occasionally theriomorphic deity, and this seems to hark back to the ancient view of the world.[26] In the pre-Ptolemaic conception of the world, the earth disc was surrounded by the sea.[27] In addition to the world-encircling ocean there was another vast sea, which was thought to reside on top of the dome of the sky. There seem to have been certain correspondences between this supercaelian ocean and waters beneath the sky in that the stellar constellations and bodies of water (seas, lakes, and rivers) on the ground often carried the same names.[28] The ancient Mesopotamians counted seven seas altogether around the earth, and these seven interconnected seas corresponded the seven moving or non-fixed stars (planets), which were also called the 'seven heavens'. In fact, there is a

Figure 1.1 Cylinder seal impression of the theriomorphic Mediterranean Sea (left).

still a portion of the night-sky that is called the 'the Sea' which features constellations bearing the names of mythical sea monsters.[29] The ancient conception of the sea seems to have contained a much wider expanse, and the deity whose dominion was the sea would naturally have been the master of both. This deity was associated with the Mediterranean Sea in particular.

In Syrian iconography, as preserved mostly in cylinder seal impressions (see Figure 1), Yamm, the god of the sea, was depicted as a winged character, capable of traversing the distance between his two realms. Most often, wings were used to mark celestial or astral deities, and while sea gods are often considered terrestrial deities, this two-fold sea ultimately explains why the god and other mythical beasts associated with the sea were depicted with wings. In cylinder seal impressions, the Sea-god is also accompanied by leaping dolphins and diving waterbirds, both creatures naturally traversing the span of the sea, the earth, and the skies.[30] This conception fits in with the adversary of the hero being portrayed as a winged dragon or the sea-serpent in later narratives, which symbolically collapses the earth, the heavens, and the seas as its domain. As mentioned previously, the dragon is found in connection with this motif especially in later Arthurian legends, but the iconographic motif can be traced through Syrian depictions of the sea god in Levantine port cities all the way down to the Hellenistic period.[31] The sky-sea explains why fantastical creatures like dragons and hippocamps featured aspects of fish, birds, and land-animals, all in one.

Taken together, these Bronze Age iconographic depictions and texts help explain why it was important for ancient kings and rulers to present themselves as the conquerors of the sea, symbolically recreating and partaking in the mythic victory of the Syrian Storm-god over his adversary, the Mediterranean Sea, following in the footsteps of Sargon the Akkadian. It must be borne in mind that in this mythology, the sea and the monster that dwells in the sea are one and the same, one representing the other in an eternal cycle. In mythological stories and legends, the divine hero conquered the monster, while in the world of men it was the king who subjugated the sea by conquering coastal regions and making real-world military campaigns to the Mediterranean Sea. Both these motifs seem to keep recurring in texts and iconography, and the tradition persisted through both Classical and Late Antiquity.

Continuation of the Tradition in Classical Antiquity

The same tradition of conquering the sea has been connected to later rulers of the ancient world. A story similar to Alexander was written regarding the Carthaginian general Hamilcar Barca, the father of the famous Hannibal that later waged war on the Romans.[32] According to the story, as recorded by the Greek historian Polybius in the second century BCE, the waters receded before Hamilcar on the river Bagradas as they had done before Alexander on the Pamphylian Sea a century prior, allowing Hamilcar a decisive military victory.[33] Both of these events, Alexander and Hamilcar marching through receding waters, were also connected to the Mosaic cleaving of the Red Sea by the Jewish historian Josephus in the first century CE.[34] This indicates that the ancient historians were well aware of the symbolic content of the narratives. While these fantastic stories have obviously been historicized and stripped of any explicitly mythological elements, it is noteworthy that the Carthaginians were the direct descendants of the Eastern Mediterranean cities where these stories had originated many centuries before.[35]

The first-century CE geographer Strabo writes in his *Geography* (16.2.28) that in the city of Joppa (modern Jaffa/Yafo), it was Andromeda who 'was exposed to the sea-monster; for the place is situated at a rather high elevation [...] so high, it is said, that Jerusalem, the metropolis of the Judaeans, is visible from it; and indeed the Judaeans have used this place as a seaport when they have gone down as far as the sea'. He does not elaborate on how the myth and the use of the port by the Jerusalemites are connected, but he seems to present the mythic story as an historical event. The myth of Andromeda and the sea-beast Cetus was also connected to the city of Jaffa by Josephus (*BJ* 3.9.3) and Pausanias (4.35.9). While the name of the maiden is different in the stories – Andromeda, Astarte, Aphrodite, Derceto – the basic structure of the story seems to remain consistent.[36]

The tradition finds continuation in the Roman cultural sphere. Emperor Caligula (12–41 CE) had a personal connection to the Eastern Mediterranean, having spent his youth in Syria with his father Germanicus. Caligula seems to have modelled his rulership very specifically after the kingship of Alexander the Great. Both Suetonius in the second century (*Calig.* 46.1) and Cassius Dio in the third century (59.25.1–3) recount a story, with the intended purpose of describing the madness of the emperor, of how, during a military campaign to Britannia, the emperor had arranged his troops and their weaponry on the shore of the sea with the purpose, implied by the authors, of waging war against the sea. According to Suetonius, the emperor even erected a lighthouse at Itium to celebrate his victory over the sea.[37] While neither of these authors was a contemporary of Caligula and clearly had no first-hand experience of the events, the purpose of the stories seems to be to emphasize the infantilism and madness of the monarch who was later fashioned a tyrant. But the incident is curious with regard to these traditions that would still have been a living tradition on the coast during Caligula's youth, as it seems that the emperor was purposefully modelling his character and story after the example set by Alexander, of whose legend the subjugation of the sea formed a part.[38]

Stories and texts in which kings plunge their weapons into the sea in front of their military troops as a symbolic staging of the mythological combat between the Storm-god and his adversary, the divinized sea, had been recounted in the Syrian area for thousands of years by Caligula's time, always with the intent of legitimizing precarious kingship.[39] According to Suetonius (*Calig.* 52.1), Caligula often appeared in public holding a thunderbolt or a trident, which Suetonius calls the 'emblems of the gods' and which are connected with the Storm-god (Zeus) and Sea-god (Poseidon) respectively, and would dress himself in the breastplate of Alexander the Great, which he had taken from Alexander's sarcophagus in Egypt. If Caligula had sought to emulate Alexander the Great, or Suetonius himself drew material from Alexandrine histories to make such implications, it is possible that the Eastern Mediterranean narrative of the Storm-god's combat with the sea underlies this curious incident, at least in the sense of an adapted intellectual tradition. In the context of the Syrian traditions, staging a combat against the sea for the benefit of the military troops at least makes some kind of sense.

The Persistence of the Tradition in Late Antiquity

The tradition of the divine hero's defeat of the sea persisted also in Late Antiquity both in mythological and historical forms. The legend of Saint George and its connection to the city of Ashkelon has been discussed previously. While the historical Saint George is located at the cusp of Classical and Late Antiquity, and the legend itself was popularized in the Middle Ages, it is important to note that the story of Saint George's battle with the dragon, in particular, was specifically founded in Late Antiquity. The oldest version of the story is recorded in the Syriac translation of the *Acts of Saint George* from the fifth century, already featuring hints of the motif of slaying the dragon. Originally written in Greek, of which only fragments survive, the Syriac translation was rendered only decades after the original. The oldest surviving complete iteration of the text is dated to *c.* 600. In this version, the epithet dragon or asp-serpent is given to King Dadianus, from whose grasp George saves princess Alexandra. In the visualization of the story, the martyr is depicted as slaying a serpent instead of a dragon.[40] But as discussed in this chapter, the serpent formed a part of what would later become dragon imagery.

It is possible that the crucial element that allowed for the Christianized translations of a story originally connected to Syrian deities was the motif of suffering, which was part of the combat of the Storm-god in the Levantine mythology. In the legend of Saint George, the martyr suffers appalling torture and a violent death for Christ, and indeed the suffering and death of Saint George forms the earliest layer of the stories connected to his character.[41] While the Syrian Storm-god is rescued from the underworld by the maiden-goddess, the suffering and death of the hero are also very much a part of the earliest narrative from Ugarit. Suffering and death are also a part of the Adonis stories that abound on the Eastern Mediterranean, the name of Adonis an *interpretatio Graeca* of the Syrian Storm-god Baal in the Hellenistic Era.[42]

However, the story of Saint George is not the only example of the motif from the Later Empire. The similarity of the archangel Michael's defeat of the Dragon with the story of Saint George has been mentioned previously. In Eusebius' *Vita Constantini* (3.3) from the fourth century, the defeat of his predecessor Licinius by the Roman Emperor Constantine is recounted. According to Eusebius, the emperor commissioned a painting of his sons and himself standing on top of a serpent pierced by a weapon as a visual reworking of the battle in Revelation with the serpent symbolizing the defeated Licinius and the emperor himself representing Michael.[43] The story of Constantine's defeat of Licinius at the site of a winged pagan deity is also recounted by Nicephorus Callistus Xanthopulus in his *Church History* (*HE* 7.50), predominantly using much older sources.

Nonnus of Panopolis, a Greek epic poet writing in the fifth century CE, tells the story of Dionysus' battle against the Sea-god Poseidon on the island of Tyre. Nonnus equates Dionysus in the story with Heracles, who in turn was the Greek interpretation of Melqart, one of the iterations of the Syrian Baal in the cities of the Eastern Mediterranean but who was etymologically connected to the Storm-god Zeus. The reason for the battle in the story was Beroë, in this version of the myth a mortal woman pursued by both gods.[44] Nina Jidejian related a similar aetiological myth from Beirut, according to which the city had been named after the nymph Beroë, daughter of Aphrodite, lusted after by the patron divinity of Beirut, the Sea-god Poseidon, who contested for the goddess with Dionysus, 'symbol of the land'.[45] This myth was commemorated on coinage from the Hellenistic era. According to Jidenian, 'Beroë thus became the possession of the Sea-god, a reflection of the city's geographical and maritime importance in the ancient world,' making Beirut the only city on the Eastern Mediterranean where the Sea-god wins the combat against the Storm-god.

A continuation of the motif is also found in the cult of Zeus Georgos, an agricultural deity worshiped, for example, at Antioch, which may have been a precursor of the Saint George legends. Erica Ferg connected the name George to the figure of the Storm-god by way of 'belonging to Zeus Georgos', the Athenian serpent-slaying god of farmland, fecundity, lightning and rain.[46] According to her, the saint was not called George due to the name of a historical person but through association with the function or mission of the saint, being the 'Christianized version of a local Levantine cult already dedicated to 'Zeus Georgos'. While an Athenian deity, the origin of Zeus Georgos was in the cities of the Eastern Mediterranean, in urban centres such as Antioch, in the local deity of the Levantine cities. This *Belus Georgeus* was an iteration of the Storm-god Baal.[47] According to Ferg, Saint George is an example of a Levantine deity becoming transformed into a saint in the Christian tradition of the late-third to early-fourth centuries, in the tradition of the cults of the Byzantine warrior saints. This translation of the myth of the Storm-god's battle with the sea took place during Late Antiquity for the specific purpose of Christianizing popular pagan cults.

The historicized narrative of the ruler symbolically subjugating the sea is found in connection with the Sassanid King Khosrow (Chosroes) from the sixth century. The story is recorded by Procopius in *The History of the Wars* wherein Khosrow breaks the

Eternal Peace with the Emperor Justinian in 540 and launches a campaign across the eastern provinces of the Roman Empire.[48] After conquering many of the metropolises of the empire, among them Antioch, Khosrow reaches the Mediterranean Sea by Seleucia Pieria (Procop. *Bell.* 2.5–13). There, the king ritually bathes in the sea to present himself as the victor and makes sacrifices to the gods before returning to his troops. Procopius cites this provocative act as the reason why Justinian found it impossible to make peace with Khosrow. Robert Rollinger suggested that bathing of the king's weapons or their symbolic plunging into the Mediterranean would also have taken place.[49] The king of kings, *Shahanshah*, as he was called by the Persians, did this to project himself as a king worthy of his predecessors, seemingly following the precedent established by multiple Mesopotamian kings.

Conclusion

The ancient Levantine king ruled with the authority of the Storm-god, wielding the god's power and prestige, and presenting himself as the representative of the divinity to his people.[50] The symbols and symbolic investiture of kingship were shared by gods and kings alike. As an icon or a proxy for the divine essence, the mortal king ritually performed the role of the divinity for his people in cult. And it was by conquering the sea that the ancient king was made. The recurring myth of the hero's defeat of the sea-monster is inexorably intertwined with the conquest of the Mediterranean Sea by Mesopotamian kings that frequently manifested in real-world military campaigns to the Mediterranean coast. As the Storm-god's victory over the divinized sea legitimized the rule of king, so did the character of the sea itself mediate kingship, presenting in the sea-monster the ancestral seat of kingship and in the hero-king its vital, living representative. The fact that the stories were used to legitimize kingship that ascertained their continued transmission in the Eastern Mediterranean for such a long time.

Mythical and legendary stories of the hero's defeat of the watery monster were also periodically historicized, connected to historical persons and locales, in order to activate (or even re-activate) them in their respective societies. Connecting the myths to real-world locations and to real, living, people ascertained that the myth stayed relevant in the area of the Eastern Mediterranean century after century. As the reader can surely deduce by the examples discussed in this chapter, most of the later stories in Classical and Late Antiquity using older Mesopotamian conceptions of conquering the sea were written down by 'western' authors writing about 'eastern' kings. Their tone is often perplexed regarding the traditions, reading them either as something fantastical or something utterly incomprehensible. While the narrative itself had proven persistent, something of its symbolic content had clearly been lost in time. This refashioning of the story seems to take place by the time that the Classical Era turns into Late Antiquity and may even have been ushered in by the Christianization of these older narratives.

It seems as though the tradition itself continued on in these later stories, but its significance was lost while the ideological trappings of Mesopotamian kingship faded from memory. There is certainly more than a hint of Orientalism[51] in their portrayal of these rulers and their strange customs and superstitions. But when we look at the succession of these stories in their historical context, waging war on the sea becomes much easier to understand. The stories also persisted in the area long after Antiquity. In 1826 the British Ambassador to the Ottoman Empire, Sir William Drummond, recorded a local myth from Byblos, according to which the water of the Adonis River (modern Abraham River or *Nahr Ibrahim*) was believed to be tinted red annually to commemorate the season 'when the festival was celebrated in his honour', Adonis being a Hellenistic translation of the Storm-god Baal in this area. The tinting of the water in the colour of blood was reminiscent of the god's combat.[52] In fact, in parts of the Levantine littoral, traces of this tradition may still exist today, for example in the Beirutian New Year's celebrations where tracer bullets are shot out to the Mediterranean Sea.[53] The local participants in this modern ritual likely have no idea of the area's long history of waging war on the sea.

Nevertheless, the ancient mythology and the employment of the symbolism within the story by subsequent rulers went hand in hand, Saint George and the Dragon an example of the former and Khosrow's bathing in the sea following his conquests an example of the latter, the over 3,000-year-old tradition still alive and well in Late Antiquity.

Notes

1. Riches 2000.
2. Collins 2018.
3. Johnson 2005. While the narrative hearkens back to chapter 12 of Revelation, the earliest depiction of the archangel Michael slaying the dragon is connected with the defeat of the Roman Emperor Valerius Licinianus Licinius by his colleague and successor Constantine near the sanctuary of Michaelion in the village of Sosthenion (modern Istinye) near Constantinople in the early fourth century. The sanctuary had been erected on the temple of an unknown local winged deity, possibly called Zeus Sosthenios. See Williams 2004: 36, Johnson 2005: 33–5.
4. Good 2009. The best-known Arthurian romances are Sir Thomas Malory's *Le Morte D'Arthur* from the fifteenth century and the four romances (*Erec et Enide, Cliges, Yvain, Lancelot*) by Chretien de Troyes from the twelfth century. See Steinbeck 1976.
5. Guiley 2001: 129–30; Walter 2003: 110.
6. Jacopo de Varazze in Italian; he lived from 1220–98. In addition to hagiographies Varagine cited early Church Fathers and historians like St Augustine, St John Chrysostom, and Cassiodorus. See Duffy 2012: xi–xiii.
7. Reames 1985; Duffy 2012. Several manuscripts of the legend that circulated in the Middle Ages survive, but two abbreviated versions, Jean de Mailly's *Abbreviatio in gestis et miraculis sanctorum* and Bartholomew of Trent's *Epilogus in gesta sanctorum* seem to have been the most popular. The work was translated into English and published in a folio volume by William Caxton in 1476 as *The Golden Legend*, being one of the first books printed in England. A critical edition of the original Latin text was prepared by G. P. Maggioni in 2007

as *Legenda Aurea. Con le miniature del codice Ambrosiano C 240 inf.* See also Duffy 2012. The quotes are from Caxton's translation.

8. Riches 2000.
9. Redford 1992: 45–6.
10. Töyräänvuori 2018: 125–69.
11. The *editio princeps* of most of the tablets in the Baal Cycle was published between 1932–1938 in CTA and the journal *Syria* X; XII by C. Virolleaud. For details on the publication of each column and tablet, see Smith 1994.
12. Smith 1994.
13. Cf. Irby 2021: 149–50.
14. *De Astronomica* (*Poeticon Astronomicon*) is a work written in the name of the first-century Roman historian Gaius Julius Hyginus but was likely written later since it seems to contain information from the *Almagest* of the Alexandrian polymath Claudius Ptolemy written in the late second century. See Condos 1997.
15. Abel 1933: 153–4.
16. Malamat 1994; Rollinger 2012; Töyräänvuori 2018.
17. Malamat 1965; Rollinger 2012; with supplementary examples in Töyräänvuori 2018: 494, lists Mesopotamian kings from the twenty-second to the sixth centuries BCE, among them Lugal-Zaggesi, Sargon, Naram-Sin, Šu-Sin, Yahdun-Lim, Šamši-Adad, Zimri-Lim, Tiglath-Pileser, Aššur-Bel-kala, Aššurnasirpal, Šalmaneser, Adad-Nirari, Sennacherib, Esarhaddon, Nabonidus and Cyrus.
18. Liverani 1993; Töyräänvuori 2018.
19. Most of the texts are Akkadian lapidary inscriptions discussed by Töyräänvuori (2018: 437–55) but they also include later Mesopotamian narratives like Birth of Sargon, Sargon the Conqueror, and Sargon King of Battle.
20. Lambert 2013, 232.
21. Töyräänvuori (2018: 455) argues that Sargon's predecessor Lugal-Zaggesi is the first monarch to reference the conquest of the sea in his royal inscriptions without having factually accomplished this feat. This is why both the physical, real-world military campaign to the Mediterranean Sea and its recording in multiple lapidary inscriptions was required of the usurper Sargon to legitimize his ideologically precarious kingship.
22. Töyräänvuori 2018.
23. Herodotus mentions the ritual in *Histories* 4.44, 4.85. The Neo-Assyrian inscriptions with which Rollinger 2012: 732 connects the ('identical') ritual are RIMA 2 A.0.87.3: 21–25, RIMA 2, A.0.89.7: iv 2f., RIMA 3, A.0.102.6: ii 33; A.0.102.8: 19´; A.0.102.2: ii 77. He also goes on to suggest that this same tradition was adopted by certain Roman officials via Alexander, setting up altars by the Strait of Gibraltar, Cape Finisterre and Alto da Vigia, all at the westernmost edge of the world at the time.
24. Diod. Sic. 17.95; Plut. *De Alex. fort.* 62; Curt. 9.4, 13; Just. *Epit.* 12.8; Plin. *HN* 6.49, 62; Philostr. *V A* 2.43; Arr. *Anab.* 5.29.1f. Most notably Cyrus and Xerxes. See Töyräänvuori 2018: 478–98.
25. Poseidon not only became the name of the Syrian god of the Mediterranean Sea in the Hellenistic period, but it also seems as though, at least in Argive pottery, the sea god identified as Poseidon was in reference particularly to the Syrian god of the Mediterranean Sea. On the Levantine coast, Poseidon was associated with the cities of Berytus (Beirut) and Sidon specifically. Langdon 1989: 201; Jidejian 1992: 58.

26. Töyräänvuori 2021.

27. The geocentric model (a globular earth as the centre of the universe) became the standard model in the second century following the writing of *Almagest* by Claudius Ptolemy, mentioned previously. However, notions of a spherical Earth had existed prior to this e.g. in Pre-Socratic philosophy from the sixth century BCE, notably by Heraclitus, whose works survive only in quotations, e.g. in Aristotle (Harris 1994). Ptolemy had also used the observations of Babylonian astronomers in the construction of his model. See Crowe 1990.

28. Day (1985, 4): writes '[…] the archaic world view shared by the ancient Israelites along with other peoples of the ancient Near East that both above the domed firmament of heaven and below the earth there is a cosmic sea. Rain was regarded as having its origins in the cosmic sea above the firmament and coming down through the windows of heaven, while the world's seas and lakes were thought of as connected with the subterranean part of the cosmic sea'. Both rivers and certain constellations carried the names of serpents, e.g. *bašmu* (serpent) referring to the constellation Serpens and *mušḫuššu* (horned snake) referring to the constellation Hydra.

29. Olcott 1911. He lists among the constellations of 'the heavenly sea' the constellations Cetus, Pisces, Delphinus, Aquarius, Pisces Australis, Capricorn, Grus, and Eridanus. He also suggested that this grouping may have been borne out of the sun's journey through this part of the sky during the rainy season in the ancient Near East. This may be accurate at least insofar as the earth's axial precession goes. Olcott (1911: 31–2) also mentions an ancient Egyptian belief that the inundation of the Nile was caused by the Water Bearer (Aquarius) sinking his urn into the foundations of the heavenly river, often connected with the Milky Way.

30. Töyräänvuori 2021.

31. Jidejian 1992: 60–1, 114. Byblian coins from the fourth century BCE feature the god Melqart riding a hippocamp, a winged horse with the tail of a serpent. The horse was also associated with the sea god both on the Eastern Mediterranean and the Aegean areas. and may have served as the symbolic representation of the crashing waves of the sea, where the wings represented the heavens and the serpent was associated with the earth. See Langdon 1989; Töyräänvuori 2021.

32. Goldsworthy 2003.

33. Recorded by Polybius (1.75.7–10): '[Hamilcar] had noticed that when the wind blew strongly from certain quarters the mouth of the river got silted up and the passage became shallow just where it falls into the sea. He therefore got his force ready to march out, and keeping his project to himself, waited for this to occur. When the right time came, he started from Carthage at night, and without anyone noticing him, had by daybreak got his army across at the place mentioned.'

34. In *Antiquities of the Jews* (16.5), Josephus explains the Biblical story of Moses cleaving the Red Sea as follows: 'As for myself, I have delivered every part of this history as I found it in the sacred books; nor let any one wonder at the strangeness of the narration if a way were discovered to those men of old time, who were free from the wickedness of the modern ages, whether it happened by the will of God or whether it happened of its own accord; while, for the sake of those that accompanied Alexander, king of Macedonia, who yet lived, comparatively but a little while ago, the Pamphylian Sea retired and afforded them a passage through itself, had no other way to go; I mean, when it was the will of God to destroy the monarchy of the Persians: and this is confessed to be true by all that have written about the actions of Alexander. But as to these events, let everyone determine as he pleases.'

35. Carthage had originally been founded by Tyrians and had received an influx of Tyrian refugees both during the Persian conquest of the Levant (fifth century BCE) and again during Alexander the Great's destruction of Tyre. See Grainger 1991: 38; Glassman 2017: 507.

36. On the role of the maiden/goddess in the story, see Töyräänvuori 2016.
37. Suet. *Calig.* 46.1: 'At last, as if resolved to make war in earnest, he drew up his army on the shore of the ocean, with his ballistas and other engines of war, and while no one could imagine what he intended to do, on a sudden commanded them to gather up the seashells, and fill their helmets and the folds of their dress with them, calling them "the spoils of the ocean due to the Capitol and the Palatium". As a monument of his success, he raised a lofty tower, upon which, as at Pharos, he ordered lights to be burned in the night-time for the direction of ships at sea; and then promising the soldiers a donative of a hundred denarii a man, as if he had surpassed the most eminent examples of generosity, "Go your ways," said he, "and be merry; go, ye are rich".'
38. Adams 2007: 40; Heckel and Tritle 2009: 263.
39. Caligula was only the third emperor of the newly established Roman Empire whose line of succession was not through primogeniture but by adoption. His predecessor Tiberius had adopted both Caligula, son of the popular general Germanicus and great-grandson of the first Emperor Augustus, and his own grandson Gemellus, intending for them to share the Principate. This made the legitimacy of Caligula's emperorship precarious despite his early popularity as ruler. See Adams 2007, and also Lampinen's chapter in this volume.
40. Kiraz 2009.
41. Morabito 2011.
42. West 1997: 57.
43. Eus. *Vit. Const.* 3.3: 'And besides this, he caused to be painted on a lofty tablet, and set up in the front of the portico of his palace, so as to be visible to all, a representation of the salutary sign placed above his head, and below it that hateful and savage adversary of mankind, who by means of the tyranny of the ungodly had wasted the Church of God, falling headlong, under the form of a dragon, to the abyss of destruction. For the sacred oracles in the books of God's prophets have described him as a dragon and a crooked serpent; and for this reason the emperor thus publicly displayed a painted resemblance of the dragon beneath his own and his children's feet, stricken through with a dart, and cast headlong into the depths of the sea.'
44. Nonn. *Dion.* 43: 'For King of Satyrs and Ruler of the Sea, a maiden was the prize. She stood silent, but reluctant to have a foreign wedding with a wooer from the sea; she feared the watery bower of love in the deep waves, and preferred Bacchos: she was like Deïaneira, who once in that noisy strife for a bride preferred Heracles, and stood there fearing the wedding with a fickle bullhorn River.'
45. Jidejian 1992: 58.
46. Ferg 2020.
47. Haddad 1969: 24–5, connects Saint George directly to the Ugaritic Baal through Zeus Georgius: 'The attributes of the Christian saint, as we shall demonstrate, link him strongly even to the ancient Baal-Hadad known to us from the Ugaritic texts of the 14th century BC'
48. See Börm 2021.
49. Rollinger 2012: 734–6.
50. Green 1993.
51. Said 1978.
52. Drummond 1826: 122–4.
53. Gall and Hobby 2009: 555.

CHAPTER 2
MIGRATING MOSAICS: TRANSFORMING IMAGES OF OCEANUS AND MARINE ENVIRONMENTS FROM THE IMPERIAL PERIOD TO LATE ANTIQUITY*

Alexandra Grigorieva

Introduction

Roman *imperium sine fine* brought Mediterranean cultural habits to places far removed from the actual sea. Indeed, people who lived nowhere near the sea and had never had an opportunity to travel beyond their actual homeland may have been aware of the Mediterranean Sea and its importance for the Roman Empire. One of the elements that certainly made such a perception possible, or indeed inevitable, was figurative art. There is no doubt that, unfortunately, not many actual *capolavori* reached the imperial backwoods, but on the other hand, any form of artistic expression may have been sufficient for displaying one's own purposes and for showing off one's status and degree of romanization. Hence, nowadays archaeologists are constantly finding the remains of Roman villas, often decorated with mosaics, even in the remotest corners of the former Empire.

The art of mosaics flourished during the Roman Empire all over the Mediterranean.[1] Despite the observable regional differences, many mosaic motifs were part of the global imperial art fashion, as pervasive and recognizable as IKEA furniture is nowadays, and it is possible to appreciate the same decorations on mosaics found in Italy, Tunisia, and Germany, as well as in other regions. Many of these mosaics represented marine topics of various kinds, which is particularly understandable when these were used for decorating water-related places such as baths (whether public or private), *nymphaeum*-style fountain environments, and in Late Antiquity even some early Christian baptismal fonts. According to Francesca Ghedini and Marta Novello, the wealth of marine motifs can be grouped by subject into two large bodies; one representing the realistic sea, and the other mirroring the imaginary mythic sea with all its 'swimming monsters'.[2] The notion of *monstra natantia* was named by Horace and later elaborated by Tacitus as 'sea monsters, part-human part-beast shapes, seen or believed in out of fear' (*monstra maris, ambiguas hominum et beluarum formas visa sive ex metu credita*).[3] In some instances, however, the two subjects do merge together and we may observe identifiable specimens of real marine fauna in the midst of cavorting sea monsters[4] or 'naturalistically' displayed fishing activities performed by cupids in sea waters teeming with marine species.[5] In this light, the question is how such marine motifs arrived – and were viewed

– in landlocked Romanized places, distant from the actual Mediterranean coastlines and their cultural conventions.

To find some answers, I will use Ghedini's double framework of the 'real sea' and the 'mythic sea' and try to trace the presence of two marine characters, one 'real', the other one 'mythic'. Both characters appear in the mosaics in the formerly 'barbarian' North (or more precisely North-West) of the Roman Empire (roughly corresponding to modern England, parts of France, Germany, and Switzerland) and in other mosaics found in different parts closer to, or along, the Mediterranean coastlines. I will be looking at works dating from the middle of the second century CE, because that is the period when, according to Katherine Dunbabin, 'the use of mosaic pavements really began to take root in the north-west provinces of the Empire'.[6] The chronological framework of the works that I am studying extends until the sixth century CE, therefore well after the fall of Rome and corresponding to the Late Antique period.

A Surfeit of Morays

For the 'real' marine character I have chosen *murena* or the Mediterranean moray (*Muraena helena*), a highly distinctive, somewhat snake-shaped fish that held a particular prominence both in the Roman cuisine[7] and as part of various *topoi* used in imperial literature.[8] Romans had started farming morays as well as a few other fish species already in the Late Republican period,[9] and these constituted a basic luxury food, somewhat like the farmed salmon of today, fatty and satisfying.[10] Indeed, Cicero prided himself in easily abstaining from eating both moray and oysters.[11] And as it is today with farmed salmon versus wild salmon, morays caught in the wild – especially along the Sicilian coasts where they reportedly abounded – were appreciated more than the 'farmed' ones and were really sought after.[12]

The earliest representation of a moray in a mosaic that we know of (end of the second century BCE), can be found in Palestrina – the ancient Praeneste. This beautiful work in *opus vermiculatum* was made according to the sophisticated Alexandrian canon,[13] and even if it is unfortunately badly damaged, it is still possible to discern that its main subject was a sea replete with colourful marine fauna, executed with incredible precision and attention to detail, and bordered at one end with an elegant coastline. And even though the moray represented there is only partially preserved, it can be appreciated that it was represented fighting an octopus and thus illustrating a marine *locus communis* that had been discussed in Classic literature by Aristotle and many of his followers,[14] being the so-called *antipatheia*, bitter triple enmity between moray and octopus, octopus and spiny lobster, spiny lobster and moray.[15] No traces of spiny lobster have survived close to the moray-octopus fight from the mosaic, but originally it could have been a triple representation. After all, this is what can be appreciated on the two extraordinary high-quality *opus vermiculatum* Pompeiian marine emblemata[16] from the Casa del Fauno (VI, 12, 2, end of the second century BCE) and Casa a Cinque Piani, a.k.a. Casa dei Mosaici Geometrici (VIII, 2, 16 early first

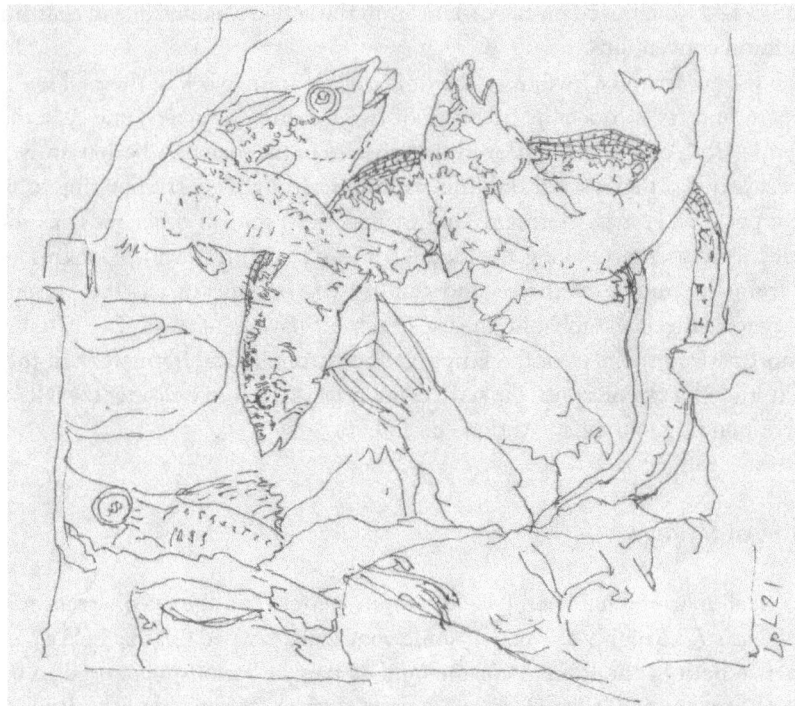

Figure 2.1 A second-century mosaic still-life with a realistic looking moray. Antiquarium of Ostia (Italy). Here and throughout the article drawings are by Lisa Plavinsky.

century BCE). These mosaics display a triple *antipatheia* of a moray, an octopus and a spiny lobster prominently featured in the centre, again presumably according to the learned literature-orientated Alexandrian prototype that was applicable both to mosaics and wall paintings.[17]

However, by the second century CE the *antipatheia* model for mosaic representations of moray, or at least the meaning of this representation (in fact, almost a scientific illustration), seems to have been forgotten. New mosaic styles were developing in Italy where ornamentality was appreciated more than verisimilitude.[18] For instance, the famous fish mosaic from Populonia,[19] dating about 100 CE,[20] discloses the main protagonists of the former *antipatheia*: the moray, the octopus and the spiny lobster and, although in this case they are somewhat realistically executed, they are also squeezed together rigidly and improbably with some other fish species just to fill the mosaic's shape. Therefore, in this mosaic the intention was not to display the actual movement of living marine fauna as happened with earlier mosaics.

Gradually, it is possible to appreciate that verisimilitude gradually went out of favour even for still-life xenia style mosaics. So, the pretty naturalistic second century Ostian still-life with moray and other fish (Figure 2.1) found in the Isola Sacra Necropolis might have been perceived as quite old-fashioned even when it was made. As mosaic styles progressed from *emblema*-oriented and painting-oriented towards more general and decorative ones in the first–second century CE,[21] the moray was fast becoming just one fish among many, with no particular meaning. However, this motif still appeared regularly represented in both 'realistic' and 'mythological' sea settings, incidentally often in the mythological ones, particularly coupled with fishing cupids, marine Venus, Oceanus and so on.

Oceanus, Father of All Things

The mythical marine character whose mosaic images seem worth exploring alongside the real ones is Oceanus, a somewhat complex and conflicting figure in Classical Antiquity. Oceanus is both a Titan and the great world-encircling river, as well as representing the future Atlantic Ocean beyond the Mediterranean and the source of all waters on earth, either fresh or salty (3,000 rivers and 3,000 Oceanids according to Hesiod).[22] Following different traditions, Oceanus could be either the son of Uranus and Gaia (Hesiod), or their father (Orphic sources) and thus the primeval father of all gods.[23] Virgil calls him 'universal father' (*Oceanus, pater rerum*).[24] He is specially prominent in Imperial Rome,[25] and there is even a Latin hymn *Ad Oceanum* addressed to him as *cunctorum partem* ('part of everything') which dates from as late as the third or fourth centuries CE.[26]

Right up to the early classical period, iconographic evidence of Oceanus is patchy and scarce at best.[27] There are a couple of early-sixth-century BCE Attic black-figure vases with labelled characters in which Oceanus is depicted as a partly anthropomorphic, partly zoomorphic figure: a bearded man with big horns whose lower torso ends in a giant fish-tail, while holding a long snake and a longish fish on one of the vases.[28] An early-fifth-century BCE red-figure vase has Oceanus (a fully anthropomorphic old man with a tall staff) and other characters of the legend of the Garden of Hesperides grouped around the apple-tree of Hesperides, entwined and guarded by the mythic snake Ladon (future constellation Draco).[29] Finally, Oceanus is also present (and labelled, miraculously enough) on the famous mid-second-century BCE Gigantomachy frieze of the Pergamon Altar[30] and, even if it is not possible to completely discern the anthropomorphic figure, there is a giant snake represented nearby that helps to complete the picture.

Green Beginnings

It is during the Roman imperial era that we suddenly find images of Oceanus, particularly his head, or the so called 'mask of Oceanus', surfacing everywhere in all kinds of artistic media: mosaics, wall paintings, carved stone and so on.[31] In Italy, the earlier images identified with Oceanus that came to my knowledge appeared around mid-first century CE in Pompeian and Herculaneum wall-paintings.[32] These images displayed stylized bearded masks with crustacean *chelae* (i.e. claws/pincers) and plant tendrils sprouting from their heads. These depictions looked more like ornamental designs than divine

Figure 2.2 A late third- or early fourth-century mosaic of Oceanus. Bardo National Museum (Tunisia).

personifications, and seemed to be executed in the Fourth Pompeian painting style that was almost certainly derived from *grotteschi* of Emperor Nero's *Domus Aurea*.[33] Still, there are also a couple of more individual-looking small bearded Oceanus mask mosaics with *chelae* claws set in a now mostly lost mythic marine milieu frieze or in a *nymphaeum* frieze among decorative plant tendrils and flowers, and respectively preserved *in situ* in Herculaneum's *Casa dei Cervi*[34] and *Casa di Nettuno ed Anfitrite*.[35] In a later development, it is also possible to find two second century CE black-and-white Oceanus mask mosaic pavements from the *Terme Marittime* baths of Ostia,[36] where the Room D has the sombre shaggy black head of Oceanus with prominent *chelae* claws encircled with four oar-bearing and horn-blowing Tritons with forked merman tails instead of legs. Instead, the image of Oceanus that can be found in Room E is very similar but surrounded by four Nereids riding sea-horses (hippocamps).[37] The nether parts of Oceanus' masks seem to end in decorative acanthus leaves, placing their iconographic style much closer to the previously mentioned grotesque Oceanus wall paintings documented in the nineteenth century, than to the surviving Herculaneum mosaics. It is quite probable that the original mask of Oceanus, a particularly Roman phenomenon, had actually evolved out of a grotesque decorative motif with masks and leafy scrolls.[38]

The original decorative motif can be appreciated on an early-second-century mosaic from Sousse in Tunisia (inv. Sousse 57.220). In this piece we can find eight love scenes (one damaged) placed between a satyr and a bacchante framed by coiling acanthus plant tendrils springing out of eight shaggy bearded masks (two damaged) and interlocking them together. No crustacean elements can be detected in the mosaic as such, but the iconography is pretty similar to an early Oceanus mask.[39] A couple of centuries later (Figure 2.2), in the late third or early fourth century CE, it is possible to find the mosaic mask of a 'green' Oceanus, characterized by crustacean legs and plant tendrils growing out of his head. The mosaic was found in an apsidal basin of *Maison de Bacchus et Ariane*, Thuburbo Maius (Tunisia), now located in the Bardo Museum (inv. 1399).[40] A third-century version of the 'green' Oceanus is also attested in Orbe (modern

Switzerland),[41] and to some extent in the Bad Kreuznach mosaic from Roman Germany (see Figure 2.7). Therefore, this early iconographic style was quite widespread even in latter times. It might have been partly influenced by green-haired images of river gods, such as the mosaic of a river god mask with lank untidy greenish hair and beard and round eyes with a surprised look, set among the greenish mosaic reeds to preside over an elegant water cascade in a colourful *nymphaeum* of *Casa della Fontana Grande* in Pompeii.[42]

In any case, the bearded mask sprouting greenery was not only reserved to characterize Oceanus. Indeed, there are two fourth–sixth century documented mosaics of bearded masks sprouting acanthus leaves from mainland Greece. One comes from an Argos villa and represents a grey-bearded old man as part of a traditional acanthus scroll, and the other consists only in a mask found in a corner of the episcopal palace of Nikopolis, capital of the former Roman province of Epirus Vetus (in parts of modern Greece and Albania), so the context is unclear.[43] The latter represents a young, bearded man crowned with luxuriant acanthus leaves (rather unusual motif in iconography). There is also a late Roman mosaic from Constantinople of a giant, green-bearded mask (Figure 2.3) set within a complex acanthus scroll.[44] In both cases, there is no marine context represented at all. Thus, based on the mosaic evidence available, it might seem that the single Oceanus mask motif was born roughly in the first century CE from green scroll grotesque ornaments decorated with many masks. The motif was finally characterized by the greenery in Late Antiquity, with its singularity remaining, but its sea-connected symbolism and links with marine environments abandoned after several centuries of ubiquitous prominence. One of the last appearances of the proper 'green' Oceanus can be witnessed on the fabulous great dish of the Mildenhall Treasure.[45] This enormous fourth-century CE silver dish weighing more than eight kilos features the mask of Oceanus in its centre, and here the figure has both a beautiful beard of acanthus foliage and dolphins sprouting from it and from his shaggy hair. Here Oceanus is surrounded by a flowing border of Nereids and other mythic sea-creatures separated with a garland of sea-scallops from a wider border featuring a Bacchic revelry of satyrs and bacchants that together with Pan and Silenus are overwhelming drunken Hercules with their music and dancing.[46] However, it seems that the image was not forgotten, and although there cannot be any direct evidence to its impact, it is highly probable that Roman 'green' Oceanus eventually morphed into the Green Man so prominent in British culture from Medieval times onwards. In this green ornamental guise Oceanus mask has never completely disappeared from the European art scene, surfacing in different countries and epochs from time to time.

The Horns Controversy

Another important recurring element in the image of Oceanus, apart from the occasional greenness and the indispensable proliferation of shaggy hair-cum-beard, is something non-human growing out of his human head. In the first Italian Roman mosaics and wall-

Figure 2.3 A first-half-of-the-sixth-century Constantinople mosaic. Great Palace Mosaic Museum (Turkey).

paintings available from the first century CE, it is possible to see crustacean *chelae* claws represented. A little later, particularly in Tunisia, other crustacean elements, such as antennae and even characteristic crustacean legs have been added to the head of Oceanus. But such abundance of crustacean elements can be found even in later mosaics from Italy, for instance in the late second or early third century Oceanus mosaic from the Villa di Baccano (Figure 2.4), where the mask of Oceanus is depicted with *chelae* claws, antennae, crustacean legs and dolphins sprouting from his beard.[47] The mosaic is set in the centre of a square mosaic with four sea monsters cavorting around and a few fish specimens to fill in the corners of the image. The villa once belonged to the Emperor Septimius Severus, and it is quite possible that with his African background, some of the people supervising the mosaics hailed from Roman Africa as well. The latter would justify the bevvy of additional marine attributes for the Oceanus' mask and the way of representing the sea environment with short broken lines, something quite common in the North African Roman mosaics.[48] However, the composition of this polychrome

Figure 2.4 An end of the second–early third-century mosaic of Oceanus (detail). The National Roman Museum, Palazzo Massimo alle Terme (Italy).

mosaic is more reminiscent of the black-and-white Oceanus *Terme Marittime* mosaics of Ostia discussed earlier.

However, the *chelae* claws are the most frequently used motives for the mask of Oceanus in mosaics, wall-paintings, sarcophagi and so on, and these elements are more or less recognizable depending on craftsman's skill. In the Villa di Baccano's mosaic, the *chelae* might have been confused for antlers if they were not coupled with antennae and crustacean legs that emphasize their marine nature. Different level of craftsmanship and different execution localities may render the same subject of the mosaicist's handbook in such a way that very few elements remain in common. Let us compare the two images of Oceanus (Figures 2.5 and 2.6) that clearly have the same origins, although they come from the opposite parts of the Roman Empire, one from near Antioch (province of Syria in Imperial times), and the other from Verulamium in Roman Britain. Both are set by themselves in a square (a very rare occasion for an Oceanus) within geometric patterns,[49] and both have the same amount of body showing and the same posture, head slightly non-frontal, turned a little bit to the left, both have lots of grey hair (another unusual Oceanus trait) although arranged slightly differently.

However, whereas the second–third century CE Antioch Oceanus (Figure 2.5) found in Harbiye (former Daphne, situated in the valley of Orontes roughly between Antioch and the sea) definitely has *chelae* claws on top of his head, the Verulamium Oceanus (Figure 2.6), found in modern St Albans and dating from 160–190 CE, is crowned with something that looks more like antlers than any kind of crustacean claws. The latter constitutes the earliest mosaic of Oceanus found in the North-West of the Roman Empire. These 'antlers' do look vaguely similar to the way *chelae* claws of Oceanus from the Villa di Baccano (Figure 2.4) are depicted, but still 'antlery' enough to give rise to many speculations.[50]

Figure 2.5 A second–third century mosaic of Oceanus. Antakya/Hatay Archeological Museum (Turkey).

Figure 2.6 A 160–90 CE mosaic of Oceanus (possibly conflated with Celtic Cernunnos). Verulamium Museum (St Albans, UK).

To this conundrum, there could be basically three explanations. First, the Verulamium craftsman could have been local and not overmuch familiar with marine fauna of the Mediterranean. So, when reproducing the Oceanus model, they might have just copied it as best they could without much ado, just not very proficiently. Second, the craftsman decided in good faith that the things on the representation's head were supposed to be antlers because they recognized them as a more familiar object. Since St Albans was located in the midst of the woods, almost a hundred kilometres from the sea, the craftsman was perhaps influenced by other horned deities they knew about. And here we return to the first images of Oceanus crowned with horns on the sixth century BCE Greek vases and to images of river gods, particularly Achelous traditionally represented with horns.[51] It could be possible that Oceanus was still depicted sometimes as a horned deity, influenced either by the image of Achelous or an earlier belief.[52] However, there are also local deities to be considered. The Celtic god Cernunnos,[53] 'the horned one', looks like a possible candidate,[54] especially since modern scholarship seems to concur that Roman cults were often reinterpreted by the Romano–Celtic British, particularly iconographically.[55] On the only stele with the actual *Cernunnos* inscription, the deity carved in stone displays short stubby antlers remarkably similar to the claws/antlers of the Verulamium mosaic.[56]

Finally, the third possible explanation of the Verulamium claws/antlers is that the craftsman was specifically ordered by his patron (or decided on his own) to pay homage to Cernunnos or some other local deity perceived as horned and acted accordingly with Roman materials and techniques at his disposal. It is quite conceivable, since we have another Cernunnos representation in stone dated roughly like the Verulamium mosaic[57] that also uses characteristic symbols from Roman art and flanks Cernunnos with figures of Mercury and Apollo, both easily recognizable, the former by his caduceus, the latter by his lyre.

We have further evidence of possible syncretism and conflation of Oceanus and Cernunnos in a mosaic found in the province of Germania Superior in 1966 as part of a Roman villa in the little spa town of Bad Kreuznach (Crucinacum/Cruciniacum,

Figure 2.7 A 234 CE mosaic of Oceanus (possibly conflated with Celtic Cernunnos). Bad Kreuznach, Germany (in situ).

originally a Celtic settlement), located close to the province's capital Mogontiacum (Mainz) to the east of Trier and just south of Bingen am Rhein (Figure 2.7). The example found there consists of an enormous mosaic (the biggest one found in Germania Superior)[58] that represents a complex marine environment very much following the North African style. In it, it is possible to find people sailing and fishing in different boats, waters teeming with realistic sea fauna, beautiful buildings on the seacoast, and in the apsidal part that would have been right beside the couches of the triclinium, a majestic bust of Oceanus dwarfing everything else on the mosaic with two sea monsters rushing from behind his head in opposite directions. Luckily enough, it is possible to date this mosaic to the year 234 CE, as it includes a partly preserved inscription mentioning the year when M. Clodius Pupienus Maximus (future Roman Emperor for three months in the year 238) and M. Munatius Sulla Urbanus were Roman consuls.[59] Thus, the Bad Kreuznach mosaic was made just about half a century later than the Verulamium mosaic. However, the Germanic Oceanus looks quite dissimilar apart from the profound gaze and the colouring: dark tanned body, light grey hair and short cropped beard, though the former is more present (the bust is even showing some chest) and the latter is done in a different style, almost in ringlets. And although the *chelae* claws are definitely replaced with antlers, in this case the antlers are different-looking, thin and branching,[60] not to mention the green leaves sprouting out of his head, which look rather incongruous for a marine setting. Placing Oceanus as mask or bust in a realistic seascape can be frequently found in North African mosaics[61] but this particular kind of Oceanus image does not seem to have a precedent. It is also the only mosaic that I am aware of which shows Oceanus with something suspiciously like a torc made out of a living snake encircling his throat. The very few images of Cernunnos that are accepted as such by researchers do have torcs,[62] as torcs were in general considered typical for Celtic/Gaulish attire,[63] even as early as the third century BCE as can be seen from the famous Dying Gaul, a copy of a Hellenistic statue.[64] For instance, the carved stone image of Cernunnos from Reims[65] has an open-ended torc around the throat, much like the snake torc of the Bad Kreuznach Oceanus. Cernunnos also has a connection to snakes and, in fact, some researchers identify the torc and the snake as the most typical attributes of Cernunnos.[66] So, in this case we have an image of Oceanus displaying three elements of Cernunnos iconography: the antlers, the snake and the torc (combined in one). The mosaic has also green leaves, underlining its connection to the forest instead of to the sea. And, unlike the case of the Verulamium Oceanus, here only one explanation is possible. It cannot be an innocent copying mistake, nor can it be explained within such a marine environment by the craftsman missing the sea connection and deciding to go for the forest imaginary instead. So the only valid possibility could be that it was a deliberate homage to a non-Roman deity, a kind of *interpretatio celtica* presumably ordered by an extravagantly wealthy local patron based in the Roman backwoods (hence the ties to the local deities) who was the proprietor of the stupendous villa in question, famous for other mosaics in a very different style.[67] The initial water nature of the Roman Oceanus is thus subsumed in the forest nature of Cernunnos who, nevertheless by his central position, is still shown as *pater rerum*, the origin of all things *terra marique*, an all-important figure.

The situation was different in Roman Gaul. There, in a more Romanized environment, Oceanus, however idiosyncratically depicted – like the fourth century '*Ocianus*' found in Le Gleyzia/Glésia, Montréal-du-Gers, southwest of France (Figure 2.8) – usually keeps his Mediterranean attributes such as *chelae* claws, antennae, water streams pouring out of the mouth over the beard, dolphins sprouting from the beard and so on.[68] However, in most masks from Gaul – like from Britain and other Northwest provinces of the Empire – Oceanus is predominantly represented as an Oceanus mask. Particularly after the third century CE, Oceanus mask mosaics are executed with much less skill and their *chelae* claws and antennae can be easily taken for horns by the uninitiated craftsmen. The latter could be perhaps justified in the fact that life in these provinces became gradually more insulated and removed from Mediterranean trade. In addition, the constant invasions from enemies and the re-emergence of piracy[69] made the sea a dangerous environment, therefore access to the sea fauna in many places had become non-existent. In this way, after the advent of Christianity Oceanus, conflated with Neptune and his trident[70] on the

Figure 2.8 A fourth-century mosaic of Oceanus. Eugène-Camoreyt Museum (Lectoure, France).

one hand and Cernunnos, Pan, and other mythic horned entities on the other hand, loses his marine nature and eventually becomes the horned demonic figure brandishing a trident[71] of Christian popular culture.

Oceanus and Morays in the Marine Environment

Only from about the second century CE onwards do we suddenly encounter a real proliferation of images of Oceanus in mosaic art. Most of the examples that have survived come from the wealthy province of Africa Proconsularis (modern Tunisia), flanked by the western coast of Libya and the northeast part of Algeria.[72] The immense prosperity of Roman Africa was closely linked to sea trade, so it is no wonder that all kinds of actual and imaginary marine environments (fishing scenes, port activities, sea *thiasos*, the toilet of marine Venus) featuring both real (fish of all kinds, sea urchins, molluscs, crustaceans and so on) and mythic marine characters (Oceanus, Neptune, Amphitrite, Triton and so on) were overwhelmingly popular in the region.[73] However, unlike other anthropomorphic marine characters, Oceanus was mainly represented there again not as a full-bodied figure, but as a huge bearded mask, with water or fish/dolphins flowing from his mouth/hair.[74] He most often had parts of crustaceans growing out of his head: predominantly *chelae* claws, but sometimes even antennae or characteristic jointed crustacean legs

Figure 2.9 A mid-second-century mosaic of Oceanus with a moray. Sousse Archaeological Museum (Tunisia).

(Figure 2.9) like in the mid-second century mosaic of Sousse,[75] where the mask of Oceanus dominates the apsidal basin teeming with realistically depicted sea fauna (octopus, sea-urchin, crab, shrimp, squid, electric ray, various other fish species), including an unmistakable moray on the left.

Although superficially similar to the early Oceanus mosaic masks of Italy, Oceanus masks found in Tunisia are substantially different. First, the latter are mostly of enormous proportions, dwarfing everything around them and dominating the mosaic composition; in addition, they usually have huge, deep solemn eyes that have given researchers cause to speak of such masks' prophylactic and apotropaic functions. The latter is justified in the fact that some of them are accompanied with explicit inscriptions,[76] and they also exist all over the Mediterranean in other mosaics clearly designed for averting the evil eye.[77] Second, Oceanus masks of North African workmanship are mostly set against a background replete with natural-looking or at least recognizable marine species. Morays seem to have played a prominent part among the latter, presumably because they were then, as now, quite common around Sicily, both on the Italian and on the North African side. Sometimes they were still placed close to spiny lobsters and/or octopodes but not in clear displays of *antipatheia* so favoured by the earlier Alexandrian mosaicists.

Far fewer depictions of Oceanus set in a realistic seascape have been found outside Tunisia. The previously mentioned Bad Kreuznach Oceanus mosaic is one of the unusual exceptions. There we can see without doubt actual specimens of marine fauna albeit (unlike the impressive hyper-realistic Oceanus proper, see Figure 2.7) represented without too much skill (Figure 2.10). The cartoonish octopus on this third century CE mosaic is a far cry from the perfectly realistic-looking octopus of the above-discussed

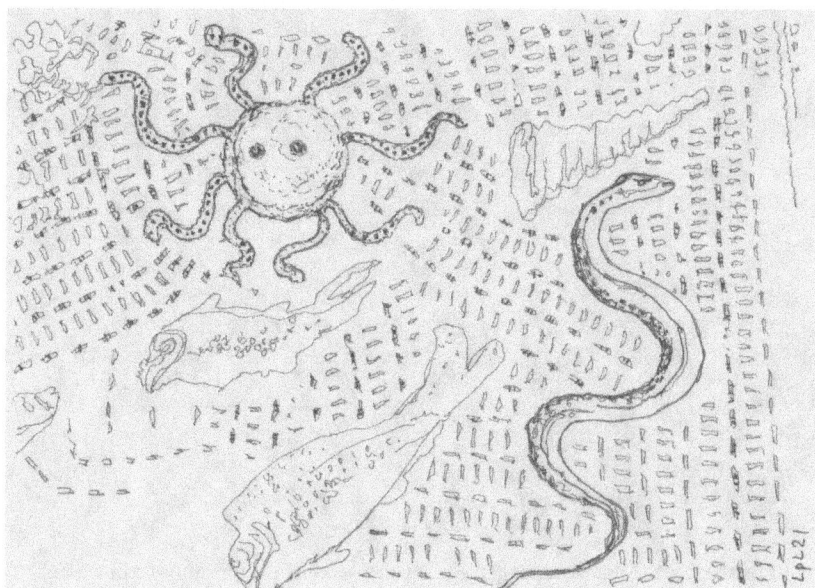

Figure 2.10 A 234 CE mosaic of Oceanus, marine fauna (detail). Bad Kreuznach, Germany (in situ).

marine *antipatheia* mosaics of the second century BCE. One might well presume that the craftsmen employed in making the seascape in Germania Superior had no previous firsthand familiarity with the marine species of the Mediterranean. However, the huge marine fauna mosaic with forty-seven specimens of fish, shellfish, molluscs etc. from the Mediterranean coast just south of Tarragona roughly from the same period[78] has octopus depicted in pretty much the same way, so the reason is less the lack of practical zoological knowledge rather than the artistic conventions of the period. Same goes for the bright yellow moray of both Bad Kreuznach and Tarragona mosaics, which inexperienced viewers can easily take for some kind of snake (compare with the realistic moray of the second-century CE Ostian still-life mosaic in Figure 2.1). This even makes one wonder whether the bright yellow snake torc of Oceanus of the Bad Kreuznach mosaic was not actually a moray torc, particularly since by Late Antiquity one of the Latin words for such an ornament was 'little moray' *muraenula/murenula*.[79] Of course, the rapprochement between snakes and morays is an old one, and has been firmly entrenched in Mediterranean popular culture at least since the time of Aristotle, who exposes the widespread belief that a moray comes out of the sea to copulate with a serpent. Oppian, in his second-century CE poem on fish and fish behaviour (*Halieutica*), mentions not only the heroic battles of morays, octopodes and spiny lobsters, but also describes the moray and serpent love scene in great detail. This is still part and parcel of Greek folklore and has even made it into modern Greek pop songs.[80]

The other slightly earlier mosaic[81] representing both Oceanus and morays (see Figure 2.11) from Roman Germania comes from the remnants of the Roman baths in

Figure 2.11 A badly damaged end-of-the-second-century mosaic of a giant Oceanus mask. Found in Bad Vilbel, a reconstructed copy in situ. The original is in Hessisches Landesmuseum Darmstadt (Germany).

Bad Vilbel, a small spa town to the north-east of Frankfurt am Main almost on the limit of Germania Superior. It was excavated in the mid-nineteenth century and it is unfortunately rather badly preserved, but it is still possible to discern the huge mask of Oceanus in the middle, as well as some real and some mythical sea creatures grouped around it (in North African style). In this case, the craftsmen might have been entirely unfamiliar with any Mediterranean marine fauna, because the octopus (if we assume that the creature is an octopus) looks more like some monstrous bug (both the body shape and only six extremities) than anything else, and it is hard to perceive the moray of the mosaic as anything but a snake.[82] Still, the overall effect of this mosaic from the less 'civilized' right bank of the Rhine must have been quite stunning and the marine connection of Oceanus and its implied *Romanitas* is unmistakable.

We can also observe a possible trace of moray depicted with an Oceanus mask[83] in Gaul in the second century black-and-white mosaic of *Maison des Dieux Océan* in Saint-Romain-en-Gal, an original Gallo-Roman settlement on the Rhone bank opposite of Vienne.[84] The part of the mosaic with the possible moray (unlike other marine specimens) is no longer preserved in museum, but it is presented as it was *in situ* on the reconstruction after the original drawings of the mosaic in the museum's archaeological park.[85] The other very similar black and white mosaic of Oceanus discovered on the opposite bank in actual Vienne does not show any morays among its sea fauna. Both mosaics are not unlike the black-and-white Oceanus mosaics of Ostia discussed earlier, but the mask of Oceanus in mosaics from Roman Gaul are surrounded with real marine animals, whereas the Ostian Oceanus mosaics show a strong preference for mythic sea creatures as the milieu for masks.[86]

What is very unusual is that in Roman Gaul we also have a possible moray depicted together with real sea fauna and zoomorphic *monstra maritima*, as far as I know an unprecedented iconographic example. A hexagonal frigidarium pool from the luxurious fourth century CE *Villa du Palat*, Saint-Émilion[87] is crammed with all kinds of real marine specimens around a sea horse and a sea bull. Some of the specimens are quite recognizable and depicted with more realism than the third-century fish mosaics of Tarragona or Germania Superior discussed above. In these it is possible to find a spiny lobster, an octopus (several of them), an electric ray and so on. And then, in the middle of the mosaic there is an obvious lamprey (*Lampetra fluvialis*) with its jawless mouth like a slit, characteristic gill dots (hence the German name for it, 'nine eyes' *Neunaugen*) and fins that no moray has ever had. If it is an accurate drawing[88] it could be the only known mosaic image of the European lamprey, essentially displaying fresh-water species, but easily explained near Bordeaux where lamprey from the Dordogne river and Gironde estuary has been a local gastronomic specialty for centuries.[89] A creative craftsman from the region with a penchant for realism could have easily included in a mosaic a fish he knew instead of a moray he could never have witnessed in Gaul. The second possible lamprey on this mosaic is situated right between a spiny lobster and an octopus, just where a real moray would be, a remnant of the old iconographic tradition of *antipatheia*. Confusion between the two species[90] was long a part of the European literary tradition, starting with the already-mentioned place in Pliny the Elder's *Natural History*,[91] where he discusses a 'starred' moray from Gaul, and finishing with twentieth century English translations of various belles lettres texts that mention morays as lampreys.[92] The latter seems to be quite absurd, since lampreys have no jaws, can only survive by sucking the blood of other bigger fish and, unlike morays, cannot be kept as pets. In this light, the two Roman literary moray *topoi*: 'cruel Romans giving slaves to their pet morays to devour'[93] and 'kind Romans cherishing their pet morays' become totally senseless.

Another mosaic from the fountain of the same villa possibly has more traces of morays, although these are even more unobtrusive. The workmanship here is very different, one may even say simplistic, and it is not easy to recognize morays in schematic blue lines interspersed with schematic fish all over the fountain base. But although the fourth century mosaic school of southwest France was highly original[94] its members obviously did use pattern books and were influenced by mosaic developments in Africa and Asia. So, the global Late Antiquity mosaic trend towards ornamentalism, appearing also in African mosaics that showed, among other things, a combination of fishes and morays just as elements of a pattern (for instance on a basin from Sbeitla)[95] might have influenced this even more schematic *Villa du Palat* decoration.

Conclusions

Unfortunately, it is impossible to enumerate in one chapter all the mosaics depicting morays and Oceanus (both together and on their own) so in this contribution I have tried to select those most relevant to the topic of marine environments and their transformation in Late Antiquity beyond the natural limits of the Mediterranean, concentrating mostly on the North-West of the Roman Empire. If we look at morays, from being represented through the rather literary *antipatheia* motif probably originating in Aristotle's *History of Animals*[96] and still-life *xenia* images, they became a regular part of general marine environment,[97] particularly in North African mosaics (both realistic and mythic – indiscriminately) and mosaics modelled after them.[98] In the end of the second century, at least in Roman Germania, morays started to be perceived as snakes and were depicted accordingly, displaying the marine environment as even more bizarre and dangerous to the eyes of land-locked inhabitants, who had never seen the sea. In the fourth century Roman Gaul it is possible to find an instance of moray (*Muraena helena*) being taken for a different fresh-water fish species, the local lamprey (*Lampetra fluvialis*), replacing the unfamiliar Mediterranean creature and thus grounding the mosaic motif in regional reality. There is also a possibility that in some Late Antique mosaics removed from the actual Mediterranean figurative morays were transformed into thin and wavy ornamental lines. So, on the whole, by the Later Roman Empire, we have at least some traces of an iconographic tendency from the North-West: from morays to snakes (or even lampreys) to wavy lines that eventually obliterate the initial connection to the Mediterranean.

It is much harder to figure out something as straightforward for Oceanus mosaics. First, there is a staggering number of Oceanus mosaics all over the Roman Empire,[99] even in its most remote corners from Armenia (Oceanus and his spouse Thalassa/Tethys, Roman baths in Garni, fourth century CE)[100] to Morocco (Oceanus mask, Roman baths in Lixus, early third century CE)[101] more than 5,000 kilometres apart. Second, their typology is quite complex and mixed, making it very hard to generalize as there are too many categories that must be considered. Yes, Oceanus can be depicted as a mask (just his head), as a bust, as a head with torso, as a full-length figure. And while the mask of Oceanus is more characteristic for Europe and Africa, and the torso and full figure for Asia, there are always exceptions. One question is what kind of cohesive typology might we use to compare a majestic figure of Oceanus depicted on a mosaic with a huge reed stalk semireclining under the apple tree of Hesperides together with guardian snake Ladon from Ma'arrat al-Nu'man museum (Syria)[102] which could be a copy of an exceptional painting by some artist, and a mosaic of standing Oceanus from Petra (Jordan)[103] holding an oar in one hand, a sailing ship in the other, with one foot on a dolphin, crude but cute, like a child's drawing? Both are fifth century CE artworks, both are signed as Oceanus in Greek, both have beards and *chelae* claws growing out of their heads, but it is hard to conceive more divergent images (though cf. Figure 2.8, discussed above).

Still, as images of full-length Oceanus and Oceanus together with his spouse Tethys (another mainstay in Asia)[104] had hardly made any impact in the North-West Mediterranean (Spain excluded)[105] and beyond, it was possible for me to confine my research to the mask of Oceanus and some busts of Oceanus. The same goes for the attributes of Oceanus such as oars, as I had to disregard the mosaics that rarely appeared in later mosaics of the provinces removed from the actual Mediterranean.[106] Since the

Migrating Mosaics

Figure 2.12 A late fifth–early sixth-century mosaic of baptism of Christ. The Arian Baptistery (Ravenna, Italy).

oar of Oceanus was supposed to bring good luck and safety for travelling around Mediterranean it might not have been much use away from it.[107]

The attributes I did explore in detail, such as greenness and *chelae* claws versus horns, have provided us with enough material to think about their reception in Late Antiquity and beyond. The greenness of an Oceanus mask stemming from decorative leafy grotteschi scrolls populated with masks and all kinds of faces – after existing for several centuries independently set in a marine environment – eventually reverted to type and became ornamental again, although in single form and contributing to the appearance of medieval Green Man in Britain, Germany and so on, and leaving behind the Mediterranean connection.

The *chelae* claws that initially were the horns of Oceanus in his early pre-Classical depictions became horns again in Late Antiquity in provinces far removed from the sea in the Christian iconography of horned demons (conflated from several horned deities, probably including Celtic Cernunnos), completed with Neptune's trident, again leaving the sea semantics behind. In a bizarre syncretic twist, the *chelae* claws of Oceanus unexpectedly appear once more on a Christian mosaic of the late fifth–early sixth century, from the Arian baptistery of Ravenna (Figure 2.12) constructed on the orders of Theodoric the Great. Young Christ is being baptized by John the Baptist in the waters of

Jordan river, whose personification sits by on a golden vessel out of which his waters flow. He is holding a giant reed and sporting beautiful red chelae claws on his head.[108] So in yet another syncretic trend the iconography of Oceanus and marine environments could sometimes even influence characteristic depictions of river-gods in Late Antiquity.[109]

Notes

* I would like to thank Lisa Plavinsky, a wonderful artist, art historian and a dear friend of mine, for our many talks on the history of art and all the brilliant sketches of the mosaics she drew for this chapter. I would also like to express my heart-felt gratitude to the wonderful people of the Finnish Institute in Rome where I spent several blissful weeks in February 2020 (just before the global hell broke loose) doing preliminary research for this chapter in the library of the beautiful Villa Lante. My thanks go also to the terrific librarians of the American Academy in Rome who provided lots of generous support to a strange researcher, *siete grandi*. And last, but not least, to my fantastic family who patiently allow me to escape from family duties (from time to time) into the realms of research.

1. Dunbabin 1999.
2. Ghedini and Novello 2005: 182–94.
3. Hor. *Carm.* 1.3.18; Tac. *Ann.* 2.24.6.
4. Compare the second century CE mosaic of Neptune's triumph decorating the so-called Neptune's baths (Terme di Nettuno) and the third century CE mosaic depicting a lighthouse and real and imaginary sea fauna around it (Terme del Faro). Available at: www.ostia-antica.org/regio4/2/2-1.htm in Ostia, Italy.
5. For instance, a cupid fishing in a boat, a second–third century mosaic decorating a swimming pool, Maison de la Cascade, Utica, Tunisia.
6. Dunbabin 1978: 8.
7. Several recipes in Apicius 10.2.2 (six recipes in total + one extra in the *Excerpta*), a mock description of a sumptuous moray dish in Hor. *Sat.* 2.8.48.
8. Sen. *Ira* 3.40.2; Clem. 1.18.2; Plin. *HN.* 9.77, 172; Plut. *De soll. an.* 959a-985c; Ael. *NA.* 8.4. For quite some time *murenae/muraenae* of classical texts were translated as lampreys in European languages, particularly English, with many bizarre results. The controversy probably hails back to Plin. *HN.* 9.76 where he describes a lamprey as a Gallic moray dotted with stars and then via some glosses (myraina *est piscis id est* lampraeda, available at: https://publikationen.badw.de/en/thesaurus/lemmata#60831) unexpectedly to Saint Albert the Great, who studied at the University of Padua close to the Adriatic coast of Italy where there are no morays and hence mistook morays for more familiar lampreys while compiling his book 'On animals' *De Animalibus* 1916–1920), Lib.XXIV, chap. 1, p. 1537, inspired by Aristotle's *Historia Animalium*.
9. Varro. *Rust.* 3.3.9-10; Columella, *Rust.* 8.17.8; Marzano 2013.
10. Nowadays it is almost impossible to buy morays anywhere but in the local fish markets of Sicily and other parts of the Mediterranean and even then, they are not a species one can find with any regularity.
11. Cic. *Fam.* 7. 26. 2.
12. Juv. 5.99.
13. Meyboom 1977; Zapheiropoulou 2006: 308–9.

14. Plin. *HN* 9.185; Opp. *Hal.* 2.253-418.
15. Conger eels are sometimes also mentioned along with morays when describing this triple *antipatheia*, for instance there is a conger eel in another part of the Palestrina mosaic, and there is an imperfectly preserved red crustacean close to it that is usually taken for spiny lobster, Zapheiropoulou 2006: 308–9.
16. Le collezioni del Museo Nazionale di Napoli 1989: 116, Zapheiropoulou 2006: 252–4, 261–2.
17. This *antipatheia* also used to appear in wall-paintings (both Pompeiian and later Roman), see discussion in *Palazzo Massimo alle Terme, le collezioni* 2013: 469.
18. Dunbabin 1978: 7.
19. Now in the British Museum. Available at: www.britishmuseum.org/collection/object/G_1989-0322-1.
20. Although Meyboom 1977: 209 dates it earlier.
21. Dunbabin 1978: 8.
22. Hes. *Theog.* 364–8.
23. *Kl. Pauly* 1972: 267–8.
24. Verg. *G.* 4.382.
25. Foucher 1963: 139; Rumpf 1939: 11–19.
26. *Anth. Lat.* 167–8, no. 718. I am indebted to Fabio Barry and his article from 2014 for this fascinating find.
27. *LIMC* 1994: OKEANOS VII/1 31–33, VII/2 22.
28. A *dinos* by Sophilos (The British Museum 1971.1101.1. Available at: www.britishmuseum.org/collection/object/G_1971-1101-1) with Oceanus clearly holding the snake and the fish, and the François vase (The National Archaeological Museum of Florence 4209. available at: https://weblimc.org/page/monument/2072256) with a less well-preserved Oceanus depiction, both featuring gods at the wedding of Peleus and Thetis.
29. *LIMC* 1994: op.cit.
30. Available at: https://weblimc.org/page/monument/2071289.
31. *LIMC* 1994–1997: OKEANOS VII/1 33, OCEANUS VIII/1 907–915, VIII/2 599–607.
32. Now unfortunately lost, drawings of them by Discanno published and so preserved in Presuhn 1878: plates XVII, XXI.
33. Dunbabin 1999: 104.
34. De Vos and De Vos 1982: 275.
35. Camardo and Notomista 2013: 187, 193.
36. Beccatti 1961: 112–13 (plates CXLV, CXLVI)
37. Available at: www.ostia-antica.org/regio3/8/8-2.htm.
38. Dunbabin 1978: 154; Yakoub 1995: 162.
39. Yakoub 1995: 70–2; Dunbabin 1978: 150, 167, 174.
40. Yakoub 1995: 162–3; Dunbabin 1978: 274.
41. Dunbabin 1978: 150; Delbarre-Bärtschi 2014: Oceanus.
42. *LIMC* 1997 considers this mask to be that of Oceanus: VIII/I 910 Oceanus 47.
43. Spiro 1978: xvl, xlv; plates 124, 588.

44. On its context Dunbabin 1999: 232–5, also considered to be Oceanus by *LIMC* 1997: VIII/I 910-911 Oceanus 54 (dating it to early fifth century, but this dating is not unanimous).
45. Available at: www.britishmuseum.org/collection/object/H_1946-1007-1.
46. On the special connection of Oceanus and Bacchus, see Foucher 1963.
47. Palazzo Massimo alle Terme: le collezioni 2013: 472.
48. Dunbabin 1999.
49. Here the resemblance ends: the Antioch mosaic is part of a great rectangle patterned with lozenges (available at: https://pbase.com/dosseman/oceanushead), while the Verulamium one is set in a bigger square patterned with meanders, flowers, and vessels (available at: https://collections.stalbansmuseums.org.uk/objects/14650).
50. Dunbabin 1999: 90 definitely identifies the figure as Oceanus, but the Verulamium museum (see n 50) is cagier and describes it as a sea or a woodland god.
51. Barry 2014: 9–10.
52. The sixth-century CE poet John of Gaza describing images of sixty pagan deities depicted around the Christian cross supposedly as a Christian allegory in his *Tabula Mundi* also called from a scholiast's remark *Description of a Picture of the World Situated in the Winter Baths* still calls Oceanus 'the horn-bearing abyss', *kerasphoros*, see Voute 1972: 659, even though we should bear in mind that the Greek word for crustacean antennae is actually the same as 'horns'. If such a depiction ever existed it would have been probably something like the second–third century CE cosmological mosaic of Mérida with Oceanus seated in the left corner below holding a snake, more on the latter in Blázquez 1993: 380–5; Dunbabin 1999: 147–50.
53. In-depth study of his various aspects by Bober 1951, update and partial reassessment by Fickett-Wilbar 2003.
54. Henig 1995: 18–19, 186.
55. Moitrieux 2014: 162.
56. Cluny museum stele, early Gallo-Roman, Bober 1951: 14, 17.
57. Reims museum stele, Antonine period, Bober 1951: 35, 43.
58. Hornung 2011: 53–61.
59. Balmelle and Darmon 2017: 105.
60. Balmelle and Darmon 2017: 167 claim these antlers to be corals (underlining the Cernunnos connection), but I know of no iconographic precedent of corals growing out of mythic marine characters' heads, it's usually crustacean elements.
61. More about it further on in the next section Oceanus and morays in the marine environment.
62. Bober 1951; Fickett-Wilbar 2003.
63. Livy 7.10; Just. *Epit.* 43.5.7. I would like to express my great thanks to Dr Antti Lampinen for kindly helping me out with many of the Celtic references.
64. Available at: www.museicapitolini.org/it/collezioni/percorsi_per_sale/palazzo_nuovo/sala_del_gladiatore/statua_del_galata_capitolino.
65. Reims museum stele, Antonine period, Bober 1951: 35, 43.
66. Fickett-Wilbar 2003: 101.
67. Covered by Parlasca 1959, unlike the Oceanus mosaic, that was discovered seven years after Parlasca's groundbreaking monograph on Roman mosaics in Germany was published.
68. Balmelle and Darmon 2017: 166–7, 248–53 for the second–third century CE mosaics such as black-and-white Oceanus masks from Vienne similar to the ones found in Ostia, but placed

in a more realistic marine setting with recognizable specimens of sea fauna, Late Antiquity polychrome mosaic masks of Oceanus, particularly from Maubourguet with a truly baleful look and enormous dolphins as moustache rather similar to the Oceanus mask of the Mildenhall dish mentioned in the previous section, but sporting proper huge *chelae* claws and unexpectedly capped with a highly stylized sea shell (see also the description of the Withington Oceanus mosaic note 68) and huge Oceanus with a soulful gaze from Saint-Rustice, an only partly preserved mask with *chelae* claws and antennae surviving only on a nineteenth-century drawing that was made after the 1833 excavation.

69. See Lampinen and Mataix Ferrándiz in this volume.
70. Compare, for instance, the fourth–fifth century British mosaic of Oceanus from Withington with an enormous dolphin moustache, *chelae* claws like branching antlers, and unexpectedly Neptune's trident. Available at: www.britishmuseum.org/collection/object/H_1812-0613-1.
71. One of the first depictions of a demon with a trident was found on a tenth-century Irish cross, Allen 1887: 164.
72. Dunbabin 1978: 299; Paulian 1979: 115.
73. Dunbabin 1999: 112.
74. Dunbabin 1978: 149–54.
75. Yacoub 1995: 162.
76. Dunbabin 1978: 151–3.
77. Dunbabin 1999: 312–13.
78. Available at: www.mnat.cat/en/artwork/20/mosaic-of-the-fish/ dated to third century CE, now in Tarragona National Archaeological Museum, MNAT 45456.
79. Available at: https://publikationen.badw.de/en/thesaurus/lemmata#60832.
80. Opp. *Hal.* 1.554–579. The same belief appears in European medieval bestiaries, later literary anecdotes and so on, including the 1979 pop song with words by Nikos Kavvadias.
81. Parlasca 1959: 115–16, he dates it to the end of the second century CE.
82. The original is preserved in Darmstadt, but Bad Vilbel has been presented with a reconstructed copy, on which the head of Oceanus suddenly bears a close resemblance to the head of the Gorgon or Gorgoneion with morays swirling out of it like snakes. Actually several cases of conflation of Oceanus and Gorgoneion images have been noted by some researchers, the most famous image of this kind is probably the carved stone Oceanus/Gorgon mask on the pediment of the Roman Bath (Aquae Sulis) temple. Available at: www.romanbaths.co.uk/walkthroughs/temple-pediment, see Paulian 1979: 131.
83. Actually, four Oceanus masks, which is quite unusual, although there are several different styles of Tunisian mosaic with four Oceanus masks (Dunbabin 1978: 1950–51), it was also possibly the case of the *nymphaeum* of Oceanus in Nola, Campania, more on the iconography of four Oceanus masks Voute 1972: 659–71.
84. Balmelle and Darmon 2017: 165–7.
85. Personal observation when visiting Musée gallo-romain de Saint-Romain-en-Gal in October 2018.
86. See the section Green Beginnings.
87. Balmelle and Darmon 2017: 243–7.
88. I have not found any photo of this mosaic, so I am describing the drawing provided *ibid*: 247.
89. Available at: www.tasteatlas.com/lamprey-a-la-bordelaise.
90. Some modern researchers even confuse morays with fresh-water eels, see Reese 2002.

91. See n. 8.
92. Available at: https://en.wikipedia.org/wiki/Lamprey#In_literature accessed on May 20, 2021.
93. This makes little sense even if applied to morays, fish of shy and retiring disposition, for they do not feed 'piranha style' and are totally uninterested in devouring humans – preferring to feed on crustaceans and cephalopods instead. For this piece of defamation the Roman pet morays had to thank Seneca, who began this nonsensical *topos* (*Ira* 3.40.2, *Clem.* 1.18.2).
94. Balmelle and Darmon 2017: 225.
95. Available at: https://romeartlover.tripod.com/Sufetul2.html.
96. Arist. *Hist. an.* 7.590b; Westgate 2000: 268.
97. One of the moray mosaics from Zliten, villa Dar Buc Ammèra under the flowery scroll is a peculiar throw-back to earlier times, sporting amazingly realistic xenia, see Aurigemma 1960: tabl. 161., there is also an interesting Libyan example of *antipatheia* mosaic from Gurgi, Tripoli, tabl. 67, with moray fighting an octopus, spiny lobster waiting for his turn to fight the moray beneath them.
98. Although in this chapter I have discussed predominantly western mosaics with morays, there are some mosaics with morays preserved in eastern parts of the Roman Empire as well, for instance fish mosaics from Rhodos (De Matteis 2004: 311, 323) or a fish mosaic from Lesbos (thanks to Dr Josephine Hoegaerts for alerting me to this one, a fishing scene with various marine species including a moray, here erroneously labelled as an eel – available at: www.kankeleit.de/fish.php). Of the western mosaics I have not mentioned, the gorgeous vivid polychrome mosaic from Toledo, Spain (Santa Cruz Museum) of marine fauna with a golden spotted moray encircled within a fruit-and-flower border dated to after the third century CE (somewhat reminiscent of colourful fish mosaics of Zliten, Villa Dar Buc Ammèra, see Aurigemma 1960: tav. 128) deserves particular attention.
99. *LIMC* 1997: VIII/1 909–11 lists over forty Oceanus mosaics and it is just a drop in the ocean, it crams busts, heads and torsos together as Oceanus heads and lists just three full figures of Oceanus separately.
100. *LIMC* 1997: VIII/1 910, VIII/2 604, Oceanus 53; Eraslan 2015: 457.
101. Dunbabin 1978: 264.
102. Source – private pictures by a friend; the Labours of Hercules cycle.
103. *LIMC* 1997: VIII/1 911, VIII/2 604, Oceanus 60.
104. Eraslan 2015.
105. The Iberian Peninsula in general being much closer to North Africa and sometimes even Asia in its mosaic art, Dunbabin 1999: 144–59.
106. *LIMC* 1997: VIII/1 914.
107. Even if we do have one unusual Oceanus mask from Roman Gaul with an oar (mostly the oar is only for full-length Oceanus images, or at the very least torsos) and no *chelae* claws, *LIMC* 1997: VIII/1 909, VIII/2 603, Oceanus 25, Balmelle and Darmon 2017: 167.
108. Funnily enough a very similar mosaic in the Orthodox baptistery in Ravenna, Battistero Neoniano, built half a century earlier has no *chelae* claws on top of its version of Jordan river.
109. It could be possible, I think, to trace the influence of such Oceanus/river god image in the development of later iconography of horned Moses with his staff that can provide water or turn into a snake, another frequent attribute of Oceanus, but this topic should be researched on its own, considering the archaic semi-serpentine nature of Oceanus and his old connections with Eastern Mediterranean cultures. See also Töyräänvuori in this volume.

CHAPTER 3
MEDITERRANEAN AS A CONTESTED ENVIRONMENT IN LATE ANTIQUITY
Antti Lampinen

Introduction

The stories Romans told about themselves did not showcase them as natural seafarers, but the Mediterranean gradually became an almost instinctive core for the growth narratives of the empire.[1] The originally fairly landbound state of Republican Rome had had to acquire a navy and some familiarity with maritime warfare during the First Punic War.[2] Similarly, during the Illyrian Wars the rule of the sea as a way of safeguarding merchants (or posing as a protector of merchants in an effort to advance the Roman elite's needs) became a part of Roman strategic thinking.[3] Finally, Pompey's campaign to suppress piracy all through the Mediterranean was not only a significant constitutional step towards one-man rule in Rome, but also towards the consolidation of the idea of Mediterranean as *mare nostrum*, with only Roman interests given full legitimation within its circuit.[4] Compared with these developments, the battle of Actium solidified trends that had already been long in development by eliminating the last independently operating naval force in the Mediterranean. A perhaps more important aspect of the defeat of Antony and Cleopatra was the way in which the nature of the battle, waged on sea and land around the entry to the Ambracian Gulf, made the pre-existing Hellenistic formula, rendered in Latin as *terra marique*, a paradigmatic expression of Roman imperial triumphalism.[5]

In the north-west, the unfathomable Atlantic fringe remained a more threatening landscape, much less amenable to domination and even knowledge. Enquiries about the Ocean had been taking place ever since the Roman state developed interests in the west, during and after the Second Punic War.[6] Yet the Atlantic retained its numinous quality until well into the Imperial Era – and arguably, until Late Antiquity. The superstitious fear of the Ocean was in all likelihood a genuine sentiment.[7] An excess of water worried the Romans, and seafaring was often seen as a necessary evil – a view which continued until the Later Empire and the Byzantine Era.[8] This seems to be what motivated a note in Aulus Gellius' *Noctes Atticae*, where he muses that the poets had conceived the sons of Jupiter, such as Aeacus, Minos and Sarpedon, as foremost in virtue, prudence and power, whereas the sons of Neptune, born of the sea, were said to have been fierce, horrible and devoid of any humanity; these included the Cyclops, the murderous wrestler-king Cercyon, the bandit Sciron, and the Laestrygonians.[9] The Ocean's violent nature could make the association with elemental and harmful divine beings much easier. Cicero had written jokingly to the advocate Trebatius who was accompanying Caesar to Britain, jesting about Trebatius' refusal to swim in the Ocean, though the younger man was otherwise a keen swimmer.[10] The numinosity of the Ocean would prove to be enduring.

The Mediterranean, by contrast, was for the Late Republican and Early Imperial audiences a comparatively familiar, circumscribed and understandable environment. While no-one would traverse the sea for pleasure, and ritual life was used to manage the risks of plying the waves, at least the threat of enemies or monsters was not normally perceived as part of it: these lay beyond.[11] Orators such as Aelius Aristides in the second century celebrated the providentiality of Rome's Mediterranean-wide unity in every bit as glowing terms as the centrality and ideal conditions of Italy were lauded by other writers.[12] Despite the seasonal natural hazards and the rigours of seafaring, the comparatively predictable environment of the Mediterranean was, in itself, presented as Nature's boon to the world-empire. Even the hazards themselves formed such a mythologized and often-repeated *topos* that the actual comparative safety of most of the sea-crossing along the Mediterranean is obscured somewhat in our sources.[13] These and other related perceptions regarding the sea as an environment have now been wonderfully explored by Georgia L. Irby.[14]

But what happened to perceptions of the Mediterranean *mare nostrum* during the centuries of the Later Imperial era, when its waves once again carried hostile fleets? This chapter will survey the Late Antique perceptions of the Mediterranean as a contested sea. It aims to explore how the social perception and representation of this great connecting and separating natural feature – an environment both bountiful and dangerous – changed in an era when it was no longer a *mare nostrum* in an exclusive sense.[15] How did the emperors make use of the renewed opportunity to triumph over seaborne enemies, and not just 'the sea' in an abstract way? I will organize this exploration in a broadly chronological way, from the third to the seventh centuries; yet with the recognition that such a synoptic and diachronic approach in itself is influenced by the way in which the Mediterranean as an environment seems unitary in an almost essentialist way.[16] First, however, I will look at some pieces of evidence for ancient 'triumphal rulership' and its relationship to the sea, after which I will go through the principal groups of outsiders who called into question the Roman rule of the Mediterranean. What I hope will emerge is a picture of a rich texture of perceptions, metaphors and rhetorical postures that used the providential-seeming unity of the Mediterranean – as well as its ruptures – to communicate different values and claims.

Triumphalism and the Sea in Late Antiquity

The sea as an environment in flux was perhaps a conceptual problem for the Roman universal rule, though, due to being basically landlocked, the Mediterranean was at least easier to subject to the Roman triumphalistic treatment than the Ocean.[17] Yet the sea had retained a role as a *materies gloriae* for Roman elites ever since Pompey's campaign against the pirates. Velleius Paterculus, tellingly celebrated Pompey's achievement in hindsight, and made it clear that his naval campaign all over the Mediterranean had ascertained the Roman power over *orbis terrarum*.[18] The emperors sought actively to promote the image of triumphing both on the land and on the sea, as already noted. But the pacification of the Mediterranean – its imperially guaranteed freedom of navigation – also led to a transfer of some of the triumphalist imagery to the Ocean.[19]

In discussing the opposing traits in the mentally disturbed personality of the Emperor Caligula, Suetonius first notes that he experienced nightly conversations with some sort of marine spirit, and then focuses on his concurrent contempt and superstition toward the gods.[20] Immediately afterwards, Suetonius tells that, when visiting the Rhine frontier, Caligula was full of threats towards the free barbarians, yet immediately took fright at the prospect of them setting an ambush and personally beat a panicky retreat. When told, not long afterwards, of an uprising in Germania, he prepared fleets in order to flee the city to the provinces across the sea, which were sure to still be left to him.[21] Apparently his imagination was immediately affixed to the double historical *exemplum* of the Cimbri breaching the Alps and the Senones menacing the city. To indulge in speculation, it is possible that in Caligula's own mind a barbarian threat and the significance of the Ocean were bound up together in some elemental way.[22]

Late Antiquity also provides some examples of the Ocean's role as an environment suited to providentialist rhetoric. One can be found in the collection of twelve Latin panegyrics, where it is not simply for the sake of a rhetorical flourish – though certainly for that purpose too – that the Panegyrist of 310, addressing Constantine, describes Constantius Chlorus gazing upon the Ocean, father of the gods. Chlorus' approach to the Ocean is implied to have been linked, following some secret plan, with his own approaching apotheosis.[23] This kind of imagery lent to the Ocean not only a sense of danger and a primeval character, but could also have associated it with the elder generation of gods, whose superseded vestiges were used to explain such impressive natural phenomena as volcanoes.[24]

The emperors were not, however, the sole beneficiaries of the rhetoric of universal triumph. From the third century we have some evidence of the old '*terra marique*' formula being used not only for the emperor, but also in provincial inscriptions in the eastern half of the empire when praising benefactors.[25] Most often, however, naval victories were attributed to the emperor even when he had not participated actively in them (a tradition neatly continuing the case of Actium). Flavius Fravitta's victory in 400 near Constantinople over the impromptu fleet put together by the renegade *magister militum* Gaïnas was represented as a full-blown imperial naval triumph by Eusebius Scholasticus.[26] In addition to consulship, we also have clear indications that the victory prompted triumphal honours for Fravitta and was reflected in at least two monuments in Constantinople; the frieze of Arcadius' column, and a monument in the shape of a marble *liburna* near the Augusteion.[27] The Sea was being reclaimed as an environment of triumphal Roman rulership after a hiatus of over a century: the previous naval victory commemorated in any way in Constantinople was the one by Constantine himself over Licinius.[28] Arcadius, who was eager to project a similar martially active and triumphal image as his father Theodosius had, no doubt seized on this victory to complement his posturing as an emperor conquering both on land and on sea, which we know to have been put forward on the basis of other written sources.[29] The defeat of the renegade general Vitalian in 515 was similarly celebrated with the full pomp of an imperial naval victory, complete with chariot races.[30]

Much like Aelius Aristides, the author of the fourth-century geographical text *Expositio totius mundi et gentium* presented the rich and constant flow of goods over the empire's sea routes as an exceptional blessing. *Expositio*, one of two Latin redactions based on a Greek original, always tracks the imperial presence among the nodes of Roman mercantile network. Antioch, in particular, forms an important node in this network, and this is clearly linked to the imperial presence.[31] The *dominus orbis terrarum, imperator Constantius*, had had the harbour of Seleucia (in Pieria) constructed by excavating out a mountain and introducing the sea in its stead, resulting in a 'large and good harbour, where ships enter for their safety and their valuable cargo is not lost'.[32] For the author of the *Expositio*, then, the imperial power was still a quasi-divine force (the word *divinus* often means 'imperial' in the text) acting on the environment of the Mediterranean itself: directing, ordering and safeguarding, but also generating demand and moving mountains themselves to tame the sea. In the *Expositio*, which was a far-from-learned work, imperial power seems to have been perceived to be on some providential level the guarantor of the boons brought by the sea environment to the empire.[33] With reflections of the rhetoric of imperial power and success so widely disseminated, the challenges to the Roman dominance of the Mediterranean in Late Antiquity could have posed a problem to the established discourse. In the next section, I will go through the major groups of outsiders who threatened the Roman rule of the Mediterranean, and the ways in which they were involved in the discourse of the time with the sea as an environment, as well as the imperial language of power.

Seaborne Threats and the Late Antique Political Discourse

Seaborne movements of Rome's enemies are considerably more difficult to track in our sources than those happening overland. This results from several factors. On the one hand, land warfare was always prioritized in ancient historiography and technical writing.[34] On the other hand, due to an influential set of ancient perceptions, many external groups – especially northern barbarian societies – were generally interpreted as being interested in taking over new lands, and also comparably inept at such activities as shipbuilding and navigation. Plying the sea was paradigmatically seen as a pursuit for complex societies, rife with all the moral corruption and hybris that such advanced cultural activities could bring.[35]

Pirates form a difficult and somewhat separate case, just like the bandits do on land: they have existed in almost all eras where coastal communities have had at least some freedom in switching between their modes of subsistence. Even after Pompey's campaign 'against the pirates' – in reality against all sorts of communities in regions hitherto only loosely controlled by Rome – some small-scale piracy probably survived.[36] It could have become more common in times of crisis or rebellion.[37] Partly this comparative silence is due to the nature of our sources, which seldom considered small-scale piracy or banditry the sort of stuff with which serious historiography should concern itself.[38] Pirates were also kept alive as a literary device by their liberal use as a plot device in the lighter literature and novels of the time, as well as a topic of debates in rhetorical exercises.[39]

Goths

Beginning with a Gothic raid against Olbia in 238, the mid-third-century attacks by a selection of northern groups against the Roman cities of the Pontic and Aegean region were certainly partly seaborne.[40] Communities of the southern Pontic coast were badly traumatized by these events. We see, in particular, an intense concern about the threat of sexual violence against local women from the 'barbarians', though there is also evidence of local groups joining in with the attackers.[41] It was not only the coasts of the Black Sea that suffered from these attacks: the enemy fleets also managed to breach the natural choke-point of the Bosporus and continued their depredations in the Aegean and even as far afield as Cyprus and Rhodes.[42] Zosimus, the early-sixth century CE historian, gives an account of the first seaborne Gothic invasions, for which he very probably relied on Herennius Dexippus' history, largely coaeval to the invasions. Inspired by the loot of the Borani, other Scythians build a fleet with the assistance of prisoners of war and foreign merchants living in their country. They take a route past Istrus, Tomi and Anchialus and reach the Philcatine Lake near Constantinople. Here, dangerously close to what in Zosimus' age was the capital of the empire, the invaders 'made an agreement' with the local fishermen – who had hidden themselves in the marshlands – and procured extra ships from their local collaborators; these allowed them to cross to Chalcedon, which they captured without opposition – the local garrison having deserted or fled in terror at their approach.[43] Noteworthy is the passage's emphasis on the difficulties experienced by the advancing 'Scythians' before they enlist the help of local fishermen. In this, Zosimus reflects a persistent fear of the Late Imperial elite about locals allying themselves with the barbarians, who then would benefit from their inside knowledge of the environment and their possible resentment of the imperial administration. It has to be kept in mind, however, that in Zosimus' own chronological context around the turn of the fifth and sixth centuries, such concerns were no doubt more acute. Thus, his account should be read as a back-projection to the third century, informed by his own pessimistic view of the fading of Rome's fortunes.[44] In such a plan, the sea could play the role of a betraying environment, together with those subalterns who depended on it for their sustenance.

Whenever an external danger finds a novel route into the 'safe' lands of the ingroup, the resulting epistemic shock tends to leave traces in literary discourse.[45] It may be that similar views were already present in Dexippus' third-century historical work *Scythica* – which it is very likely that a set of palimpsest fragments recently uncovered in Vienna belong to.[46] Though the new fragments relate primarily to warfare in the Balkans under Decius or Gallienus, parts of Dexippus' narrative are known to have been autoptic. He was an Athenian nobleman who was chosen to lead his city's contingent against Herulian or Gothic marauders sometime during the invasions of the 250s and 260s.[47] He wrote his historiographical work in the classicising idiom, which included calling all the northern invaders 'Scythians' and his narrative was peppered with plentiful allusions to the Persian Wars of the Classical Era.[48] It is true, of course, that the empire had witnessed traumatic incursions by barbarians into the heartlands of Italy and Greece a few generations earlier, during the rule of Marcus Aurelius, but these had never used the Mediterranean as a route of access, and had conformed to the established historical *exempla* of barbarian incursions from the north.[49]

Dexippus' *Scythica* no doubt described the seaborne invasions of the era, too, but most of the surviving fragments pertain to land-based battles.[50] In a set-piece speech from Dexippus preserved in the Porphyrogennetan *Excerpta de Sententiis*, however, a speaker addressing Athenians in this time of crisis seeks to lift their confidence by reminding them of the nearby presence of an imperial fleet.[51] Yet the speech of Emperor Decius to his troops, preserved in the 'Vienna Dexippus', and the anonymous rhetor's exhortation to the Athenians in the Porphyrogennetan fragment of Dexippus resemble each other in the inclusion of admissions of the suffering intrinsic to the human life.[52] Speeches from an age of anxiety. While the sea was, for the first time in generations, an environment bringing danger and anxiety to the shores of Greece, it could still be presented as equally bringing the salvation by the imperial fleet. By the time of writing of the *Historia Augusta*, the 'Scythians' were imagined as having been defeated in a naval battle by a certain Venerianus in a fairly early stage of the invasions.[53]

Vandals

It is conventionally accepted that the Vandals had an operational navy by 429 when they crossed into Africa.[54] They had perhaps been building ships since 419, judging by the censure that the *Codex Theodosianus* metes out, in a rescript from that year, to Romans who have betrayed the secret of shipbuilding to the barbarians – usually interpreted to have been the Vandals.[55] After the capture of Carthage in 439, they were strategically very well placed at the centre of the Mediterranean sea-route system, and the disruption to the Roman shipping and naval mobility has been seen as significant, even if some scholarly characterizations of the Vandal state as a sort of 'corsair kingdom' are quite overblown.[56] This image, in fact, has been shaped by Roman, especially Justinianic, propaganda, as will be seen below.

Seafaring during the 'Vandal century' could have become more closely associated with the threat of violence due to actual changes in the nature of Central Mediterranean shipping based on Carthage: as Chris Wickham has concluded, the archaeological record of trade goods tallies with the impression that Vandals focused their navy for military rather than fiscal purposes.[57] The old Roman fears of local seafaring professionals joining in with the barbarians and bringing with them their intimate knowledge of the environment and the technology seem also to have been reawakened, as Andy Merrills has discussed.[58] As noted by John Pryor and Elizabeth Jeffreys, the Vandals 'had broken the Romanized homogeneity of the Mediterranean for the first time'.[59] The range of the Vandal raids would have made the coastal cities as far as the Aegean and the Balearic islands seem much less safe than before.⁶⁰ It is probably not an exaggeration to suggest that for the contemporary citizens of the empire, 'the sea had become more dangerous than it was during the earlier decades'.⁶¹

That the Vandal King Geiseric saw claims of controlling the Mediterranean and its islands as a significant part of his royal propaganda is emblematized by Theophanes' mention of his adoption of the title '*rex* of the earth and sea'.⁶² In this, he tapped right into the imperial language of universal rule, which in this volume is also explored by the chapters of Töyräänvuori, Mataix Ferrándiz and Minale. By the time of Justinian's reconquest of North Africa, Procopius' hindsight detected in Geiseric's early and devastating raids a callous misuse of religious excuses: safe in his dominance of the sea, Geiseric presents himself as God's punishment to whichever people he attacks.⁶³ It is a typical – almost stereotypical – expression of barbarian *hybris* when enjoying success. Other sources, too, refer to how Geiseric's treatment of East Roman envoys was reported as supremely arrogant.⁶⁴ It is not inconceivable that this view could have approximated the feelings of those communities targeted by his raids in the 450s and 460s. After the sack of Rome, there was hardly any other direction for the perceptions to develop at. The epistemic 'just-so' quality of a Carthage-based foreign power ending up sacking the Eternal City, the victor over Carthage centuries earlier, could easily have made the developments impinge on the way in which the rule over Mediterranean was affected by these events.

There is further evidence in the sources – beyond those already quoted – that the old triumphalistic idea of the true-and-tested emperor having defeated his enemies both on land and on sea remained strong. The yearning for an active military emperor, such as has been observed above in some of the Constantinopolitan celebrations of the defeat of Gaïnas' party, was palpable also in Sidonius Apollinaris' reference to the old *terra marique* victory imagery:

> We need now an armed prince who in the manner of our sires shall not order wars but wage them, one before whom land and sea shall quake when he advances his standards, so that at last with power regained the Roman war-trump may direct Rome's dormant navies.⁶⁵

The Roman attempts to dislodge the Vandals from Carthage were fruitless until Justinian, and the most famous debacles may well have dented the Roman confidence regarding naval operations in the Mediterranean. These defeats were not what enabled the Vandal sea power to rise in the first place (the relative indifference by the Romans to maintaining standing fleets in the Imperial Era has been seen as the main reason), but they enabled their operations to continue.⁶⁶ It was, as Zeev Rubin put it, a political and military problem, even if not an economic one.⁶⁷ The symbolic need for the emperors to triumph over their transmarine enemy was paramount, as to leave a former part of the empire unrecovered would have caused a serious dent in the rhetoric of the emperor's universal rulership over land and sea.

In 440/1, Theodosius II sent a strong army against Vandal Carthage – a deed that he, very tellingly, represented as a return to the Republican-era politics of expansion 'to the edges of the earth'.[68] This venture was, however, recalled after Attila posed a more immediate threat to Thrace, and another expedition in 448 got similarly only as far as Sicily.[69] Overseas ventures across the Mediterranean were becoming a troublesome exercise for the empire, risking weakened defences elsewhere. The divisive aspects of the sea as an environment perhaps loomed larger in the calculations of the Roman decision-makers. This only increased the resolve of several emperors to retake Africa. Priscus describes Leo I's expedition to Carthage in 467 as having been undone by Geiseric bribing the naval commander, who then 'willingly suffered defeat'.[70] In fact, it seems that the Vandal forces also defeated the Roman navy on the sea, and what Priscus reported is the official version of the Constantinopolitan court, emphasizing the Vandals' subterfuge (a proverbially 'Punic' quality) and the untrustworthiness of the emperor's subordinates.[71] Moreover, as is clear from Procopius' description of Justinian's Vandal war, the Roman defeat of 467 had led to a genuine fear of a naval confrontation with the barbarians – joined to that of the more general 'dangers of the sea' – and this fear had dented the Roman armed forces' capabilities.[72] Procopius' narrative also makes it clear why this would be so: Geiseric devised a stratagem which, as soon as the Vandals gained a favourable wind, allowed them to release fireships at the packed Roman navy. The Vandal navy then arrived to ram and sink the fleeing survivors.[73]

A most frightening combination of elements – fire and water – had thus engulfed the Roman fleet in 467, and Procopius dwells on the horror: the emotive impact of the passage is an obvious one, and the panic of the Romans is explicitly spelled out. The Vandals in this passage are presented as clearly superior to Romans at naval warfare – at least when using stratagems – and the cunning of Geiseric seems to assimilate him to the earlier *exempla* of wily barbarian leaders. Indeed, he seems somewhat like a combination of Brennus and Hannibal – except that this time the barbarian guile hits Romans not from behind the Alps, but in an environment where they had not experienced serious defeat since the Punic Wars. The resulting insecurity endured until Justinian's rule Romans avoided a confrontation with the Vandals, even though they did use their navy to put pressure on other barbarian kingdoms; in 508, Anastasius, for instance, ordered the coasts of the Ostrogothic Italy (which seems not to have possessed a naval force) to be raided with a sizable fleet. It may be that in response to this, Theodoric did have some kind of navy constructed.[74]

With the Mediterranean not wholly under Roman control, any naval operation on its shores was a vast undertaking that left the empire vulnerable on its other frontiers.[75] As an environment, it could no longer be dominated, and even presenting it as such may have strained credibility. It is, of course, very possible that the anxieties visible in some of the contemporary sources led them to paint a fairly pessimistic picture of the times, and even to portray the sea itself as having turned against the Roman Empire. During the 'Vandal century' the Mediterranean no longer knit the empire together but instead carried danger into its heart. In some ways – in stark contrast to previous conditions – the sea as an environment could have ended up emphasizing the limited nature of Rome's resources and reach. The attempt of Constans II to lead the operations in Italy and the Mediterranean from Syracuse, where he was accused of attempting to set up an alternative capital and where he was finally murdered in 668, may have been an experiment in finding an alternative command node in the Mediterranean network.[76] The most crucial explanatory factor for this radical experiment was the rise of the Caliphate as a challenger to Rome's remaining naval power. After a brief interlude, the loss of Egypt, the Levantine coast, and North Africa had brought the weakness of Rome's Mediterranean communications lines back to the foreground.

Arabs

The attacks of Muʿāwiyah ibn Abī Sufyān, later the first Umayyad Caliph, against Cyprus in the late 640s seems to have made a big impression even on western perceptions of the safety of the Mediterranean – at least if the apocalyptically framed reference in the *Cosmographia Aethici Istriotae* is anything to go by.[77] This puzzling, but very popular, early-eighth-century Latin text contains a surprising number of details about seafaring and naval matters. Not only are there frequent references to the eponymous character Aethicus and his students sailing the world between Taprobane in the east and Ireland in the west in search of wisdom (*Cosm.* 24–25), but an entire excursus – and a very imaginative one, at that – is devoted to different ship types (44–57). The reference to the Arab naval threat takes place in a prophetic passage branching off from the author's discussion of Macedon. Alexander-matter is very prominent in this section, but the geographical emphasis is located quite squarely in the Syro-Palestinian area. 'Great and most famous Macedonia', and 'your great charioteer, Alexander' are addressed at the height of their glory, but the next section switches abruptly into a more sombre mood:

> Return, return to Mount Sion! They are penetrating Cyprus and the coastal regions and Ahilon along the path of your foot soldiers on the backs of the sea; the violent depredation of the cavalry seizes the shores of the sea. Persians, Medes, Birrones and Varri, Phoenicians, Maeones, Mesopotamians and Tyrians cross and pass from region to region from the gates [of the sun] and the hinges and to all the ends of the earth, bringing with them their dromedaries, laden with conquered treasures.[78]

Premonitions of naval confrontation litter the *Cosmographia*. Later, in a section that resembles a *periegesis* of the Eastern Mediterranean, there is a reference to some of the ship types of the Cretans, *carpatas naves et dromones* being 'masterly against the Tyrians' (*magistra erga Tyrios*), which could perhaps be a reflection of the Roman-Umayyad naval warfare between the 640s and 680s.[79] 'Tyrians' seems to be the cosmographer's tag for Muslims or Arabs.[80] This may be related to Akko being an important base for the early naval operations of the Caliphate, and to the author's taste for choosing antiquarian or otherwise obscure place names and ethnonyms instead of familiar ones – often creatively repurposed from Isidore of Seville or Orosius.[81]

The significance of the new Cibyrrhaeot theme for the maritime defence of the Aegean – it stretched on the mainland from close to Rhodes and Carpathos (the eponym for the *carpatae naves*, which Aethicus himself is claimed to have designed: *Cosm.* 95) all the way to the coast opposite Cyprus – may also have been a factor affecting the visibility of these areas and topics in the *Cosmographia*.[82] Cyprus itself had supposedly been praised in an elaborate *laus* by 'Aethicus'. Perhaps aptly for the island of Aphrodite, the language is eroticized.[83] An external threat facing an island described in such feminized and adoring fashion – an island environment not *of*, but *as* Aphrodite, even – could have obtained associations of sexual violence. Yet the passage also contains the peaceful image of the naturally abundant island hosting newcomers: this and the reference to covenants (*foedera iura*) probably reflects the shared Roman-Arab taxation of Cyprus, which was affirmed by a treaty by 688.[84]

The emphasis on Cyprus in the worldview of this early-eighth-century Latin author cannot be satisfactorily explained without briefly considering the origins of the *Cosmographia* – a difficult question which has been best and most recently elucidated by Michael Herren in his edition-translation-commentary. We are dealing with a very layered, not entirely serious text that may have been begun in the British Isles, but was almost certainly finished either in the Frankish realm or Northern Italy shortly after the *Apocalypse* of Pseudo-Methodius was translated into Latin in the 720s.[85] The writer seems not to have known Greek very well, but had a definite interest in Greece – possibly partly due to the pagan and philosophical identity constructed for the purported original writer of the text, Aethicus. If, as Herren has suggested, the author of *Cosmographia* studied under Theodore of Tarsus, this interest in Cyprus could reflect not only its contemporary significance but the Cilician origins of Theodore, who himself had experienced the Byzantine-Sassanid wars of the 610s, which saw many Syrians escaping the Persian occupation to Cyprus.[86] They might even be glimpsed dimly in the 'weary sojourners' (*inquilina familia . . . fessis*) of Aethicus' Cyprian *laus*.

Western Syrian chronicles, similarly, highlight the attack on Cyprus as an important event, especially as it preceded the even more extensive raids against Crete, Rhodes and Sicily during the rule of Muʿāwiyah, as well as his navy's clashes against the Romans along the Asiatic coast all the way to the Sea of Marmara in 654 and 655.[87] In a likely fragment from the *Chronicle* of Dionysios of Tel Maḥrē (early ninth century), the description of the setting forth of Muʿāwiyah's task force is clearly included as an impressive ekphrastic passage, where the wealthy island appears as a sheltered land which had been spared the ravages of war by its geographical boundedness.[88] Anchoring off the coast of Cyprus, Muʿāwiyah decides to wait for the peaceful submission of the island, but after several days 'a cruel doom of destruction took shape against the unfortunate population' in his own mind, which was, moreover, swayed by the 'hostile recriminations and angry insults' of his Egyptian contingent, with the Alexandrian marines singled out in particular.[89] The legendary ill-temper and destructiveness of Alexandrians – a commonplace stereotype in Late Antiquity – is here turned into an invasive form of aggression against a previously blissful island.[90]

Dionysius' description of the ensuing sack of Cyprus and the enslavement of its people is every bit in the tradition of the pathos-inducing '*urbs capta*' topos of ancient historiography, with clear allusions to sexual violence – much like in the *Cosmography*.[91] Descriptions of seaborne invasions, such as the raid on Cyprus, would have influenced, partly via the *Apocalypse* of Pseudo-Methodius, the mood and tone of even such western texts as the *Cosmography*. A renewed period of intense naval warfare in the Eastern Mediterranean in the 670s may have further highlighted the tumultuousness of the sea as a contested environment in contemporary perceptions, and the reverberations seem to have been noticed in Italy, too.[92] Perhaps significantly, a recent study has demonstrated how the Arab conquest caused a sizable relocation of populations from the coastal cities of the Levant both through individuals' initiative and through imperial evacuations by sea: many of these Syrians ended up in Italy.[93]

A *Mare Nostrum* no More?

Metaphors of the sea had always kept the theme of danger salient in Greek and Roman minds; in this, the tradition is remarkably consistent.[94] Sea metaphors, generally, are noted to have continued their popularity unabated in Late Antiquity, and perhaps even increased their ubiquitous presence.[95] Partly, of course, this depended upon the entirely conventional understanding of disasters at sea being a supernatural punishment for moral failures of various types.[96] This last section aims to look at the more metaphorical and generalized reflections of the new, contested nature of the Mediterranean. Very real and actual changes in the safety of former heartlands of the empire did not leave people's worldviews and perceptions untouched. Occasionally, historical *exempla* were used to make the new insecurity more understandable; at other times, the old rhetorical clichés about the dangers of the sea obtained new urgency.

To avoid deterministic assumptions, it will be useful to bear in mind that for the writers from the late fourth and early fifth centuries, Rome's Mediterranean connectivities did not seem to be in danger. Ammianus Marcellinus' description of the Isaurian banditry and piracy does not give much of an impression of the Mediterranean having turned into a markedly more dangerous environment. For him, the operative topographic element is the mountainous landscape of the Isaurian homeland, so much more distinctive as an ethnographic explanatory factor than the sea.[97] Vegetius – like Ammianus, another military man with no reason to doubt his confidence in the eternity of Rome's Empire – introduces his short section on naval warfare by using the lack of seaborne threat as one of his justifications for treating the topic as late in his book and as perfunctorily as he does. This has been usually taken to indicate a date for the *De re militari* preceding the Vandal threat (*c*. 419).[98] Winds and storms are explicitly said to be a greater danger to warships than enemies, but Vegetius does seem to acknowledge that there had also been a time when the Romans had had a standing navy, with no need to raise improvised ships in times of crisis.[99] In a recent article on Vegetius' naval appendix, Craig Caldwell points out that in the late fourth century, the technical vocabulary relating to naval warfare was present even in ecclesiastical texts, where the metaphor of first practicing and then actually fighting the naval battle acts as a simile for the importance of learning to avoid fear through preparation.[100]

At the outset of the fifth century the Mediterranean could even be an environment offering safety from the barbarians who threatened on land: a seaborne escape from his pursuers is conjured up by Orosius in a dramatized autobiographical vignette. Yet the sea in this scenario, too, would carry the pursuer and the pursued alike. It was only the divine providence that turned the sea into a route of escape:

> When I tell, if I may mention my own life, how I first saw barbarians from unknown lands, how I escaped from their hostility, flattered those in power, guarded myself against those I could not trust, outwitted those who lay in wait for me, and finally, how, when they pursued me by sea with their rocks and spears, and had almost laid hands upon me, I escaped them when I was covered by a fog which suddenly arose [...].[101]

Naturally, the metaphor of the surging and violent sea was just as available to Orosius as to earlier writers, and he put it in vehement use when describing times of upheaval and warfare. In his case, due to his need to demonstrate that the pre-Christian period had been much worse for humankind than his contemporary era that seemed so troubled, the watery metaphors were particularly paraded in the case of the wars of the Roman Republic.[102] The sea as a metaphor for wars is very vividly used for instance in Book 5, though Orosius makes it clear that the numerous wars of the Late Republic tossed the 'ship of state' even worse than any rough sea could.[103] Such a storm-tossed 'ship of state', beset by the hostile forces of the sea – though the metaphor tends to make every iteration seem as urgent as the previous ones – was in need of a skilled and steady steersman, such as in Agapetus' advice to the Emperor Justinian.[104] Beyond the metaphors lay the perceived risks involved in seafaring; this was the social reality of shared imagery that made these metaphors function and stick.[105]

In addition to the continued rehearsal of such well-established *topoi* – as well as the concrete enemies making the Mediterranean dangerous – it will be crucial for this volume's theme to see whether the sea as an *environment* had begun to obtain markedly more sinister qualities by the Later Empire; if so, when does this become noticeable in our sources? Partly such imagery of danger or corruption could derive from the well-established ideas about the nature of the elements, and the processes resulting from these. In Orosius' description of a locust plague in Africa and a following epidemic, the Mediterranean functions as a source for the noxious disease; the locusts from the land were swept into the sea, where they rotted, generating the plague.[106] As has been noted by Peter Van Nuffelen, the passage is an excellent example of the emotionally laden and vivid way in which Orosius (and many of his contemporaries) amplified their ekphraseis.[107]

Victor Vitensis, who wrote his *History of the Vandal Persecutions* in the 480s, tells how Quodvultdeus of Carthage and other homoousian clergy are put 'naked into dangerous ships' on which they were forced to sail to Italy.[108] It is unclear what made these ships particularly dangerous – how is any ship safe to a naked bishop? – and the best guess is that this simply made the narrative better. This torture story may have been especially apt due to the by-now established association of Vandals and sea power: Geiseric's expulsion of non-Arian clergy was morphed into a purposefully dangerous quasi-execution from which the clerics only survived due to the grace of God. In section 26, similarly, the emphasis is on the sea journey that was necessary to reach the Vandal Africa: the captives taken by Geiseric from Rome arrive in weak state, as they were unfamiliar with sailing.[109] Rome is made to sound like a solidly land-bound city, with denizens unused to the sea. Passages like these clearly use the sea as a distancing environment, emphasizing the separateness of the story of the Vandal/Arian persecution of homoousians and making their plight seem all the more pitiful and hagiographic.

Although it is true that the emphasis on the dangers and rigours of sea voyages forms a solidly entrenched *topos*, in a turbulent era the sea remained a traditional but certainly no less effective a metaphor. Rutilius Namatianus created a particularly vivid image of himself at the mercy of a hostile environment in the surviving sections of his homecoming poem *De reditu suo*.[110] Waters of the 'Ocean' flood fields and farms during the autumn storms, and the sea of the Tuscan coast are depicted as bringing crashing waves 'from another world'.[111] The mixing of the land and the sea, as Jacqueline Clarke notes, could, in such a situation, be a reflection of a world turned upside down, the familiar mixed with the unfamiliar, and the entire order of nature seemingly threatening to slip free from the tethers of human understanding.[112] Equally poignant is the way in which the Mediterranean – a practically tideless sea – behaves similarly to the strange, remote Ocean.[113] But what is notable is the fundamental reversal of the established ideas of security for the respective environments: the land has become the more dangerous of the two.[114] The instability and the violence of the sea, and the juxtaposition of this environment with those on land, was a potent tool in Rutilius' poem, which flavoured his *nostos* with epic tones while celebrating what seemed like the returning fortune of the Roman Empire.

During Justinian's wars in Italy, it seems that the Mediterranean was again presented as a 'Roman' environment, and the Roman dominance of the sea was, for Procopius, something that gave them an advantage over the Goths.[115] Phyllis Culham has evocatively illustrated this through the iconography of Christ Pantocrator at the apsidal mosaic of Ravenna's San Vitale: the world is represented as a blue globe of water.[116] The sea, indeed, was the only viable route of propagating imperial power into the Exarchate of Ravenna. It is, however, perhaps safest to connect this apparent newfound confidence with Justinian's propaganda rather than seeing it as a widely diffused sentiment.[117] As for actual triumphs on the sea, Justinian's many wars do not offer much back up. The Vandal campaign did use a vast fleet for transportation purposes, but the Vandal kingdom itself was defeated on land.

Finally, it is interesting to return to the *Cosmographia Aethici Istriotae*, which shows how the Mediterranean could be defamiliarized in western imaginaries from the period when the Byzantine navies were seriously on the defensive against the Caliphal naval forays. The islands and the seaborne warfare of the Mediterranean get a lot of attention, but overall the Mediterranean emerges as a wholly fantastical environment in the text, with many marvels sprinkled among its geography. Sections 90 to 101 of *Cosmography* treat the Mediterranean islands, with a particular emphasis on the Cyclades (the topic of sections 94–97), Crete, Cyprus, as well as Sicily and the Stoechades; yet several semi-fictionalized islands are mentioned as well. When in the Cyclades, Aethicus is said to have invented and built 'powerful and very fast ships' of his own design, which he called 'palace ships' (*aulonas*) used for repelling enemies 'in this sea and in Greece'.[118] The island of *Carpatos* (Karpathos) is strongly associated with ship-building in the text, and *naves carpasiae* (or *carpatae*) are frequently cited as a standard for excellent warships, 'built with wondrous skill to transport units of armies, cavalry and infantry alike'.[119] The 'Carpasia' is a ship type mentioned also in Isidore's *Etymologies*, which presumably is where the author found it.[120]

Despite its name, the *Cosmography* has many novelistic aspects. The rest of the passage on *Carpatos* includes several elements that attest to the idea of a dangerous, contested Mediterranean. In a cryptic statement, the philosopher Aethicus is claimed to have said: 'The Great Sea is heavy with limbs because of the bitter whirlpools, waves [and] riptides of Carpasia. Enemies and neighbouring friends reluctantly bring and exchange booty money [and] captured plunder for their exiled kinsmen. Parents travel dolefully to assuage the contemptible deportations of their children.'[121] Here, we might have a reflection of the old hub of slave-trade on Delos but transplanted slightly – as well as no doubt mixed with the more contemporary rumours of conflict and displacement in the Eastern Mediterranean. In *Cosm.* 103b, there is an apparent reference to a deportation (or other forced population movement, perhaps a resettlement) of Aethicus' 'own' Istrian community to 'Cassiopan Islands' (*captivati ab Histria Casiopas insulas pervenerunt*), which Michael Herren – no doubt correctly – relates to the disturbances caused by the Slavs, and the moving of significant populations from the mainland to the relative safety of the Ionian (as well as other Greek) islands.[122] In practical terms, the safety of islands was clearly recognized in Late Antiquity. After all, the early stages of the founding of the communities that later grew into Venice – a city with an almost unique attachment to the sea, and in its early stages built in a decidedly non-monumental form from the local materials of the lagoon – are firmly datable to the invasions of Northern Italy, and especially Aquileia.[123]

Concluding Thoughts

Was the Mediterranean perceived during the Later Imperial centuries as having become more dangerous? To what a degree did the sea as an *environment* feature as adverse or dangerous to the Romans? The sea had never been characterized through the category of *amoenitas* – a term which betrays its land-based associations immediately. But even more so, the element of water was seen as a cruel one, and the sea – naturally – had it in excess. By the time Constantine Porphyrogenitus wrote his *On the Themata of East and West* towards the middle of the 900s, even such an oft-plied sea as the Aegean could be emphasized to pose dire and dangerous conditions that required an expert navigator aboard.[124]

Of course, perceptions of danger do not need to have (and often indeed do not have) a direct correspondence with actual levels of risk. From our point of view – at least when based on the simple truisms we 'know' about these times – the societies of the Late Roman Empire *ought* to have felt themselves more vulnerable to sea-borne dangers compared with previous centuries. What the sources do seem to confirm is an increased perception of the Mediterranean as an environment that could separate instead of unifying. This was accompanied by a renewed imperial interest in the sort of triumphalism that also extended over the sea as a component part of the whole world; enemies beyond the sea – particularly the Vandals but also the Goths of Italy – were to be subjugated by a victorious emperor. The Arab-Roman naval struggle, on the other hand, seems to have cast reverberations around the broader Mediterranean periphery in the seventh and eighth centuries.

There is also clear evidence that metaphors of decay and danger were eagerly deployed in connection with the sea in our sources: often they were expressed through time-honoured tropes. We should probably not imagine the cruel, dangerous or adversarial qualities of any sea environments in the Roman perceptions as a binary proposition, but as a sliding scale with strong contextual underpinnings. The Mediterranean was clearly regarded in its usual state as a safer and less adversarial environment than the Ocean. But a warlike and disturbed context could easily prime associations of danger even in an environment as enclosed as the Mediterranean. Defeats, whether resulting from enemy fleets or natural disasters, could be interpreted as signs of a loss of divine favour. Seaborne disasters had, after all, been seen as a sign of supernatural anger at human moral failings ever since the *Odyssey*.

It does seem clear, in any case, that between the fourth and eight centuries a qualitative change had taken place in the perception of the Mediterranean. Naval warfare had returned as a major preoccupation, first during the 'Vandal century' and then, after a brief lull, due to the Slavic and Arab raids. With the seaborne threats colouring people's perception of the sea as an environment, we have some indications of both concrete and metaphorical imagery of the dangerous sea becoming foregrounded in the Late Antique audiences' minds, and writers clearly interacting with this. The developing Christian spiritual imagery of the Late Antique centuries found ample use for the idea of sea as a metaphor, mixing much-earlier Biblical imagery to the symbolism about natural environments inherited from the Greco-Roman tradition.[125] If there is a certain degree of divergence and variation visible among the Late Antique references to the nature of the Mediterranean and its navigation, this is quite understandable. Meanings were created on a more local basis, and the local conditions and experiences of the nature of the inland sea qualified the world views and agendas of each writer in each individual context – perhaps more so than during the Early Empire, when the unitary narrative of a single Mediterranean wielded stronger influence.

Notes

1. Rubin 1986: 15–18.
2. For the narrative, see e.g. Rubin 1986: 18–26. See also Engels 2016: 305–9.
3. See Wilkes 1992: 170–81; Gruen 1984: 359–73.
4. Cic. *Leg. Man.* 314; cf. *Balb.* 6.16; Plut. *Pomp.* 24–30. See also De Souza 2008: 78–81, 85–9; Engels 2016: 309–10.

5. For the forebears, see Momigliano 1942: esp. 62–4; Engels 2016: 292–305; on the Augustan stage see Reitz-Joosse 2016; also Bowden 2007; though Engels 2016: 311–12 sees Augustus as fundamentally turning his back to thalassocratic posturing. Cf. Aug. *RGDA* 25; Str. 3.2.5; Vell. Pat. 2.73.3; Plin. *Pan.* 4.7.
6. For Eratosthenes' writings on the Ocean, Roller 2010. For Polybius and Posidonius, see Roller 2006: 99–105; Clarke 1999: 139–54, 172–9.
7. Cf. Mela 3.2; Tac. *Germ.* 34.2–3; Suet. *Calig.* 50.2, 51.1–3.
8. The complex of ideas is examined for instance by Bruun 1992; also see Horden and Purcell 2000: e.g. 411–23; Nesselrath 2005: esp. 163–5. For the Byzantine Romans' views, see Veikou and Nilsson 2018: *passim* but esp. 272.
9. Gell. *NA* 15.21.1. On the representations of Ocean in Late Imperial mosaics, see Grigorieva in this volume.
10. Cic. *Fam.* 7.10.2.
11. Cf. Plin. *HN* 7.9. On religious rituals connected to seafaring, see Blakely 2017.
12. Ael. Ar. *Or. ad Rom.* 10–13; cf. Vitr. *De arch.* 6.1.11.
13. Cf. Horden and Purcell 2000: 443–4.
14. Irby 2021: esp. 45–62, 157–70.
15. Cf. Rubin 1986: 15–26.
16. See e.g. Harris 2006: 20–8; Herzfeld 2006: 45–6; as well as Engels 2016: 289, 309 and *passim* on the ideas of thalassocracy fostered by the Mediterranean.
17. E.g. Ael. Arist. *Or. ad Rom.* 10–13.
18. Vell. Pat. 2.32.4; cf. App. *Mith.* 121 with a similar sentiment.
19. On the Mediterranean as *mare clausum*, blocked from Rome and her allies by the pirates: Cic. *Leg. Man.* 32.
20. Suet. *Calig.* 50.2, 51.1. The *species pelagi* might be linked, at least on the level of contemporary rumours, to the more famous instance of fighting the ocean and then parading the *spolia Oceani* (*Calig.* 46.1).
21. Suet. *Calig.* 51.2–3.
22. Ibid. 51.3. If Suetonius is correct in saying that Gaius believed himself to be suffering from an illness of the mind (50.2), the emperor might have regarded this as a form of divine punishment.
23. *Pan. Lat.* 6(7).7.2.
24. For the best-known case, Etna, see Buxton 2016.
25. E.g. *CIL* III 12376; *IGRRP* III.481.
26. On Eusebius Scholasticus, see *PLRE* II 'Eusebius 8'; cf. Socr. 6.6.36.
27. *Notit. Urb. Const.* 5.11; Zos. 5.20.3–4; *Suda* Λ.490, *s.v. líberna*. For these, see McCormick 1986: 49–50, 52–55; Cameron and Long 1993: 238.
28. As noted by Cameron and Long 1993: 238.
29. See Burns 1994: 174, 348 n. 118; Lampinen 2015: esp. 25–9.
30. McCormick 1986: 62.
31. *ETMG* 23, 32.
32. Ibid. 28.
33. See also Chapters 1 and 9 of this volume.

34. E.g. Maur. *Strat.* 12.21 modelling naval strategies exactly after military ones.
35. Cf. Dunsch 2015; Engels 2016: 311; Purcell 2017: 323.
36. E.g. Arr. *Epict. diss.* 3.13.9. On the probability of piracy continuing, Starr 1989: 74; also De Souza 2008: 89–90; Merrills 2018: 498–502. See also Mataix Ferrándiz in this volume.
37. E.g. during the Jewish revolt of 66–70 CE: Joseph. *BJ* 3.414–431.
38. Cf. Cass. Dio 55.28.3 on such matters 'not being worthy of record'.
39. On pirates in ancient novels and rhetorical exercises, see De Souza 2008: 92–3; also see Merrills 2018: 500.
40. Martin and Grusková 2014b: 728. On the Black Sea raids, see Kulikowski 2007: 18–20.
41. E.g. Greg. Thaum. *Can.* 1, and cf. *Can.* 5, giving the name of these barbarians as 'Boradi and Goths', though *Can.* 7 also refers to locals joining in with the raiders. For a funerary epigram, see Kaygusuz 1984; also Palumbo Stracca 1997.
42. Reddé 1986: 608–17. See also the chapter of Zavagno and Olgun in this volume.
43. Zos. 1.34-35 (translation R. T. Ridley 1982). Cf. the episode in Zos. 1.71.2, discussed by Le Bohec 2017: 490.
44. On Zosimus' pessimism: Kaegi 1968: 134.
45. Cf. Merrills 2005: 87 on the role of the Caucasus (which the Huns had penetrated in 390-91) in Orosius' *Historiae*.
46. See the different suggestions about the chronological context of *Scythica Vindobonensia*'s material: Martin and Grusková 2014b: 745–8; Mallan and Davenport 2015: 215–20; Suski 2017: 309–12.
47. For Dexippus, see still Millar 1969: esp. 19–24; for the description of the battle at Thermopylae against Scythians (*Codex Vindobonensis Hist. gr.* 73, ff. 192^v–193^r), see the translation in Mallan and Davenport 2015: 206; Martin and Grusková 2014a: 112–13 identify the commander Dexippus with the historian.
48. See Millar 1969: 24–5; Martin and Grusková 2014b: 742; Rollinger 2019.
49. The Costoboci attacked Greece even as far south as Eleusis in 170: Paus. 10.34.5; Ael. Arist. *Or.* 22; *CIL* VI 31856 (*ILS* 1327); the Marcomannic-Quadic invasion of Italy: Cass. Dio 71.3.2; Amm. Marc. 29.6.1; SHA *Marc.* 14.5-7.
50. E.g. describing the siege of Side in Lycia, which was probably only reachable by a naval force: cf. Millar 1969: 24.
51. Dexipp. *ap. Exc. de sent.* 47.
52. *Scyth. Vind.* f. 194^v, translation in Martin and Grusková 2014b: 736; cf. *Exc. de sent.* 47 (see Suski 2017: 306).
53. SHA *Gall.* 13.7; cf. Zonar. 12.26, attributing this to Cleodamus.
54. On the Vandal conquest, see also Chapter 6.
55. *CTh* 9.40.24. See Moss 1973: 725. Similar fear is relevant to Malch. F 20 (Blockley) *ap. Exc. de leg. Rom.* 1.120-125.
56. Cf. Rubin 1986: 26–7; on the image of a 'corsair kingdom', Pryor and Jeffreys 2006: 12; also Egea 1997.
57. Wickham 2005: 711.
58. Merrills 2017: 501.
59. Pryor and Jeffreys 2006: 12; see Merrills 2017: 496–8.

60. E.g. the raiding of Nikopolis in 467 and 474: Chrysos 1981: 50–5; Snively 2007: 740.
61. Lounghis 2018: 21.
62. Theoph. *Chron. a.m.* 5941.
63. Proc. *Bell.* 3.5.22–25.
64. Priscus F 41.1 (Blockley) *ap. Exc. de leg. Gent.* 15.
65. Sid. *Carm.* 2.382–86 (translation W. B. Anderson).
66. Cf. Rubin 1986: 29 on the basis of Jean Rougé; but against this view see Pryor and Jeffreys 2006: 7. On Roman 'contribution to piracy', De Souza 2008: 89–90.
67. Rubin 1986: 30.
68. *Nov.* 7.3. Cf. Lounghis 2018: 21.
69. Prosp. Aq. *s.a.* 441; Theoph. *Chron. a.m.* 5941–2, 5961, 5963. For the two expeditions under Theodosius II, see Pryor and Jeffreys 2006: 8–9; Merrills 2017: 503–4.
70. Priscus F 53 (Blockley) *ap.* Theoph. *Chron. a.m.* 5961. Cf. Procop. *Bell.* 3.6.1–2, 5–25, which in Blockley is F 53.3.
71. Cf. Rubin 1986: 45; and on the interweaving of the themes of cunning and thalassocracy, Engels 2016: 308. As Merrills 2017: 497 points out, the Vandal hostilities were dubbed by Sidonius Apollinaris the 'Fourth Punic War'.
72. Procop. *Bell.* 3.14.2; cf. 3.15.20.
73. Ibid. 3.6.17–21. As Pryor and Jeffreys 2006: 9 note, the Roman commander had left his fleet at anchor in a vulnerable position off Cape Bon. On Procopius' manipulation of his narrative, see also Merrills 2017: 507.
74. Marc. Com. *Chron. s.a.* 508. Cf. Pryor and Jeffreys 2006: 14–15 on the tenuous evidence for Ostrogothic navy.
75. Cf. Rubin 1986: 42.
76. See Pryor and Jeffreys 2006: 25–6; see also Lounghis 2018: 23.
77. Herren 2011: 294; Berg 2013: 7.
78. *Cosm.* 84. All the translations of this text are those of Herren 2011.
79. Ibid. 91.
80. Ibid. 84, 91.
81. On Akko/Acre, cf. al-Balādhurī, *Kitāb futūh al-buldān* 117. On ethnonyms, cf. *Cosm.* 29, 59, 62, 84b, 110.
82. On Cibyrrhaeot theme, see Lounghis 2018: 24–6, 29–30.
83. *Cosm.* 90.
84. Herren 2011: xxxi. On the conquest and the Roman-Arab 'condominium' of Cyprus, see Pryor and Jeffreys 2006: 25; Zavagno 2013; Lynch 2016; Picard 2018: 189–90, 193–4.
85. See Herren 2011: xxxviii, lx; lxii, lxvii, lxxii, lxxvii–lxxviii; also Berg 2013: 12.
86. Herren 2011: lxix; on Theodore, see Lapidge 2006: 8–10.
87. Dion. Telm. *Chron.* 93 (AG 960) *ap. Chron. AD 1234* (Palmer 1993: 173–4); [Sebeos] *Hist.* 50(170–1) on Muʿāwiyah's attack and the divine intervention saving Constantinople. The historicity of this attack is considered doubtful: Pryor and Jeffreys 2006: 25.
88. Dion. Telm. *Chron.* 94 (AG 960) *ap. Chron. AD 1234* (transl. Palmer 1993: 173–4).
89. Ibid. 95 (transl. Palmer 1993: 174).

90. Cf. Amm. Marc. 22.11.4, 16.15, 16.23; SHA *Tyr. trig.* 22 *Aemil.* 1-4; *ETMG* 37.
91. Dion. Telm. *Chron.* 96 (AG 960) *ap. Chron. AD 1234* (transl. Palmer 1993: 174–5)
92. See Pryor and Jeffreys 2006: 26–7. Cf. also Fischer 2014, 56–9 on the *Chronicle of Fredegar*.
93. Theodoropoulos 2020: 265–7, 278–80; cf. Fischer 2014, 59.
94. Cf. Beaulieu 2016: 24–5, 181 for the early, Greek stage of the metaphoric usages. For sea metaphors in the Byzantine material, see Veikou and Nilsson 2018: 270–1.
95. Cf. Brooke 1987: 289–90; Whitby and Roberts 2018: 231; also Wade 2018.
96. Cf. Blakely 2017: 362–79.
97. Amm. Marc. 14.2.1–20.
98. Moss 1973: 724.
99. Veg. *Mil.* 4.38, 4.31.
100. Caldwell 2021: 217.
101. Oros. *Hist.* 3.20.6–7 (transl. A. T. Fear 2010).
102. Ibid. 5.24.9–13, with both stormy sea-swells and torrential storms (of blood) used as metaphors.
103. Ibid. 5.24.9–10. Cf. Van Nuffelen 2012: 130. Another metaphoric use of the sea is Oros. *Hist.* 6.14.1.
104. Agap. *Exp. capitum admonitionum* 2, 10.
105. See Dagron and Rougé 1982 on fifth-century CE horoscopes; cf. dream signs in Byzantine *oneirocritica*, translated in Oberhelman 2008: 86, 136, 157, 185–6, 206–7.
106. Oros. *Hist.* 5.11.2–3. On the sea and the generation of plagues, cf. also Irby 2021: 117–19.
107. Van Nuffelen 2012: 126–7.
108. Vict. Vit. *Hist. pers. Vand.* 15.
109. Ibid. 26; cf. Basil. *Ep.* 2.1.
110. See Clarke 2014: 96; Veikou and Nilsson 2018: 268 on the general rhetorical *topos*, for instance in Synesius. See also Horden and Purcell 2000: 138–40, 443–4.
111. Rut. Namat. 635–44.
112. Clarke 2014: 96.
113. Devecka 2019: 253.
114. Rut. Namat. 37–42.
115. Procop. *Bell.* 5.7.20, 6.7.17, 12.16–17. See Pryor and Jeffreys 2006: 14–18.
116. Culham 2017: 288.
117. Cf. Procop. *Aed.* 1.2.1, still using the old 'peace by land and sea' trope when reporting an inscription of an equestrian statue of Justinian.
118. *Cosm.* 95.
119. Ibid.
120. Isid. *Etym.* 19.1.11; cf. how the *meoparae/mioparae* of *Cosm.* 53, 56 (cf. 19, 22, 36, 63) are from *Etym.* 19.1.21.
121. *Cosm.* 95.
122. Herren 2011: lxxv. On the safety and comparable prosperity of the Greek islands in the seventh century, see Wickham 2005: 628; also cf. Zavagno's and Olgun's chapter in this volume.

123. The Lombards are the usual culprits (Paul. Diac. *Hist. Lang.* 2.14) although back-projections to the Hunnic disturbances of the fifth century have been popular; cf. Pryor and Jeffreys 2006: 19; D'Amico 2017: 217–19.
124. Const. Porph. *De them.* 17(43) (p. 83 Pertusi).
125. For the significance of this to the Byzantine attitude towards environment, see Olson 2020: especially Ch. 8 'Conclusions'.

PART II
A NETWORKED ENVIRONMENT

CHAPTER 4
CONNECTING PEOPLE IN THE MEDITERRANEAN: MOBILITY AND MIGRATION IN OSTIA AND PORTUS

Arja Karivieri

Introduction

The mutual dependence of the two harbour cities, Ostia and Portus, and their connection to the metropolitan area of Rome, the Mediterranean area and the provinces of the Roman Empire provide interesting material and new aspects to the ongoing discussion of migration in Antiquity, especially as compared to Laurence Tacoma's definitions of migration to Rome. As Tacoma did not include the analysis of migration to Ostia and Portus in his study of 2016, this chapter aims to raise the specific character of the harbour cities of Rome to the centre of attention with the help of archaeological evidence, literary sources and inscriptions. The geological development of the coastal area of Ostia-Portus since the Late Bronze Age onwards has had a decisive impact on human mobility and the urban development of the harbour cities of Rome. The estuary with its saltworks and the surrounding landscape with its fertile soil enabled the development of agriculture, and the coastal area created a favourable environment for the creation of a large settlement and a system of harbours by the sea. Furthermore, this chapter undertakes a comparison to the latest geological studies of the coastal area of Latium and the River Tiber, and discusses the development of this area from the Roman period to modern times.

Various Definitions for Migration

According to Charles Tilly, there are four forms of migration: local migration, circular migration, chain migration and career migration.[1] However, as Tilly's typology has been adapted to European migration history, Laurence Tacoma emphasizes that Roman migration cannot easily be classified into one of Tilly's four types. Therefore, Tacoma developed further the definitions of Tilly in his study *Moving Romans. Migration to Rome in the Principate* (2016), suggesting that migration consists of ten more specific categories.[2] These have been labelled as: elite migration, administrative migration, educational migration, movements of intellectuals, permanent mobility of performing artists, seasonal and temporary labour migration, immigration by the poor, migration of traders, immigration of slaves to households, and, finally, military migration. In addition, Greg Woolf includes three features for the study of human mobility in antiquity: first, different kinds of mobility and different kinds of migrants; second, variable mobility over time; and, third, quantitative claims for mobility in history.[3]

Elite Migration

In his study of migration to Rome in the Principate, Tacoma did not include the material from Ostia and Portus.[4] However, the ten categories of migration listed by Tacoma provide an interesting basis to study the mobility of the inhabitants of the harbour cities of Rome, as well as the reasons for the mobility of temporary inhabitants, visitors and workers in the coastal area which need some more comments. The first category, elite migration,[5] is connected to geographical mobility of the provincial elite, as many members of aristocratic families from the provinces moved to Italy and Rome, especially to promote their political career. However, they were also expected to own property in Italy.[6] Emperor Trajan himself, who was born in Italica in the Roman province of Hispania Baetica, ordered office-holders to own at least one-third of their property in Italy.[7] Trajan thought that it was 'unseemly that candidates for office should treat Rome and Italy not as their native country, but as a mere inn or lodging-house for them on their visits.'[8] Consequently, candidates rushed about to buy up anything they heard was for sale, and the price of land increased, particularly in the neighbourhood of Rome. Pliny the Younger advised his friend Maecilius Nepos to sell out his Italian estates and buy new estates in the provinces, as the same candidates for offices sold their estates in the provinces to be able to buy land properties in Rome and Italy: 'So if you are tired of your Italian estates, now is the time, believe me, for selling out and buying in the provinces – the same candidates are selling there to be able to buy here.'[9] In the middle of the second century CE, there were already almost as many senators from the Greek-speaking eastern provinces as from the West. The Senate had become multinational and representatives of the most important families from various parts of the empire had gathered in Rome.[10]

Later in the second century, Marcus Aurelius ordered *senatores peregrini* to own a fourth part of their property in Italy: *utque senatores peregrini quartam partem in Italia possiderent*, thus reducing the earlier requirements for senators who came from the provinces, as compared to the requirements of the Trajanic period.[11] As Werner Eck states, the senatorial mobility to Italy created a concentration of wealth in Italy and lack of funds locally.[12]

In Late Antiquity, several senators lived at Ostia. Russell Meiggs suggested that 'Volusianus v(ir) c(larissimus) ex praefe(c)tis' who celebrated a *taurobolium* at Ostia, could probably be connected to C. Caeionius Rufus Volusianus Lampadius, who was praetorian prefect in 355 CE and *praefectus urbi* in 365–366 CE.[13] Meiggs wished to see the *Domus dei Dioscuri* as the Ostian residence of Volusianus. The house has a large mosaic floor depicting Venus and the Nereids, flanked by the inscription '*plura faciatis meliora dedicetis*', a motto used especially in Africa, where the family of Volusianus had land property.[14] Another family, *Anicii*, who came from Praeneste, had links with Africa. Anicius Auchenius Bassus in the late fourth or early fifth century declares the Christian faith of the family, and Anicia Italica with her husband Valerius Faltonius financed a water-pipe.[15] Symmachus owned a large estate in Ostian territory and, in his letter from 398 CE,[16] he was a guest in the wedding at Ostia of the son of Sallustius who had been *praefectus urbi*.[17] These examples show that several senatorial families had residences at Ostia.

Administrative Migration

The second form of migration listed by Tacoma, administrative migration, is especially well-attested by *cursus* inscriptions, showing the positions Roman citizens held in the provinces both in military offices and in imperial administration, providing especially interesting facts for the study of military careers in the Roman army.[18] An example of this kind of career is provided by a member of an important Ostian family, *Egrilii*, A. Egrilius Rufus, who reached the equestrian status, held several Ostian offices in the late first century CE, and he also held a military tribunate in the *Legio V Alaudae* in Germany.[19] Another member of the same Ostian family, Q. Egrilius Plarianus, was suffect consul in 144 CE and the proconsul of Africa in 159 CE.[20] Another prominent Ostian family, *Sextii*, had several members who travelled abroad from Ostia during their career. T. Sextius was governor of Africa in the Late Republican period, and thereafter several members of the family had the *cognomen Africanus*. In 112 CE T. Sextius Africanus, another member of the family, was the consular colleague of Emperor Trajan.[21] The family of the *Fabii Agrippae* and *Agrippini* was an important Ostian family from the second century CE onwards.[22] C. Fabius Agrippinus was a member of the senatorial order, he was *quaestor* in the province of Cyprus until *c.* 140 CE, governor of the province of Thrace, and in 149 CE suffect consul.[23] Another family member with the same name became the commander of the *Legio I Minervia*, stationed in Bonn in 211 CE and the governor of the province of Syria until 219 CE.[24]

Educational Migration

The third type, educational migration, is connected to the travels conducted by young men who travelled for educational purposes.[25] As Rome was a centre of education, many came to Rome through Ostia and the harbour of Portus, and some of them very probably stayed in Ostia to study in the local schools or *collegia* there.[26] Another form of educational migration concerns apprenticeship, i.e. moving to become disciples in the workshops of artisans, sculptors, painters, or students of famous doctors or architects.[27] There were both pottery and glass workshops in Ostia and Portus in Late Antiquity[28] that could provide training in various tasks of the production processes.

The Movement of Intellectuals

The fourth form of migration consists of the movement of intellectuals. This was a widespread form of mobility, as large cities, such as Alexandria, Antioch, Athens and

Rome were desirable for all those who 'wished to move up on the social ladder'.[29] Some intellectuals are attested at Ostia, such as a sophist called P. Aelius Samius Isocrates, who was native of Nicomedia in Bithynia and a citizen of Ephesus.[30] Two doctors are also known by name, Titus Statilius and *pansophos* Ygeinos.[31] At the end of the second century CE, one Ostian doctor, Marcus Rubrius Zosimus, *medicus cohortis,* served at the hospital (*valetudinarium*) of the Fourth Praetorian cohort of Aquitania, *Cohors IIII Aquitanorum equitata,* stationed at the Main river of the Limes. Zosimus dedicated an altar to Jupiter, Apollo, Aesculapius, Salus and Fortuna, emphasizing his origin with the expression *domu Ostia*.[32] The decoration of this altar also refers to the origin of Zosimus, showing the god of the sea, Neptune, protective god of the harbour city, represented in the relief holding the trident. Yvonne Schmuhl suggests that the Greek name of Zosimus may be an indication that the doctor came as a slave to Ostia and served the family of *gens Rubria,* before he as *libertus* started his military service. Greek doctors were highly valued by the Romans and Galen refers to the contacts he had with the doctors of Ostia and Portus.[33]

In the fourth century CE, when Christianity had become the official religion with the emperor as its protector, Rome with its new churches, St Peter's and the Lateran basilica, attracted Church fathers and bishops from the whole Mediterranean area to Rome. Simultaneously with the construction of these new churches, Constantine the Great also built a large Christian basilica in Ostia where various specialists worked on the project.[34] Possibly at least some of these specialists came from the same workshops that worked to build St Peter's and the Lateran basilica in Rome.

Some decades later, St Augustine arrived with his brother and his mother Monica to Ostia where they settled in a house with a garden.[35] Augustine writes vividly in his *Confessiones* about their life and living in Ostia, how his mother Monica got ill and died in Ostia in 387 CE.[36] Monica was buried in Ostia according to the local customs, which was her own wish, as Augustine describes it. Meiggs[37] interpreted that the friends that Augustine mentions in his Ostian letters as senatorial officers with African connections, including a Volusianus,[38] Pammachius,[39] the *Anicii,*[40] an Italica and Anicius Bassus, who dedicated a poem to Monica soon after her death. This epigram is partially preserved in an epitaph discovered in a tomb excavated in 1945 adjacent to the Basilica of Santa Aurea in Ostia Antica, and copied in Early Mediaeval manuscripts.[41] In his turn, Tacoma emphasizes the importance of combining various categories of evidence. In his article, he compares the results of isotope analyses, the information from inscriptions, and the narrative in *Confessiones,* and shows how different sources can tell different stories.[42]

The letter of Jerome from 397 CE to his friend, the Roman senator Pammachius,[43] provides further evidence for the increased amount of travelling from various parts of the Roman Empire to Rome, Portus and Ostia. The Senator travelled to Italy to visit the new churches and the basilicas donated to local saints, and in contrast, travelled from Rome to the Holy Land, Alexandria and other parts of the Roman world. Jerome wrote this letter to his friend Pammachius who had settled with his wife Paulina at Portus to build a *xenodochium* for Christian pilgrims. In Jerome's letter to Oceanus on the death of Fabiola, Jerome returns to the importance of Pammachius' *xenodochium* at Portus:

... a hostel was purchased and a crowd flocked to it for hospitality ... The sea brought in travellers for the land to welcome. Rome sent others, who hastened to enjoy the comforts of the mild shore before they set sail... What Publius did once in the island of Malta for a single apostle and ... for a single ship, they did many times for many men ... The whole world heard that a Home for Strangers had been founded in the port of Rome, and Britain knew in the summer what Egypt and the Parthians had learned in the spring.[44]

Jerome's letter provides evidence of the multicultural nature of the harbour of Rome in the late fourth century and the many inscriptions of Portus, written in Greek, show also the eastern origin of many inhabitants and visitors to Portus.[45] These inscriptions include dedications to traditional Roman gods, to Egyptian and other Eastern divinities, as well as Christian and Jewish inscriptions from Late Antiquity.[46]

At Portus, Latin inscriptions are more numerous than Greek, but the origin of the individuals is provided more often by Greek inscriptions.[47] As Olli Salomies has emphasized, the origin of the deceased cannot be determined from personal names only, since slaves, freedmen, as well as Jews, could use Roman names.[48] However, as Emanuela Borgia suggests, foreign individuals who attained a higher social status preferred to use Latin in their grave monuments, showing a higher grade of integration as migrants, when workers of eastern origin at Ostia and Portus used Greek in their epitaphs.[49]

Permanent Mobility

One large group of migrants was formed by people who were permanently moving, i.e. performing artists, such as gladiators, actors, *venatores*, charioteers, athletes, musicians and reciters of poetry, as well as pantomime artists.[50] There are several individuals attested by graffiti and grave inscriptions found in Ostia that may be accounted in this group. There are also small objects decorated with representations of actors, gladiators, *venatores*, wall paintings representing charioteers in the Casa degli Aurighi, and floor mosaics representing dancers, athletes and boxers in baths and bars in Ostia provide evidence of their activities and popularity in the area.[51] A pantomime artist from Scythopolis in Syria Palaestina, M. Aurelius Pylades, was praised in an inscription from the mid-third century CE by the *seviri Augustales* in Ostia.[52] Pylades had previously performed in Ascalon and Damascus in his home province and the inscription is also a tribute to the late father of Pylades, by the name Iudas, apparently a member of the Jewish minority in Ostia.

Seasonal and Temporary Labour Migration

A central group of mobility is connected to seasonal and temporary labour migration, such as sailors travelling between the harbour cities of the Mediterranean.[53] As Ray

Laurence emphasizes,[54] the epitaphs from Ostia's cemeteries show that the members of the imperial fleet in Ostia were recruited from various parts of the empire, such as Thrace, Pannonia, Sardinia and Corsica. However, epitaphs reveal only the names of those who died in Ostia, and there were numerous others who only resided in Ostia and Portus for short periods. In this light, Erdkamp has pointed out that the economy of ancient cities was subjected to an annual cycle of expansion and contraction, with additional work during summer.[55] The building and construction industry involved both workers with special skills and numerous unskilled workers who offered their labour force and could both move soil and transport building material.[56] The unloading of supplies from ships to smaller boats (*navis caudicariae*) that would carry the goods along the Tiber to the city of Rome and the loading of outgoing large merchant ships with a cargo at Ostia and Portus required a large number of workmen. Paul Erdkamp compares the circumstances of Rome to modern Shanghai, and suggests that more than 20,000 dock workers could have been employed in the harbours of Rome from April to October,[57] coming from smallholding households in the countryside.

To the activities of the shipowners and *navicularii,* in the harbours of Rome, we may also add other groups who were active in the harbour, like the *curatores* and labourers such as *saccarii*, and shipbuilders.[58] The members' list of the shipbuilders guild from Ostia and Portus includes a small number of free foreigners, whose names are scattered among the local names, which Meiggs interpreted as evidence that all names were listed according to their seniority.[59] In his turn, Christer Bruun highlights the list of *fabri navales* that included seven newcomers who do not have the typical Roman *tria nomina*; instead they have only one name and a patronymic referring to their father, which has allowed him to identify them as *peregrini*.[60] One of them bears the name Ostiensis Isidori f(ilius) suggesting that he got his name in Ostia. Six of the names are Greek *cognomina*, indicating that these carpenters had their origins in the Eastern Mediterranean.[61] Two inscriptions, among others, can be provided as examples of migration to Ostia from Gaul. L. Antonius Epitynchanus who was a *sevir Augustalis* at Aquae Sextiae (Aix-en-Provence), was also a *quinquennalis* of the *collegium fabrum tignuariorum* at Ostia.[62] Finally, one grave monument, shaped as a small pyramid and located in the necropolis of Isola Sacra, is dedicated to Gaius Annaeus Atticus, from Poitiers in Aquitania.[63]

Almost 40 inscriptions from the area mention *navicularii*, many of them being located into the floor mosaics of the Piazzale delle Corporazioni in Ostia.[64] One of them was active in the Adriatic Sea as *curator navicularior(um) maris Hadriat(ici)*,[65] while another inscription in Greek refers to *navicularii* of ships belonging to the Alexandrian fleet importing grain to Rome.[66]

The importance of North Africa as supplier of grain increased from the first century CE onwards, which is reflected both in the increased amount of grain, wine and wild beasts coming from Africa to Italy, as well as inscriptions erected by people from African provinces.[67] David L. Stone has suggested that, during the main period of port construction in North Africa, from the first to the third century CE, the relationship between North Africa and Rome stimulated agricultural production, economic development, and social relations, creating a new phase of connectivity.[68] The connection to Africa was emphasized in Ostia and Portus from the late second century CE onwards and especially during the reign of Septimius Severus, the first African emperor. During the Severan period the theatre, the Piazzale delle Corporazioni, and the Barracks of the Vigiles were restored in Ostia, as well as large warehouses were built in the harbour of Portus. The new mosaic floors with their inscriptions decorating the long porticoes by the theatre of Ostia reveal the names of *navicularii* from many African provinces, but also from Gaul and Sardinia. One grave epitaph from Ostia mentions the *curator navium* Lucius Caelius Aprilis Valerianus of the Arnensis tribe, from Carthage, and his wife, who were buried in Ostia.[69] Valerianus is an example of a migrant from Africa who decided to stay in Ostia and did not return to his hometown Carthage.

Migration and Mobility by the Poor

A significant part of migration and mobility was conducted by the poor in the Roman world,[70] who sought new labour opportunities. Port cities offered plenty of opportunities to work in the warehouses and the dockyards of the harbours.[71] The city of Ostia was famous for the amount of opportunities it could provide for those who were looking for a job or to meet a new employer. Juvenal describes in a vivacious manner how the clientele of an Ostian *popina* could look, when he criticized the lavish lifestyle of consul Lateranus, who disgraced himself at Ostia:

> Despatch your lieutenant to Ostia, Caesar, but first look for him in a huge – diner. You'll find him reclining next to some hit man, mingling with sailors and thieves and runaway slaves, among executioners and coffin-makers and the now silent tom-toms of a priest sprawled flat on his back. There, it's 'freedom' for all alike, shared cups. There, no one gets a separate couch or a table set apart. What would you do, Ponticus, if you happened to have a slave like that? You would surely send him off to Lucania or the Etruscan chain gangs. But you of Trojan blood, you forgive yourselves. Behaviour that would disgrace a labourer is fine for a Volesus and a Brutus.[72]

This passage of Juvenal emphasizes how Roman citizens could behave more freely than workers or slaves, as well as referring to the varied and multifaceted clientele of Ostian bars and inns. Seneca's *Ad Helviam* likewise lists the various groups of people that gathered in Rome and all the possible reasons for their mobility.[73]

Migrant Traders

An important group of migrant itinerants consists of traders, who had to stay in a harbour during the winter months, as commercial navigation was suspended during the *mare clausum*.[74] Many *negotiantes vinarii*, *frumentarii*, and *mensores frumentarii* are mentioned in inscriptions.⁷⁵ Some sailors and traders would stay in Portus or Ostia over the winter months to take care of ships and the merchandise stored in warehouses, when also the riggings of large square sails and ropes had to be repaired and checked.⁷⁶ When the grain trade from Alexandria shifted from Rome to Constantinople in Late Antiquity, the nature of contacts and commercial navigation from the Eastern Mediterranean to Rome and Ostia changed. A change in ship technology from large, square-rigged ships to lateen-rigged vessels in Late Antiquity has previously been connected to the termination of grain trade between Alexandria and Rome and population decline.⁷⁷ Julian Whitewright has challenged this interpretation in his studies where he compared the literary evidence for square-sail voyages to lateen/settee voyages.⁷⁸ Whitewright suggests that 'differences in performance are more likely to have occurred as a result of differences in hull-form, rather than in sailing rig'.⁷⁹ The preference for lateen sail was due to the fact that the lateen sail provided the opportunity for cost reduction, as it required less component parts than the square sail to make it function effectively, and could operate on a range of vessel types.⁸⁰ The lateen rig thus offered economic advantages for maritime traffic in the Mediterranean in Late Antiquity.⁸¹

In their study about Roman ports and Mediterranean connectivity, Andrew Wilson, Katia Schörle and Candace Rice emphasize the importance of regular mercantile connections on established routes, and how maritime export flows affected the articulation of production in certain goods using the glass industry as an example.⁸² Roman glass production was dependent on the long-distance movement of raw materials, and raw glass ingots were imported to Ostia, Portus and Rome, where evidence for Late Antique glass-blowing workshops have been found.⁸³ The Embiez Ouest wreck found off the southern coast of France, a small ship carrying almost 18 tons of raw glass, has been interpreted as a possible example of the redistribution of raw material from a major Italian port such as Portus or Puteoli, a ship that was on its way to a port in Southern Gaul.⁸⁴

At Portus, several individuals from Nicomedia are known, and an organized association of Bithynians may have existed at Portus.⁸⁵ The profession of a person from Nicomedia is given in a grave epitaph of second or third century CE⁸⁶ as *leukourgos* and, according to Borgia, this may refer to a person who was involved in the marble trade. Nicomedia had specialized in the shipment of marble, which plausibly explains the amount of Bithynians at Portus, as marble for the building projects of Rome was distributed through Portus.⁸⁷ The existence of one woman from Nicomedia, Chrysa Markiane, who is mentioned in a funerary monument from Isola Sacra, plausibly from the third century CE, suggests that whole families of Bithynians had settled at Portus.⁸⁸ Furthermore, there is another separate group of Greek inscriptions attesting the existence of many individuals from Alexandria in Egypt,⁸⁹ two individuals also as *fabri navales*.⁹⁰ The Egyptian Quintus Lusius Rufus who died at Portus in the second century CE, was a *miles* of the *classis Misenensis*.⁹¹

Giulia Boetto has identified five main patterns of trading voyages on the basis of the evidence from five shipwrecks.⁹² The first consists of direct voyages with single cargoes between main emporia (the shipwreck of La Madrague de Giens from *c.* 75–60 BCE); while the second concerns voyages with mixed cargoes between emporia (*Cabrera III* wreck, dated by the treasure of *sestertii* to 257 CE). The third pattern dwells with mixed cargoes from a major emporium to a secondary port (shipwreck *Culip IV*, dated to 75 CE); whilst the fourth pattern deals with homogeneous cargoes transported from one port to another connected to a specific order (shipwreck *Cavalière* from *c.* 100 BCE). Finally, the fifth patterns concerns casual movement from port to port (shipwreck *Barthélemy B*, from the second quarter of the first century CE). The five shipwrecks analyzed by Boetto represent different periods, but the *Cabrera III* shipwreck that was found near Mallorca provides an example from the Later Empire, including, except for the treasure from 257 CE, an assemblage of amphorae from Baetica, Byzacena and Lusitania, and it has been suggested that the cargo was loaded in Gades and was headed towards Portus.[93] This and other trading ships could also have taken passengers, providing various possibilities for those willing to move to another part of the Roman Empire to study, to look for a job or to create a new career. Woolf suggests that if 1,000 vessels made two round trips annually across the Mediterranean, each carrying *c.* thirty passengers, that would give a total number of around 60,000 travels in a year.[94]

According to Wilson, Schörle and Rice, there were regional hierarchies, as the available harbour area, wharfage and depth controlled the amount of incoming and outgoing traffic.[95] For example, the total area of the harbour at Portus was 234 hectares after the addition of the Trajanic basin. The sides of the Trajanic hexagon at Portus measured 3,058 meters and might have allowed up to 130 large merchant ships. Together with the capacity of the Claudian basin and the Darsena basin, other canals and basins, the total wharfage may have been up to 330 large ships and several hundred small-to-medium vessels, with others waiting at anchor in the harbour basins.[96] The amount of ships and smaller vessels shows the capacity of the harbour area of Ostia and Portus for trade, export and import, and, simultaneously, the need for labourers at the docks for loading and unloading the goods.

Immigration of Slaves

Furthermore, immigration of slaves was always a central phenomenon of Roman society, which affected not only the import of foreign material culture, objects, languages, customs, religions and cults to Rome, but also the development of Roman society into a more multicultural and multi-religious society.[97] Numerous slaves and workmen were needed for work in the harbour of Portus, the river harbour of Ostia, to take care of the continuous traffic between Portus and Ostia through the canal of Isola Sacra,[98] as well as in agriculture in the rural area providing the products that were needed by the inhabitants of the harbour cities. However, it is very difficult to identify or quantify the migration of slaves, as Bruun rightly states.[99] The prevalence of slaves in the grave inscriptions of Isola Sacra can also be seen as a hint of migration and mobility, further emphasized by the existence of Greek texts among the Isola Sacra inscriptions.[100]

Military Migration

This development of Rome, Ostia and Portus into a more multicultural society characterized by many religious groups and followers of various, both traditional and new cults, was further enhanced by military migration,[101] when soldiers from various provinces of the Roman Empire moved with the army from their places of origin into new areas during their years of service. A specific example of mobility includes *vigiles* who had a four-month period of service in Ostia, from the Early Imperial period until the third century CE.[102] The excavations of the Barracks of the Vigiles revealed several inscriptions including important details of the men participating in the force, and their activities are also attested by numerous graffiti, the majority dated by Heikki Solin to the first half of the third century CE.[103] Some of the *vigiles* were recruited from the Latini Juniani, who had restricted citizen rights. By the second century CE, they could receive full citizenship after the service of three years.[104] A significant detail is the fact that there are no inscriptions connected to *vigiles* after the mid-third century CE from Ostia.

Warships were stationed at Ostia during the Imperial period, even though the command of the fleet had been transferred to Misenum. Thus, some men serving in the Misenum fleet were on service at Ostia. Indeed, Meiggs suggested that the triremes were at Ostia to police the harbours and control shipping, and occasionally carry governors or emperors who sailed from Ostia.[105]

Christer Bruun has analyzed in detail an inscription from 218 CE that lists around 180 soldiers who were discharged after long service in the two urban cohorts of Rome.[106] Twenty-four of the retiring soldiers indicated Ostia as their origin. However, the special onomastic features suggest that this group of *urbaniciani* constituted a mixed group, indicating various social and geographical backgrounds. Bruun proposes that several men in the group were recent immigrants to Ostia who brought both their *gentilicium* and the *cognomen* to Ostia, and these new recruits in 197–198 CE may have been registered at Ostia, some of them possibly seamen who were recruited in the harbour city.[107]

A grave epitaph from Isola Sacra, dated to the second century CE, is dedicated to Q(uintus) Gargilius Q(uinti) f(ilius) Iulianus, also called Semelius, a soldier who came from Carthage to Rome.[108] David Noy suggests that Gargilius came to Rome in order to enlist in the Praetorian Guard and he died at Ostia while in transit.[109] The grave epitaph of L. Caecilius Aemilianus from a funerary altar in the necropolis near Porta Laurentina describes a different type of career: he was a veteran of the Praetorian Cohort I, *decurio* and *duovir* in Aelia Uluzibbira in Africa, who became wine trader in the second century CE and seems to have created a prominent career at Ostia.[110]

Fluvio-Coastal Mobility and Migrant Workers

Férreol Salomon together with an international team has recently published results of a geoarchaeological and archaeological study at the mouth of the River Tiber. They suggest that urban fabric analysis and paleoenvironmental analysis may be combined to reconstruct the evolution of Ostia in relation to the fluvio-coastal mobility. The mobility of riverbanks and shores due to the problem of sedimentation affected the infrastructures and the organization of the port of Ostia.[111] Salomon et al. use the term resilience in connection with Ostia to describe a city that had to face fluvio-coastal hazards that at times affected dramatically the navigability of the River Tiber, the possibility to transfer the goods to or from the harbour, its warehouses and further to or from Rome, as well as the amount of labour force needed in various phases. Thus, the urban resilience of Ostia would involve 'change in *form* but not in *structure* of the urban area', as the urban centre had the capacity to adapt to fluvial and coastal disruptions that had a direct impact on human mobility and migration. Salomon and his team suggest that we may see Ostia's resilience decrease in the Early Middle Ages, and end when a new urban centre, the so-called Gregoriopolis, was built east of Porta Romana, east of the large meander of the Tiber.

Migration and Mobility, Isotopes and Ancient DNA Studies

Scientific methods utilized for the study of migration and mobility include anthropology and osteoarchaeological research, i.e. isotope analyses and DNA-analyses of the bone material from the necropoleis of Ostia and Portus and the surrounding area, compared with the results from Rome and Italy.[112] The research team of Tracy Prowse published in 2007 the analysis of oxygen isotopes from the teeth of 61 individuals from the necropolis of Isola Sacra, a study that created a lively discussion for years.[113] Another study included the analysis of strontium isotopes in 107 skeletons from the necropoleis of Casal Bertone and Castellaccio Europarco in the suburbs of Rome. The geographic origins of these individuals could not, however, be determined because similar isotopic profiles exist in various parts of the Mediterranean.[114] More reliable results can only be obtained by combining the studies of stable isotopes to the analysis of ancient DNA. The results combined with the evidence from ancient literature, epigraphy and information from archaeological contexts and finds will provide new important information for the study of migration and mobility to Ostia and Portus.[115] However, we can already confirm that a significant part, possibly up to 30 per cent of the people residing at Ostia and Portus may have been immigrants.

The latest larger study consists of 127 genomes from 29 sites in and around Rome, and covers a time span from the Neolithic until modern times.[116] Although the sample of individuals included in the study is restricted, the results provide interesting first results concerning the mobility and migration to Rome, Ostia and Portus in the Imperial period and in Late Antiquity, to be compared with other categories of evidence. The migration in the Imperial period seems to have had more genetic influence from the Eastern Mediterranean, and in Late Antiquity from Europe, as a mixture of the preceding periods and individuals from Bavaria and the Basque Country.[117]

For the first to third centuries CE, samples from 48 individuals from Rome and central Italy were analyzed (including nine individuals from the necropolis of Isola Sacra, with date range from the second to the late third–early fourth century CE): the population substructure shows that of these 4 per cent had North African ancestry, 40 per cent Eastern Mediterranean, 28 per cent Near Eastern, 24 per cent Central Mediterranean and 4 per cent European, including very few individuals of primarily western Mediterranean ancestry.[118] People and goods came from the provinces by ships that docked at Portus. The nine analysed individuals from the necropolis of Portus, Isola Sacra, provide an interesting example of the mixed population of the harbour cities from the first to the third centuries: four individuals have Near Eastern genetic influence, four have Eastern Mediterranean ancestry and one female (Sample ID=R37) is identified as European, with a genome that has nearest resemblance in the genome of individuals from Western provinces.[119]

In Late Antiquity, for the time period from 300 CE until 600 CE, the results from the samples of 24 individuals are different, reflecting the political changes and the split of the Roman Empire: 30 per cent of individuals have Eastern Mediterranean ancestry, 30 per cent European, 38 per cent Central Mediterranean and 4 per cent Sardinian. There is a substantial ancestry shift towards Central and Northern European populations and away from Near Eastern populations, and continued high variability in ancestry.[120] The results suggest that in Late Antiquity, networks of trade and routes were reshaped and grain supply rerouted to the new capital of the empire, Constantinople, which affected mobility and diminished the traffic from the Eastern Mediterranean to Rome. Instead, new groups of people from the North, Visigoths, Vandals and Lombards came to Italy and created a new mixture with the genetic diversity from the earlier centuries that may have been the result of trade, migration, slavery, and conquests.[121] Ostia and Portus were still important in Late Antiquity The results reflect well the information presented in this article from the various inscriptions from Ostia and Portus.

Conclusions

Finally, going back to the definitions used by Tilly, i.e. local migration, circular migration, chain migration and career migration, it is important to point out that Ostia and Portus also received migrants from the city of Rome,[122] people who moved to the coast to find new working opportunities provided by the expanding building industry of the harbours, as well as the large building projects with imperial funding, from the second century CE onwards. The impact of Rome is visible also in funerary customs and tomb architecture at Ostia and Portus, as well as other port cities around the Mediterranean, in Puteoli, Patras, Corinth, Djerba and Tarraco,[123] where columbarium architecture of Rome with collective tomb monuments was adopted. Dorian Borbonus sees this as evidence for efficient networks, movement, migration and social conditions. An inscription from Portus may perhaps be seen as a piece of evidence for chain migration: Valerius Veturius, African citizen, *civis Afer* is identified in his grave epitaph also as *colonicus*, which according to Noy was probably used as a message to compatriots, and he may have been involved in trade between Africa and Italy.[124] An army career was for many men from the provinces a process of circular migration.[125]

Another aspect connected to mobility and migration is, naturally, religious mobility. Simon Price made a distinction between ethnic cults and elective cults.[126] Ethnic cults include the adoption of Roman religious strategies in *coloniae* and provincial communities and the eastern ethnic cults that were brought to the West.[127] The Jewish communities in Rome and Ostia belong thus in this context. A Jewish community existed in Ostia in the Early Imperial period, as Price suggested, for commercial reasons. Among the ethnic cults from the East, the Egyptian cults that arrived with the merchants to the estuary of Tiber had a prominent role in Ostia and Portus. Price defined Mithraism as an example of elective cults,[128] and the cult of Mithras had a prominent role in Ostia. I may add another proposal: the *mithraea* of Ostia may have had impact on the transmission of the cult to the provinces, when people moved from the area to other places, or the other way around; for example, a veteran of the Roman army may have retired to Ostia and created a new *mithraeum*.

Price discussed in detail the religious landscape of the third-century town Dura Europos in Syria, which includes 15 religious places, representing Greek gods, Palmyrene deities, deities from the village of Anath, Aramaic cults, cults of Mithras and Jupiter Dolichenus, a Jewish synagogue and a Christian church.[129] Crucial for the development of economic, social and religious life was the access to the Euphrates, being a major trading route providing access to Mesopotamia and the Far East. In conclusion, Price suggested that the variety of the religious landscape in Dura Europos was the product of its economic life and movements of people, comparable to Mediterranean harbour cities, like Ostia.

However, epigraphic evidence from the sanctuaries of foreign cults at Ostia and Portus includes names of both local people as well as immigrants.[130] For example, C. Valerius Serenus who made a dedication in Greek to Septimius Severus and his family in 201 CE, was *neokoros* of the cult of Serapis at Portus and *epimeletes* of the Alexandrian fleet.[131] Valerius Serenus could either have settled down at Ostia or visited Ostia and Portus only during his mission as the curator of the grain import from Alexandria.[132] As David Noy states, it is difficult for modern scholars to know if an act of migration was intended to be temporary or permanent.[133]

In Prudentius treatise *Contra orationem Symmachi*, published in the early fifth century CE after the death of Symmachus, we find a perfect description of the perceived unity of the Roman world in Late Antiquity, the success after the *Constitutio Antoniniana* of 212 CE:

> A common law made them equals and bound them by a single name, bringing them by conquest into bonds of brotherhood. We live in countries the most diverse like fellow-citizens of the same blood dwelling within the single ramparts of their native city, and all united in an ancestral home. Regions far apart, shores separated by the sea, now meet together in appearing before one common court of law, in the way of trade in the products of their crafts they gather to one thronged market, in the way of wedlock they unite in legal marriage with a spouse of another country; for a single progeny is produced from the mixed blood of two different races. Such is the result of the great successes and triumphs of the Roman power.[134]

According to Prudentius, this unity was emphasized with the new success of the Christian church, uniting the fellow citizens of the various parts of the Roman world under a common religion.

Notes

1. Tilly 1978: 51–5; de Ligt and Tacoma 2016: 8.
2. Tacoma 2016a: 35–48.
3. Woolf 2016b: 442.
4. Tacoma 2016a: 28.
5. Cf also Tacoma 2015 for elite mobility and social mobility.
6. Tacoma 2016a: 36–7.
7. Plin. *Ep.* 6.19.4. See also: Eck 2016: 104.
8. Transl. B. Radice.
9. Plin. *Ep.* 6.19.6.
10. Eck 2016: 102.
11. SHA *Marc.* 11.8; Eck 2016: 104; Tacoma 2016a: 37, n. 32.
12. Eck 2016: 106–7.
13. Meiggs 1973: 212.
14. For more on mosaics, see Grigorieva's chapter in this volume.
15. Meiggs 1973: 212–13.
16. Symm. *Ep.* 6.35.
17. Meiggs 1973: 213.
18. Tacoma 2016a: 38.
19. *AE* 1955: 168; Salomies 2020: 160. Cf. also Bruun 2016: 190–1, comments on the 'onomastic profile', the method employed by Olli Salomies for the study of the population of Ostia.
20. Fronto *Ep. ad am.* 1.4; Salomies 2020: 160–1.
21. Salomies 2020: 161.
22. Salomies 2020: 162–4.
23. *AE* 2007: 303; Salomies 2020: 162.
24. Cass. Dio 80.3.4; Salomies 2020: 162–4.
25. Tacoma 2016a: 38–40.
26. Karivieri 2020d: 376–80.
27. Tacoma 2016a: 40.
28. Karivieri 2020a: 126–7; Karivieri 2020b: 212–5.
29. Tacoma 2016a: 40–1.
30. *AE* 1947: 162; *SEG* 13.472; Meiggs 1973: 215; Lazzarini 1980: 197–8; Borgia 2020: 41.
31. Nutton 1969: 96; Meiggs 1973: 216; Borgia 2020: 41.
32. *CIL* XIII 6621; EDCS-11000655. From Obernburg am Main in Germania superior, Stiftsmuseum Aschaffenburg, inv. 185; Meiggs 1973: 233, n. 7; Schmuhl and Steidl 2008: no. 27.

33. Galen *Comm. in Hippoc. de articulis* 303 (Kühn 18.348); Meiggs 1973: 233.
34. Karivieri 2020d: 371–3.
35. Meiggs 1973: 213.
36. August. *Conf.* 9.8–12.
37. Meiggs 1973: 213.
38. August. *Ep.* 132, 135, 137.
39. August. *Ep.* 58.
40. August. *Ep.* 92, 99.
41. *IG* XIV 942; Lazzarini 1980: 193–7; Boin 2013: 229–31; Tacoma 2016b; Karivieri 2020d: 375–6, 517, cat. no. 167; Melotti 2020: 388–90, fig. 2; Noy 2020: 54–5.
42. Tacoma 2016b.
43. Jer. *Ep.* 66.11: Meiggs 1973: 403.
44. Jer. *Ep.* 77.10 (tr. Fremantle, Lewis and Martley).
45. Keay 2012: 5–7; Van Haeperen 2019: 297–304.
46. Cf also Lazzarini 1996. For the synagogue at Portus, see Van Haeperen 2019: 291.
47. Helttula et al. 2007; Borgia 2020: 40.
48. Salomies 2002: 150–3; Borgia 2020: 40.
49. Borgia 2020: 46–7.
50. Tacoma 2016a: 41.
51. Karivieri 2020c.
52. *CIL* XIV 4624; Meiggs 1973: 423; Cébeillac-Gervasoni, Caldelli and Zevi 2010: 292–3, no. 88; Karivieri 2020c: 297–8; Noy 2020: 56.
53. Tacoma 2016a: 41–2.
54. Laurence 2020: 59–61.
55. Erdkamp 2016: 34–5.
56. Erdkamp 2016: 38; Woolf 2016b: 442, 456; Noy 2020: 53.
57. Erdkamp 2016: 41, 48.
58. On *navicularii* and *curatores* in Ostia, cf. van der Ploeg 2020; on various categories of work in the harbour, cf. Larsson Loven 2020: 228–30.
59. Meiggs 1973: 318; cf Licordari 2020: 170–1.
60. Bruun 2016: 184.
61. Bruun 2016: 184, 189.
62. *CIL* XIV 296; Noy 2020: 59.
63. Helttula et al. 2007: 24–5, no. 21; Noy 2020: 60.
64. Bruun 2017: 217; Mustakallio and Karivieri 2020; van der Ploeg 2020: 183–5.
65. *AE* 1987: 191; Bruun 2017: 217.
66. *IG* XIV 918; Meiggs 1973: 59, n. 1; Sacco 1984: 12–13, no. 2; Bruun 2017: 217.
67. van der Ploeg 2020b: 181.
68. Stone 2014: 595.
69. *CIL* XIV 4626; van der Ploeg 2020b: 185–6.

70. Tacoma 2016a: 42–3.
71. Larsson Loven 2020: 228–30; Noy 2020: 53.
72. Juv. 8.171–182 (transl. Morton Braund).
73. Sen. *Cons. ad Helv.* 6.2, 7.1, 3–4; Tacoma and Lo Cascio 2016: 6–8.
74. Beresford 2012: 3–7; 29; Tacoma 2016a: 43–5; Woolf 2016b: 256.
75. Bruun 2017: 217–18.
76. Cf Martelli 2013: 4–21; Tacoma 2016a: 44.
77. Polzer 2008: 241–2.
78. Whitewright 2011: 3–4, 9–10, 1, tables 1, 4–9.
79. Whitewright 2011: 13–14, table 10.
80. Whitewright 2018: 40–2.
81. See also Forsyth in this volume.
82. Wilson, Schörle and Rice 2012: 374–6.
83. Wilson, Schörle and Rice 2012: 376, fig. 20.3, and p. 378, table 20.10: Simon Keay, excavations at Portus; Karivieri 2020a: 127; Karivieri 2020b: 212–13.
84. Jézègou 2008.
85. Borgia 2020: 41–3.
86. Sacco 1984: 57–8, no. 38; Helttula et al. 2007: xxvi, no. 7; Borgia 2020: 42–3, table 1.
87. Borgia 2020: 47–83.
88. *SEG* 29: 980; Sacco 1984: 111–13, no. 92; Helttula et al. 2007: 167, no. 21^{GR}; Borgia 2020: 43.
89. Sacco 1984: nos 2, 3, 6, 16, 21, 23, 39, 63.
90. *CIL* XIV 256; Meiggs 1973: 216, 319; Sacco 1984; Borgia 2020: 42–4, 48.
91. *CIL* XIV 239; Meiggs 1973: 216; Borgia 2020: 44.
92. Boetto 2012: 155–6.
93. Boetto 2012: 156; Bonifay and Tchernia 2012: 320.
94. Woolf 2016b: 460.
95. Wilson, Schörle and Rice 2012: 382–4.
96. Keay 2020.
97. Tacoma 2016a: 45–6; Woolf 2016a: 36; Woolf 2016b: 441–3, 455–6.
98. Keay 2020.
99. Bruun 2016: 186–7.
100. Tacoma 2016b: 142–3.
101. Tacoma 2016a: 46–7: Woolf 2016a: 36.
102. Laurence 2020: 61.
103. Meiggs 1973: 307; Solin 2020: 320–3, 325–6.
104. Meiggs 1973: 307.
105. Meiggs 1973: 304.
106. Bruun 2020; *CIL* VI 32526.
107. Bruun 2020: 153–5.
108. *CIL* XIV 4488; Thylander 1951–1952: A 125; Helttula et al. 2007: 239–41, no. 223.

109. Noy 2020: 57–8.
110. Bloch 1939: 37; *AE* 1940, 64; Meiggs 1973: 214–15; van der Ploeg 2017; Noy 2020: 53, 59. See also van der Ploeg 2020a for wine traders and foreign middlemen at Ostia.
111. Salomon et al. 2018: 280.
112. Cf Prowse 2016.
113. Bruun 2016; Prowse 2016: 212–18.
114. Prowse 2016: 212–13.
115. Bruun 2016; Lo Cascio 2016: 30.
116. Antonio et al. 2019.
117. Antonio et al. 2019: 708, 712–13.
118. Antonio et al. 2019: 710–11, 713, fig. 4; cf. also supplementary material, p. 35, figs. S15, S18, S20, table S28.
119. Antonio et al. 2019: 713.
120. Antonio et al. 2019: 710–11, 713, fig. 4.
121. Antonio et al. 2019: 713. On Vandals, see also Chapter 6.
122. Tacoma 2016a: 168; Laurence 2020: 61.
123. Borbonus 2020: 33–5.
124. *CIL* XIV 481; Meiggs 1973: 215; Noy 2020: 58–9.
125. Noy 2020: 59.
126. Price 2012: 1–19.
127. Price 2012: 3–5.
128. Price 2012: 7–8.
129. Price 2012: 14–15.
130. Bruun 2016: 192–3.
131. *IG* XIV, 917; Sacco 1984: 13–16, no. 3; *RICIS* 2, 503/1207; Meiggs 1973: 387; Bruun 2016: 192–3; Van Haeperen 2019: 297–8, 300–1.
132. For a detailed discussion on the contacts between Ostia and Alexandria, see Mustakallio (forthcoming).
133. Noy 2020: 55.
134. Prudent. *C. Symm.* 2. 608–20 (transl. H.J. Thomson).

CHAPTER 5
... διά νήσων πλέειν ...
TAKING THE ISLAND ROUTE: TRADE AND EXCHANGE ALONG THE COAST OF SOUTHERN NAXOS*

Hallvard R. Indgjerd

Introduction

In the past five years, three separate projects have conducted a field survey on Southern Naxos and the islands of the Lesser Cyclades located immediately to the south of Naxos. This chapter uses preliminary results from these projects as a starting point to discuss the structure and extent of trade networks and long-distance connections in the Central Cyclades between the Roman and the Early Medieval period. It will stress the value of combining data from different landscape types by surveying offshore, coastal and inland areas, and the importance of covering space where habitation is not expected as well as previously known settlements.

Evidence for maritime distribution network structures is hard to gather from land-based archaeology alone as both direct and indirect connections would allow for export of produce and bring consumer goods back for consumption. At the same time, underwater data reveal little about local settlement and consumption patterns. A goal of the present project is to achieve both by aligning land surface survey data with underwater finds from the same area.

Southern Naxos and the Lesser Cyclades are home to several important Early Bronze Age sites, including Kavos and Dhaskalio on Keros[1] and Spedos and Korfari ton Amygdalon in Southeast Naxos.[2] In fact, this exact region is the area chosen by Cyprian Broodbank as the ideal case study for an EBA *small-world* island network.[3] Only in the last years, however, have Late Roman and Byzantine finds seen any serious interest. In addition to a surface survey, research has begun on the Byzantine fortified hilltop settlement at Kastro Apalirou[4] and in the proposed Late Roman monastic complex in Gyroulas, both near Sangri on Naxos, on Late Roman and Byzantine agricultural production facilities around the Hellenistic tower of Cheimarrou,[5] on an Early Byzantine chapel on the islet of Dhaskalio,[6] and on a major Late Roman (port) settlement on Schinoussa.[7]

The study region is surrounded by established Hellenistic-Roman *poleis* and trade hubs, but there are no known major centres within it. Thus, this chapter is not approaching the discussion from the perspective of commercial centres that were the start and end points of long-distance trade,[8] but is instead focused on an area in-between the major nodes to examine how a rural landscape (and *rural seascape*) interacted with maritime contacts and transport routes.

Taking the Island Route

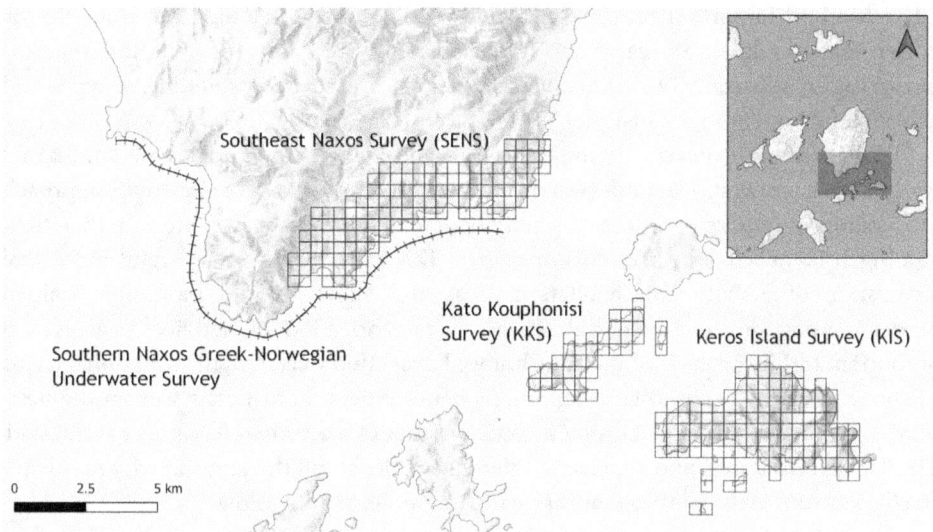

Figure 5.1 Survey projects included in the South-East Naxos Survey.

Approaches to trade routes and patterns are often based on written sources, technical calculations and simulations, or material culture. While this chapter taps into all three, the focus will be on the archaeological data which is only now becoming available for this micro-region.

The Dataset

The following discussion is based on material from the three surface surveys of the Keros-Naxos Seaways Project and on the Southern Naxos Greek-Norwegian Underwater Survey (Figure 5.1). Between 2012 and 2018, the Keros-Naxos Seaways Project surveyed the entirety of the islands of Keros (KIS) and Kato Kouphonisi (KKS), and a 1,000 ha area of the south-eastern part of Naxos (SENS).[9] The project followed an adapted version of the 'Kythera survey methodology', with a 15 per cent coverage extensive collection of feature sherds in all areas, and additional intensive collection, including 100 per cent vacuum sampling, within areas of interest.[10] Approximately 9,000 sherds were analyzed from each of Keros, Southeast Naxos and Kato Kouphonisi, with a temporal span covering the full spectrum of ceramic production from the Neolithic to recent times. In addition to typological and macroscopic ceramic analysis, a sample of the Late Roman and Early Medieval pottery has been studied petrographically.[11]

With a combination of free-diving and scuba-diving, the Naxos Underwater Survey (2016–2018) covered the coastline and reefs between Aliko and the cape of Panormos from the shore down to a 30-40-metres depth.[12] Key areas of deeper waters were investigated with ROV and side scan sonar. While this methodology is likely to have discovered all important remains of activity visible on the seafloor, the resolution is lower than on land. Similarly, far fewer objects were recovered, but the superior preservation, especially of ceramic vessels, ensures a high understanding of types and chronology present in the material.[13]

While there are necessary differences in the field methodologies of land-based pedestrian surveys and an underwater survey, all four projects have shared the approach of looking for discrete patterns of activity across the investigated areas, rather than aiming at identifying 'sites' as dots on a map. This has encouraged a careful individual evaluation of activity and habitation areas and allowed for a more fine-grained understanding of functional differences. A categorization of activity areas is still important for the analysis of the data, but we have found that applying functional terms without rigid and exclusionary definitions better reflect the patterns seen in the field. Rather than mechanically defining a pottery scatter of a certain size, e.g. as a farmstead, similar find situations may represent different activities, and the same activity may leave vastly different material traces, as discussed for landing spots below.

A key element for the present discussion is traces of maritime activity, both on- and offshore. The identification of ports, anchorages and sailing lanes, however, is far from straightforward, especially in a rural area without major harbour constructions.

The logistics of the Keros–Naxos Seaways survey project, where every day the field crew were dropped off and picked up by boat from varying points along the coastlines of Keros, Kato Kouphonisi and Southern Naxos, provided a first-hand experience of how approachable these coasts are for smaller vessels like the traditional Cycladic *caïque*, even in fairly rough weather. Little or no infrastructure was needed to transfer people and goods between sea and land, and places that at first sight looked like dangerously inaccessible cliff-faces proved to be quick and reliable landing spots. For repeated entry, simple wooden structures that could easily be dismantled at the end of the season were used to improve the local topography (Figure 5.2). The use of such minimal installations has been common on the smaller islands until recently and should not be seen as a sign of minimal interaction.[14] The prevalence of similar port solutions, known as landing stages, or *scalae*, has been argued for the ancient Aegean.[15]

As Justin Leidwanger reminds us,[16] these 'opportunistic ports' will typically be archaeologically invisible in themselves. Thus, the focus on visible harbour structures has skewed our understanding of coastal interaction and trade.[17] With a case study from Cyprus, Leidwanger argues that a combination of land and underwater data, and a careful evaluation of find compositions, is necessary to identify most ports. Wooden wharves, piers and pontoons were important elements of large and complex harbours and seem to have become more common in the Byzantine period.[18] Since wood is only preserved in exceptional cases in the Aegean, this adds a possible temporal bias, obscuring Byzantine structures more than Roman ones. As shown by Michael McCormick,[19] landing at beaches, minimal ports or anchoring offshore is commonly referred to in texts from the Late Roman and Early Medieval period, both as commercial destinations and safe harbours in case of bad weather.

Figure 5.2 Ad-hoc wooden structures used to ease the access to a sand beach on Kato Kouphonisi with the help of a few boulders fallen from the escarpment behind (top), and the limestone rocks at the foot of Dhaskalio (bottom).

Anchorages are areas, typically protected and close to land, where ships would lower anchor, either seeking shelter, waiting for changing wind conditions or harbour space, or to transfer cargo.[20] The find assemblage of an anchorage is likely to include disposed items from the ships, such as broken personal and ship equipment and emptied storage vessels, incidentally lost transport vessels from offshore loading and unloading, and lost or intentionally cut anchors.[21] Unlike wreck sites, an anchorage will not include any one full ship assemblage, but a mix of objects deposited over the period of activity of the site.

This is similar to what would be expected from a port assemblage and, as seen above, the difference between a coastal anchorage and a landing spot cannot be decided on the basis of missing port structures. A discrepancy between on- and offshore find densities, however, is a good indication, together with topographic features and the occurrence of ballast.

The quickly changing and potentially dangerous wind conditions in the Aegean make well-protected emergency anchorages valuable and frequently used.[22] An incident from Milos described in a late sixteenth-century travel account must be typical for pre-modern sailing in the Cyclades.[23] When faced with a sudden storm, the captain immediately sought shelter behind a projecting cliff (*Berg*) and set anchor, thus saving the ship and crew. A Roman example is found at Grammata, a protected bay close to the north-western tip of Syros. The use of this bay as a harbour of refuge is attested in over a 100 Hellenistic to Byzantine inscriptions carved into the rock on the northern shore.[24] Mostly they contain standardized short texts of *euploiai* and thanks for safe haven (Figure 5.3). Within the surveyed areas, remains of port infrastructure have been identified only in the bay of Panormos.

This bay in the south-eastern corner of Naxos forms a naturally protected harbour, only open to the south-west through a narrow inlet. The name itself is a common and old place name for well-protected natural harbours (πάν-ορμος translates to *offering moorage at all points* or *convenient for landing*, as used, e.g. in Hom. *Od.* 13.195). The Naxian Panormos is named in the Hellenistic-Roman *Stadiasmus* (see below), and the important EBA settlement Korfari ton Amygdalon, 350 metres north-west of the present shoreline in the bay, shows that the location has been favoured through all periods.[25]

The Panormos-Irokastro activity area (Figure 5.4) is by far the largest and most complex cluster of Late Roman material on Southeast Naxos, covering an area of close to 60 ha north and west of the bay.[26] The pottery, CBM and building remains display internal functional divisions, potentially delineating administrative, mercantile, habitational and defensive spaces within the settlement.

A stone structure running into the bay from the south-eastern edge, has been interpreted as a jetty or a ramp constructed out of ballast material as part of the bay's harbour. Close to this, more than 20 ballast piles of basalt cobbles are clear evidence of ship loading taking place in the bay (Figure 5.4).[27] The largest of these ballast piles has an estimated weight of 47 tons and contains pottery sherds from the fifth and eighth centuries CE.

West of Panormos, transport amphorae and minor ballast piles in the shallow and sandy Andrios bay are matched by ceramic finds on land.[28] While the ballast stones are

Figure 5.3 Grammata Bay, Syros. Euploia by Eunomios (top), identifying as a Jewish sailor from Naxos (possibly first century BCE) and a fourth-fifth century Christian invocation by Eulimenios from Ephesus (bottom) (Photo: Rebecca Sweetman).

Figure 5.4 Aerial view of Panormos Bay and Irokastro (top) and Aerial orthophoto of the ballast piles in shallow water in the bay of Panormos (bottom).

similar to the Late Roman piles in Panormos, the ceramics recovered from the bay do not give a clear date for these events but show activity from Hellenistic or Early Roman times to the fifth or sixth century. Together, the land and offshore finds might indicate the presence of a farmstead or other minor habitation unit in use between the fifth and the seventh century, but the material could also originate in more intermittent opportunistic use of the area. The ballast shows that cargo has been loaded, and possibly also unloaded, but on a much smaller scale than in Panormos. It is not unlikely that smaller ships after dropping their ballast further out in the bay could have landed on the beach and been loaded by hand without any further infrastructure.

A variety of ceramic vessels off the steep coast south of Cape Panormos, in an area named Tourkospilia, however, is interpreted as a *roadstead* type anchorage. The pottery consists of both transport amphorae and utilitarian wares with a date range of more than a millennium between the Hellenistic and the Middle Byzantine period. The assemblage does not contain large groups of identical vessels and there is no visible ballast on the seafloor. It is not clear if the spot has been used for ships too large to enter the bay of Panormos, or if ships anchored there waiting for free space or the right wind condition to enter the harbour, but it seems unlikely that any large-scale loading or unloading has taken place (a similar relationship between anchorage and port has been suggested for the bay of Skiros and the harbour at Apollonas on the northern part of Naxos).[29]

Close to the southwestern tip of the island a second anchorage has been discovered. On a stretch of about 300 metres off the steep south-faced coast of Cape Moni a large assemblage of pottery and anchors (of stone, lead and iron) were deposited over a time span of more than a millennium and a half, from the Archaic to the Middle Byzantine period. As in Tourkospilia there is no evidence of cargo loading or of the material coming from shipwrecks, and in Cape Moni the time span of deposition is even longer than in Tourkospilia. The combination of deep water close to land and good protection from the *meltemi* provided by the central mountain range on Naxos makes this bay the last good anchorage before tackling the exposed straight between Paros and Naxos.

Underwater prospection has not taken place along the coasts of Keros and Kato Kouphonisi. Potential anchorages would thus not have been identified and, without visible port structures, the landing spots on these islands can only be proposed based on the land find densities and general topography.

On Kato Kouphonisi a major settlement has been localized around the natural southeast-facing harbour in the bay of Panagia.[30] A very high density of Late Roman and Early Medieval transport amphorae is evidence of an active port, possibly including exports of agricultural surplus from the island. A concentration of Roman and Late Roman sherds on the north-western coast indicates that Limni Bay served as an alternative landing spot when Panagia was exposed to the weather. Scattered Roman transport amphorae sherds close to the coast elsewhere on the island show the occasional use of other protected bays, including Dhetis and Fykio.

On Keros, the recent village at Konakia stands out as the centre of activity in the Roman and Early Medieval period, and the settlement must have been served by a port in continuous operation.[31] The coastline along this plain is, however, heavily eroded, and no traces of ancient landing activities on or close to the shore are present. The southern side of Keros has several deep bays, well protected from all but straight southerly winds, and with access through *remas* into the uplands of the island. Sherds of Late Antique ceramics in these valleys and in the uplands suggests that the bays have occasionally been used for landing, but anchoring while waiting for better wind conditions may have been more common. Another likely anchorage is close to the islet of Dhaskalio at the western tip of the island. Here a small Early Byzantine chapel was built using spolia from the Early Bronze Age settlement. Apart from the chapel itself and some ceramic and glass from its excavation, this part of Keros is devoid of Roman and Byzantine finds. Elli Tzavella argues the chapel and the islet may have served as a landmark marking a safe anchorage and natural short time stopping point.[32]

Several of the straits and coastlines in the study area have reefs and eroded sharp limestone rock outcrops close below the sea surface. In strong wind and high waves, they present a serious navigational hazard which has not always been successfully overcome. The archaeological remains of these encounters are either shipwrecks, or cargo, anchors and ballast jettisoned from a grounded ship in an attempt to lift it off. While wrecks would originally contain an intact ship assemblage, poor wood preservation and the impact of wave and current activity near the surface will, in many cases, break up and scatter the remaining material.

The largest reef in the area covered by the underwater survey is found about a kilometre south of Panormos. Today, several parts of the reef raise to between two and four metres below sea level, compared to the surrounding 15–20 metres depth. With an estimated 1–1.5 metres lower sea level in the Late Roman period, the top of the reef would have been only decimetres below the surface, and, in large waves, would present a considerable danger to passing ships.

Dense scatters of ceramics as well as anchors were found throughout the reef area. While it is in some instances difficult to ascertain whether the finds are the results of wrecks or of dumping, some large assemblages of identical vessels can only be explained as wreck sites. The largest of these are in the south-eastern part of the reef and was identified by the remains of several hundred vessels of a Middle Roman amphorae type known as Dressel 2–4 similis (Figure 5.5).[33] Several Late Roman amphorae of the North African Keay 62, LRA1 and Samos Cistern types were found across the reef, but not in concentrations that could indicate the presence of wrecks.

Chronology and Provenance

The Late Hellenistic to Middle Roman period is poorly represented in the surface survey material in general, and the possibilities of pinpointing provenance are very rare. There are few, if any, examples of the typical fine-ware productions one would expect to see in the Aegean, neither Eastern Sigillata, Italian Sigillata, nor early African Red Slip have so far been identified.[34] Diagnostic transport amphora sherds roughly datable to the period are found on Keros, Kato Kouphonisi and in the Panormos area, but although they have

Figure 5.5 Dressel 2–4 similis amphorae on the sea floor at Panormos reef (Photo: Frode Kvalø, Southern Naxos Underwater Survey).

been identified as imported and as such show a connection with a wider trade network, no place of origin has been proposed.

On the seafloor, however, the evidence is more plentiful. The large concentration of Dressel 2–4 similis amphorae scattered over the south-eastern part of the Panormos Reef, can only reasonably be interpreted as a full cargo load carrying a single type of transport vessel – no other amphora types were identified within the wreckage scatter (Figure 5.5). This uniformity would suggest that the amphorae were being used for the first time, and that the ship carried a single type of goods, possibly produced and loaded near the origin of the amphorae. Andrei Opaiţ and Aris Tsaravopoulos claim the area of Chios, Erythrai or Kyme in the North-Eastern Aegean as the most likely production centre for the amphora type.[35] It has also been found in a wreck-site near the islet of Mavronisi in Naoussa Bay on Paros,[36] showing that the load that went down outside Panormos was not a one-off occurrence in the area. Several other amphora types are represented in the underwater material by individual vessels, not attributed to specific ship loads. All the identified types have in common a provenance east of Naxos, from the coast and islands from Western Asia Minor, or from Cilicia in the south-east of Asia Minor.

The Late Roman centuries are far more visible in the land survey record than the preceding periods. At first sight, this mirrors the general image of landscape surface surveys in the Aegean, which has led to the idea of the Late Roman 'busy countryside'.[37] Interesting, however, is the clustering of the pottery and the apparent lack of finds in the remaining part of the survey area. The activity is centred around one area on Keros, one on Kato Kouphonisi, and one on South-East Naxos, where the concentrations of Late Roman material are very high compared to any other period, and many times higher than the Late Roman material anywhere else in the surveyed areas. Most of the countryside, then, might be less 'busy' than described elsewhere in the Eastern Mediterranean with farmsteads in every bay. Only the find concentration in Andrios Bay fits the expected pattern of a farmstead.

Part of the explanation for this is likely to be that neither of the surveys contain particularly fertile areas. SENS, for example, covered the most remote parts of modern-day Naxos, and the arid south-facing hills and small catchment basins along most of the southern coast of the island offer little fertile agricultural ground. It's possible that surveying a larger part of Southern Naxos would have altered this picture, and the fact that the second largest concentration of Late Roman pottery is in the very corner of the included area, where it touches on the Dhistomos valley leading down to Kalandos, might well indicate this. Still, along the southern coast of Naxos, there are both more (Early) Modern farmsteads and more Bronze Age settlements than Late Roman sites.[38] The increased activity around Panormos should be considered in relation with its strengthened position as harbour and connecting node in a changing trade network, and not as part of a general ruralisation.

A few standardized types of amphorae with several production centres over a wider area make up a large part of the amphora mass-production in the Eastern Mediterranean during the Late Roman period. These Late Roman Amphorae (LRA) have a wide distribution throughout (and beyond) the Mediterranean and often occur with several of the shapes in the same assemblages as a Late Roman 'package' of transport vessel types.[39] The relative frequency between the types varies, however, and is a good tool for understanding trade and transport connections.

LRA1, LRA2 and LRA13 are the most common types in both SENS and KIS, especially later varieties dated between the sixth and the seventh or eighth century.[40] The most widespread of these, both in terms of production, prevalence, and distribution, is the LRA1-type, for which production sites have been established on Kos, Rhodes, the Datcha peninsula, Cyprus, Cilicia and Paros.[41] Based on macroscopic fabric description it is assumed that the overwhelming majority of the LRA1 examples from Keros and South-East Naxos belongs to a common production. Petrographic samples of 11 of these ceramic types support this assumption, showing little variation in the fabric and a distinctive combination of mineral inclusions.[42] This fabric is elsewhere linked with the Cilician production, with a possibility that the clay source could also originate from Cyprus.[43]

As expected, Late Roman vessels are also found under water, but they do not dominate the assemblage in the same way they do on land. In part, this discrepancy might be explained as a methodological error; Late Roman Amphorae, especially LRA 1 and LRA2, are easily recognisable even from small feature sherds, and could be overrepresented among the identified vessels in the highly fractured surface survey material. Underwater, where preservation is, on average better, this bias is likely to be minimized. Other Late Roman types than LRA1, LRA2 and LRA13 lack a classifying term in the land surface material but are not uncommon under water.

Variations of the Samos Cistern type,[44] compatible with the fifth-to-seventh-century types, were present in Panormos, at the anchorages of Cape Moni and Turkospilia and on the reef. The production of these amphorae was probably limited to Samos and the nearby coast of Asia Minor.[45] The upper part of a LRA 5/6 bag-shaped amphora, similar to sixth century versions originating in Palestine or Lower Egypt, was also found at Cape Moni.

The North-African pottery production centres, concentrated mainly within the borders of modern-day Tunisia and Western Libya, were responsible for the massive export of both transport vessels and fine ware pottery between the second and the seventh century,[46] but in the survey material from Naxos and the Lesser Cyclades, North African products only appear from the (fourth or) fifth century. Although there is a general trend in the Aegean for African Red Slip and amphorae becoming more frequent at this time, the change from a complete absence in the collected material to constituting a visible part of the assemblage is notable and might reflect local conditions.

Keay 61 and 62 amphorae have been found both in Panormos and on the northwestern part of Panormos reef. The underwater find is possibly a little earlier than the types from the land survey, dated late fifth to the end of the sixth century and sixth and seventh century respectively.[47] In the petrographic study, the Tunisian production stands out due to the inclusion of aeolian desert sand. In addition to the sampled Keay 61 and 62 amphorae, four more sherds could be identified as North African that had not been recognized typologically or macroscopically.[48] This shows that the number of North African imports is likely higher than what is found in purely typological studies. While pre-fourth century Roman fine wares hardly figure in the survey data, a number of mould-made lamps from excavations and surface finds on Naxos and Kato Kouphonisi have been, or are about to be, published.[49] Leonidas Bournias' catalogue includes finds from within the SENS area.

The lamps dated to the first and second century CE seems to come overwhelmingly from production centres in Western Asia Minor. Four of the lamps from of the temple in Hyria are ascribed to the 'Romanesis' workshop in Cnidus, while another eight from Hyria and one from excavations in the Chora of Naxos are of the red-on-white type thought to originate in Ephesus – a concentration Bournias finds remarkable compared to finds elsewhere in Greece.[50] Three late-second or third century lamps, however, are attributed to workshops in Corinth, Patras or Athens, although for one of these, the attribution is based on the discus motif alone.[51]

In the fourth to seventh century assemblages the picture is more varied. The find of kilns and lamp moulds in Gyroulas proves a local production, which, however, includes imitations of types originally from Syro-Palestine, Sicily and North-Africa.[52] Four lamps from Chora are of a type generically termed 'Aegean', which Bournias[53] speculates might be a Cycladic production based on their relative rareness outside of the islands, and good parallels on Thera. Sherds of this type was also found at the Ag Stephanos in Aggidia together with a seventh-century North African lamp fragment.[54] Lamps from the Asia Minor coast – Ephesus and Samos – showing up in Chora, Gyroulas, on Kato Kouphonisi, and in the Keros survey material, are common in the Cyclades in this period, but the large Athenian production is only represented by a few fragments from Aplomata in Chora,[55] which Arja Karivieri identifies as two fourth-century lamps and one from the mid-fifth century.[56] In addition, one fifth-century lamp from Cyprus found in Chora, two fifth-to-seventh century North-African lamp fragments found during SENS, and a sixth–seventh century Constantinopolitan one from Kato Kouphonisi complements the local imitations in showing that types from beyond the Aegean were well known.[57]

Local Production?

Despite the clear evidence for Late Roman export from Panormos, there are no signs of local amphora production in that area. Based on the high concentrations of wasters, kiln furniture and broken vessels at other known production sites,[58] it is unlikely that a workshop and kiln would have gone unnoticed within the surveyed area. This lack of local production combined with contemporary evidence for export might add to the discussion on re-use and trade of empty amphorae. In the Late Roman assemblage, Cilician LRA1 and (non-local) LRA2 constitute the bulk of the transport vessels, with some North African and other types filling the rest. An explanation for this pattern would be that these containers arrived in Panormos empty, either new and un-used, or as empty return cargo from a previous trip.

The possibility of wine and oil being transported from an inland production centre to the coast in skins before being transferred to amphorae for ship export would further facilitate the use of amphorae arriving directly at the port, as little overland transport of the vessels would be necessary. The use of skins for land-based liquid transport has been discussed based on ostraca inscriptions for the cases of second and third-century Chersonesos on Crete and fourth-century Carthage.[59] but is likely to have a much wider applicability. Skins are lighter and more flexible than amphorae, which would have clear advantages for the use of pack donkeys in rough terrain, as opposed to ship or cart transport, where the amphora's strength and stackability would be more important. The concentration of amphora workshops close to coastlines and navigable waterways supports this hypothesis.[60] An increased re-use of amphorae may have opened for the use of ports and hinterland productions without readily available pottery resources and Panormos could be an example of this.

This argument relies on the assumption that the exports from Panormos were liquid produce requiring amphora containers. While not certain, olive oil and wine are the most likely exports from Southern Naxos. Oil or wine presses have been found in a Late

Roman to Early Medieval production context at Cheimarrou, and in the upper part of the Early Medieval settlement on Kastro Apalirou.[61] Some grain cultivation is likely, but the plains of Central and Western Naxos would have yielded far better crops, making grain export more probable from Chora.

On Paros, several large amphora production centres have been excavated, mainly in the bay of Naoussa and on the east coast near Glyfades.[62] Parian amphorae used for Naxian exports has been suggested by Konstantinos Roussos.[63] If there was already a large production, and the two islands were administratively and economically closely integrated, this might have been a cheaper and better option than using an inland or potentially lower quality clay source on Naxos. The distance to transport empty amphorae across the straight is short and would add little to the total cost of transport. However, the petrography has shown that Parian amphorae were not dominating the assemblages, either in the Late Roman period or in the Byzantine Early Middle Ages.

Networks and Connectivity

A large majority of the evidence for Roman and Byzantine activity consists of pottery. This is, of course, the expected situation in a survey context, thanks to the near indestructibility of ceramics and the diagnosticity offered by typo-chronologies and petrography. Even if this often allows for some fundamental properties – time and place of production, and place of deposition – of individual sherds to be established with fairly high probability, it is far more complicated, often impossible, to describe the use-life of the object. Was it traded directly from the production centre to where it was consumed and depositioned? Was it sold in a bulk shipment from the producer to a wholesaler at a commercial hub, later to be redistributed in smaller quantities via mixed cabotage cargoes and potentially being bought, resold and transported several times before reaching its final place of deposition? Did it travel as the personal possession of an owner who was moving between places? These are, however, the kinds of questions that need answering if pottery is to be used for understanding networks and connectivity.

Despite the difficulties interpreting the life cycles of individual artefacts, the necessary – direct or indirect – link between the places of production and deposition remains and, with careful contextualization of find assemblages, the evidence for patterns of connectivity does build. Vessels found in an urban context of luxury consumption must be differentiated from those found in the agricultural production setting of a farmstead, the commercial hub of a large emporia, the export-oriented port, or the wreck of a trade vessel. It is also useful to make a distinction between ceramics as consumer goods – fine wares, lamps and possibly coarse wares such as cooking pots and tiles – and ceramics that served as containers for consumable goods – transport amphora, in some cases pithoi, dolia and unguentaria, or other vessels for smaller quantities.

Ceramic containers will often be used as a proxy for their contents, but that assumption introduces an extra layer of abstraction. Again, identifying the source of production for a vessel only proves an indirect connection, and vessel provenance cannot, *a priori*, be equalled with origin of content, which still does not prove a directly connected node. Amphorae have no doubt worked as single-use disposable containers in some situations and periods, the oil trade from Guadalquivir to Rome and the resulting Monte Testaccio of Dressel 20 amphorae being a famous example. However, convincing evidence for reuse, including shipping containers found in the seventh- and eleventh-century Yassiada and Serçe Limanı wrecks show that generalizing the idea for the Late Roman and Byzantine vessels is too simplistic.[64] It is likely that a high degree of correlation between the origin of a transport vessel and the produce intended for its primary use is more common in direct, long-distance and large-scale trade than in cabotage serving to distribute goods from larger hubs and tramping moving varied and changing cargo.

Still, pottery's ability to functions as a 'flow tracer', lighting up the nodes of a trade network, remains invaluable. For periods of very broad diffusion of highly visible and datable shapes (e.g. Late Roman Red Slip in the fifth–seventh centuries and LRA2 body sherds with spiral grooving), nearly the entire settlement structure will light up. The lack of a tracer agent, however, does not mean people and settlements are not present, they are just not visible with the current toolset. As argued by Smadar Gabrieli, Mark Jackson and Anthi Kaldeli[65] for the situation on Cyprus, a lack of a fine ware or other easily identifiable production does not necessarily equate an absence of pottery production, nor does it prove a complete breakdown in trade connections. The availability of imported Late Roman fine wares – ARS, LRC and LRD – reached far deeper in the social strata than the Early and Middle Roman Eastern Sigillata productions, and, to an even stronger degree, the Early Medieval Glazed White Wares, thus skewing the chronological analysis of the dataset.

The Structures of Maritime Networks in the Central Cyclades

To gain a fuller picture of possible and probable travel patterns, the field data can be supplemented with modelling data and textual sources. An attempt at simulating connectedness based on travel time and cost in the Roman period has been developed by Walter Scheidel and Elijah Meeks in the frame of the ORBIS project.[66] The ORBIS model is impressively large and complex, with 632 nodes, nearly 3,000 land segments and over 1,000 sea routes, but covering the entire Roman world (nearly 10 million km^2), this still results in a resolution too coarse for the study of local and regional connectivity.[67] This is a result of the stated aim of the project – 'to understand the dynamics of the Roman imperial system as a whole' – but also the decision to base the sea connections mainly on routes known from ancient literary sources. For the Aegean, that means giving unbalanced authority to the routes described in the *Stadiasmus of the Great Sea* (see below) and ignoring the diversity of sailing possibilities through the islands.

Still, such models highlight the probabilities of long-distance connections and network configurations and, used in combination with local archaeological data, may help understanding large-scale patterns. Due to the policy of making data open and available for other projects, ORBIS has been used in several further network analysis

Taking the Island Route

Figure 5.6 Travel time to reach Naxos in summer, based on ORBIS (http://orbis.stanford.edu).

studies.[68] Figure 5.6 shows calculated travel times to reach Naxos in typical summer sailing conditions.

The *Stadiasmus of the Great Sea*

A periplus of the Mediterranean, known as the *Stadiasmus of the Great Sea*,[69] has recently been a popular source for discussing Roman shipping routes in the Aegean.[70] The *Stadiasmus* is preserved as part of a fragmentary manuscript from a *codex* created in Constantinople, now in the National Library in Madrid (MSS/4701).[71] The *codex* has been dated to the third quarter of the tenth century, but both the date of the original compilation of the *Stadiasmus*, and the date of the information provided in it are subject to debate.[72] Pascal Arnaud[73] argues it took its final form as part of the writings of Hippolytus in the first half of the third century CE, but that the sources it is based on are all Hellenistic and Early Roman. Inmaculada Pérez Martín[74] points out, however, that it contains some placenames otherwise only known in sixth century and later sources, indicated that the text was updated in the centuries after its compilation, as is also suggested by Arnaud.[75]

Even if the text might originally describe a Late Hellenistic or Early Roman context, the repeated copying and possible addition of new placenames may show its relevance for later periods. Pérez Martín[76] suggests that a main reason for its inclusion in the MSS/4701 *codex* was a renewed interest in navigation in the Aegean and around Cyprus connected with the successful campaigns against Crete and Cyprus in the 960s. He draws parallels to the near contemporary Stadiodromicon in *De Cerimoniis* giving a similar route description from Constantinople to Crete in connection with the attack on Chandax in 949.[77]

While the routes mentioned in the *Stadiasmus* should not be used uncritically, it does provide an exceptionally detailed overview of possible sailing routes and seaways of the period for the areas that are covered. For Cyclades and the South Aegean, it appears to be using known connections and have mostly accurate distances between ports. Still, only the first part of the *Stadiasmus* has survived, and the chapters concerning the Aegean are close to the end of the preserved text.[78] It is, then, possible that other routes passing through the Cyclades or including Cycladic Island destinations are missing, and that these would have changed the impression of the main thoroughfares.

Among the sailing directions for the many possible routes between the Cyclades, there is an entry reading: 'From Kereia, keeping Kereia on the left, to Panormos of the Naxians, 65 stades. From Panormos to Delos 420 stadia' (§281). This would equal 10–12 km from Kereia to Panormos, and an approximately 70 km to Delos. From Konakia on the north side of Keros, that is precisely the distance to Panormos if one keeps Kato Kouphonisi to the left. The distance to Delos is realistic, too. The *Stadiasmus* later gives the distance between Delos and Naxos to 350 stadia, placing Naxos (presumably the city) a good bit closer to Delos than Panormos is. Not only does the text place Panormos as an active landing point in the Hellenistic-Roman period, potentially the second most important on Naxos, it also shows an established link between Keros (and the Kouphonissia) and South-East Naxos.

By plotting the stops and directions for the remaining routes (Figure 5.7), it becomes apparent that a further two of the trans-Aegean routing alternatives may have passed right south of Naxos. These lines connect Asia Minor and Rhodes with Attica and the Peloponnese, suggesting that the strait between Naxos and the Lesser Cyclades would have been a very busy shipping line.

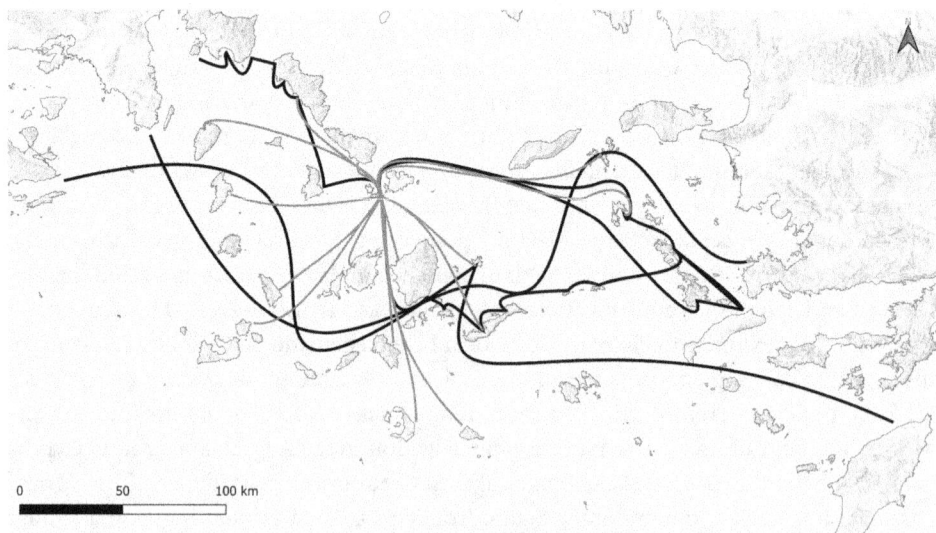

Figure 5.7 Graphic rendition of the route descriptions in the *Stadiasmus of the Great Sea* for the South Aegean. Dark showing through routes, grey links to Delos.

The *Stadiasmus* seems to describe three distinct types of routes. One is the long, direct lines from one major port to another or passing through from one side of the Aegean to the other (e.g. Kos to Delos, §280, Rhodes to Skyllaion in Peloponnese, §273, and Kos to Petaleia on Euboea, §283). Here, intermediate place names are for navigational purposes, rather than trade ports. Another is the many direct connections between major commercial ports and islands with smaller settlements in their vicinity, as seen with Rhodes (27 nodes) and Delos (16 nodes). These are structured similarly to later medieval *pieleggi* where the connections may not represent individual routes as such, but rather serves to situate the port within the region.[79] Finally, there are routes stopping over at as many places as possible on the way – 'διὰ νήσων πλέειν' – such as the alternative slow route given in §281 recording eight stops between Kos and Delos.

Hub-and-Spoke Networks

A combination of the two first types correspond to Andrew Wilson's idea of maritime trade in the Early and Middle Empire,[80] with direct point-to-point links between emporia served by large freight carriers and smaller vessels connecting the main port with lesser harbours and anchorages on the surrounding islands. The way in which Aperlae and other cities on the Lycian coast without proper harbour facilities were connecting with the hubs of Andriake or Patara might be a good illustration of this.[81]

This hub-and-spoke network design is not unlike modern-day commercial aviation networks that feed passengers into airport hubs like Schiphol and Frankfurt on small planes from surrounding cities, and re-board them onto large long-haul aircraft. An even more apt parallel, however, might be modern container shipping networks, with most of the long-distance transport guided through a few large hubs e.g., as shown by Ducruet and Notteboom.[82] These hubs have the specialized large-scale infrastructure to handle the largest container ships, and both ships and port infrastructure have been designed around a standardized container unit (the *TEU*) for optimal efficiency. While this has opened for cheap global transport, the dimensions and special adaptations of ships and ports limit the flexibility in goods types and available ports of call.[83] A similar interdependence could be argued between Hellenistic-Middle Roman massive constructed port facilities, mega-carriers of hundreds or thousands of tonnes of cargo and large, mass-produced amphorae adapted to loading and handling in these port facilities and on these ships.[84] The re-loading onto smaller ships from the emporia hubs parallels the transhipment ports of the modern network with more flexible vessels (e.g. ro-ro ferries or land transport) serving the hub's hinterland.[85]

Cabotage

Coastal and small-scale shipping, Wilson argues,[86] was not a significant factor of the Roman Mediterranean trade, in contrast with the Byzantine Early Middle Ages, in which he sees as 'a world of coastal voyaging by small lateen-rigged craft, between harbours that were often an inherited infrastructure from previous ages'. This position has been criticised using the argument that direct long-distance trade came in addition to, not instead of, a large number of smaller vessels and a high level of cabotage that remained important throughout antiquity, perhaps especially in the island-sea of the South Aegean.[87]

Peregrine Horden and Nicholas Purcell see decentralized and easily shifting cabotage and coastal tramping as a constant element of Mediterranean trade and connectivity which has existed as a background noise since prehistory, nearly invisible both archaeologically and historically.[88] The third route type in the *Stadiasmus*, 'through the islands', could indicate a less centralized distribution network, more along the lines of the cabotage trade that is likely to have always made up an important part of inter-island connectivity.

Network Resilience

The layout of trade networks and the nodes they consist of can change over time with changing political and economic conditions. Delos and Rhodes stand out in the *Stadiasmus* as the main hubs in the South Aegean, which, in the case of Delos, might reflect a Hellenistic network structure.[89] The strong position of Delos as commercial emporium was boosted by Roman tax exemptions in the Late Hellenistic period, but its importance diminishes from the first century BCE onwards.[90]

What happens when a large node such as Delos 'goes bust' depends on the structure of the network and its *robustness*. A strongly hierarchical network where nearly all long-distance connections (or *bridges*) go through the main hub, with a few intermediary level sub-clusters, is likely to have low resilience against the breakdown of the main hub and will easily disintegrate. However, if smaller, localized hub-and-spoke networks exist and already have bridge edges reaching outside the main cluster, these may absorb the traffic from a failing central hub and increased as a result.

Leslie Dossey presents a relevant example of this 'growth of the periphery in response to the weakening of the core' from the third-century CE North Africa.[91] When North Tunisian African Red Slip A production centres collapsed due to disruptions of the shipping network to the main markets in Italy in the 230s, regional productions in central Tunisia and Tripolitania immediately emerged to fill the gap in the local market, resulting in the large and decentralized production of Late Roman ARS wares exported across the Mediterranean in the following centuries.

In the Early Roman Cyclades other islands had built up a considerable export to Roman markets, such as Paros with marble, and Milos with minerals. Combined with an underlying pattern of less-structured cabotage trade, this might have prepared these ports to take on more of a hub function at the decline of Delos. Alkiviadis Ginalis argues for the existence of a hierarchy of maritime nodes – 'primary ports, secondary harbours and staple markets' – in the Aegean through the Late Roman and Byzantine period.[92]

Depending on the connections between them, a similar resilience might be expected from this pattern.

Based on a slightly modified version of the ORBIS dataset, Dominik Heher, Johannes Preiser-Kapeller and Grigori Simeonov calculated possible clusters and sub-clusters in the connectivity of the Roman Empire.[93] They argue for a nested model of networks from the micro (e.g. settlement level clusters) to the macro (empire-wide connectivity) level, where each higher-level cluster depends on the connecting lines between its sub-clusters. This leaves room to incorporate both models focusing on micro-connectivity, and those highlighting the integration of the ancient Mediterranean. By reducing the maximum travel time allowed between nodes they simulate the effect of high-level cluster fragmentation to model a breakdown in long-distance connectivity in the Late Roman and Early Medieval period. This approach found the most resilient maritime networks to correlate with the core area of the Byzantine Empire after the mid-seventh century, centred in the Aegean and including the Sea of Marmara and the south coast of Asia Minor. This does not imply a direct correlation between possible connectivity and the extent of the Byzantine state in the Early Middle Ages, but it indicates that trade and contact could be kept on a high level within this area despite a decrease in long-distance travel.

East to West through Southern Naxos

The identified Late Hellenistic to Middle Roman pottery types have in common a provenance east of Naxos, from the coast and islands from Western Asia Minor, or from Cilicia in the south-east of Asia Minor. As pointed out by Catherine Bouras,[94] this eastern dominance can also be seen in the Grammata inscriptions. All non-local ships mentioned departed from harbours east of the Cyclades, mainly along the Western coast of Asia Minor (Ephesus, Miletus, Smyrna, Perge), but also from the Eastern Mediterranean coast.

The agreement between the survey material, the *Stadiasmus* and the Grammata epigraphy is a strong argument for seeing the Late Hellenistic–Middle Roman long-distance shipping through the Central Cyclades as following a predominately unidirectional East-West route. This is not a general pattern in the Southern Aegean, however, as seen, e.g. on Kos,[95] where the origin of Roman Imperial imports is far more diverse. It is likely that north- and south-bound traffic in the Aegean would follow the coasts of Mainland Greece and Asia Minor, rather than traverse the Central Cyclades. It is also likely, however, that the diversity in Kos reflects the size and importance of the(those) city(ies). Major centres will always be well-connected, and the occurrence of imports does not necessarily reflect dominating trade routes and patterns.

An Aegean Network?

Based on the Grammata inscriptions, Élisabeth Malamut sees a change in the third century, when the routes that connected Asia Minor and the Greek mainland through the Cycladic islands became less important and local and regional traffic took their place.[96] She argues that the role of the Cyclades as an intermediary point in long-distance shipping disappears completely. As seen in Figures 5.6 and 5.7, Naxos and the Lesser Cyclades would be ideally positioned for intra-Aegean trade, with most major centres including Corinth, Thessalonica, Ephesus, Rhodes and Crete within three days travel. Grammata also reveals direct involvement from Naxiote ship captains and sailors with the *euploiai* from Eunomios, Asteris and Thremistas.[97]

While the data from the underwater survey supports the view that the dominance of the east-to-west long-distance traffic is weakened in the third or fourth century, the amount and geographic variation of long-distance imports increases both under water and on land. Scheidel, using the ORBIS model to compare proximity and accessibility with Rome and Constantinople as capital centres, argues that the move to Constantinople would make the Aegean basin the 'new core' in centrality of the empire, and the natural hinterland of the new capital based on both travel time and cost of transport.[98] An increased direct contact with Constantinople and, through the *Quaestura exercitus*, the Black Sea has already been suggested, and is supported by this model. Some degree of diffusion of products from the capital as a result is likely in return for the exported evidenced in Panormos. However, direct long-distance contacts with Mediterranean ports cannot be ruled out. In the limited body of historical sources, there is some evidence of routes between Constantinople and the wider Mediterranean passing through the islands, such as Pope Martin's stop on Naxos in the mid-seventh century.[99]

Conclusions

The extensive set of survey data that has recently been collected from Southern Naxos and the Lesser Cyclades shows that despite the (presumed) peripheral location of the investigated area, it was a frequently used node in long distance trade and travel networks. There is also evidence for export-related production and shipment harbours. The deposited ballast piles show that Naxos was not just a passive node at the receiving end of trade routes, as discussions focusing heavily on imported vessels might sometimes imply. Only when it is possible to map both imports and exports, can the area be analyzed as a fully integrated part of the trade and contact network. The work is still ongoing, and further analysis of the material will broaden and possibly alter the current conclusions, especially with regard to the position of Kato Kouphonisi, where higher, and possibly longer-lasting, Late Antique activity than expected was encountered.

In the Late Hellenistic to Middle Roman period there is evidence for long-distance, single-cargo transport. Anchorages and harbours were in use, and Keros and Panormos are mentioned by name as ports en-route through the Cyclades. Despite the coast being heavily trafficked, however, most of the long-distance trade passed by Southern Naxos without leaving a large material footprint on land. The settlements in the area were likely rather connected with the surrounding urban centres on Naxos, Amorgos, Ios, Paros and Santorini via small-scale cabotage trade, and possibly also connected with larger commercial hubs at Delos and Rhodes. The local fleet must have been adapted to utilizing 'opportunistic ports' without large structures, and the flexibility this system provides.

Delos, and possibly also Rhodes and Corinth, may have functioned as a hub for Naxian imports and exports. A decentralization into more, but smaller hubs in the Roman period, as suggested, e.g. by Rebecca Sweetman[100] would not necessarily be visible in our material if the coast of South-East Naxos remained a viable route choice. There is not enough data to read high resolution chronological variation of activity.

Both the survey data and contemporary written sources indicate that the majority of interregional travel through the central Cyclades originated east of Naxos and that eastbound sailing followed a different route. From the fourth century onwards, more long-distance transport vessels and fine wares reached the shores of Southern Naxos and the Lesser Cyclades. This coincided with a gradual denser habitation within the surveyed area, with a particular increase of pottery dated to the fifth century and onwards. The direction of travel may have changed too. The east-to-west pattern is no longer obvious, and imported pottery arrived from most parts of the Central and Eastern Mediterranean. In part this may be explained by the transfer of the imperial capital to Constantinople, redirecting trade and communication routes to pass through the Cyclades (as seen e.g. in the route used to transport Pope Martin from Italy to Constantinople in the mid-seventh century). However, an increased importance of the agricultural produce from the islands in supplying the capital and the army (evidenced by the inclusion of the Cyclades in the *Quaestura exercitus* and the later *kommerkia* system), will have led to more direct trade and a change in the network structure.

However, the observed change in provenance of fine wares and transport vessels is not necessarily proof of new direct trade contacts. Changes in the distribution pattern of fine wares in the Eastern Mediterranean, increased re-use of transport amphorae, and an overall expansion in pottery circulation accompanying a growing economic importance of the area could lead to similar patterns. Except for the harbour basin at Panormos, the Late Roman expansion is not mirrored in the underwater material. Pottery from the period is present, but far less dominating than on land. It is possible that there was no or little overall increase in the shipping activity through the area, only a different type of transits.

A reduction in cargo ship sizes in the Late Roman period, together with a stronger impetus for exploiting available agricultural resources in the Aegean, may have made Panormos a more viable option for long-distance exports, both technologically and economically. The strongly increase in activity in Panormos in the seventh century with construction of harbour structures and port facilities on land may plausibly be set in connection with the Byzantine supply system for the capital and the army. Ballast in Panormos bay shows that goods were exported from the port. The size and composition of the ballast piles make it clear that this was not local small-scale cabotage trade. Tonnage estimates based on the calculated weight of ballast piles suggest that the ships being loaded would be of the larger vessels operating in the period, and geological analysis rules out a local origin for the stones used. The total number of piles does not seem to indicate a very long or intensive use. However, while only stone ballast remains visible, sand and other forms of ballast are thought to have been more commonly used.[101]

While Panormos itself is not a site that could support a large settlement and surplus production, it is well positioned to serve as a transhipment port for produce from the fertile inland valleys of South-Eastern Naxos. This, combined with the prevalence of transport amphorae that have been connected with the *annona* system (Cilician LRA1, LRA2 and Spatheia), and the construction of a fortification in the seventh century, all indicate that the site was integrated in the state supply system, and saw external investment. It is possible that a *kommerkia apotheke* was located in Panormos.

The decision to cover the same stretch of coastline on land and in the water resulted in valuable links between underwater, coastal and upland data being made visible, overcoming the barriers often encountered when the data stops at (one side or the other of) the shoreline. In this case neither land nor underwater survey alone gives a complete picture of coastal communication. The conclusions drawn from seeing them individually would be contradictory, but when put together they complement each other. Under water, the evidence shows continued sailing along the south coast of Naxos throughout the long first millennium CE, from the Early Roman to the Middle Byzantine period, but the use of the port of Panormos is concentrated around the Late Roman centuries.

Notes

* I wish to thank the Ephorate of Antiquities of the Cyclades and the Ephorate of Underwater Antiquities for support and cooperation in my work on the Central Cyclades, as well as directors and colleagues at the Keros-Seaways Project and the Naxos Underwater Survey. The research has been carried out with funding from the British School at Athens, the Mary Jaharis Foundation and the Douglas and Gordon Bonnyman Scholarship.

1. A summary of previous work in Renfrew 2013.
2. Angelopoulou 2014.
3. Broodbank 2000: 207–10.
4. Hill, Roland and Ødegård 2017; six papers in Crow and Hill 2018.
5. Philaniotou 2003; Vionis 2016: 329.
6. Tzavella 2013: 2018.
7. Chatzilazarou 2018.
8. That approach has already been taken by, e.g. Bouras 2016.
9. Renfrew, Marthari et al., forthcoming(a); Renfrew, forthcoming(b).
10. Boyd, Brodie and Wright, forthcoming.
11. Indgjerd 2020; Indgjerd and Diamanti, forthcoming.
12. Ahrens et al. 2018: 55–6; Ahrens, Indgjerd, Kvalø, Simosi et al., forthcoming.
13. As observed by, e.g. Leidwanger 2013a: 180.
14. Constantakopoulou 2007: 22; cf, e.g. the Siphnian export of cooking pots.
15. Constantakopoulou 2007: 22; Horden and Purcell 2000: 142; cf. Ginalis 2014: 20–1; ibid. 2017: 13, n. 25.
16. Leidwanger 2013b.

17. Ibid. 221–2.
18. Ginalis 2014: 33–7, 245; as found in the Yenikapı excavations.
19. McCormick 2001: 419–21.
20. See, e.g. Ginalis 2014: 19–20.
21. Leidwanger 2013a: 181.
22. Constantakopoulou 2007: 23–4; Ginalis 2014: 19; Roussos 2017: 268.
23. Villinger 1603: 166.
24. Kiourtzian 2000: 173–5; Bouras 2016: 217–18.
25. See Angelopoulou 2014.
26. Renfrew, Marthari et al., forthcoming.
27. Ahrens et al. 2018: 57.
28. Ahrens, Indgjerd, Kvalø, Simosi et al., forthcoming; Renfrew, forthcoming(a) and forthcoming(b).
29. Roussos 2017: 268.
30. Renfrew, forthcoming(a) and forthcoming(b).
31. Renfrew, Marthari et al., forthcoming.
32. Tzavella 2013: 90–1; ead. 2018: 181.
33. Ahrens et al. 2018: 58–9.
34. Stisi and Meens, forthcoming.
35. Opaiț and Tsaravopoulos 2011.
36. Papathanassopoulos and Schilardi 1981: 140–1.
37. Cf., e.g. Bintliff 2013: 127–9; Caraher, Nakassis and Pettegrew 2006: 21–6; Pettegrew 2007: 745–9.
38. Renfrew, Boyd et al., forthcoming.
39. Rauh, Autret and Lund 2013: 161–2; Pieri 2005: 68–139; often referred to as 'Riley's package' after Riley 1979.
40. Dellaporta et al.; Renfrew, forthcoming(a) and forthcoming(b).
41. Pieri 2005: 80–1; Demesticha 2013: 170–1; Diamanti 2010: 2016.
42. Indgjerd 2020: 391–3.
43. Cf. Leidwanger, Greene and Tuna 2015: 304–5.
44. Arthur 1990; LRA8 in Pieri 2005: 132–7.
45. Pieri 2005: 136.
46. Bonifay 2004: 2.
47. Ibid. 139–41.
48. Indgjerd 2020: 394–6.
49. Bournias 2014, Bournias pers.com./in prep.
50. Ibid. 787.
51. Ibid. 789–90.
52. Lambrinoudakis et al. 2002: 403–4; Bournias 2014: 788–91.
53. Bournias 2014: 789–91.

54. Pennas 2005.
55. Bournias 2014: 790–1; Dellaporta et al., forthcoming.
56. Karivieri 1996, 261.
57. SENS; Bournias 2014.
58. E.g. Paros: Diamanti 2016; ead. 2010; Kos: Autret, Kızılarslanoğlu and Rauh 2016; Cilicia: Leidwanger, Greene and Tuna 2015, and the Datça peninsula.
59. Gallimore 2014; Peña 1998: 212.
60. See note 58.
61. Vionis 2016; Hill and Ødegård 2018.
62. Diamanti 2016; Roussos 2017: 130–1.
63. Roussos 2017: 112.
64. Abdelhamid 2016.
65. Gabrieli, Jackson and Kaldeli 2007.
66. Scheidel and Meeks 2019.
67. Scheidel 2015: 2–3.
68. E.g. Heher, Preiser-Kapeller and Simeonov 2017.
69. Paragraph numbers used here refer to the *GGM* edition in Müller 1855: 427–514; see also Helm 1929.
70. Arnaud 2005; ibid. 2017a; Bouras 2016; Tzavella 2016.
71. Pérez Martín 2016: 79.
72. Ibid. 88; Arnaud 2017b: 702–4.
73. Arnaud 2017a: 16–17.
74. Pérez Martín 2016: 88.
75. Arnaud 2005: 236, but emphatically contra in 2017a: 16.
76. Pérez Martín 2016: 89–90.
77. Ibid. 89–90; see Huxley 1976; Pryor 2004.
78. Arnaud 2017b: 704.
79. Ibid. 714.
80. Wilson 2011.
81. Hohlfelder and Vann 2000: 132–4.
82. Ducruet and Notteboom 2012.
83. Cf. Blumenhagen 1981.
84. Bevan 2014: 402.
85. Ibid. 401.
86. Wilson 2011: 54.
87. Cf. e.g. Parker 1992: 89; McCormick 2012: 63–4.
88. Horden and Purcell 2000: 145–72, building on Braudel 1972: 103–67.
89. E.g. Constantakopoulou 2017.
90. Zarmakoupi 2015.
91. Dossey 2010: 89–90.

92. Ginalis 2014: 22–5, 252; ibid. 2017: 5–7.
93. Heher, Preiser-Kapeller and Simeonov 2017: 204–9.
94. Bouras 2016: 218.
95. Kokkorou-Alevras et al. 2016: 178–87.
96. Malamut 2001: 29–30.
97. Kiourtzian 2000: 173–7.
98. Scheidel 2013: 20–2.
99. See, e.g. McCormick 2001: 502–8.
100. Sweetman 2016.
101. Parker 1992: 90–2.

CHAPTER 6
'STEPPING ACROSS THRESHOLDS': ISLANDS AS RESILIENT SPACES OF CONNECTIVITY IN THE PASSAGE FROM LATE ANTIQUITY TO THE EARLY MIDDLE AGES (c. 500–c. 700)*

Luca Zavagno and Zeynep Olgun

Introduction: Islands as Thresholds across a Mediterranean in Transition

Islands have been regarded as indefinite worlds hidden in the wilderness between isolation and connectivity, interaction and solitude, which are often analyzed according to their specific and self-contained geographies.[1] As Rabun Taylor states, 'Islands were understood as distinct closed worlds, ideal locations for the extraordinary and the bizarre, but at the same time they were also perceived as parts of a complex reality of interaction'.[2] Therefore, we can think of them as a sort of embodiment of the Roman God Janus whose name is linked with the idea of *ianua*, the Latin word for doorway and passageway.[3] As a two-headed god, Janus was in charge of beginnings and endings (in particular those related to the start and end of wars) guarding the threshold of space and time.[4] Indeed, when describing the so-called 'island paradox', what often resurfaces is the concept of double-headed places ('facing' land and sea at the same time) acting as 'connecting thresholds'.[5] On the one hand, as chunks of land surrounded by water, islands are – as Elisabeth Malamut concludes – opposed worlds where 'active networks of communication and exchange encounter *la terre fermée*: a world closed to its surroundings'.[6] On the other hand, it is the ambiguity intrinsic to the concept of threshold, regarded at the same time as a barrier and junction, that allows us to link islands to the concepts of border and frontier.[7] At the same time, it 'lends itself to the maximum variety of interrelatedness and variability of connectivity [both] making islands so important to historians'.[8]

But the comparison with Janus is also relevant to the function that islands had in the political (and military) history of the Great Sea.[9] This stems from the strategic importance of islands as connecting hubs across maritime frontiers which were less impenetrable than often believed.[10] Indeed, during the Roman and Byzantine (and even Ottoman)[11] periods, the islands of the Mediterranean played a central role in the construction of modalities of violent or peaceful interaction in period under scrutiny here.[12] Quite often, historiography prefers to stress conflicts, which seem to shape the history of Late Antiquity and Early Medieval Mediterranean. There is no space here to mention but a few of these episodes, such as the Vandal incursions in the central Mediterranean after their conquest of North Africa in 439, the Justinian '*reconquista*' of Malta, Sardinia, and Sicily in 530s; the naval coup by (the future emperor) Heraclius reaching Constantinople from Carthage via Cyprus in 610 and the Battle of the Masts in 655 which ushered in an era of repeated raids and confrontations between the Byzantine and the Arab fleets culminating with the two sieges of Constantinople in the late seventh–early eighth centuries.[13]

In particular, and since the publication of Henri Pirenne's *Mohammed and Charlemagne,* the arrival of the Arabs in the Mediterranean has been regarded as the main catalyst for the end of a unified and peaceful Great Sea under the Roman thalassocracy.[14] This episode, like the so-called LALIA (Late Antique Little Ace Age) or the Justinianic Plague – in reality, a long pandemic spell lasting well into the eighth century – and despite the lack of any real consensus about when the fragmentation of the Mediterranean started and how much single environmental crises involved, acted as an accelerator of a crisis.[15]

Nevertheless, Mediterranean shipping routes remained frequented in the period under scrutiny for diplomats, pilgrims, merchants and slaves crisscrossed the Great Sea.[16] We could regard them as the main actors of what Peregrine Horden and Nicholas Purcell describe as 'the normal rhythms of Mediterranean exchange, the 'background noise' of [...] movement which we have found in the supposed Dark Ages [as] vastly more fluid in their pattern and that, whether they take the form of cabotage, slave-riding, piracy or pilgrimage, they act to bind micro-ecologies together'.[17]

Islands are one of the best listening posts for intercepting the abovementioned background noise. This not only because the dominion over the ancient and medieval Mediterranean has always depended on the control of the maritime routes and the islands,[18] but also due to the fact that, on islands, one can trace intense encounters with new people and accommodation of artistic forms. In addition, these hubs also host forms of expedient political settlements and forms of cultural brokerage between the Arab and Byzantine worlds.[19] These, in turn, stemmed from the resilient economy of insular spaces which remained prosperous well into the late eighth century as shown by material indicators such as globular amphorae and coinage.[20]

In light of the abovementioned points, this chapter will use material culture (particularly, ceramics and seals) as well as archaeological evidence to discuss the importance of large Mediterranean islands like Cyprus, Malta, and Sardinia as hubs of connectivity in the passage from Late Antiquity to the early Middle Ages. In particular, it will examine how these insular sites turned from strategic hubs across the *annona civica* shipping routes unifying the Mediterranean in the Late Antique period to 'thresholds' at the face of the Arab conquest of the Mediterranean's southern basin. These inquiries will allow us to show how these islands experienced a Late Antique period of economic prosperity, being particularly visible in Cyprus where an intensification of coastal settlement patterns went hand-in-hand with an extensive building activity. In fact, the early Middle Ages offers to us a different snapshot of the insular Mediterranean. Although Cyprus, Malta and Sardinia were caught in the crossfire of the Arab naval raids throughout the seventh and eighth centuries they continued to act as more active economic spaces than the so-called Byzantine continental heartland.[21] It is indeed important to notice that large Byzantine islands became part and parcel of a larger trans-Mediterranean cultural and political *koine* as indicated once again by material culture. As will be seen, this included insular hubs as they weaved into a network of gateway communities under Byzantine rule.[22]

These factors are reflected by the peculiar trajectories of socio-political and administrative changes experienced by the local insular structures of power which – as it will be seen in Cyprus and Sardinia – often betrayed expedient structures of shared government between the Caliphate and the Empire. These stemmed less from the centrifugal inclinations of local secular (and religious) elites than from the ability of the so-called insular peripheries to produce fluid, creative and expedient socio-political arrangements when faced by peculiar military or political challenges.[23]

Consequently, and in tune with a coda to this chapter, we will briefly try to propose a different conceptualization and interpretation of the idea of a frontier, conceived less as specific borders separating political entities and more as complex zones embodying the cultural interactions including adaptation, acculturation, assimilation and the cultural ambiguity of ethnic and religious groups.[24] This process is often more visible on islands because of their ontological character of being a piece of land surrounded by the sea: they are concurrently vibrant embodiments of connectivity and personifications of isolation. In fact, in our opinion, it was often their strategic location along the shipping routes enlivening the Great Sea that allowed them to emerge as stepping-stones moulded by the ebbs and flows of the waves of Mediterranean political and economic history. Through islands one can indeed fully grasp the permeability and porosity of frontier environments, and nevertheless decide to sail parallel to it until the next crossing point.

The Great Sea and its Islands from Rome to the Early Byzantine Era

In Ancient Greek, the word νῆσος, used for island, stems from the verb νέω meaning 'to float' or 'to swim', and Katérina Kopaka argues that this reflects how islands were seen in movement and unstable compared to the solid land (literally στεριά).[25] Although conceptualized as erratic, islands were in fact crucial to Mediterranean navigation. The prominence of islands is firstly due to the anchorage and harbourage that these provide as 'connective points of the waterways'.[26] The anonymous Σταδιασμός ἤτοι περίπλους τῆς μεγάλης θαλάσσης (*Stadiasmos or Voyage of the Great Sea*), dating to the Roman Imperial period, is similar to the later portolans in that it gives distances and directions from one port to another, and islands are listed as prominent nodes in the network.[27] These provided the seafarers with crucial necessities: shelter, protection and natural resources.[28] Horden and Purcell also suggest that the islands have a particularly important role to play in the sacred topography of pilgrimage in the Mediterranean.[29]

Connected to these attributions of islands, their economic prominence stands out. The *Expositio totius mundi et gentium*, the original of which is dated to late fourth century, gives an economic geography of the Roman Empire and islands are shown as important producers integral to the economic network.[30] The Roman (and later, Byzantine) perception of the sea envisioned it both as a carrier of civilization and wealth as well as dangerous and life threatening.[31] This idea is traceable from Homer's works and rather oddly coalesced into the negative moral connotations associated with commerce – sea trade was not considered a noble endeavour.[32] As William V. Harris remarks, 'the perceived private character of commerce [should be seen] within the framework of the somewhat "achievement-oriented" ethos of the Roman aristocracy'.[33] It was aristocratic to accumulate land and to distance oneself from 'morally dubious ways to make money' (*loc. cit.*). The moral prejudice against sea-trade and profitable enterprises was on the one hand 'neutralized' by the sheer ease of transportation of bulk-goods by water, but above all by the need to feed a growing urban population. The development and maintenance of a state-supported doling-out system, so-called *annona civica*, became the spine innervating the Roman Mediterranean.[34] With the foundation of Constantinople, demand for grain also increased and the new capital gradually imposed a new direction and organization on Egyptian exports.[35]

There is no space here to propose a detailed study of the *annona civica* in order to examine the economic implications of this subsidized shipping system.[36] It is rather our intention to dwell upon its influences in shaping the settlement pattern of the coastal and insular regions which were involved in the traffic of food (grain, wine and oil) and supplies which Michael McCormick describes 'as dictated by the political and strategic imperatives of the imperial economy'.[37] In this light, we will consider the 'long' fourth century as the first of two chronological watersheds; for the foundation of Constantinople in 324–30 CE and – above all – the Vandal conquest of Carthage in 439.[38] The latter at first crippled and then finally severed the traditional shipping routes of the *annona* linking North Africa (and partially Sicily) with Rome. In fact, as will be seen, the second crucial moment coincides with the fall of Egypt to the Rashidun caliphate in 640s which de facto dried up the second source of the *annona* system. Within an 'economic chain' linking Egypt and partially Sicily with Constantinople, islands as well as coastal gateways, were one of the essential elements in this network and their prominence depended on the existing sea routes.[39]

In particular, we would like to mention here the island of Cyprus, while briefly referring to Lycian and the Carian coast as control test-cases. This is not only because 'the Eastern Mediterranean exchange network was quite different to the west, for the Alexandria-Constantinople grain *annona* did not – unlike in the African case – result in the dominance over any other exchange item in the East [...] leading to the continuous existence of a multiplicity of routes',[40] but rather due to the fact that we have appropriate archaeological material and stratigraphically controlled excavations for Cyprus, which was located at the heart of the cabotage routes linking Egypt with Constantinople. Cyprus also provides important hagiographical sources attesting both to the important political and social role played by the *annona* in a large seventh-century city like Alexandria as well as its impact upon the economic life of the neighbouring island.[41]

Cyprus was administratively reorganized by Justinian in 536, who allocated it to a peculiar administrative district, the *Quaestura exercitus*, which comprised of a collection of territories around the Lower Danube, the Aegean Islands and Asia Minor.[42] The role played by Cyprus as a bridge and mandatory maritime staging post on the route that led from Egypt to Constantinople is confirmed by both documentary (such as the sixth-century travel log of the famous pilgrim Antoninus Placentinus) and material evidence. The latter is attested by the costly imported Proconnesian marble, from the island of Marmara (hauling on the transports from the capital to Egypt), as well as Phocaean Fine Wares and Late Roman amphorae 1. These vessels were also produced on Cypriot sites, attesting to the exportation of local wine or olive oil.[43] The best evidence, however, is provided by a changing trend in local settlement patterns which already started in the fifth century and lasting well into the seventh century. It concerns the rise of smaller coastal settlements, which are not immediately major port cities, that connect the sea and the hinterland but are 'facing the sea'.[44]

One good example of this trend is offered by Agios Georgios at Cape Drepanon, which shed light on the *annona* connection between Alexandria and Constantinople. The rural settlement is located on the western point of the island and 21 km north of Paphos. The cape was cut from the hinterland by the Akamas Mountains, and it cannot be located in the written sources from the period.[45] Excavations yielded three sixth-century basilicas similar in plan (although not always in size) to those dotting the island in rural as well as urban areas.[46] Despite having limited connections to the hinterland, Agios Georgios developed drastically in the period under scrutiny, as showed by the analysis of the ecclesiastical buildings like the so-called Basilica A.[47]

This was the biggest structure in the settlement and also occupied a prominent position on top of the ridge of the promontory: thus it would have been the most visible to the sailors as navigational landmark, and several attributions of this basilica points to a maritime connection.[48] The column shafts, Corinthian capitals as well as church furniture are made of imported Proconnesian marble.[49] In fact, due to its lavish decoration, Demetrios Michaelides argues that Basilica A was one of the most 'opulent' basilicas on Cyprus, meanwhile the ambo and the baptistery associated with the church on the other hand are described as of a Constantinopolitan type by the excavators.[50]

In particular, the sixth-century 'church wreck' of Marzamemi, off Sicily, witnesses the movement of Proconnesian ambos shipped around the Empire, from which disassembled pieces of an ambo belonging to this monumental bridge type were recovered.[51] An inscription found on the ambo, ΥΠΕΡ ΕΥΧΗΣ ΝΑΥΤΩΝ (for the blessing of sailors) shows a clear maritime connection for it implies that the ambo was put up 'as a vow by sailors or seamen'.[52] Although no trace of an ancient harbour has been located, Cape Drepanon was identified as an important harbour on the sea routes from Hellenistic to the Byzantine Period.[53] The lack of a visible harbour can be due to the erosion of the coastline, as several anchorages visible from the administrative centre of the settlement have been discovered.[54] As a result of its apparent maritime connectivity, the site had indeed been identified as an *annona* stopover by its excavator.[55] Indeed, two types of finds from the excavations create a link between Cape Drepanon and Egypt: high-quality pottery from Egypt, and ampullae from the shrine of Saint Menas, close to Alexandria.[56] Since the latest coin found during the excavations so far is a *follis* of Constans II of the year 641–642 CE, the abandonment of the settlement by the Christians seems to coincide with the Arab conquest of Egypt in 642 CE, and thus the cessation of grain shipments from Alexandria to Constantinople.[57] An alternative but concurrent function of the site has, in fact, been proposed by Michaelides, who argues that 'the site at Cape Drepanon acted as a stopover for pilgrims travelling to and from the Holy Land'.[58]

Here, a comparison can be drawn with the small site of Aperlae on the Lycian coast. Aperlae also boasted several ecclesiastical buildings albeit rarely being mentioned in textual sources. Robert L. Hohlfelder suggested that the development of Aperlae developed both as local pilgrimage site and a small commercial exchange centres along the Lycian coastal shipping routes.[59] Similarly, along the coast of Lycia an islet off the west tip of Dolichiste (Kekova) has yielded a three-aisled basilica with carved decoration of high quality dated to the fifth century. Next to it is an octagonal baptistery and a vaulted building of uncertain purpose that shows Late Antiquity masonry over Hellenistic foundations.[60] West of Lycia the Carian coast provides similar evidence. Indeed, Vincenzo Ruggeri has concluded that Caria (on the south-westernmost corner of the Anatolian peninsula) boasted 'considerable wealth in the late fifth to sixth centuries'.[61] Indeed, neither-urban-nor-rural settlements dotted the Carian coastline, as shown for instance by the early Byzantine settlement of Torba endowed with a small church, a bath and a 'mausoleum' preserving a rather elaborate mosaic decoration.[62] Farther to the west in Aşağı Mazı a Byzantine complex by the sea has been surveyed. It must have been a large one, though what remains of it today is the central and southern part of a large basilica church (the south aisle touches the sea), a building, possibly a mausoleum (its shape resembles that of Torba), and a series of vaulted rooms, aligned along the seashore.[63]

Evidence from Lycia and Caria points to a different level of economic activity, as less state-orientated and more in tune with the abovementioned background noise of Mediterranean regional connectivity. Indeed, the bustling economic life characterizing small but well-frequented coastal sites can also be documented by shipwrecks. A good example is offered by the Fig Tree Bay shipwreck on the south-eastern coast of Cyprus, dating to the second century CE.[64] The ship should be considered a 'small' (around 5.5 tons) vessel, possibly departing from Cilicia or North-Western Syria.[65] It would point to a regional connectivity between Cyprus, Cilicia and Syria often relying on 'opportunistic ports' like those identified at the nearby sites of Avdimou Bay and Zygi-Petrini.[66] Therefore, the above-mentioned small-scale sites were a part and parcel of a fragmented and locally based connection which did not require elaborate harbours and did continue function as local loci of economic activity after the seventh century.[67]

In this light, a recent documentary survey along the southern coast of the Karpas peninsula offers another good example of networks of economic activity. This has yielded architectural evidence of three settlements centered around Early Christian basilicas (Agia Varvara and Panagia Aphendrika in Sykhada) as well as a third site (Trachonas) couched on a larger stretch of gently descending terraces.[68] It is indeed possible that these could have hosted small communities benefiting from the presence of small harbours and seafaring activity. In particular the Church of Panagia Aphendrika in Sykhada boasted at least three chronological phases: a fifth-century large basilica, a smaller eighth-century three-nave church and eleventh-/twelfth-century rural chapel. In the same vein, in Agia Varvara (located a few metres away from the coast), glass mosaic *tesserae* seem to point to the existence of an earlier phase of the building whose current structure dates to the eighth century.[69]

Contrary to the case of Agios Georgios, these rural sites were not abandoned; they continued to be frequented well into the eighth century and possibly later, witnessing a changing but resilient role played by islands vis-à-vis the post-*annona* Mediterranean exchange networks. Our next section will broaden the geographical horizons described until now, as it will be focusing on the political, economic and cultural role played in the early Middle Ages by three insular environments (Sardinia, Cyprus and Malta) spanning the two halves of the Mediterranean.[70] We will mainly rely on material and archaeological evidence, yielded in recent years from these islands. Through this evidence, we will show how these islands remained functional stepping-stones across the routes of a politically divided and economically fragmented Mediterranean. However, the sea still managed to keep its coherence partly thanks to these islands, because they acted as places where local elites and common people seem to have adjusted the tone of their daily socio-economic, cultural, and even religious interaction.

Three Islands in the Medieval Mediterranean

As the previous section of the chapter examined extensively the importance of the eastern basin of the Mediterranean (and in particular the island of Cyprus) across inter-regional (*annona*-driven) and regional shipping routes, this section considers the political and economic trajectories of the western basin of the Great Sea. The reason for taking this approach is twofold. On the one hand, historiography has often regarded the western basin of the Mediterranean as irredeemably lost to Byzantium, which supposedly turned its back to it after the death of Constans II in 668 in Syracuse.[71] A partial exception to this assertion is represented by Sicily, which remained essential for the grain supply of the imperial capital until the Aghlabid invasion on the early ninth century.[72] In fact, we will prove that Sardinia and Malta remained central to the imperial economic, administrative and fiscal structures in the so-called Dark Ages of Byzantium.[73] Cyprus performed a similar function in the Eastern Mediterranean as it remained a Byzantine province, although tax revenues were somehow shared with the Caliphate until 965 (of which more below). On the other hand, although the local elites from Sardinia, Malta and Cyprus looked at Constantinople as a source of political legitimacy and status, they were also able to perform acts of political expediency as well as boosting the economy, as a result of their role in different exchange systems and cultural areas. This image has been enhanced thanks to the archaeological evidence and material culture recently yielded from these islands.

For instance, one must admit that the recent developments in the analysis of the production and distribution patterns of local ceramics have been essential for assessing the role of an island like Cyprus at the centre of interlocking economic networks.[74] Indeed, the analysis of deposits from the so-called Imperial Baths in Umayyad Beirut has revealed the presence of globular amphorae whose fabric suggests an origin from Cyprus.[75] This peculiar type of vessel is particularly relevant because not only they are the best evidence for the period under scrutiny here, but also because they are ideally paired with different types of evidence pointing to cross-cultural interactions.[76] Here, one can for instance mention the journey of pilgrims like Willibald (in the early eighth century) and the Frankish Bernard (in the mid-ninth century) as good examples of the inter-regional travel of people and goods which crisscrossed the supposedly impermeable barrier between two Mediterranean worlds.[77] We can picture these pilgrims traveling on small boats similar to the one of Fig Bay as well as to the ship found off the Israeli coast at Tantura.[78] As the latter seems to have been built in Southern Anatolia in the tenth century, it shows the continuous use of more modest boat types, allowing coastal regions and islands to be supplied with goods (like oil and wine bottled in the abovementioned small-sized globular vessels) traveling alongside occasional passengers.[79]

Indeed, Cyprus continued to act as a convenient place from which to find a passage to the Levant. One can mention here those Cypriots who regularly ferried to and from Syria as mentioned in the *Acts of the Seventh Ecumenical Council* (787 CE), or the Cypriot monk Anastasius the Sinaite who travelled extensively to Syria and Palestine in the early eighth century.[80] These could be simply dismissed as a by-product of a resilient maritime connectivity.[81] However, we should stress that connectivity was not univocal or unidirectional; different kinds of sources could help to frame it within human or material cross-cultural exchanges which caused the construction of complex local social identities.[82]

Indeed, material evidence also suggests a certain common cultural unity with the Byzantine world.[83] As Paolo Delogu remarks, the production and distribution network of ceramics (globular amphorae and chafing dishes) point to 'a [*koiné*] which seems to coincide with the territories and the seas on which the Byzantine Empire retained a political and naval rulership'.[84] Otherwise, it is possible to trace the locally made Cypriot ceramics reaching Palestine and Egypt well into the eight century.[85] It is clear that Cyprus remained central to the shipping routes carrying goods and people from the Levantine coast well after the end of the so-called Egyptian tax spine in 640s.[86] Here one can mention for instance that some Arab cargo owners wrote Kufic inscriptions on some amphorae unearthed in Paphos. In addition, one can add some Muslim funerary inscriptions reflecting an Arab presence in the city between the late seventh to the late eighth century. An Arab population in Cyprus is indeed hinted at by the ninth century Arab *Chronicle* of al-Balādhurī.[87]

It is possible to propose a comparison with Sardinia where Kufic inscriptions have been unearthed, although they have often been hastily linked to the Arab raids which hit the western Mediterranean in the first half of the eighth century.[88] Instead they may point to Arab settlements, in particular if one considers that Sardinians had to settle for the payment of the *jizya* (poll-tax) as result of their peace treaty with the Arabs in 752.[89] As Marco Cadinu concludes, 'there are sufficient reasons to believe that the Islamic presence in Sardinia may have led not only to conditions of political and economic control but also to the migration of a large number of settlers.'[90] Indeed, the architecture of some Sardinian rural churches has revealed that they may have reused and adapted previously existing Muslim buildings.⁹¹ In a rather similar vein, analysis of a decorative motif boasted by two eighth-century Cypriot rural churches has revealed traces of interlaced frescoed patterns which were either directly borrowed from the decoration of Muslim secular palaces or represent the artistic expression of a common cross-cultural 'Eastern Mediterranean' *koine*.⁹²

The presence on these islands of graffiti and craftsmen familiar with trans-cultural artistic motifs bespeaks of a type of interaction from below, foreign to what has been often label as international court culture with shared values based on gift-exchange of luxury objects.⁹³ The latter belongs to a rather non-commercial circuit of transaction as opposed to the commercial cycles.⁹⁴ In this light, part of the importance of material evidence like graffiti lies in the fact that they were produced by non-elite members of the local society and are therefore a way to understand how individual Muslims internalized and expressed political and religious ideology.⁹⁵

However, these factors did not imply that the peculiarity of the insular cross-cultural interaction was lost to the imperial secular and religious elites. Here, a further kind of evidence can be summoned to shed light on the complex fiscal and administrative structures and praxis documented in Sardinia and Cyprus: lead seals. Since seals were once attached to the official correspondence traveling within a hundred-kilometre radius from its issuing authority, lead seals – coupled with the scant Arab and Byzantine literary sources – point to rather creative ways of defining local structures of governance. For the Arabs, the political status of islands like Sardinia and Cyprus was uneasily described as between independence – as ruled by local *muluks* (i.e. kings) – and a loose dependence on the Byzantine capital.⁹⁶ For Constantinople, the same islands were regarded as imperial provinces, although governed by *archontes* – a title encompassing a wide array political, judicial and military functions.⁹⁷ In the Byzantine hierarchy an *archon* was indeed not on the same foot as the *strategos*, the general who was directly appointed as military governor of one of those regions (called *themes*) regarded as essential to the survival of the empire.⁹⁸ It is not by chance that only Sicily was elevated to the rank of theme in the late seventh century, owing this status to its central role as 'granary of the empire'.⁹⁹ *Archontes* were often chosen among local elite families; together with other subordinate officials of the imperial military and administrative machinery as well as or secular or religious elites, they could also be effectively employed as interpreters, diplomats, or cultural brokers when the need arose.¹⁰⁰

As we will come back to the role played by elites as intermediaries across a permeable frontier in the last part of the chapter, it is important to notice that the Sardinian and Cypriot sigillographic evidence indicates another distinctive characteristic. On both islands we can indeed document eighth- and ninth-century lead-seals belonging to both Caliphal and Imperial authorities.¹⁰¹ In particular, the Islamic seals yielded in Cyprus bear the peculiar denomination *Qubrus*, pointing to the presence of Umayyad fiscal authorities on the island, as also hinted at by a treaty which – according to Theophanes' *Chronicle* – forced the islands to equally share the local tax revenue between the Caliph and the Emperor.¹⁰² Similarly, in Sardinia a large cache of sixth-to-eighth-century lead seals has been yielded in Sinis; these included specimens issued by the Byzantine military, administrative and religious authorities as well as four boasting Kufic inscriptions.[103] Some of these latter seals clearly belonged to Islamic fiscal officials as they certified the payment of the *jizya* levied on the local non-Muslim population.[104]

Muslim fiscal and administrative officials were, however, not the only ones frequenting Sardinia. Material evidence points also to the role that Muslim traders played in linking the island to the *Dar al-Islam*. Excavations in Tharros have documented two glass tokens as well as a precious stone and a ring all bearing Kufic inscriptions. In particular, the glass tokens were indeed used as monetary weights to validate transactions paid with Islamic coins.[105] Indeed, both in Sardinia and Cyprus it is possible to document a large amount of so-called seventh-century Arab-Byzantine coins as circulating together with post-reform eighth-century Muslim and Byzantine coins.[106] These point to a trans-regional, trans-cultural, and trans-political acceptance of different monetary units (Byzantine and Umayyad) as referring to commercial activities. It is interesting to notice here that a similar numismatic profile can be documented for the Balearics in the period under scrutiny and even beyond.[107]

After revising the abovementioned evidence, it is clear that islands like Sardinia and Cyprus remained resilient and were oft-frequented hubs of cross-cultural interaction both at an elite and state level as well as testifying to familiarity and coexistence at the grassroots of local societies. The former has been documented mainly through lead seals and literary evidence, whereas the latter has been enhanced by ceramics and coins partially revealing a network of commercial relationships between Muslim and Christian traders. This does not obviously exclude violence. Indeed, and leaving aside the repeated Arab raids hitting Cyprus and Sardinia between the late seventh and tenth centuries, we should indeed return to ceramic evidence. Recent research has indeed proposed that the abovementioned eighth-ninth century globular amphorae, often yielded together with contemporary Byzantine coins and lead chafed dishes, could also point to the 'a more controlled system of state dirigisme that was in place during the centuries of severe economic and financial crisis in the Mediterranean'.[108] This stemmed from the ability on the part of the Byzantine state to fully control its tax base and – more importantly – to supply its army and its navy squadrons detached in the Tyrrhenian and the Eastern Mediterranean.[109]

The ambiguous role played by globular amphorae – shipped to the military and political outposts of a Byzantine cultural and administrative sphere, as well as easily travelling with merchants to Egypt and the Levantine coasts (where they also have been documented) – bespeaks of peculiar forms of daily interaction across the sea.[110] The island of Malta is a good example of this complex nexus of political, diplomatic, cultural and commercial ties using islands as convenient nodal points. In Malta the reassessment of old archaeological surveys and the numismatic and sigillographic evidence have all demonstrated that from the mid-seventh century until the Aghlabid invasion in the 870s, the Maltese Archipelago remained not simply a distant outpost on the imperial frontier.[111] Instead, the island shows a 'degree of autonomous action in communal terms, managing to economically bridge the political divide existing between the Byzantines and the Arabs'.[112] Ceramic evidence and globular amphorae (as well as the presence of a large warehouse) point to its redistributive role for the Byzantine Tyrrhenian fleet.[113] Nevertheless, the local military authorities were also acting as brokers. The best example of this phenomenon is an eighth/ninth-century seal of Niketas, *archon kai drouggarios* of Malta, which was not found on the archipelago or in a nearby region under Byzantine control, but rather surprisingly in Tunisia: tantalizing evidence of political contacts across the supposed North–South Mediterranean divide as well as the active role of insular authorities in maintaining open political backchannels with the Muslim world.[114]

Conclusions

In this chapter, we have argued that, despite their double character as isolated and connected spaces at the same time, islands have been central to the historical trajectories of the Mediterranean in the transition from Late Antiquity to the early Middle Ages. The latter has been clearly demonstrated by the role that Cypriot maritime stations played in serving the needs of the Constantinopolitan *annona* convoys. As most of these sites were abandoned in the aftermath of the fall of Egypt to the Rashidun and as Arab fleets started roaming the Eastern Mediterranean (gearing up to the two sieges of Constantinople in 674 and 717) one could be tempted to make the case for an almost total desertion and depopulation of coastal and insular sites as the inhabitants ran for the hills and sheltered themselves in a fortified *kastra*.[115] In other words, as the Byzantine Empire lost its richest eastern provinces and the Egyptian *annona* as the last remnant of the Roman 'mondo Mediterraneo' or *mare nostrum* came to an end (see also Lampinen in this volume), the population dwindled as economic-commercial activities ceased almost completely and fortified hilltop settlements replaced the coastal sites, whereas islands like Cyprus simply became peripheral strongholds or no man's land at the frontier of empires.

In fact, this historiographical narrative has been reassessed and partially dispelled by the re-examination of the chronology of Early Medieval pottery as well as the release of better archaeological publications. As a result, the end of the Egyptian fiscal tax spine, the contraction of production and distribution and the marked decline in supra-regional trade did not ring the death knell for islands. A reassessment of the pattern of distribution of one of the best material evidences of the period (globular amphorae), yielded from sites across the Byzantine and Muslim Mediterranean, has confirmed that the fragmented regional and interregional shipping routes remained frequented in the eighth and ninth century. These two centuries have been labelled as the *nadir* of Mediterranean exchange as they separated the end of the Roman resurgence from the advent of the Macedonian dynasty. The former is what Chris Wickham famously described as the first trade cycle spun by the Roman state fiscal system.[116] In fact, the second cycle took off around 800, that is, roughly one and a half centuries after the Roman tax spine (embodied by the *annona civica*) ended for good.[117] In our opinion, tracing the socio-political and economic history of the Mediterranean island environments has helped us to bridge this chronological gap, in particular with regard to the mechanism of production and distribution in the Mediterranean world during the so-called Dark Ages – i.e. between the seventh and the ninth centuries.[118] After all, as Jody Gordon and Anna Kouremenos conclude, islands played a far greater role in Mediterranean history than their size suggests.[119]

In other words, as we have seen in the case of Sardinia and Cyprus, the economic resilience boasted by islands tapped into and at the same time enhanced their strategic location along the connecting shipping routes. This, in turn, allowed them to become crucibles of not-always-conflicting empires, as both the eastern and western halves of the Mediterranean basin remain integral to any political and military discourse about Medieval Byzantium. We have not only documented the strategic presence of Imperial and Caliphal authorities on islands, but also forms of local and regional coexistence at the grassroots of local societies. Although often invisible in literary sources, these are clearly documented by material evidence. This does not subtract from the 'other' role that islands played as Byzantine administrative and military bulwarks vis-à-vis the Arab threats.[120] After all, the small boats repeatedly mentioned in this chapter also carried slaves: human cargo resulting from Arab raids like the one which caused the forced mobility of the Cypriots whom Anastasius the Sinaite met in the early eighth century, working in a Caliphal household near the Dead Sea.[121]

One should not forget that the complex socio-cultural frameworks that insular people and communities created and lived in not only had 'obvious' violent or economic corollaries (for instance in trade), but also resulted in the construction of peculiar political and even religious structures. These, however, often remain foreign and unfathomable to outsiders as exemplified by a famous episode reported by a tenth-century Byzantine hagiographer and referring to a pilgrim reaching Cyprus from Anatolia. He said: 'While he was performing prayer in one of the churches of the island the Ishmaelite Saracens came upon the sanctuary, for they had part in the government of Cyprus. This prompted the blessed man quickly to leave the island.'[122] For if an island is a creation made from the encounter of waves and land, it should also be regarded as the creator of new theorizations for the workings works of powers in cross-social situations, what accounts not only for physical forces but also cultural and ideological ones.

Notes

* The first five pages of the contribution have been written by Luca Zavagno and the rest by Zeynep Olgun.

1. Braudel 1996: I.150; see also Fébvre 1922: 207–8.
2. Taylor 2000: 1.
3. Constantakopoulou 2017: 3.
4. Livy 19.2; see Green 2000: 302.
5. Gordon and Kouremenos 2020: 3. On the so-called 'island paradox' see Rainbird 2000; Van Dommelen 1999; and Kardulias 2020.
6. Malamut 1988: 598.
7. Darley, Jarrett and Zavagno 2019.

8. Purcell 2013: 374; see also Horden and Purcell 2000: 74–7, 123–71.
9. Constantakopoulou 2017: 1–8.
10. Lilie 2013: 14–15.
11. For the dichotomic role of Mediterranean islands in the Ottoman period see Hadjikyriacou 2017; also Gürkan 2018.
12. Valérien 2014: 80–1.
13. Jeffreys and Pryor 2006: 3–27; Ahrweiler 1966: 17–47. On the Battle of Masts, see Cosentino 2008 with further bibliography. See also Lampinen's chapter in this volume.
14. Pirenne 1936: 17–20. On the concept of Roman Mediterranean 'thalassocracy', see Carile and Cosentino 2004: 7–32 with further bibliography. For a reassessment of the so-called Pirennian debate, see Hodges and Whitehouse 1983.
15. On the Justinianic plague and its demographic and economic impact see Mordechai and Eisenberg 2019; *contra* Meier 2020. On LALIA (and the role played by environmental crisis in the Fall of Rome and creation of Medieval Europe) see Sessa 2019 and Izdebski 2013.
16. See also McCormick 2001: 123–281.
17. Horden and Purcell 2000: 172.
18. Picard 2015: 235.
19. Vionis 2013.
20. Cosentino 2018: 94–5; also Cosentino 2013.
21. Wickham has defined the Byzantine heartland as the 'uneasy coupling of two wildly different geographical zones: the Anatolian plateau and the Aegean, one of them ecologically poor and devastated by political events [of the seventh century], the other in parallel systemic crisis'; Wickham 2005: 32.
22. Cf. Shepard 2014.
23. Zavagno 2019.
24. Eger 2015: 11; see also Darling 2012.
25. Kopaka 2008: 184.
26. Cosentino 2018: 91; Kopaka 2008: 190; Pryor 1988: 7.
27. *Anonymi Stadiasmus Maris Magni*, in *GGM* (Müller 2010 [1855]) I.427–514.
28. Kopaka 2008: 191.
29. Horden and Purcell 2000: 440.
30. *Anonymi Totius Orbis Descriptio* in *GGM* (Müller 2010 [1861]) II.lii–lx. On *Expositio totius mundi et gentium*, see also Lampinen's chapter in this volume.
31. Carile and Cosentino 2004: 7–11.
32. Cosentino 2013: 66.
33. Harris 2011: 209.
34. Wickham 2005: 708–18.
35. Teall 1959: 89.
36. Durliat 1990.
37. McCormick 2001: 89.
38. On the Vandal conquest, see also Chapter 3.

39. Wickham 2005: 72–4.
40. Wickham 2005: 714.
41. See, for instance, the seventh-century *Life of Saint John the Almsgiver*: Dawes and Baynes 1948.
42. Gkoutzioukostas and Moniaros 2009.
43. Armstrong 2009.
44. See for instance Vionis 2018: 45–70.
45. Papacostas 2001: 118; Raptis and Bakirtzis 2008: 89.
46. Procopiou 2018.
47. Fejfer and Mathiesen 1995.
48. Michaelides 2001: 43.
49. Bakirtzis 2020: 27.
50. Michaelides 2001: 43; Bakirtzis 2020: 27.
51. Kapitän 1969; Leidwanger 2018.
52. Michaelides 2001: 51.
53. Bakirtzis 2020: 25.
54. Raptis and Bakirtzis 2008: 87.
55. Bakirtzis 1995; Bakirtzis 2020: 29–30.
56. Bakirtzis 2020: 31–2.
57. Raptis and Bakirtzis 2008: 89.
58. Michaelides 2001: 53.
59. See Hohlfelder 2005; Hohlfelder and Vann 2000.
60. Foss 1994: 46–7; on the eighth-century settlement pattern in Lycia see also Armstrong 2006 and Ruggeri 2001.
61. Ruggeri 1998: 206.
62. Ibid. 205.
63. Ibid. 204.
64. Leidwanger 2013c.
65. Leidwanger 2013c: 200–02.
66. Leidwanger 2013b: 233–6. On opportunistic ports, see the chapter by Indgjerd in this volume.
67. Harpster 2019.
68. Zavagno and Kızılduman 2018: 233.
69. Megaw 1950.
70. Wickham 2018.
71. Haldon 2016: 110.
72. McCormick 1995.
73. Cosentino 2013: 72–3.
74. Zavagno 2011–12: 131–2.
75. Reynolds 2018: 93–4.

76. Decker 2016: 177–8; Vroom 2012: 371–5.
77. Talbot 1954; Tobler and Molinier 1880: 310–20.
78. Barkai, Kahanov and Avissar 2010: 88–101; Barkai 2009; Barkai and Kahanov 2016.
79. Vroom 2016: 190–1.
80. See Zavagno 2011–12 with further bibliography, in particular concerning the primary sources.
81. Horden and Purcell 2000: 168.
82. Fairchild Ruggles 2004: 87.
83. Arthur 2012: 339–40.
84. Delogu 2012: 463.
85. Ballet 1995: 17–20; see also, Gabrieli, Jackson and Kaldelli 2007.
86. Wickham 2005: 789–90.
87. Hitti 1916: 117.
88. Fois 2011.
89. Fois 2016.
90. Cadinu 2017: 500.
91. Cadinu 2013: 407.
92. Farace 2015.
93. Brubaker 2004; Cutler 2001.
94. Wickham 2005: 694–8.
95. See Lindstedt forthcoming.
96. On the *muluks* see Vallejo Girvés 2012: 470–5 with further bibliography.
97. See Treadgold 1997: 378.
98. On the themes and their origins see Haldon 2016 with further bibliography.
99. Laiou and Morrisson 2007: 23–42; Wickham 2005: 780–94.
100. Zavagno 2011–2012: 144 with references to the sources in question.
101. See Prigent 2012; and Metcalf 2014: 57–65 for Cyprus and Spanu and Zucca 2004 for Sardinia.
102. Mango and Scott 1997: 506.
103. Spanu and Zucca 2004: 142–5.
104. Pinna 2010: 27–8; see also above.
105. Fois, Spanu and Zucca 2013: 258–9.
106. See Zavagno 2011 with further bibliography.
107. Moll 2005; McCormick 2001: 354–7.
108. Arthur 2018: 285–6.
109. Lounghis 2018.
110. Zavagno 2018.
111. Bruno and Cutajar 2013.
112. Bruno and Cutajar 2013: 28–9.
113. Bruno and Cutajar 2018: 111–12.

114. Bruno 2009: 84.
115. Veikou 2012.
116. Wickham 2004: 164.
117. Wickham 2005: 780–93.
118. Varinlioğlu 2019: 101.
119. Gordon and Kouremenos 2020: 3.
120. See Lounghis 2010: 188–90.
121. Munitz 2006: 96.
122. Delahaye 1925: 638.

PART III
BRAVING THE SEA IN THE LATER EMPIRE

CHAPTER 7
'WASHED BY THE WAVES': FIGHTING AGAINST SHIPWRECKING IN THE LATER ROMAN EMPIRE

Emilia Mataix Ferrándiz

Introduction

For the Romans, their relationship to the land had a legible history of law and politics that was violently inscribed through territorial lines, borders, and divisions, while the sea was perceived of and positioned outside the realm of governance of Roman civil law.[1] While land could be fenced in and enclosed, and so was fair game for conquest and control, flowing water and the sea laid outside the threshold of individual patrimony, and were seen as belonging to humanity at large.[2] In that respect, shipwrecks appear as events that bridge the gap between the land and the sea, because of the different legal remedies provided to deal with these catastrophes, which in turn enlarged the scope of land-based legal rulings. Indeed, the imperialistic efforts of Rome were first translated into treaties, and later into statutes that little by little allowed them to increase their power throughout the Mediterranean. In addition, private remedies such as edicts and advice from jurists also reflect the Roman propaganda of a Mediterranean Sea that was peaceful thanks to their rule. Later, imperial jurisdiction, manifested through imperial constitutions, also reflected how the authority of Rome was translated into the governance of events occurring at sea, overseen by an all-powerful emperor.[3]

Shipwrecking throughout Roman History (in a Nutshell)

Before the Establishment of the Roman Hegemony throughout the Mediterranean[4]

The archaic conception of shipwrecking was unavoidably linked with the ancient understanding of the sea and its shores. In a Mediterranean embedded in a semi-permanent state of war, the *ius naufragii* constituted a practice by which a shipwreck, or its remains, when reaching a foreign coast outside a trading hub recognized as such, belonged to those who took them as their own.[5] This practice was initially conceived of as an individual right, but later developed into a right of the diverse communities around the Mediterranean,[6] whose governments supported it since they found in this activity a means of subsistence and enrichment as well as an affirmation of their power.[7] The potential limitations on the *ius naufragii* were based on exercising power, negotiating, or simply threatening each other.[8]

In contrast, piracy constituted acts of threatening or looting,[9] performed by groups acting outside the law of war and its limitations as established by the state.[10] Since acts of piracy were considered as operating outside the law of war, when indeed that seems to have been the permanent state of affairs in the archaic Mediterranean, it is thus quite difficult to establish the nuances of the term in that period.[11] To make this picture even blurrier, merchants and pirates were not only entangled in an intricate interdependence,[12] but were also psychologically and practically parts of a single, age-old historical structure, the 'raid mentality', which essentially represented a specific mode of economic activity.[13]

Overall, the *ius naufragii* was practiced outside areas that were either labelled as commercial hubs or identified by the authorities as safe spaces by public declaration. The latter highlights the political dimension of this practice in the Archaic Mediterranean, where the safe spaces were designated by public authorities and thus indicated their connections (or their absence) with individual populations. What is significant here is the link between violence and space since suppression is necessarily connected to the establishment of control over territory and trade routes.[14] The latter can be perceived in the treaties or agreements between different populations that established limitations on the practice of wrecking, as well as the legitimacy or unlawfulness of violence at sea.[15] These treaties may have prevented the exercise of *ius naufragii* between political communities that were united by a consensual commitment of their members to a shared conception of law and rights, and were thus bound by a common purpose.[16]

The Emergence of the Idea of Prosecuting Violence during the Roman Republic

The Late Republic was a period known for its violent events,[17] and in the case of seafaring the data provided by underwater archaeology have been interpreted as proofs of the intensity of piracy during the first century BCE.[18] During that time, Cicero referred to pirates as 'enemies of all mankind',[19] not specifically of the Roman people.[20] That qualification legally justified that combating pirates was an obligation of all countries, who could take the measures that they considered appropriate, even justifying crossing borders and jurisdictions.[21]

The legal problem with suppressing piracy was a question of jurisdiction,[22] to which the Romans responded in different ways, for example, by classifying provinces in different ways and establishing their rule of law.[23] The *Lex de provinciis praetoris* (which survives in three inscriptions, two from Delphi and one from Knidos),[24] the *Lex Gabinia de bello piratico* (67 BCE),[25] and the *Lex Manilia* (66 BCE).[26] These legal sources are indicative of the will and need of the Romans (and their allies) to legally change the Mediterranean maritime landscape to provide safe spaces in which to navigate. That was obviously a political act, but within that act, there was a conceptual spatial change that bridged the gap between the civilized land and the 'unruly' sea.

The first century BCE saw the enactment of the *edictum de naufragio*, which set limitations on the conduct described in the *ius naufragii*. As for the provision itself, the Digest states:

> D. 47.9.1pr. (Ulp. 56 *ad Ed.*) The praetor says: 'Of those of whom it was said they have looted or wrongfully received anything from a fire, a building that has collapsed, a wreck, a storm-wrecked raft or ship, or to have inflicted any loss on such things, I will give an action for fourfold against them in the year when proceedings could first be taken on the matter and, after that year, for the simple value of the things. I will likewise give an action against a slave or household of slaves.'[27]

The *edictum de naufragio* includes a civil action which addressed cases of *rapere* (violent theft), *recipere* (take) and *damnum dare* (causing damage) performed at the same time and in the same place as a catastrophe occurred (*incendio, ruina, naufragio*).[28] In turn, the edict also applied when these behaviours occurred when a ship had been assaulted,[29] and during the assault.[30] The edict changed the paradigm of shipwreck as a legal concept so that it was perceived as an event from which the subject must be protected, both in terms of their integrity and property rights.[31] Although these behaviours may already have been considered wrongful by some prior to the enactment of the edict,[32] the essential aspect set out in this disposition was that shipwrecking was to be considered an act of private violence that must be legally targeted.[33] In the context of the edict's enactment, *vis* (violence) became an ethical label adjudged by social practice and the political notions that identified not only the act of shipwrecking as violent but also the actions deriving from it.[34]

An essential feature of this edict is its persistence through time. While approved during the Late Republic, it was included in the perpetual edict of Hadrian (131 BCE),[35] which is why Ulpian and other authors could comment on it, as can be appreciated in the different fragments compiled in the title *de incendio ruina naufragio rate nave expugnata* (D. 47.9).[36] The edict was also considered by the emperors or their secretaries when writing their rescripts which, in turn, extended its original scope. Finally, the edict was preserved in later compilations, which highlights that this disposition was applied in different social and political circumstances from when it was enacted.[37]

The (Apparent) Calm and Peace of the High Empire

In the Earlier Imperial era, the whole 'world' was Roman, so there was no point in maintaining the pretence of an international prosecution of piracy.[38] Augustan propaganda,[39] as well as the *princeps*' creation of magistracies to survey the sea,[40] have convinced some scholars that shipwrecking and piracy were practically extinct during the Roman Empire, especially during the *Pax Augusta*.[41] However, although seafaring and trade were safer during the High Imperial period due to several factors,[42] small-scale, opportunistic piracy persisted.[43] In addition, piracy became a more serious problem during the third-century crisis, forcing the Roman authorities to take extraordinary measures to suppress it.[44]

Many provinces that became Roman had a long tradition of practicing shipwrecking and piracy, which at some point was even strongly linked to the formation of their communal identity and power.[45] In addition, since the formation of the empire implied a progressive conquest, while some of the provinces that were taken in by the Romans may have tried to eradicate piracy within their boundaries, other neighbouring areas might have just kept on committing raids against these newly Roman provinces.[46] In these cases, many attacks would not have been carried out solely as a way of obtaining booty, but also as a defensive act against piracy committed by others against them.[47]

Some fragments included in the title *de naufragio* reveal different ways in which the scope of the *edictum de naufragio* was extended to the provinces.[48] One last example – even if it does not belong to the *edicto de naufragio* – would be a fragment of Marcian's *Institutes*[49] in which the jurist first refers to the punishment for shipwrecking, first by the *Lex Iulia de vi privata*, and later by the *cognitio extra ordinem*, as mentioned in an imperial constitution from Antoninus Pius.[50] By including these references to the punishment for shipwrecking in his book, Marcian was detaching them from their statutory or casuistic origin and raising them as abstract principles of general applicability.[51]

Regarding these fragments, on the one hand, there is the advice provided to provincial magistrates by Ulpian in his books, as he was himself part of the imperial chancellery during Caracalla's reign,[52] and therefore, represents the official narrative of the empire. On the other hand, there are the rescripts compiled and commented on by Paul in his book 54 on the commentary on the edict,[53] and in the second book of *quaestiones* from Callistratus.[54] Both of them were assuredly well acquainted with the imperial archives when they included these observations in their books, as they were expanding their impact and promoting the values of the empire regarding how to punish shipwrecking in the provinces.[55]

Shipwrecking, Law and the Socio-Political Landscape of the Later Empire

Many epigraphical and literary sources demonstrate that piracy became a more serious problem during and after the third century.[56] These inscriptions and texts should not be interpreted as evidence of a maritime 'crisis' *per se,* but as references to run-of-the-mill activities, indicating the continuity of piracy and plundering activities all throughout Roman History. However, one key element here is that many of the measures taken happen to come from the beginnings of a period of political instability and somewhat before the Gothic raids in the middle of the third century CE.[57] These raids were serious and damaging for the eastern provinces of the empire, but they do not indicate a complete breakdown of the framework that had helped Rome to keep piracy at reasonable levels during the previous centuries. However, these were just the beginning of more damaging invasions to come later (Saxons,[58] Vandals, Visigoths and later the Arabs).[59] These developments are also discussed in Antti Lampinen's chapter in this volume.

These events, and the subsequent measures taken by the Romans to counter them, reveal an empire in transition, threatened by external forces that were testing the strength and power of the Roman Empire. To these pirate attacks committed by populations alien to the empire, we need to add the plundering activities from privateers and subjects belonging to the Roman Empire, which did not cease during this period.

Plundering in Late Antique Legal Sources

This section mostly deals with sources which, some in a more direct manner than others, refer to shipwrecks, and give evidence of the unstable and changing political situation of the empire. One of the limitations of the sources from this period is that they are scattered throughout different codices and private law compilations, and that all these legal works were constructed following a particular aim, which in some ways could cover up the socio-political reality behind them.

The first text studied is an imperial constitution compiled in the *Codex Iustinianus* (*CI*) from the age of Diocletian paraphrasing the *edictum de naufragio*:

> CI 6.2.18. The Emperors Diocletian and Maximian to Dionysodorus. The rule of the Perpetual Edict declares that an action for fourfold damages is available for a year to him, whose property is lost, against him, who is said to have taken or caused any loss to property from a shipwreck or fire, and after that time an action lies for the simple value, apart from the existing statutory penalty (transl. Corcoran et al. in Frier's edition).

This is a rescript dated to 30 December of 294 CE, in which the two *Augusti* and Caesars were replying to one Dionysodorus from Nicomedia (in modern Turkey), who was probably asking about a ruling on the law concerning a property loss due to a shipwreck or fire. Since we only have the reply, it is impossible to know which of these catastrophes was mentioned by the petitioner, but perhaps the fact that the shipwreck was mentioned first indicates that this was the unfortunate event suffered. If that was the case, it would imply that, as I have mentioned in the previous section, even if the official discourse established the unlawfulness of stealing from a wreck, as well as plundering, these events nevertheless took place in every period of Roman history.

The text refers to the penalty established in the *edictum de naufragio*, meaning the private *actio*, as well as to the existence of a statutory penalty that should be the *quaestio de naufragii*,[60] which occupied one title from the *Codex Theodosianus* (13.9) and another from the *Codex Iustinianus* (11.6).[61] The text appears compiled in the title dealing with theft (*de furtis*), which would correspond to title 47.2 of the Digest, which indicates that this rescript was probably included because the compiler was associating the ideas, and not because he knew the specific action. Since the rescript was quoting the *actio de naufragio*, that would have been the legal remedy indicated, not the *actio* available for theft, the penalty for which was double the value of the things stolen.[62] The distinction between theft and robbery is not always crystal-clear. In that sense, §5 from the title *de naufragio* contains a text in which Gaius establishes some differences between ordinary theft or robbery and stealing from shipwrecks.[63] According to the fragment, someone who took something from the shore that was rescued from a shipwreck was liable for theft or robbery, if it happened sometime after the wreck. However, if that same person took the object from a sinking ship, a vessel under attack, or from the coast as the wreck was happening, or knew that the thing came from a wreck, then the *edictum de naufragio* applied. However, when this rescript was enacted most actions had lost their individuality, which is the reason why the compilers' arrangement may not have seemed strange.

Another compilation in which we can find references to the *edictum de naufragio* are the *Pauli Sententiae*, an anthology compiled about 300 CE[64] from various works of Paul's by an unknown hand.[65] The fragment belongs to the title addressing issues taking place during a tumult (*de his quae per turba fiant*), and says:

> PS 5.3.2. Where any property obtained from a fire, the ruin of a building, shipwreck, or the plunder of a vessel, has been stolen or concealed, and whoever concealed, hide, or rob with violence, can, within a year, be sued for fourfold damages, and, after the lapse of a year, for simple damages (transl. Scott, with amendments).

The *Pauli Sententiae* probably represented a tool to remedy the existing chaos in the sources available for solving cases and studying the law, offering a decisive synthesis of jurisprudential doctrines and imperial constitutions.[66] The inclusion of this fragment in the *Pauli Sententiae* indicates that it was going to be studied by law students, and also used to solve cases in trials. In addition, the general validity of this compilation was extended over time and authoritatively validated in one Constitution of Constantine.[67] Therefore, the inclusion of this fragment indicates the importance of the *edictum* and could, perhaps, be linked to the persistence of the practice of plundering in Late Antiquity.[68]

The fragment includes some differences with respect to the original text of the *edictum de naufragio*. The fragment addresses the behaviours of *suppresserit* (sink, make disappear) and *celauerit* (to hide from), that were not included in the original phrasing of the *edictum*.[69] The use of these two verbs is something that needs further attention since, in the first part, *supprimere* refers to a ship, and therefore needs to be read as 'sink'. However, in the second part, its meaning contrasts with that of the verb *celare* and it makes me think that it could not only be referencing the concealment of booty, but also the ransom of people, since the verb has been associated with the *plagium*, and these terms are mentioned in the *Lex Fabia* (64 BCE).[70] That hypothesis fits well with the fact that the text was inserted in a title labelled *turba* (tumult).

By including the behaviour targeted by the *edictum de naufragio* in the title regarding *turba*, it may seem that these conducts needed to be committed when taking advantage of an element of disorder or disturbance caused by a crowd.[71] One characteristic element of the *actio de naufragio* with respect to other similar legal remedies concerning violent robbery is that the behaviours targeted in this disposition were not conditioned upon being committed by a gang.[72] The latter points in two related directions; the first is that the disposition will target the behaviours indicated in the fragment when committed by a group of people, and the second is that it will also address situations when they are conducted so as to take advantage of the confusion created by a tumult, for example when a ship is being attacked. The latter was referred to by Ulpian in his extensive comment on the *edictum de naufragio*,[73] but it is unsure whether that was the scope of the original edict when it was enacted in the first century BCE. The text indicates that the original scope of the *edictum de naufragio* was enlarged in the *Pauli Sententiae*, by including the concealment of people or booty in addition to the robbery of salvaged goods, and also encompassing behaviours committed individually or in groups. The latter could be a reflection of the social reality, but what it probably indicates is that the author of the *Pauli Sententiae* knew the context of the *edictum de naufragio* and its connections with other unlawful behaviours besides those in the Digest's title. That seems to be what the authors of the *Libri Basilicorum* were following, summarizing Ulpian's commentary of the edict in a single text.[74]

The first fragment from the *CI*'s title *de naufragiis* includes a rescript from Caracalla, in which the emperor indicated that a wrecked ship washed to shore by the waves still belonged to the original owner(s):

> CI 11.6.1. The Emperor Antoninus A. Maximo. If at any time a ship has been pushed to the shore as a shipwreck, or if at any time it reaches the land abandoned, it shall belong to the owners (transl. Kehoe et al. in Frier's volume).

The latter followed the principle that goods salvaged from a wreck could only be subject to appropriation if the original owner abandoned them.[75] That was the general trend of the title *de naufragio* and was promoted in other imperial texts, which indicated that the archaic custom of the *ius naufragii* was – at least, officially – not allowed by law in the Roman world. In addition, the emperor underlined that the Roman treasury did not have any right to the wrecked ship or the salvaged goods.[76] The latter fit well with other Digest texts forbidding the interference of public authorities with a wreck or its remains.[77] Ulpian was probably referring to this same imperial constitution in D. 47.9.12pr. (Ulp. 8 *De Off. Proc.*), a fragment belonging to Book 12 on the duties of proconsuls, therefore setting the text in a provincial context[78] and referring to any kind of ship and to anyone interacting with the remains of a wreck.[79] These fragments underline that, at the time of Caracalla, it seems that the *fiscus* can demand the payment of toll taxes but had nothing to do with wrecked cargoes.[80] Solazzi interpreted this fragment as the emperor being forced to take the tone of a preacher, to reiterate to his agents from the *fiscus* (and I am imagining to the common people too) that they should not interfere with the remains of a wreck.[81]

One fragment of Fortunatianus' *Ars Rhetorica* (from before the fourth century CE) indicates the opposite view, what can, perhaps, be considered a sign of change in Caracalla's policy, which was again in force during Justinian's reign and was included in his work.[82] Otherwise, it could be considered either as ignorance on the part of the writer of the actual practice in force, or simply a reflection of the activity of the *publicani* as witnessed by the writer, who considered such actions to be lawful (even if the *publicani* may have simply been abusing their power).[83]

Bearing in mind the role of this fragment, and considering the title in which it is included, the first thing to acknowledge is that the title includes several imperial constitutions ranging from 372 until 412 CE, by which the emperors provided responses for issues concerning the *annona*'s food supply to different *praefecti pretorii, navicularii*, and even the Senate. This title needs to be considered in parallel with title 13.9 (also entitled *de naufragiis*) from the *Codex Theodosianus* (*CTh*), and from which many fragments were copied to be included in the *CI*. However, that our fragment 11.6.1 is included in this title does not mean that the text was only referring to ships involved in public supply. What could be the significance of including this fragment in the title *de naufragiis* from the *CI*? The fragments of this title refer to an investigation (*quaestio de naufragii*) that was meant to determine whether a wreck causing the loss of a public cargo was caused by weather conditions, by lack of diligence or expertise in navigation, or by fraud. The different particularities appear to be first described in title 13.9 of the *CTh*, from which many texts were copied, modified, and adapted into title 11.6 of the *CI*.[84] The fragments from both titles describe the procedure to carry out the investigation of a shipwreck, and none of them describe the case of a public authority interacting with the remains. However, the rescript of Caracalla does not appear to be mentioned in the *CTh*, which could make one consider whether the behaviour of the imperial agents and local privateers with respect to wrecks was more reckless during Justinian's reign, thus motivating the compilers to include this text in the title. But the latter should be justified by the different nature of both compilations, being that the *CTh* was restricted to laws of general efficacy (*edicta*) versus the *rescripta*, which would have been compiled in the previous *Codices Hermogenianus* (*CH*) and *Gregorianus* (*CG*), and which were tacitly recognised in the *CTh*.[85] Perhaps the texts dealing with plundering in the private sphere were compiled in these codes, which titles also followed the sections of the Praetor's Edict,[86] in which the *edicto de incendio ruina naufragio rate nave expugnata* was compiled.[87]

In addition, several fragments of title five from the *Codex Theodosianus* (*de naviculariis*) also refer to frauds committed while transporting cargoes on behalf of the *annona*.[88] The interest in establishing these measures regarding the *annona* supply should not be simply justified by the increasing importance of the state management of the *annona* during the Later Empire, since the shippers derived benefits from working for the state but were not completely dependent on it.[89] These texts describe the process of demonstrating and proving that the wreck by which a public cargo was lost was caused by natural forces. Corresponding with the historical context of the fragments, the procedure followed was the *cognitio extra ordinem*.[90] The investigation was led by the provincial governor from the area where the wreck took place, but the decision on the matter was then transferred, depending on the historical context, to the praetorian prefect,[91] or to the prefect of the *annona*.[92] In one constitution from 380, the Emperors Gratian, Valentinian and Theodosius establish guidelines for the type of evidence that can be used by sailors to facilitate their revindications, and include the stipulation that their close kin can be called as witnesses in cases when the shipper has not survived.[93] In case it was demonstrated that the shipwreck occurred due to natural causes, the shipper was to be exempted from having to compensate for the lost cargo, but the finding would not offer to make up for the damage suffered by the ship.[94] However, it seems that quite frequently the shippers actually caused the wrecks,[95] taking advantage of the fact that the state was assuming the risk for the transport.[96]

From my point of view, these texts reflect the need to establish a special rule for cases of *stellionatus* (swindling), which did not have any specific penalty and therefore needed to be fixed *extra ordinem*.[97] Even if that was not the aim, however, Ulpian does provide an extensive list of the conducts targeted in this category (perhaps such a list was unnecessary and restrictive),[98] and the jurist actually mentions 'in particular, a person who conceals merchandise can be charged with this offense',[99] which is indeed quite illustrative and fits with other similar topics addressed by the Severan jurist in his book eight on the duties of the proconsul.[100] Concretely, the fragment *D.* 47.11.6pr. (Ulp. 8 *De Off. Proc.*) addresses the problem of fraud committed by subjects working for the corn supply and refers to *merces supprimunt*.[101] In his text, Ulpian indicates that this problem was addressed by imperial constitutions and *mandata*, however it seems to me that these may have not been efficient enough to control these behaviours, so later emperors needed to enact further imperial decrees to deal with these cases.

These texts highlight the importance of the documentation used to declare what was actually loaded and unloaded from a vessel, and in relation to this several texts talk about the corruption of provincial officers who committed fraud in these matters.[102] Some fragments prescribe that the shipper should provide proof about the circumstances that could have caused damage to the cargo, a serious reduction of the expected load, or the jettisoning of part of the goods to avoid wreckage.[103] The latter is justified because the shippers could say that they have jettisoned part of the load, but instead keep it somewhere in order to sell it for a profit. However, some fragments from an imperial constitution compiled in 409 CE reflect the warranties provided by the imperial constitutions for cases involving shippers working in the eastern part of the empire, and indicate that when their fault in a case of shipwreck was proven, the guilt would be shared amongst the entire council of shipowners.[104] In that way, these subjects would not aim to commit fraud so as to avoid confrontation with their peers and losing the privileges of being part of the council.[105]

One of the first thoughts that comes to mind when reading these sources is why the authors kept copying the *edictum de naufragio* and its related texts, while other sources, which may have also addressed these events, only appear in the Digest but not in other private compilations.[106] The *edictum de naufragio* was part of the perpetual edict and, in that sense, it would have been a source accessible to the different authors writing their compilations. Here we must differentiate between private compilations and the codes that gathered and organized imperial constitutions. In the first type, we can see authors at work, compiling the sources available to create manuals aimed at teaching and explaining the law,[107] which is why these sources did not always need to be up-to-date, meaning that they were an existing element in the legal framework presented, but were not necessarily in use at the time. For example, the penalties included for the behaviours targeted by the *edictum* were fixed *extra ordinem* when these writers were compiling the texts. Notwithstanding that, the persistence of this edict probably indicates the importance of this source as symbolizing the changes in the paradigm of *ius naufragii* since the Roman Republic.

In the case of codifications, such as those of *Theodosianus* and the *Iustinianus,* they also compiled sources which were hand-picked by the compilers, thus forming a subjective whole. However, even though these imperial constitutions were edicts or rescripts (with their subsequent applicability and impact), the result would be the same since their inclusion in these codes extended their effects to become general rules. Many of these sources concerning plundering were probably included in the codes because they needed to remind that the behaviours included in these rulings were still being committed, and existing laws were being violated or avoided, or there was a need to reclassify these practices from merely anti-social or inconvenient behaviour to legal offences. Either way, the repetition of the laws added strength to the imperial anti-plundering crusade that was a constant throughout different periods, despite the variations in the activity of both privateers and gangs.[108]

Concluding Thoughts

Based on the analyzed texts, it seems that the criminalization and prosecution of *ius naufragii* and piracy in antiquity was based on unilateral solutions arrived at in response to specific situations. Thus, it was closely related to the notion of, if not empire, at least a politically organised community.[109] This was the general trend followed by the official rulings since Rome's hegemonic governance of the Mediterranean Basin after their victory in the Punic Wars and its progressive imperialistic expansion.

In that sense, the guiding principle appears to have been that violence and acts of war at sea should be avoided, but that the exercise of private violence was perhaps more difficult to control. Thus, we need to bear in mind that while there may have been an official or established framework of understanding regarding certain practices that depended on the power of the central government, other traditions and customs could and would have remained in force and interfered with these generalized principles. In that sense, for the people for whom looting had always been part of their economic income, it would have been difficult to be told that this practice was no longer acceptable.[110] Therefore, this perspective needs to be considered when examining the culturally diverse Mediterranean regions. After all, any landscape is made up of multiple ideological and interrelated components, which are best understood by considering their previous inhabitants.

In addition, the Later Empire witnessed several threatening invasions and events which, as we know, would eventually destroy the framework of Roman control, first in the West, and later in the East (although this is another story). In that general environment of disorder and violence it was even more difficult to control plundering, something that many shippers working for the *annona* would have taken advantage of. In addition, many areas of the empire, being threatened by external forces, may have gone back to plundering not only as a way to overcome piracy, but also, perhaps, as a defensive measure against assailants in general.¹¹¹ In that way, even if it may seem to be a cliché, the Later Empire and its sources regarding plundering leave an image of a fragmented political community reflecting the decline in imperial stability, and the progressive disappearance of the *mare nostrum* and its social and political significance for the Roman world.

Notes

1. Tuori 2018: 204–14.
2. See *D.* 1.8.2pr-1 and *D.* 1.8.4pr-1 (Marc. 14 *Inst.*). Also, *D.* 43.8.3.1 (Celsus 39 *Dig.*) 'the sea, like the air, is for the common use of humankind'.
3. See also Minale in this volume.
4. Following the original title of one paper written by Rougé 1966: 1467–79.
5. Hdt. 3.137–138; Polyb. 2.8; Strab. 5.4.2, 89.5.2, 17.3.20; Plin. *HN* 2.73 (71) and 7.57.11; Apollod. *Epit.* 6.7; Dionys. Per. 47–49; Amm. Marc. 15.2.2–3. The existence of coastal areas with a large number of wrecks sunk near the sandy shores probably indicates that wrecking vessels by attracting them to the coast with signs was a common practice, see *D.* 47.9.10 (Ulp. 1 *Opin.*); Purpura 1986: 156.
6. Andrich 1904–11; Rougé 1966: 109; Moschetti 1977; Velissaropoulos-Karakostas 1980: 162.
7. Chic García 2013: 17.
8. Rougé 1966, quoting remedies such as the ἀνδροληψία, σύλαν (right of reprisal), or the use of συμβολά (objects symbolizing a relationship between two parties). For an overview, see: Dem. *De cor.* 21.82; 23.82.4; Polyb. 8.50–51; *Lexeis Rhetorikai* in *Lex. Seg.* 213–30. 214.2; Bravo 1981; MacDowell 1963: 27–8; Velissaropoulos-Karakostas 1980: 141–50 (ἀνδροληψία); *SEG* II² 1132; *SEG* IV² 1.68; *FD* III 2.68; *SGDI* II 2506; *CID* IV 12; *CID* IV 114; *SEG* IX 1²; *SEG* IX 2.573; *SEG* XII 9.191; *IMT* Skam/NebTaeler 192; *SEG* II 533; *SEG* XL 609. Purpura 2002; Bravo 1980; Pritchett 1991: 68–132; Garlan 1999: 108; Cassayre 2010; Dillon and Garland 2010: 164; Cecarelli 2013: 38 (σύλαν), and Velissaropoulos-Karakostas 1977; Cataldi 1983; Herman 1987; Zuccotti 1992: 305–439; Purpura 1995: 468–9 (συμβολά).
9. Hom. *Od.* 3.69.12; 3.71–74; Thuc. 1.4–5; Dem. 53.3; Lys. 22.14; Arist. *Pol.* 1.1256; Eur. *Hel.* 765–69, 1125.9; Apollod. *Bibl.* 2.1.5; Polyb. 2.8–9; 2.4–5.
10. Gabrielsen 2001: 225; Arnaud 2016: 24.
11. As indicated by Ormerod 1997: 59–73. It is different in later periods, when the state of war is something exceptional, and then it is easier to establish differences between privateer and private, between prize and booty. Privateers would seize spoils and are justified by being part of a just war, while pirates only act for their own good and their acts find no legal justification. The latter is the approach as phrased by Grotius, see, Kempe 2009: 393–95.
12. De Souza 1999: 22, 56, 201–2; Alonso-Núñez 2007.
13. Cassola 1968: 28; Gabrielsen 2001: 237; Bresson 2016: 418, referring as using the 'economic rationality of violence'.
14. Vlassopoulos and Xydopoulos 2015: 8–9.
15. Frezza 1949: 29; Bederman 2001: 192; Ando 2020: 123. Some examples of these sources were six treaties agreed between Rome and Carthage from 509–279 BCE (Polyb. 3.22.4–7); or the treaties concluded by Maroneia from 167 BCE (*SEG* XXXV 823. ll.6–11) and Astypalaia from 105 BCE (*SEG* XII 3.173. ll.26–29 (=*IGRRP* IV 1028).).

16. That was the main point of Cic. *Rep.* 1.39; Cic. *Parad.* 27.
17. E.g. Lintott: 1999.
18. Parker 1992: figure3, Parker's graph shows a progressive increase in the number of known wrecks from about 600 BCE to 200 BCE, followed by a rapid rise to a peak in the first century BCE; Parker 1992: 84, 196. However, although archaeological evidence can indicate that a wrecked ship suffered a violent attack, it does not necessarily mean that these violent marks on the ship correspond to a pirate assault, Arnaud 2016: 22.
19. Cic. *Off.* 3.107 *pirata non est ex perduellium numero definitus, sed communis hostis omnium, cum hoc nec ides debet nec ius iurandum esse commune*: '... for a pirate is not included in the number of lawful enemies but is the common foe of all the world; and with him there ought not to be any pledged word nor any oath mutually binding' (transl. W. Miller).
20. Which would have implied a series of procedures in terms of declaring war according to the *ius fetialis,* such as the *ius iurandum* as indicated in Cic. *Off.* 3.108. See also, Catalano 1964; Loreto 2001: 69–73; Bederman 2001: 55–7.
21. Tarwacka 2009; ead. 2012, 70, 73; ead. 2018: 302, 309; Policante 2015: 26–50.
22. Anderson 1995: 178.
23. Str. 10.5.4; 14.5.2; Ando 2020: 119.
24. *SEG* XXVI 1227.
25. Asc. *Corn.* 72a–c; Cass. Dio 36.
26. Cic. *Leg Man.* 56: *itaque una lex, unus vir, unus annus non modo nos illa miseria ac turpitudine liberavit, sed etiam effecit, ut aliquando vere videremur omnibus gentibus ac nationibus terra marique imperare.* 'And the result was that one law, one man, and one year not only set you free from that distress and that reproach, but also brought it to pass that you seemed at last in very truth to be holding empire over all nations and peoples by land and sea' (transl. H. Grose Hodge).
27. Lenel thought that the last phrase was an interpolation, see Lenel 1889: 765–6 (§ 189); id. 1927: 396. For more details on the origin, chronology, and features of the disposition, see Mataix Ferrándiz 2019: 153–95,
28. Being fire, collapse of a building or wreck. D. 47.9.1.2–5 (Ulp. 56 *ad Ed.*); D. 47.9.2 (Gai. 21 *ad Ed. Prov.*).
29. *D.* 47.9.3.1. (Ulp. 56 *ad Ed.*) *Deinde ait praetor 'rate navi expugnata'. Expugnare videtur, qui in ipso quasi proelio et pugna adversus navem et ratem aliquid rapit, sive expugnet sive praedonibus expugnantibus rapiat.*
30. *D.* 47.9.4pr. (Paul 54 *ad Ed.*).
31. Some fragments of the Jerusalem Talmud show that this conception is not shared in other cultures, see Talmud of Jerusalem, *Schequalim.* V II.2.; Talmud of Jerusalem, *Baba Qama.* X.2.
32. Indeed, Plautus' comedy *Rudens* refers to the unlawfulness of seizing property coming from a wreck (esp. 955–1065) and it was probably written in 181–180 BCE.
33. Balzarini 1969; Vacca 1972.
34. Labruna 1971: 10–11; id. 1972: 528; id. 1986: 11.
35. Lenel 1927: 391–6, § 189. On the perpetual edict, see Tuori 2006: 219–37 for a review of the literature available.
36. Esp. Ulpian's book 56 and Paul's book 54, both on the praetorian edict.
37. For a similar kind of issues concerning text transmission, see Minale in this volume.

38. This principle was interpreted differently by Grotius to help his own interests. See Grotius 2009: 26–7; Straumann 2015: 130–65; Tuori 2018: 214.

39. Augustus indeed claimed to have stopped piracy in the Mediterranean, proclaiming 'I freed the sea of pirates' (*mare pacavi a praedonibus*), see *CIL* III.2 769 (=*RGDA* 25.1). However, the line alludes to his rival Sextus Pompey, see Livy *Per.* 123; 127–28, and Fuhrmann 2012: 95 n. 23. Other sources that claim the benefits of the *Pax Augusta* are, Hor. *Carm.* 4.5.17; Str. 3.25; Philo *Leg.* 146; Plin. *HN* 2.118; Prop. 3.4.1, 3.4.11, 3.4.59; Suet. *Aug.* 22.

40. Purpura 1985: 106.

41. Ormerod 1997: 257; Braund 1993: 106–7; Noy 2000: 142. For example, the wreck *Cabrera D* (1–15 CE) included helmets in its cargo, something that according to Parker could only be justified by the presence of soldiers on board and not on the self-defence of the crew, since this wreck dates to the *Pax Augusta*. see: Parker 1992: 84.

42. For a general view, Wilson 2011: 33–9; 54.

43. De Souza 1999: 205–13. However, the boast had some merit: piracy did not become a serious problem again until Late Antiquity, see Moschetti 1983: 873–910.

44. De Souza 1999: 218–24.

45. E.g. Cilicia and Crete, see Shaw 1997: 199–233; Avidov 1997: 5–55. For the case of the Roman takeover of the Polemonid kingdom of Pontos in 63 CE, see Tac. *Hist.* 3.47–48 and De Souza 1999: 208–9.

46. See the case of the Chauci, who carried out raids into Gaul in the first century CE (Tac. *Ann.*11.18).

47. The Frisians attacked a ship from the Usipi, crewed by men who had deserted the Roman army in Scotland in 83 CE and sailed across the North Sea to the German coast, Tac. *Agr.* 28; Cass. Dio 56.20. Judea was widely known as an area where piracy was perpetrated before the Roman occupation of the province, as when Pompey attacked the area in 63 BCE, Joseph. *BJ* 2.9.2, 2.12.1, 3.9.2, 3.414–17; De Souza 1999: 209.

48. See §10; §4.1; §7 and §12pr.

49. Marcian's book was a kind of sourcebook written in the late Severan period and probably in an oriental province, see Andres Santos 2004, with bibliography.

50. *D.* 48.7.1–2 (Marc. 14 *Inst.*).

51. Coriat 1997: 649–52.

52. Dell'Oro 1960: 119; Honoré 1962: 209.

53. Written during Caracalla's reign, see Honoré 1962: 224; Klami 1984: 1834, while Maschi 1976: 676, locates his work in a broad chronological timeline, between Commodus and Severus Alexander.

54. Probably written under Septimius Severus, Honoré 1962: 216.

55. This phenomenon has been described as the 'maximation of imperial constitutions' and involved an extensive knowledge of the archives of the imperial chancellery. See Archi 1986: 161; Volterra 1971: 832; Palazzolo 1980; Coriat 1997: 635–64; Varvaro 2006: 381.

56. *BÉ* 1946–47: 337–38; *IGRRP* 4.1057 lines 11–20; *IGRRP* 3.481 lines 8–10; *CIL* VI 1638 SHA *Tyr. trig.* 26.2; *Pan. Lat.* VIII.12.1, VIII.18.1; Amm. Marc. 14.2; 16.9; 19.13; 27.9; Zos. 1.71; De Souza 1999: 218–24.

57. Zos. 1.27–28, 1.32, 1.34, 1.42, 1.46; SHA *Claud.* 6–12, 9.7; *Gall.* 12.6, 13, 13.6.

58. On the Saxons, Sid. Apoll. *Ep.* 8.14, *ad hoc exercent illos naufragia, non terrent. est eis quaedam cum discriminibus pelagi non notitia solum, sed familiaritas. nam quoniam ipsa si qua*

tempestas est huc securos efficit occupandos, huc prospici vetat occupaturos, in medio fluctuum scopulorumque confragosorum spe superventus laeti periclitantur. 'Moreover, shipwreck, far from terrifying them, is their training. With the perils of the sea they are not merely acquainted—they are familiarly acquainted; for since a storm whenever it occurs lulls into security the object of their attack and prevents the coming attack from being observed by victims, they gladly endure dangers amid billows and jagged rocks, in the hope of achieving a surprise' (transl. W. B. Anderson).

59. For a summary, see De Souza 1999: 225–40.

60. Manfredini 1986: 135–48.

61. Even if *CI* 11.6.1 includes a rescript from Caracalla that refers to the interference of public authorities in case of shipwreck, therefore not dealing with a *quaestio*, and placing itself in line with §7 from the title *de naufragio*.

62. Gai. *Inst.* 4.37.

63. *D.* 47.9.5 (Gaius 21 *ad Ed. Prov.*) *Si quis ex naufragio vel ex incendio ruinave servatam rem et alio loco positam subtraxerit aut rapuerit, furti scilicet aut alias vi bonorum raptorum iudicio tenetur, maxime si non intellegebat ex naufragio vel incendio ruinave eam ese. Iacentem quoque rem ex naufragio, quae fluctibus expulsa sit, si quis abstulerit, plerique idem putant. Quod ita verum est, si aliquod tempus post naufragium intercesserit: alioquin si in ipso naufragii tempore id acciderit, nihil interest, utrum ex ipso mari quisque rapiat an ex naufragiis an ex litore.* 'If someone removes or seizes something salvaged from a wreck, fire, or collapse of a building and put it in another place, they will be liable on the action for theft or that for things taken by force, even though they were unaware that it comes from a wreck, fire, or collapse of building. Many are of the opinion that where someone appropriates from a wreck something which is lying washed up by the waves, the same applies. This is true if some time has elapsed since the wreck; but if what happens occurs at the very time of the wreck, it is irrelevant whether the seizure be made from the sea itself, the wreck or the shore.'

64. The dating of the work has been a much-discussed issue, summarized by Ruggiero 2017: 20–49.

65. The authorship of the work has also been a debated question, of which Ruggiero 2009: 270–76, summarizes the literature available.

66. For further details on the context of this work, see Ruggiero 2009: 288–91.

67. *CTh* 1.4.2.

68. Moschetti 1977: 551; De Souza 1999: 218–40.

69. However, these behaviours are mentioned in other fragments related to the purpose of the *edictum*, see *D.* 47.9.3.8 (Ulp. 56 *ad Ed.*); *D.* 48.8.3.4 (Marc. 14 *Inst.*).

70. Cic. *Rab. perd.* 8.7, 5; *D.* 48.15 (*De Lege Fabia de Plagiariis*); Coll. 14.2–3 (14.2.1 = Paul. Sent. 5.37.1–2; Molè 1971: 74 n.1; Lambertini 1980: 77–84; Manfredini 1984: 2219–220.

71. *D.* 47.8.4 (Ulp. 56 *ad Ed.*), also Bianchi Fossatti Vanzetti 1995: 106, interpreting the first text of the title as referring to *multitudine* (crowd).

72. Balzarini 1969: 262–4; Vacca 1972: 48–51, as happened with the *edictum* of Lucullus.

73. *D.* 47.9.1.5 (Ulp. 56 *ad Ed.*) *Item ait praetor: 'Si quid ex naufragio'. Hic illud quaeritur, utrum, si quis eo tempore tulerit, quo naufragium fit, an vero et si alio tempore, hoc est post naufragiumque: nam res ex naufragio etiam hae dicuntur, quae in litore post naufragium iacent. Et magis est, ut de eo tempore* … 'The praetor also says: "if anything from a shipwreck." Here one may ask whether this concerns someone who takes something when the wreck happened

or also at another time, that is, after the wreck; for things are said to come from a wreck which lie on the shore after the wreck. And it is true that the edict applies to the time, ...'

74. B. 53.3.25.
75. D. 41.2.21–2 (Iav. 7 *ex Cass.*), 41.1.58 (Iav. 11 *ex Cass.*), 41.7.7 (Jul 2 *ex Minicio*), 14.2.8 (Jul 2 *ex Minicio*), 41.1.9.8 (Gaius 2 *Rer. Cott. Aur.*), 14.2.2.7 (Paul 34 *ad Ed.*), 47.2.43.11 (Ulp. 41 *ad Sab.*), 41.7.2.1 (Paul, 54 *ad Ed.*), 47.2.43.5 (Ulpian, 41 *ad Sab.*).
76. CI 11.6.1 *fiscus meus sese non interponat. Quod enim ius habet fiscus in aliena calamitite, ut de re tam luctuosa compendium sectetur.* 'My treasury must nor interpose itself. For what right does the treasury have in another's calamity, that it gain a profit from that grievous a situation?' (transl. Kehoe).
77. D. 47.9.7 (Call. 2 *Quaest.*), 47.9.12pr. (Ulp. 8 *de Off. Proc.*), 39.4.16.8 (Marc L. *Sing. de Delat.*).
78. Dell'Oro 1960: 51–60.
79. D. 47.9.12pr. (Ulp. 8 *de Off. Proc.*) *Licere unicuique naufragium suum impune colligere constat: idque imperator Antoninus cum divo patre suo rescripsit.* 'It is established that it is lawful for anyone to collect with impunity his wrecked property; so ruled the Emperor Antoninus and his deified father in a rescript.'
80. Ferrarini 1963; Solazzi 1939: 254; Purpura 1976: 72.
81. Solazzi 1939: 254–5.
82. Fortunat. *Ars. Rhet.* 1.13. *Quae est simplex definitio? Cum unam rem simpliciter definimus ut: naufragia ad publicanos pertineant. Cuiusdam naufragae corpus cum ornamentis ad litus expulsum harena obrutum est, id publicani eruerunt.*
83. Solazzi 1939: 254–5, who thinks that the abuses of the *publicani* may have forced Caracalla to use that sentimental tone in his rescript compiled in *CI* 11.6.1 (*Quod enim ius habet fiscus in aliena calamitate, ut de re tan luctuosa compendium sectetur?*).
84. *CTh* 13.9.3 (=*CI* 116.2), 13.9.3 (=*CI* 11.6.3), 13.9.4 (=*CI* 11.6.4), 13.9.6 (=*CI* 11.6.5), 13.5.32 (=*CI* 11.6.6; *CI* 11.2.4).
85. Matthews 1993: 25–6; Connolly 2010: 8–9; Corcoran 2013: 4.
86. Corcoran 2013: 4–5.
87. Mataix Ferrándiz 2019: 178–81.
88. E.g. *CTh* 13.5.26, 13.5.34.
89. Broekaert 2009: 169–73; *contra,* Sirks 1992: 158–68.
90. Several scholars have remarked on incoherencies among the fragments as to the time available for presenting the evidence to a judge, which seems to have been settled at two years. Cuiacius 1758, *ad CI* 11.6.2, highlighted some incoherencies, later refuted by Manfredini 1986: 138–48 and Solazzi 1939: 258; De Salvo 1992: 356–7. It may have taken one year to make the accusation from the date that the wreck happened, and one year more for the investigation.
91. *CTh* 13.9.1 (=*CI* 11.6.2), 13.9.4 (=*CI* 11.6.4).
92. One fragment refers to the praefect of the *annona* of Africa in *CTh* 13.9.2 (372 CE); while later (397 CE), *CTh* 13.9.5 mentions the *praefectos annonae* from Rome.
93. *CI* 11.6.3.
94. Solazzi 1939: 256; De Salvo 1992: 361–2.
95. *CTh* 13.9.1 (=*CI* 11.6.2), 13.9.3.1 (=*CI* 11.6.3), 13.5.32 (=*CI* 11.6.6), 13.9.4.1.
96. *CTh* 13.9.5.

97. *D.* 47.20.3.2 (Ulp. 8 *ad Off. Proc.*); Mentxaka 1988: 306–13.
98. Harries 2007: 31–2.
99. *D.* 47.20.3.3. (Ulp. 8 *ad Off. Proc.*) *Qui merces suppressit, specialiter hoc crimine postulari potest.* Mentxaka 1988: 312–13.
100. Lenel 1927: 981–4.
101. *D.* 47.11.6pr. (Ulp. 8 *ad Off. Proc.*) *Annonam adtemptare et vexare vel maxime dardanarii solent: quorum avaritiae obviam itum est tam mandatis quam constitutionibus. mandatis denique ita cavetur: "Praeterea debebis custodire, ne dardanarii ullius mercis sint, ne aut ab his, qui coemptas merces supprimunt, aut a locupletioribus, qui fructus suos aequis pretiis vendere nollent, dum minus uberes proventus exspectant, annona oneretur". Poena autem in hos varie statuitur: nam plerumque, si negotiantes sunt, negotiatione eis tantum interdicitur, interdum et relegari solent, humiliores ad opus publicum dari.* 'In particular, forestallers and regraters, speculators generally, interfere with and disturb the corn supply, and their avarice is confronted both by imperial instructions and by enactments. By imperial instruction, it is provided: "You must further ensure that forestallers and regraters, speculators generally, indulge in no commerce and that the corn supply is not incommoded either by those who conceal what they have bought or by the wealthier who do not wish to sell their merchandise at a fair price because they anticipate that the next harvest will be less fruitful." The penalties for such persons are varied; for, generally, if they be merchants, they are only banned from trading or, in some cases, relegated to an island, while those of the lower, orders are condemned to forced labour.' See also Pollera 1991: 406–18.
102. *CTh* 13.5.38; *CI* 11.2.5; *CTh* 13.5.29. See also Sirks 1998, 331, 341.
103. *CTh* 13.9.4, 13.9.5.
104. *CTh* 13.5.2 (=*CI* 11.2.4; *CI* 11.6.6).
105. See for example *CTh* 13.8.
106. For example, one script released by Antoninus Pius and compiled by Marcian referred to the *Lex Iulia de vi privata* to address the theft of salvaged goods (*D.* 48.7.1.1–2 (Marc. 14 *Inst.*).
107. For example, for the case of the *Collatio Legum Mosaicarum et Romanarum*, see: Frakes 2011: 66–98. Also, on the role of the jurists as masters, see Mantovani 2018: chapter 4.
108. Harries 2009: 80, 82, 86.
109. Benton 2011: 239–40.
110. Raids were a source of economic income in the archaic Mediterranean for several Mediterranean populations, such as Dalmatia, Cilicia and Liguria, see: Diod. Sic. 5.39.8; Str. 4.203.
111. As appears to be referred to for an earlier period in Petron. *Sat.*114.14 and Macrob. *Sat.* 3.6.11.

CHAPTER 8
UPWIND SAILING CAPABILITIES OF SQUARE-RIGGED SHIPS IN LATE ANTIQUITY AND THE RAMIFICATIONS FOR TRADE NETWORKS

Doug Forsyth

Introduction

Pre-industrial societies developed a variety of solutions for maritime transport likely in response to different environmental conditions.[1] Egyptian society developed flat-bottomed craft with large square sails in response to a river environment that allowed them to utilize the force of the current to float northwards headed down river and the force of the wind to then sail southward against the current.[2] In Northwestern North America, indigenous societies developed large paddled canoes to deal with an environment dominated by strong tidal current flows and fickle winds.[3] In the South Pacific, islanders developed large sail-powered craft capable of extended voyages taking advantage of predictable trade winds.[4] Mediterranean societies were no different in the development of watercraft designs that fit their environmental conditions. Commercial trading vessels developed hull, rig and sail designs in an adaptive approach to Mediterranean wind conditions that blew predominantly from the northwest in the summer months and were more variable in other seasons. By Late Antiquity, we can observe the full suite of nautical innovations that Mediterranean people developed to optimize sailing efficiency given the materials and technologies available to them.

This chapter will consider these developmental steps of vessel and rig designs observable in Late Antiquity and the ramifications these designs had for vessel movement relative to wind direction. As will be shown, the technical limitations of a ship's capacity to advance its position relative to wind direction had a profound impact on networks of connectivity. Scholars have focused on two types of maritime trading relationships, either direct long-distance voyaging or stepping-stone near-shore cabotage. These two models often focus on the written record preserved in legal codices or taxation practices to understand the trading patterns. Overlooked, I suggest, has been an evaluation of just what ancient square-rigged Mediterranean sailing ships could and could not do in response to seasonal weather constraints.

In this chapter, we will first discuss the Mediterranean wind and sailing environment. Secondly, we will investigate the ship and rig designs of Late Antique sailing craft to understand the human response to weather constraints and, lastly, to consider the ramifications of these practical implications for seasonal trade networks.

Weather Patterns

Wind roses are diagrams developed from observations of wind direction taken over a given period of time, delineated by month. The longer the line, the more days the wind blew from that direction, expressed as a percentage of days in the month. The number in the centre of the diagram is days of calm. From modern metrological data, the Mediterranean wind direction in the months of April, July, and October are presented in Figure 8.1.[5]

To apply these wind roses derived from modern wind observations, one does have to consider if ancient winds were the same as modern winds regarding direction and seasonality. In what is a rare case of corroborative information, Aristotle (*Meteorologica*) and Theophrastus (*De Ventis*) provided data regarding wind direction and duration from observations taken across the whole of the Mediterranean in the fourth century BCE. Their data corresponds closely with modern data in the Eastern Mediterranean where they had more reporting stations, less so in the Western Mediterranean, and in almost all wind directions except southerly winds where the correlation is not as high.[6] Wind directions are often a function of the heating and cooling of the Earth's surface and the Earth's rotation.[7] If the Sahara Desert was a hot region in antiquity as it is today and the Earth rotated in antiquity as it currently does, it suggests we are on safe ground regarding the application of modern wind data to antiquity as long as we don't take it too far.

Assume for the moment that sail-powered craft performed best when the wind came from astern. From an examination of the wind roses in Figure 8.1, in April and October there are some days when the wind would be favourable for travel from the southeast to the northwest. In July, though, travelling in the same direction would be near impossible as the wind blows from the northwest over 90 per cent of the month. A Roman grain ship wanting to sail from Alexandria to Puteoli in July is just not going to get there; the voyage will have to wait several months before the summer winds are replaced by more directionally variable conditions in the fall.[8]

Across the Mediterranean the general wind flow is from northwest to southeast. Wind-driven currents augment this.[9] Briefly presented here and discussed in detail below, this wind flow facilitates direct downwind sailing from a northwest origin port to a destination in the southeast, especially in the preferred summer sailing season. This weather pattern cannot continue indefinitely, with the wind-pushed water stacking up in the southeastern corner of the Mediterranean; at some point this must flow back to the west.[10] The counter flow of water is observable in a north-flowing current along the Levant which then turns west along the south coast of Asia Minor.[11] A ship can hop from stop to stop along this route working against the prevailing northwesterly winds at propitious times.

Ship Design and Sailing Practices

Three angles of vessel movement relative to wind direction need to be considered, with the wind coming from behind the ship, across the beam of the ship, and from the bow

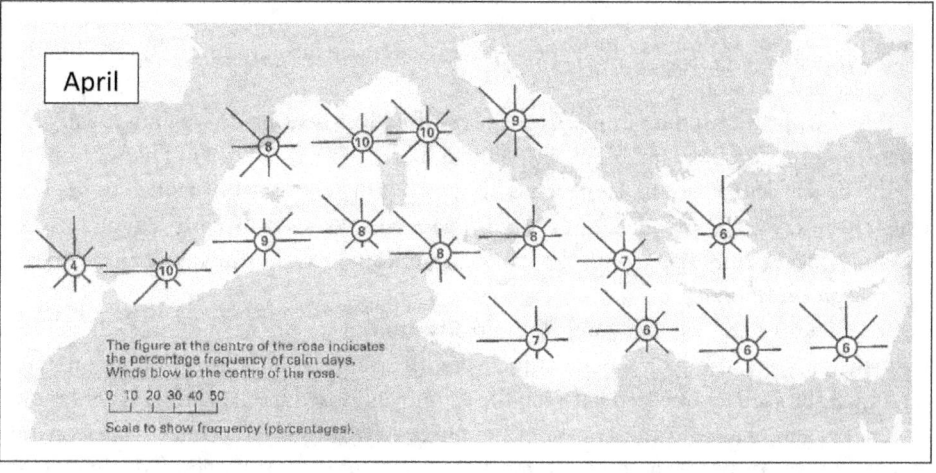

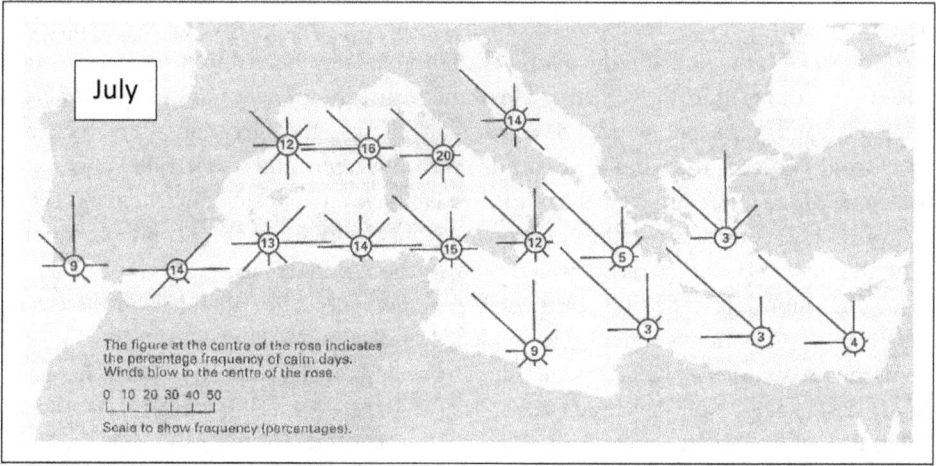

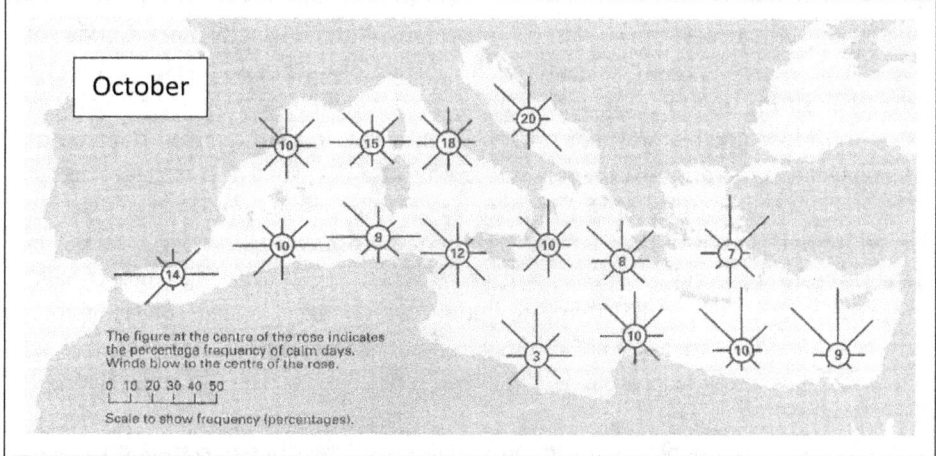

Figure 8.1 Wind Roses for April, July, and October. Used with permission of Rod Heikell, *Mediterranean Cruising Handbook*, Imray, pp. 110–11.

(into the wind). To successfully proceed in each scenario requires three different technological developments.

To sail with the wind is simple. Consider a dried leaf floating on a pond: it will go in whatever direction the wind blows, but only in that direction. If the wind blows from the north, the leaf will go south. If the wind blows from the east, the leaf will go to the west. Flat-bottomed vessels with large square-rigged sails, as seen in early Egyptian tomb carvings, successfully sailed with the wind. Large Roman grain ships were successors to this design tradition.

To sail across the wind requires the introduction of an off-setting force. Consider a watermelon seed sitting on a plate. If flicked with a finger it goes in the direction it was hit. But, if the seed is squeezed between the thumb and forefinger, it will squirt out more-or-less perpendicular to the two forces applied. A wind-powered craft works on this principle. It needs opposing forces to move in a direction other than directly downwind. One of these forces is active – the wind; the other is resistive – the water. On a sail-powered craft, the force of the wind is caught by the sail. The resistive force is applied by the keel beneath the hull and the part of the hull that is immersed in the water. The two forces are in opposition, thus creating a forward-thrust component.[12] If we have sufficient resistance and sufficient wind power, we can change the direction of travel from downwind to across the wind. Evidence from iconography and shipwrecks suggests an understanding gradually developed of the need to have an opposing force to make a craft go in a direction other than in the direction the wind blew. Early in the second millennium BCE, the first evidence of sail-powered craft in the Mediterranean is seen on Minoan seals. The smooth rounded hull shapes of these depictions are notable.[13] In the Greek Classical period, the iconographic evidence indicates keelless flatter hull shapes predominated.[14] By the late first millennium BCE, shipwreck evidence shows a change in vessel design with well-developed keels. The Madrague de Giens wreck near Toulon dated to mid-first century BCE had a keel with a depth of about one metre. The floor timbers turn deeply into a keel sump.[15] By the Roman Imperial period, when evidence of keels and deeper hulls is abundant, the sailing capabilities of ships had been considerably enhanced. Roman period iconography shows distinctly more rounded hull shapes with more wetted area – meaning the portion of the hull immersed in the water rather than sitting on top of the water – all of which would have provided greater lateral resistance. Most notable are depictions of a Roman merchantman on the side of a sarcophagus from Sidon in Lebanon and graffiti of a deep-hulled merchantman from Pompeii.[16] Representations of ships preserved on funerary monuments show an ever-deepening hull design during the Imperial period.[17] Some preserved frames and hull planking from a second or third century CE Roman wreck near Marseilles suggest a rather steep-sided, deep hull.[18] Two Late Antique wrecks from Yassiada, one from fourth century CE and the other seventh century CE, show deep-draft, full-keel boats, designs that would have provided a great deal of lateral resistance marking the full trajectory of development.[19]

The third condition, being able to sail into the wind, requires a vessel and rig design that in effect causes the wind to bend around the ship, thereby creating a high-pressure and a low-pressure side just as an airplane's wing does. The ship effectively moves from the high-pressure, on the lee side of the sail where the bent wind flow reattaches, into the low-pressure zone created by the bending of the wind upwind of the rig.[20] Ancient square or rectangular sail shape was modified by adjusting the sail shape to enhance its wind bending capability.[21] Brails are a series of ropes that run from the yardarm (or boom) on top of the sail around the foot of the sail and back up to the top that, when cinched up, allow a broad sail to be furled. Brailing a sail is a very ancient practice as seen in Egyptian carvings and Minoan iconography from Thera, both dated to the second millennium BCE. Adjusting the brails asymmetrically can alter the sail shape to suit various wind conditions allowing a square sail to be turned into a triangular sail by raising some of the brails while leaving others loosened.[22] Achilles Tatius (3.1.1-2), writing in the second century CE, described sailors adjusting the brails to create a smaller triangular shape during a fierce squall.[23] Technical data on the lift coefficient generated by single square-rigged sails is sparse, but what we have indicates an effective lift coefficient net of drag of under 2.0. The lift coefficient is a measure of the high- and low-pressure zones created by a close-hauled craft. The higher the coefficient, the greater the ability to sail into the wind. Tests on schooner rigged (meaning fore and aft sails) craft have a lift coefficient of over 4.0 whereas a three-masted, square-rigged barque was only 1.5.[24]

A subsequent development, the lateen sail, has traditionally been given considerable credit for improving windward sailing ability.[25] The lateen rig is a more fore and aft design and would seem to assist sailing into the wind, especially on the tack where the mast did not compromise the sail shape.[26] Whitewright has argued persuasively against the traditional view and concludes that the windward sailing performance of the lateen and settee rigs were generally equivalent to square sail rigs in windward ability.[27] When the lateen rig entered the Mediterranean is a matter of debate.[28] The traditional view is that the lateen rig arrived in the Mediterranean in the early seventh century CE with the Arab conquests. Whitewright argues that iconography of rigging elements from a graffito of a ship found in Corinth dated to the fifth or sixth century CE and a mosaic from Kelenderis in Southern Turkey showing a settee rig dated to the late fifth or early sixth century CE suggests a pre-Arab date is more appropriate.[29]

With the implementation of a fore and aft rig design and deeper keels at some point in Late Antiquity, the full suite of commercial trading ship design advances developed in the ancient world can be observed.[30] It must be noted that the technological developments are cumulative. A lateen rig on a flat-bottomed hull would still be blown sideways. It was the understanding of the need for resistive force created by the keel that changes the physics. No matter the sail shape, if the hull form is unchanged, one would still just blow sideways – the rig design would be irrelevant.[31]

An appreciation for a sailing vessel's speed potential is a necessary component of this discussion. Maximum speed for a displacement hull is a function of its waterline length. This can be expressed in the formula $HS = 1.34 \times \sqrt{LWL}$: Hull Speed (HS) in knots (nautical miles per hour) equals 1.34 multiplied by the square root of the water line length (LWL), expressed in feet. The governing principle is the distance a vessel moves between the bow wave and the stern wave the vessel creates as it moves through the water.³² A vessel with a 50-foot waterline length can travel at a theoretical speed of 9.48 knots (9.48 = 1.34 × √50). Speed over the ground can be enhanced when the water the ship is sailing though is moving as well, either in the form of wind-driven waves or currents. A sail-powered, keeled vessel can sail at full theoretical hull speed towards a destination that is downwind or across the wind from it. A sail-powered vessel cannot sail directly into the wind, but rather must move at an acute angle towards it.³³ A modern fore-and-aft rigged-sailing vessel with a modern hydrodynamic keel design can sail at about a 45° angle to the true wind direction, net of leeway. As an example, to sail towards a destination due north, 000° or 360°, a sail-powered vessel must sail a course of 45° to a latitude half-way to its destination, then tack (bring the wind to the other side) and sail a course of 315° for the second half of the latitude to be gained (see Figure 8.2).

The ramifications for time and distance relative to wind direction are significant. Our theoretical 50-foot water-line-length vessel traveling downwind or across the wind could make a 50-nautical-mile journey in five-and-a-half hours if it could sail at full theoretical hull speed. But if the journey was upwind, for a modern design, the 50-mile trip would take seven-and-a-half hours as it would need to sail two legs of 35.35 nautical miles each, at an angle of 45° to the wind, a total of 71 nautical miles (hereafter nm).³⁴ The reality would be an even longer voyage as the vessel now has to work back into the wind-driven waves rather than going with the wave pattern when sailing downwind. Remember the angle of 45° is for a modern fore-and-aft rigged-sailing vessel. The angle to the wind at which ancient square-rigged ships could make progress to weather is discussed below.

The 'into the wind' versus the 'with the wind' dichotomy is fundamental to the analysis of networks of communication. It might be helpful to consider an analogy. Consider the case of paddling a boat in a river. If one could paddle at a rate of three knots in still water, and the river flowed at a rate of two knots, the speed one could paddle moving with the current is the sum of 3 plus 2, equal to 5 knots. Moving ten nautical miles downstream would take two hours. To paddle upstream, the numbers flip, and it is 3 knot speed of paddling minus 2 knots of current for a net rate of just 1 knot. To paddle ten miles upstream takes ten hours.

Safadi and Sturt (2019) have attempted to capture the dichotomy of sailing with the wind and into the wind in an interesting cartography project.³⁵ Much like a topographical map attempts to add a vertical dimension to a spatial map of distances by the use of contour lines of elevation, or a weather map that shows isobars to mark atmospheric pressure gradients, they have added the third dimension of sailing time to an otherwise two-dimensional spatial map. Sailing times upwind are represented by widely spaced lines denoting slow progress and downwind destinations by closer lines suggesting faster transits. The resultant cartogram of the Eastern Mediterranean shows how closely ports were connected by sailing conditions (or not) and how those degrees of connection changed with seasonal weather patterns. Imbedded in the analysis are assumptions on the speed and angle at which vessels could sail into and with the wind.³⁶

Recent scholarship has added much to our understanding of windward sailing performance of square-rigged ancient ships. Gal, Saaroni, and Cvikel explored sailing routes in the Eastern Mediterranean between Egypt, Cyprus and various ports in the

Levant through extensive modelling of weather and sea state conditions to project crossing routes and voyage durations.[37] These observations were cross-referenced with experimental archaeology of voyages undertaken by the *Ma'agan Mikhael II* replica ship. Whitewright has drawn on experimental archaeology as well as ancient literary accounts of voyage durations and conditions across the broader Mediterranean.[38] Palmer considered a wide range of vessel experiments of various rigs and from a variety of areas and periods, not just the ancient Mediterranean.[39] The common goal of these investigations was to develop an understanding of how ships could perform on various points of sail relative to wind direction towards an objective, a rate denoted as VMG, velocity made good (towards that objective). The conclusions of these studies are broadly uniform in coming to an understanding that ancient square-rigged ships sailed very well across the wind and with the wind but could make minimal progress into the wind. Whitewright concluded that in optimal conditions, a square-rigged ship could sail at best 60–65° to the true wind direction and make a maximum VMG of about 2 knots.[40] Sailing off the wind, either reaching or running, he suggests an average speed of 4–6 knots and a maximum of 10–12 knots. Whitewright argues in calculating Red Sea voyage times that steady, if slow, progress in typical wind conditions towards upwind destinations could be made.[41] Gal et al. suggest that progress into the wind is compromised by the leeway (drift) a ship makes while sailing close hauled which they calculate as 10–15°, a view shared by Palmer.[42] Gal et al. suggest an apparent wind angle of 68° plus leeway of 15° results in an effective angle of sail relative to true wind direction of 83°. This is in optimal conditions. Experimental tests using a replica Hanseatic cog showed the vessel could make good a modest +0.18 knots upwind in light winds and flat seas but actually lost distance to weather and moved backwards in strong winds and waves.[43] Similarly, for the *Ma'agan Mikhael II*, once wave heights reached just 0.3 m, positive VMG to windward was no longer achievable. Leeway in choppy seas increased up to 25 per cent and tacking angles were 190–200°.[44]

The effective wide sailing angle including leeway of about 80° off the true wind makes a directly upwind destination hard to achieve. Tacking at such wide angles makes beating towards an upwind destination very difficult. To move two nautical miles directly into the direction the wind was coming from, a ship would have to sail two legs, one out and then one tacking back of 5.5 nm each, total 11 nm sailing distance to advance the 2 nm to weather in an hour to achieve 2 knots VMG. If the angle of sail into the wind could be improved by five degrees to 75°, the two legs would be reduced to 3.67 nm each, total 7.34 nm.[45] Neither scenario is very likely as the speed the vessel would have to sail at is too great to cover the required distance. I suggest that the proposed VMG to weather calculations are more in keeping with an ancient vessel's ability to sail *across* the wind on a long reach rather than *into* the wind. Wainwright's research that a square-rigged ship of the Imperial Roman period with a suitable keel could make 2 knots VMG to weather sailing slightly above perpendicular is plausible and supported by experimental archaeology, especially the *Kyrenia II* discussed below.[46] This is a close reach, not sailing close hauled into the wind (see Figures 8.2 and 8.3).[47] Palmer observed that sea state and the condition of the ship's hull fouling were important factors in upwind progress. Large waves and an unclean hull significantly impeded a sail-powered ship's progress to weather.[48]

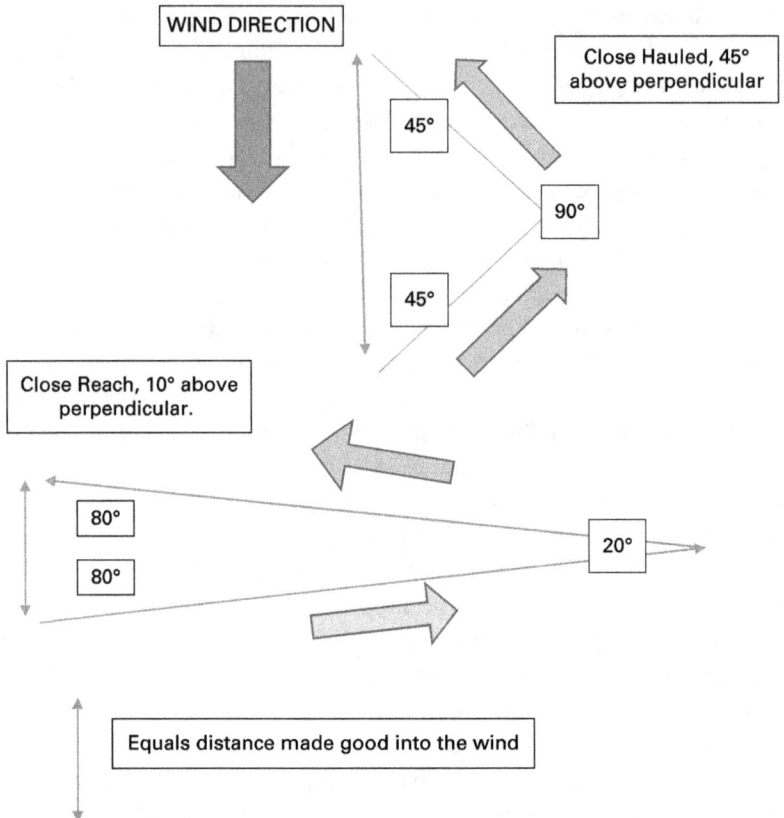

Figure 8.2 Close hauled and close reach sailing angles.

To put the distinction between close hauled and close reaching into context, consider a journey from Northern Paros' Bay of Naoussa, to Delos. Delos is 15 nm due north of Paros, directly into the wind. Under the normal July wind conditions, the wind blows from the north or northwest 70 per cent of the month.[49] In order to sail to Delos in the summer, the achievable course would be to sail to Kythnos, on a day when the wind was from due north, on a heading of 280° true (passing south of Syros) for 39 nm, then sail from Kythnos to Delos on an average heading of 84° true (passing north of Syros) on a day the wind backed to the northwest for a distance of 40 nm.[50] A total of 79 nm sailed to move north 15 nm. Practically speaking, in the summer months, Delos is much further from Paros than the spatial distance marked on a chart would suggest due to the prevailing wind direction and windward sailing abilities of ships of the period.[51] We will return to this theme when we discuss networks of communication and models below.

Sailing into the wind in square-rigged ships did not become any easier in the following centuries. Captain William Bligh of the *HMS Bounty* had been assigned the task of sailing to the South Pacific to obtain breadfruit trees. Bligh was late getting away, so

Wind direction from top towards bottom
Dark = no go zone, Light = maybe, Grey = good sailing

Figure 8.3 Diagram of sailing angles relative to wind direction.

rather than taking the traditional downwind route east around Africa, which was longer but went with the wind and waves, he chose to go west – into the wind and waves off Cape Horn at the bottom of South America. The *Bounty* tried to get around Cape Horn from 2 April to 17 April 1788, 15 days, going tack on tack getting constantly pummelled by wind and waves. Eventually, Bligh relented, writing in his log that 'the Sea has beaten us', and they headed east, giving up trying to move west into the prevailing wind and waves.[52] Rice Holmes (1909), writing near the end of the age of sail, after consultation with a retired captain of a square-rigged cargo ship, argued that seven points off the wind was the sailing angle a single-sail square-rigged ancient ship could achieve.[53] Seven points is 78.75° off the wind, just 11.25° above perpendicular.

This author suggests that square-sailed ancient sailing ships could not make steady progress sailing a series of short tacks into the wind. In reality, no sailor would take their ship out into a contrary wind hoping to beat their way upwind for days on end to reach an upwind destination, rather they would stay in port, wait for the wind direction to change and make sail with all haste under favourable conditions. Whitewright reached a similar conclusion: 'The practice of waiting for a suitable wind-direction must have been the norm'.[54] If the wind became adverse whilst in route, the sailor would seek temporary harbour in an interim port and wait once again for favourable conditions. Progress into the prevailing wind would come in short chunks or bursts when conditions allowed. Progress was not steady but was rather sporadic. The concept of an 'average' speed is not applicable in this interpretation, movement comes in chunks when conditions permit movement in the direction one wishes to go, not as a constant.

Two letters from Cicero to Atticus further demonstrate this practice of moving against the wind in chunks. Cicero was traveling from Rhodes to Athens, a northwest-bound transit. Cicero had to book two separate voyages to accomplish his journey. The first leg was to slowly travel north up the Asia Minor shore to Ephesus, waiting at various islands for favourable winds along the way. In Ephesus he changed ships, then sailed west to Piraeus. From the dates of his letters we know it took 15 days to make the passage from Ephesus to Piraeus a distance of 360 km, an average of 25 km per day, slower than walking, suggesting that on some of the days the vessel remained in port.[55] The total journey took about one month. The modern reconstruction *Kyrenia II*, modelled after a fourth century BCE shipwreck found off Kyrenia, Cyprus, travelled from Piraeus to Cyprus and back. The outbound leg from Piraeus to Cyprus in September 1986 was downwind. They then waited until April 1987 to make the return voyage again under downwind conditions.[56] Gal et al., modelling a voyage from Dor in the Levant to Pharos (Alexandria), shows that in August the VMG would have been 0.6 knots with an average voyage duration of 19 days over a sailed distance 3.1 times the direct track. In October, the same voyage would have achieved a VMG of 1.7 knots, taken on average 6.4 days and been nearly a straight-line course sailing 1.3 times the direct distance.[57] In the example of sailing from Paros to Delos given above, the alternative strategy would be to move from Paros to Delos in either April, when the wind blows from the south 15 per cent of the month, or in October when the wind blows from the south 12 per cent of the month. In a southerly wind, Delos is an easy two- and-a-half-hour sail away.

A close examination of the wind roses presented above show that the Mediterranean winds are indeed variable in direction. In the Eastern Mediterranean, northwest winds dominate the summer months but are variable in direction in the spring and fall shoulder seasons. In the Western Mediterranean, winds clock from all around the compass throughout the year.[58] These weather patterns suggest the strategy of waiting for opportune weather conditions rather than attempting to sail against the wind would be efficacious. Beresford argued that ancient sailing was more a year-round practice than is traditionally thought and extended into seasons when winds blew in directions opposite the summer wind patterns.[59]

The wind roses give us percentage of the total days per month the wind blew from a particular heading. It does not tell us the number of consecutive days the wind blew from that direction. Applying this observation to a potential voyage, let us examine the route from Tyre on the Levantine coast to Piraeus during the month of April, a generally propitious time to undertake such a voyage, breaking it up into possible chunks or bursts of movement. For this analysis, assume a speed of six knots sailing downwind over a 24-hour period for a daily run of 144 nm.[60] If we had a favourable southerly, south-easterly, easterly, or north-easterly wind, the combination of which should be present 43 per cent of the month, we could sail from Tyre to Cyprus in one day, 133 nm. If the wind remained favourable, Cyprus to Rhodes is two days further away, a hop of 260 nm, with a shorter stop on the south coast of Anatolia available at 160 nm if necessary. From Rhodes to the central Cyclades is another 24-hour sail of 147 nm, and from there to Piraeus a one-day sail of 90 nm. Moving by chunks along this route during the 43 per cent of the time the wind blew from a favourable position while remaining in port for the 37 per cent of the month when the wind blew in opposition, or the six days, 20 per cent of calm, seems like a prudent sailing plan, more efficacious than heading out into a known contrary wind and making virtually no progress towards the desired goal. Predicting the duration, the wind would blow from the desired position, not turn foul and would be a product of the seasoned knowledge of the sailors based on experience. Human agency is a significant factor in the routing and timing of movement throughout all historical periods. The corollary of this route would be the return journey from Piraeus to Tyre, a probable downwind run from May through September that could be done in one continuous passage. From the wind rose data, in July it would be from a favourable direction, i.e. suited for downwind or broad reach sailing 96 per cent of the time with only three days of calm during the month (see Figure 8.1).

Networks

The suggested interpretation of sailing practices has profound ramifications for our understanding of how networks of communication were pursued. Damian Robinson's and Andrew Wilson's edited volume *Maritime Archaeology and Ancient Trade in the Mediterranean,* contained many erudite pieces about aspects of marine voyaging including examining the extant literary evidence of institutional developments in terms of shipping contracts, ship construction loans, laws and regulations regarding maritime commerce as well as the archaeology of ships and harbours.[61] In general, the authors developed a well-documented thesis that direct sailing was the norm from Classical times through the Hellenistic and well into the Roman Imperial period. Pascal Arnaud's chapter 'Ancient sailing routes and trade patterns: the human factors' suggested that, by Late Antiquity, the pattern of direct sailing had changed to shorter, multi-stop voyages in part due to changing social conditions.[62] The analysis focuses on the interrelationship between maritime trade and politics. The short hop 'tramping or cabotage' model describes how ships traded goods as they moved along, perhaps in an organized manner, and perhaps *ad hoc*. This contrasts with straight-line, long-distance trade between known markets adhering to regulations and contracts.[63] Both models have implications for network affiliations, one suggesting tight local networks and the other long-distance networks with more formalized patterns of contact. Generally, the *ad hoc* tramping pattern is considered as both an Iron Age precursor and a Late Antiquity successor to the organized long-distance trade that has been regarded the norm from Classical Greek through to Roman Imperial times.[64]

In a persuasive article, Candace Rice examined trade and sailing patterns based on a comprehensive analysis of shipwreck evidence primarily from the Roman Imperial period.[65] Her analysis provided archaeological evidence that both tramping and direct sailing practices were utilized.

Archaeological evidence of tramping is found in the cargo assortment of several shipwrecks. The Late Bronze Age Uluburun cargo from the south coast of Asia Minor had a very mixed cargo of raw copper, tin and other items.[66] A first-century CE shipwreck off the mouth of the Rhone and another off Elba had mixed cargoes of wine amphorae with Cretan wine on the bottom of the hold and later loaded amphorae from Ibiza (Ebusos) on top.[67] Other wrecks with similar assortments suggest that multiple-stop sailing was not unusual. Two wrecks on the Skerki Bank, about 80 kilometres northwest of Sicily in the Tyrrhenian Sea, had mixed cargoes from multiple destinations. Wreck F loaded building stone sourced from Aswan in Egypt on the bottom of the hold, loaded on top of the stone cargo were Italian and Spanish wine amphorae, Spanish *garum*, and Carthaginian coarseware in commercial volumes. The cargo loading suggests the ship moved from east to west, tramping along the North African coast. Wreck B had wine from Egypt, Crete, Campania, and oil from Tripolitania. Both wrecks date to late-first century CE.[68]

Direct sailing is recorded in formalized trade practices, and this evidence extends across all periods. Bottomry loans provided to ship owners by lenders strictly stipulated what cargoes could be loaded, what the sailing routes were to be and their destinations. Legal cases from the fourth century BCE into Late Antiquity were brought by holders of bottomry loans that stipulated sailing routes in the loans, against defendants accused of not adhering to the loan agreements.[69] The bottomry loans are probably a very convincing argument for regulated direct sailing, but these cases suggest there were numerous divergences from the prescribed practices.[70]

The best evidence of direct sailing would be Roman grain ships, specialized craft designed to haul large quantities of grain from Egypt, North Africa and elsewhere to Rome. Sadly, no physical remains of these survive to my knowledge. The Athenian practice is revealed in the corpus of Demosthenes's cases pertained to grain shipments. Athenian law required that two-thirds of the grain arriving in Piraeus had to go to Athens and no resident of Athens was permitted to ship grain or to loan money against a grain cargo going elsewhere. The Roman imperial grain trade was more nuanced and apparently imperial-controlled inventories and private citizen trades in grain were managed with an eye to maintaining steady market prices. There is no direct statutory authority for this practice though, just innuendo in Tacitus, Suetonius and Josephus of the market manipulations.[71] In the Late Antique period edicts preserved in the Theodosian and Justinian codices seem to be trying to exert imperial authority over sailing routes.[72] However, as mentioned in Demosthenes' litigations and shipping loans recorded in tablets from Murecine near Pompeii, what appears on paper and what occurred in practice may have frequently been two different things.[73]

A mixed-cargo assortment, as opposed to a uniform cargo, does not automatically equate with tramping. A third-century CE wreck from near the Balearic Islands is comprised of a mixed cargo of wine, oil and *garum* from multiple Spanish locations (Baetica, Lusitania and Africa Proconsularis). In this case, the mixed nature of the cargo suggests the ship was loaded in one port, probably Gades (Cádiz), and was destined for one port, probably Ostia, providing evidence of direct sailing from one emporium to another.[74]

An examination of port regulations provides another category of evidence of trading practices. In the Greek world access to ports was regulated, most famously perhaps was the Athenian prohibition against Megarian ships entering harbours of the Delian League (Thuc. 1.129). From Thasos in the North Aegean *c.* 250/200 BCE an inscription was found relegating certain size ships to certain harbour basins, presumably separating the smaller local vessels from the larger direct sailing ships.[75] The port of Rhodes was regulated as has come down to us in the *Vita Porphyri* 55, where a ship could enter the harbour for up to three hours to take on water, whereas for trading operations different types of access and control procedures applied. Similarly, from second century CE, port regulations of Caunus in Caria distinguished between ships making short 'in transit' stops, ships calling for trading and ships needing shelter or refitting.[76]

This regulation of trade was surely driven by the state wanting to get a portion of the profits of trade for itself. Greek records indicate there were two types of tax: first, *ellimenion* probably levied by port authorities for access to harbour facilities and services. Second, *tele emporika* was a customs duty levied both on incoming (*eisagoge*) and outgoing (*exagoge*) goods. These fees were significant – Aristotle considered these the second largest source of income for the city state.[77]

Under Roman administration, these fees and taxes were called *portoria* or *portus* and were applied both to individual provinces such as Asia and groups of provinces as a block such as the Gallic provinces. Some cities or ports were given free status or at least lesser taxes. A badly preserved document, the *Lex Portorii Asiae,* lists ports between the mouth of the Pontus and Side following the order in which a ship would sail along the coast. This seems to indicate some differential conditions between ports including cargo valuation for tax purposes and recording requirements.[78]

Conclusion

We have two well-developed models: multi-stop tramping or straight-line, one-stop, long-distance regulated trade. Based on an understanding of how ancient sail-powered craft could manoeuvre relative to wind direction, I suggest that both models are correct and worked in concert. It is the nature of how sail-powered craft work that dictates this. Simply put, because sail-powered craft cannot sail into the wind, almost *per se,* straight-line sailing is only possible on one leg of a round-trip voyage. In a continuous journey, the other leg must be multi-stop tramping. Only for specialized craft, such as the Roman grain ships, was two-way direct sailing the practice.[79] This limited the grain ships to one round-trip voyage per year as they had to wait for the winds to cycle to the correct position for downwind sailing on each leg of the journey. Whitewright argues that while deep-keeled ships with better windward sailing ability such as the *Kyrenia* were known from at least the fourth century BCE, flat-bottomed ships designed with no regard to their weatherly sailing ability continued to be built into Late Antiquity. This suggests that windward sailing ability was not that important in many cases and that the maritime routes and trade networks of antiquity had developed with this in mind.[80]

As per the evidence presented, this combination of models applied across all periods including Classical through to Imperial. When sailing on a downwind route, highly structured trade was very much the norm, between known ports under state authority or at least with state knowledge. But when working back against the wind, the point-to-point cabotage model of sailing would be more interpretive. It may not mean a completely *ad hoc* arrangement without any preplanning but more a coastal sailing pattern arranged around good anchorages, wherein one returned to known ports, with known goods for known customers on a regular basis. Changes to ship design in the Common Era, and accelerating after *c.* 200, enhanced the sailing capabilities of merchant craft and reduced the practical difference between the two models.

One last piece of archaeological evidence to consider when debating these two models is how many anchors ships carried onboard. Vessel wrecks from the third century CE on into the Byzantine period were found with numerous small iron anchors aboard. The fifth-century CE Dramont E wreck had ten onboard, and the seventh century CE Yassiada wreck had eleven. This large number of anchors has been interpreted as evidence of a changed trade pattern from direct sailing in Late Antiquity.[81] The carrying of multiple anchors, though, was not a new practice. The Late Bronze Age Uluburun wreck had at least 24 stone anchors on board, which indicates that Mediterranean sailors long appreciated the difficulty of working back into the wind and had developed practices both technologically and in trading patterns, to deal with it.[82]

The argument put forth in this chapter is that the natural conditions of wind and weather are a considerable, if not the dominant factor, in sailing routes and practices for wind-driven craft. This condition trumps human constructs that suggest otherwise. For most cargo ships, the best solution was to rely on a combination of sailing practices utilizing direct sailing when the wind was from behind and a tramping approach when working back against the prevailing wind in a series of short hops or chunks when conditions allowed. Moreover, this practice occurred across all periods and under various legislated or prescribed regulatory schemes.

Notes

1. The author would like to thank the organizers of the 2018 XXV Finnish Symposium on Late Antiquity and the editors of this volume, Emilia Mataix Ferrándiz and Antti Lampinen for this opportunity. This chapter is significantly altered from the original presentation with more emphasis on the physics of upwind sailing. The conclusions regarding networks of communication are unchanged. I would also like to thank the anonymous reviewers of this chapter for their insightful comments and information on sources that I had not consulted. Any mistakes that remain are solely my own.
2. Casson 1971: 16–22.
3. Stewart 1977: 57, 89, 107; Drucker 1965: 27–31.

4. Lewis 1994.
5. Beresford 2013: figs 2.3 a–d.
6. Murray 1987.
7. See Beresford 2013: 54–6 on Mediterranean weather.
8. Beresford 2013: 178–80 described seasonal grain ship transits.
9. Cunliffe 2008: 49–51, fig. 2.12.
10. Similar to the Southern Pacific's *El Niño* and *La Niña* oscillation cycle. See https://oceanservice.noaa.gov.
11. Cunliffe 2008: fig. 7.19; Rauh 2003 on pirates; De Souza 1999: 15–26 on Carian pirates waiting along this route.
12. MacGibbon 1982: 78–82; Marchaj 1985.
13. Casson 1971: 32–4, 38–9, figs 34–6.
14. Casson 1971: figs 80, 90, 117.
15. See Casson 1994: fig. 78 for an excellent photo of hull frames bending into a deep keel.
16. Throckmorton 1972: plate 2, fig. 11.
17. See Casson 1971: figs 142 (dated 200 CE), 143 (dated third century CE), 149 (ship at sea late third century CE).
18. Throckmorton 1972: 81, plate 5. Second or third century CE wreck now in Musée Borely.
19. Casson 1971: figs 152, 153; Johnstone 1974: 72; Development of the keel in ship design and its impact on vessel performance has generally been overlooked. Beresford (2013: 163–6) never mentioned keel design or its role in hull design in an otherwise excellent presentation on ancient sailing. Wilson 2011: 40–2 provided a good discussion on the keel and Whitewright 2011: 5–6, fig. 3 has a good diagram of diachronic keel development.
20. See Marchaj 1985; id. 2000 for full discussion on the physics of windward sailing; see Maloney 1983: 187–8 for a concise explanation of the physics involved.
21. Beresford 2013: 158–63 on sail design including lateen rigs.
22. Beresford 2013: 166 on brailing a broad sail.
23. See Casson 1971: chapter 12, n 24 on ancient authority for brailing.
24. Palmer 2009: 320–1, figs 10, 11, 12, 13, 14, on coefficient tests.
25. See Casson 1971: 243–5; Whitewright 2009: 97 for bibliography of traditional view.
26. Palmer 2009: 321.
27. Whitewright 2011: 13–14, table 10, fig. 5.
28. Whitewright 2018 for full discussion; Casson 1971: figs 180, 181 are two representations dated to third century CE of vessels he describes with lateen sails, but I suggest they could be interpreted differently; Beresford 2013: 158–63.
29. See Casson 1971: chapter 11, n. 77 for traditional view; Whitewright 2009: 98–9, 102, figs 3, 4.
30. Construction materials, techniques and building practices are a separate discussion.
31. See Palmer 2009: 314–16 on the interaction of sails and keels.
32. See article by Doane, C. 2010. 'Crunching Numbers: Hull Speed and Boat Length.' Accessed at boats.com. search term 'theoretical hull speed'. Accessed 7 November 2020.
33. Maloney 1983: 171.

34. Law of cosines see keisan.casio.com for an isosceles triangle calculator.
35. Safadi and Sturt 2019.
36. Safadi and Sturt 2019: 5–6, table 2.
37. Gal, Saaroni, and Cvikel 2021.
38. Whitewright 2008; id. 2011.
39. Palmer 2009.
40. Whitewright 2011: table 6; 2007: 43, 44, table 6.1, reached a similar conclusion in a 2007 analysis focused on voyages in the Red Sea.
41. Whitewright 2007: 85.
42. Gal et al. 2021: 3; Palmer 2009: 316–17.
43. Palmer 2009: 322–3, fig. 18.
44. Gal et al. 2021: 4, fig. 3.
45. I have not included in this calculation that a square-rigged ship cannot tack into the wind but rather must wear-ship, or gybe around, to bring the wind onto the other tack over the stern rather than the bow, a manoeuvre that loses several precious boat lengths of distance gained upwind.
46. Whitewright 2007: 84.
47. See Maloney 1983: 171–2, fig. 801 on terminology for points of sail.
48. Palmer 2009: 318–19, 325–6.
49. Taken from wind rose, fig. 8.1.
50. Distances and headings taken from DFMA Chart 54320 based on Greek chart *Kikladhes Nissoi to Kriti*.
51. But it should be noted, downwind Paros is not very far from Delos which is the condition that Safadi and Sturt 2019 were trying to demonstrate in their mapping.
52. Bligh [1792] 2005: chapter 2, log entry Monday 21, Tuesday 22; Alexander 2004.
53. Rice Holmes 1909: 27 considered the Voyage of St Paul and interviewed a captain of a square rigger, then harbour master of Dover. For refence, the compass is divided in 32 points, 11.25 degrees each.
54. Whitewright 2011: 10.
55. Cic. *Att.* 8.9; Craik 1980: 8.
56. Beresford 2013: 120–2; Katzev 1990.
57. Gal et al. 2021: 7, fig. 7.
58. Prolonged calms (and the threat of fierce mistrals coming without warning) are the challenges in the Western Mediterranean.
59. Beresford 2013: 3–7.
60. The *Kyrenia II* (14 metres in length) sailed from Piraeus to Paphos, Cyprus and back, outbound in September 1986 and returning in April 1987. Speeds were widely variable as winds were often very light, less than 3 Beaufort. Katzev 1990 produced a daily sailing log. Speeds ranged from nearly becalmed to over 12 knots during a squall lasting several hours. In reasonable sailing conditions of Beaufort 3–4, speeds were about 4.5 knots. *Kyrenia II* was able to comfortably sail on a beam reach (see run 2 from Sounion to Kythnos and run 6 Schinousa to Kos as examples). Maintaining a constant 6 knots for 24 hours, as used in this example, is admittedly a sailor's dream come true.

61. Wilson and Robinson 2011.
62. Arnaud 2011: 61, 75–6.
63. See Arnaud 2011 for a compelling analysis of the argument and presentation of the documentation.
64. Arnaud 2011: 61, 75–6; McCormick 2001: 569.
65. Rice 2016: 165–6.
66. See Pulak 2010; 2005; Bass 1991 on Uluburun wreck.
67. See Rice 2016: 180–1, 184, table 2; Heslin 2011; Marlier and Sibella 2002; Santamaria 1984 on wrecks with wine cargoes.
68. McCann et al. 2004; Rice 2016: 53–4 disagrees that Wreck B was tramping.
69. Dem. 34.37, 35.51.
70. For ancient authority on Bottomry Loans see Lysias against Diogeiton (*Or.* 23); Demosthenes against Aphobus (*Or.* 37), against Zenothemis (*Or.* 32), against Aparturius (*Or.* 33), against Phormio (*Or.* 34), against Lacritus (*Or.* 35), against Polycles (*Or.* 50), against Dionysiodorus (*Or.* 56); *PVindob.* 19792 (CE 149), *PVindob* 40.822. (mid–second century CE); Plut. *Cat. Mai.* 21.6; Cic. *Rab. Post.* 40.5; Cato, *Agr. prooem*; D. 22.2, 45.1.122.
71. Tac. *Ann.* 2.87, 6.13 on Tiberius' strategies; Suet. *Claud.* 18 on Claudius' approaches; Joseph. *BJ* 2.383, 386.
72. *CTh* 13.5.33; *CI* 4.33.4.
73. Arnaud 2011: 68, n. 73.
74. Rice 2016: 187–8; Bost et al. 1992: 200–1.
75. *IG* XII Supplement 151, no. 348 = *SEG* XVII: 417.
76. Arnaud 2011: 66–8.
77. Arist. [*Oec.*] 2.1–6; Xen. *Oec.* 3.12–13; See Rice 2016: 185–5 of import and export duties and the wide variability in rates; Arnaud 2011: 66.
78. *Lex Portorii Asiae* (Monumentum Ephesenum) *IG* 112.8; AE 1989, no. 681; Arnaud 2011: 66.
79. Garnsey et al. 1983; Rickman 1980; Casson 1971.
80. Whitewright 2018: 40, 42; id. 2011: 5–6.
81. Arnaud 2011: 63.
82. Pulak 2005: 46.

CHAPTER 9
ON THE BYZANTINE TRADITION OF *D.* 14.2.9 (MAEC. *EX LEGE RHODIA*): A NOTE CONCERNING THE EMPEROR AS RULER OF THE SEA

Valerio Massimo Minale

A Mysterious Fragment

The fragment by Volusius Maecianus preserved in the Digest's text 14.2.9 presents several problems, the first one of them being the fact that the text is written in Greek.[1] The corresponding translation of the text reads:

> Petition from Eudaimon of Nicomedia to the Emperor Antoninus: lord and Emperor Antoninus, after a shipwreck in Icaria, we were robbed by the agents who live in the Cyclades islands. Antoninus replies to Eudaimon: it is truth that I am the lord of the earth, but the law is the lord of the sea; it is necessary to obey to the sea law of the Rhodians, until when none of our laws will be in opposition. Also, the *divus* Augustus decided in this sense.

The fragment has been studied since the time of Gothofredus (sixteenth–seventeenth centuries)[2] and also questioned due to being considered as the result of an intrusive postclassical intervention.[3] It is true that the received text has been altered; an example of these corrections is the generally accepted use of Ἰκάρια instead of Ἰταλία.[4] Another modification – accepted by fewer but still a considerable number of scholars[5] – is the passage which changes the use from δημοσίων (δημόσιοι, *servi publici*)[6] to δημοσιωνῶν (δημοσιῶνοι, *publicani*). The alteration implies that the text, instead of referring to a fiscal context, evokes a connection with custom duties, more concretely with the tax of the *portorium* (applied on the basis of the fourth part of the shipment, known as the *quadragesima*).[7] As a consequence of these modifications, the text is still difficult to read.

There are several signs indicating that the fragment could be a forgery, such as the fact that it does not quote the volume from which the excerpt has been taken, not even as *liber singularis*. It is also surprising that the *inscriptio* mentions both the *nomen* and *cognomen Volusius Maecianus*, when in other texts this jurist is always referred to as *Maecianus*. In addition, the *Index Florentinus* lacks a title on the *Lex Rhodia* ascribed to Maecianus, and moreover, βασιλεύς would be a Byzantine term, therefore it would not have been used as such in the original fragment.[8] Finally, the passage may have been placed outside its original title, that is to say the Digest's title 47.9 (*De incendio, ruina, naufragio, rate, nave expugnata*).⁹ This hypothesis is based on the fact that it would represent better a *direptio ex naufragio* than a *iactus* (or ἐκβολή), since this last institution ruled the practice of jettison – throwing goods overboard to lighten the ship in case of danger[10] – which, in turn, caused a sort of collective contribution to help the owners (συμβολή) of the cargo thrown from other owners whose cargo was not affected by the jettisoning.[11]

Furthermore, the anomalous use of the formula *ex lege* instead of *de lege* has persuaded some scholars to think that the fragment came from a version, obviously in Greek, of an extract from a work belonging to the Antonine jurist Maecianus.[12] Something similar can be appreciated in D. 43.10.1 (*Sing. De cura urb.*, L. 28), in which the beginning of the text uses the preposition ἐκ and the genitive related with an ἀστυνομικὸς μονόβιβλος of Papinian.[13]

However, against those who have even refused Maecianus' authorship[14] it must be said that the jurist held the role of *praefectus annonae* and then of *praefectus Aegypti* from 13 February 161 CE for several months and even perhaps for one whole year.[15] Besides, Maecianus' involvement in patronage activities tied him to some relevant guilds. Based on his relationship with the guilds, some scholars have pointed out that the law quoted in the fragment D. 14.2.9 could have been the statute of one of those guilds operating in the commercial harbour of Ostia.[16] Such a connection with the world of the seaborne trade could have emphasized the relationship of the jurist with maritime practices and their regulations.

The most relevant questions about the text are twofold: on the one hand, the real meaning of the words κύριος and νόμος, and on the other hand, the opposition between κόσμος and θάλασσα.[17] Otherwise, the reference to Augustus could be a simple addition, although we have to admit that the use of the verb κρίνω gives the impression of an authentic resolution.[18] Apart from the event itself, we are faced with a complex mechanism that submitted the issue to be solved to an already assumed foreign customary regulation (the *Lex Rhodia*) into the Roman legal system of the sea if other imperial constitutions were not prescribing something else.

The request for justice is represented by the noun ἀξίωσις (from the verb ἀξιόω),[19] was written by Eudaimon of Nicomedia, and addressed to an emperor bearing the name Antoninus – almost certainly Antoninus Pius.[20] In the petition, Eudaimon described how during a shipwreck some men stole his cargo, more or less violently based on the meaning of the verb διαρπάξω, a derivation of the noun ἁρπαγή, referring to 'part of the shipment'. However, the emperor's answer to Eudaimon is rather enigmatic. Indeed, in response to the demand of Eudaimon – who probably was the ship's owner – the emperor affirms his status as the κύριος and so lord (in the double sense of governor and judge) of the world, while the νόμος would equally be a lord, but of the sea.

Thus, if the main problem is to assign the right value to νόμος, it is relevant to note that it is used in a way that is firmly connected with the relationship existing between the law ruling the sea and the figure of the ruling emperor, who is κύριος τοῦ κόσμου, literally, again, 'lord of the world'. The term appears in the fragment 14.2.9 three times, but every time with a different connotation, first as customary law, then invoking the *Lex Rhodia* and finally, as referring to the Roman legal system. The term κύριος recalls quite an unequivocal concept which is used fairly recurrently in the Antonine cultural environment,[21] while the words νόμος and κόσμος are mentioned in other settings in which the respective meanings of the terms are less easily recognizable. The first word, νόμος, can either refer to the customary sea law or to local legislation;[22] these are two types of rulings with diverging nature, even though they are both destined to acquire effectiveness through an imperial sanction.[23] The second term, κόσμος, embodies the order of the Roman legal system,[24] which is based on the principle that every norm should automatically be submitted to the authority of the emperor himself, who is identified as the lord of the world but not as a tyrant.

In any case, the main framework for solving Eudaimon's issue would be provided by the incorporation, or at least acceptance[25] – maybe through a mechanism gradually promoted by the edict of the praetor[26] – of a foreign law of customary origin, attributable to the Hellenistic period and connected only with the island of Rhodes, but assimilated in the Roman tradition to the regulation of the *iactus* (jettison).[27] In this view, the Emperor Antoninus Pius embodies the lawgiver, and his answer to Eudaimon provides a precise indication of the ideological relation between his will and the customary sea law, known and respected by everybody[28] and historically represented by the *Lex Rhodia* (*de iactu*).[29] Such a relation would develop through the reception of an alternative rule, while always respecting the limit set up by what was established in the laws of the Romans. The latter is mirrored by the mention to Augustus,[30] founder of traditions, who would have decided likewise; here we would like to stress again the use of the verb κρίνω based on the agreement between Romans and Rhodians.[31]

If we consider the fragment from *D*.14.2.9 as original, it is possible to see in the text an opposition of elements mirrored in the use of κόσμος and θάλασσα (without ignoring the presence of μὲν and δὲ). Understood in a rhetorical sense, these terms could assume an additional value and even means the contrast between structures organized by humans and the primordial chaos of the forces of nature, represented by storm waves and sea abysses.[32]

The Byzantine Tradition of *D*. 14.2.9 (Maec. *Ex Lege Rhodia*)

Considering the preceding observations, I propose to study the Byzantine tradition of the fragment *D*. 14.2.9 to offer some further reflections. The first echo of the fragment appears in *Basilika* 53.1.1, belonging to the elaboration of the Justinian's compilation made by the *antecessores* and the *scholastikoí*:

> Evidently, the matters concerning seafaring are ruled by the Rhodian sea law, unless any other law contradicts its matters.

It is immediately noticeable that this short sentence is clearly a copy of the last part of Maecianus' passage, omitting the reference to Augustus. Its position in the opening of the fifty-third book of the *Basilika*[33] is of great importance and provides evidence that the Byzantines were interested in extrapolating the fragment beyond its original placement in a title generally devoted to the *Lex Rhodia de iactu*, a sort of universal norm intended to rule everything that would happen at sea when not conflicting with Roman law.

Unfortunately, because the book collecting *D.* 14.2 in its first and third title has been reconstructed, it has reached us without any *scholia* which could have furnished useful pieces of information. It should be enough to indicate that the *Nomos Rhodion Nautikos*, which we will mention later in this contribution, contained several fragments (not the Maecianus' law) stemming from *D.* 14.2. The fragment 14.2.9 is also placed in *B.* 53.8 of the Heimbach edition, even if the fragment is better understood as a simple appendix in the Groningen edition.[34]

Following the tradition of 14.2.9 through these examples may give the impression that the story of Eudaimon was useless and thus had disappeared completely from the written record. We would like to focus now on the *Synopsis Minor* N.15, which strongly develops the original sentence from 14.2.9:

> All things concerning seafaring and what is decided at sea are judged according to the Rhodian law and solved through the rules of the Rhodians, unless there is another contradicting law. Sure enough, the [Rhodian laws] are much older than the other maritime laws, and they are suitable for the majority of the cases and they seem as perfect for the most important events. But then later some men maliciously used the laws of the Rhodians, and their distortion of the facts caused that necessarily the new norms stood out as a consequence, by filling up the lack of the old laws and by transforming them into a more organised and remarkable structure, and there should be no doubt that such rules were highly estimated by the emperors who levied justice. When a new norm is not conflicting with the ancient law of the Rhodians, the maritime matters must be decided by it; but when other norms contradict the Rhodian sea-law, then the Rhodian law will not be used and the other norms will apply.

The fragment's most important phrase for our argument here is 'then later some men maliciously used the laws of the Rhodians, and their distortion of the facts caused that necessarily the new norms stood out as a consequence' which tries to show the attempt of a renovation of the ancient tradition by a new legal system.

The *Synopsis Minor* (Μικρὰ Σύνοψις κατὰ στοιχεῖον) is a collection of laws dating from the end of the thirteenth century, organized following the distribution of the topics among the 24 letters of the Greek alphabet.[35] We do not know the concrete dating of the compilation, even if it certainly appeared before Constantine Harmenopoulos' *Hexabiblos*, which was published in 1345.[36] However, we know that three-quarters of the *Synopsis Minor* are composed by sources from the Michael Attaleiates' *Ponema Nomikon* (1072–1073)[37] and the *Synopsis Maior* (Μεγάλη Σύνοψις τῶν Βασιλικῶν) (second half of the tenth century).[38] Both works constitute summaries based on the *Basilika*. The remaining quarter from the *Synopsis Minor*, by contrast, is composed of sources taken from still-unknown origins.[39] Theodosios Zygomalas, at the end of the sixteenth century, paraphrased the collection in *dimodikí*, the vernacular Greek language.[40] In addition, the same paraphrasis, together with another one of Harmenopoulos' *Hexabiblos*, has been found in a manuscript entrusted at the National Library of Moscow.[41]

Nevertheless, the Attaleiates' *Ponema*, a work dedicated to Michael VII Doukas and characterized by a proem which is a sort of idealized history of the Roman law, preserves one sentence at the beginning of the forty-eighth title which is almost identical to *B*. 53.1.1:

> Of course, the matters concerning seafaring are ruled by the Rhodian sea law, unless any other law contradicts its matters.

On the other hand, the N.1 (Περὶ ναυτικῶν) of the *Synopsis Maior* does not reflect such sentence. It is quite certain that the N.15 of the *Synopsis Minor* was amended by an anonymous compiler who compared its parallelisms with Attaleiates' *Ponema*. The author seems to have a particular tendency for such a way of working,[42] suitable for the aim of creating a juridical lexicon.[43] In any case, the collection reached us without the proem and therefore it is impossible to propose further conjectures.

The sentence 'and they are suitable for the majority of the cases and they seem as perfect for the most important events' notes that the laws of the Rhodians were good for most issues, while in some cases they lacked a punishment (from ἐπιπλήσσω). In this point, the text includes an explanation indicating the historical reasons – later some men maliciously used the laws of the Rhodians – which would allow that the *Lex Rhodia* could apply instead of the imperial constitutions (and there should be no doubt that such rules were highly estimated by the emperors who levied justice). In this way, new laws could replace old customs by transforming them into a more organized structure. In the end, the idea seen in Maecianus' fragment comes up in connection with the prescription that the *Lex Rhodia* would be applied only if it does not collide with another Roman law ('when a new norm is not conflicting with the ancient law of the Rhodians, the maritime matters must be decided by it; but when other norms contradict the Rhodian sea-law, then the Rhodian law will not be used and the other norms will apply').

The history of how this long text was published and edited helps to contextualize its relationship with *D*. 14.2.9. It was Georg Tanner (*c*. 1520–*c*. 1580) – Francois Badouin's pupil in Bruges, who studied the Greek text of the *Novellae*[44] and taught them in his courses in Vienna[45] – who for the first time envisioned an edition of the *Synopsis Minor*, even if he was unable to bring this project to completion.[46] In the end it was Simon Schard (1535–1573) who put together an edition of the *Nomos Rhodion Nautikos* (*De varia temporum in iure civili observatione* ..., *item leges Rhodiorum navales* ..., Basileae, per Ioannem Oporinum, 1561). The N. 15 (from page 266 onwards), which was also compiled in the fragment 135r of Vindobonensis iur. gr. 17, is the oldest manuscript referring to this set of rules,[47] even if it is mutilated in some parts (and in particular, between f. 134v and f. 135r, where there is the word in red ink δοκίμιον, lack two pages), and also inserts the title Περὶ τῶν νόμων ῥοδίων ναυτικῶν, ἐκ βιβλίου τινὸς νομίμου τοῦ Δοκίμου (the Rhodian-sea-law, including diverse comments on civil laws). Johannes

Leunclavius also included the same fragment 14.2.9 in the title devoted to the *Lex Rhodia*, always at the end of the section devoted to the sea law in the second volume of *Jus Graeco-Romanum* (Francofurti, impensis heredum Petri Filcheri, 1596), and only using the variation Δοκιμίου in page 278. Later on, in 1828, Jean-Marie Pardessus, with the help of Georgios Alexander Rhallis, composed in Paris a complete edition in which the N.15 was located in the *Collection des lois maritimes antérieures au XVIII siècle* (vol. I).[48] Their edition collated two manuscripts from Paris (Par. gr. 1382 and 1387) and one from the Vatican (Vaticanus Pii II 39), which was made available thanks to the intervention of the cardinal Angelo Mai. The *editio princeps* was finally composed by Karl Eduard Zachariae von Lingenthal in the year 1856 in Leipzig, and afterwards reproduced by the brothers Panagiotis and Dimitris Zepos in Athens in 1931. The first edition included the *Synopsis Minor* from 1869, as well as Vindobonensis iur. gr. 17, which was considered by von Lingenthal the ancestor of the alpha family, in the tradition of the *Synopis Minor*. In his edition, von Lingenthal also labelled the fragment with the number 14.[49] The latter may seem like a touch of irony, adding up to a rather intricate sequence of philological events.

After all the intricacies that can be found in the tradition of *D.* 14.2.9, we finally address the fragment 2.11.1 from the *Hexabiblos* (1344–45):

> All the nautical issues and those which are connected to the sea must be decided and judged following the *Lex Rhodia* and that justice must be administered through those instructions, in case there is not another law contradicting these belonging to the Rhodians: as a matter of fact, the laws of the Rhodians are the oldest among the other maritime legislations.

After the word παλαιγενέστεροι, the rest of the passage is (identical to that) preserved in the *Synopsis Minor* N.15, and only copied by Constantine Harmenopoulos. After all, we know that the jurist from Thessaloniki used extensively the collection labelled as *Synopsis Minor*. This compilation could have been written, according to an idea of Andreas Schmink, by the local *dikaiophylax* Georgos Fovinos, called ἐπιστήμων μετρητής, who lived between the thirteenth and fourteenth centuries.[50] This sentence was preserved in the second book of the *Hexabiblos* under the title Περὶ ναυτικῶν, and offers several points of interest. On the one hand, there is the use of the verbs κρίνω, τέμνω and δικάζω that everyone has linked to a particular aspect of a solution provided for a juridical question.[51] On the other hand, there is the issue about the meaning attributed to the *Lex Rhodia* itself. It is first presented in the singular, then in the plural, maybe referring to the *Nomos Rhodion Nautikos* and to the single fragments composing it, while in the end the laws of the Rhodians (οἱ τῶν Ῥοδίων νόμοι) are defined as the oldest among the remaining sea legislations (τῶν ἄλλων ναυτικῶν νόμων παλαιγενέστεροι). This point is directly connected with the previous subordinate clause which, in turn, is introduced by the temporal preposition ὅταν, explaining the principle of the 'residual' use of the *Lex Rhodia*, that is to say that it could apply only when nothing else contradicts it.

Still, all these elements do not solve the doubts concerning the customary nature attributed to the *Lex Rhodia*. That qualification was partly validated by the adjective παλαι(ο)γενής in its superlative form, because the *Nomos Rhodion Nautikos* collected both old common uses and passages coming from the classical jurisprudence and taken from the *Digesta*, which, in turn, was ratified by imperial law. More precisely, it is possible that when the Byzantines evoked the law of the Rhodians in their texts, they were actually referring to the *Nomos Rhodion Nautikos* and not to the *Lex Rhodia de iactu*. Indeed, the nature of the *Nomos Rhodion* was twofold because it was composed partly of fragments coming from *D*. 14.2 (and distributed, as we have seen, between *B*. 53. 1 and 3) and partly of customary norms belonging probably to a Hellenistic background. In addition, the fragments reproducing the passages of the *Digesta* were perceived as usages universally accepted at sea and in the meantime recognized by the emperors. The latter connects with a certain legal mentality and should be connected to the transmission of the *Nomos Rhodion Nautikos* often as a simple appendix of *B*. 53 (in addition to the *Ekloge*).

However, it is generally accepted that Constantine Harmenopoulos only decided to preserve a short part of the *Synopsis Minor* N.15, the source which he used as reference. Moreover, the discussions concerning the selection of the fragments stems up from the fact that the *Hexabiblos*, which would experience a remarkable diffusion in the Slavic circles, mainly in the Balkans,[52] was also object of rich commentaries preserved in at least a couple of manuscripts.[53] However, these arguments are not enough to explain the circumstances of our fragment 14.2.9. Indeed, we need to step back and look again at the *Nomos Rhodion Nautikos*; not to the normative compilation, but to the *Prooimion*,[54] which is preserved in several manuscripts.[55]

The text is known from two versions, of which the longer could be the older one, dating to a period between the eleventh and the twelfth centuries, and therefore pulling back the date of the passage from the Macedonian dynasty to the Comnenians and the Doukai.[56] Thus, the text would have been composed in a legal culture imbued with historiographic literature by an unknown intellectual, who has been identified by Gothofredus as Michael Psellos,[57] but who more probably could have been John Xiphilinus (the younger) or Michael Attaleiates himself. The text includes the already-mentioned issue of the incorporation of the *Lex Rhodia* into the Roman sea-law. According to this view, the question asked of the emperor by sailors (ναυταί), captains (ναυκλήροι) and merchants (ἔμποροι), about receiving protection in the case of shipwreck, testifies to a collective need among a mercantile demographic: more specifically, maritime trade. Therefore, the emperor answered by referring to a law universally used in the Mediterranean Sea and consequently, decided to adopt it in Rome.[58]

Another element that should be stressed here is the list of the names presented in the source, both in the first and in the second version. In the *Recensio* I, we can find the names of Hadrian, Tiberius, Lucius (Ulpius) Trajan after a textual corruption with Lucius Verus,[59] Septimius Severus and Pertinax. The fragment then evokes Tiberius, Nero, and again Tiberius, who is sometimes mentioned in the text in contexts where the reference must be to Claudius.[60] Also mentioned are the consul Antoninus,[61] Laurus and Agrippinus; these last two were consuls themselves, but unfortunately, we do not know much about them. Finally, there are mentions of Vespasian, Trajan and Augustus. Otherwise, in the *Recensio* II we find Tiberius and Nereus – the latter apparently corresponding to a mythological figure, most probably the maritime divinity, but who in reality could be Nero. Then we read again the names of Tiberius and Antonius instead of Antoninus, the consuls Clarus instead of Laurus and Agrippinus, Vespasian and then Trajan, again Nereus/Nero, Hadrian together with the consuls Clarus and Alexander[62] and the usual mention to Tiberius Claudius.

The starting paragraph is a kind of short preface in which it is told that the *Lex Rhodia*, which is identified with the *Nomos Rhodion Nautikos* itself, would be enforced and accepted by a series of emperors, being Hadrian until Pertinax in the shorter version, while the longer and older one attributes this decision – ἐκτεθεὶς, from ἐκτίθημι – only to Tiberius Claudius. The term used is ἐθέσπισαν, from the verb θεσπίζω, originating in turn the technical term of θέσπισμα, which wavers between the older term 'prophesy' and the actual meaning 'order'. The rest of the text, which is much more difficult to understand, starts with the episode of Tiberius and Nereus/Nero. There, the emperors answer the requests presented by these who worked at sea. In addition, it follows with Nero sanctioning that every norm included in the *Lex Rhodia* would be taken into consideration with great attention. In this case, the word ἐμπλέοντες substitutes the ναυταί, while the ἐπιβάται, the travellers, are added to the other categories just mentioned. Tiberius gives his approval to the vote by using the phrase ταῦτα πάντα ψήφῳ θεματίσας, which probably implied a particular intervention of the senate. Thus, after placing his seal as confirmation and giving the law to the consul Antoninus, the text will be transmitted to the consuls in Rome, specifically Laurus/Larus and Agrippinus, and through this process, otherwise transmitted to Vespasian and Trajan.

Even if there are doubts concerning the improved senatorial cooperation during Tiberius (or better, Claudius), Trajan's role appears more cogent because it is literally told that the use of the imperial seal through the vote of the senate as an authentic *confirmatio* (validation) connects with the verb σφραγίζω (from σφραγίς) which we found other times in the two additional versions of the text. The discourse in its first version closes with the declaration that Augustus would also have reached the same decision. The other fragment, which forgets to mention Augustus (even if there Tiberius instead of Claudius could be the *princeps* himself), is better connected to the role of the senate and the mechanism of the *confirmatio*, which is, in turn, related to all the quoted emperors. Finally, Tiberius simply reports the fragment of the *Nomos Rhodion Nautikos* where it is indicated that, in case of danger of shipwreck, the main mast will be cut to keep the vessel safe, and the expenses later divided among the participants to the enterprise.[63]

Thus, it is clear that such a list of emperors was destined to have an ideological, almost mythographic significance because it was directed towards establishing a hypothetical continuity for the Rhodian sea law within the Roman law through the series of imperial validations. That said, it is the mention of Augustus, coming to light after centuries of oblivion, that attracts our attention:

> The law of the sea is ruled by maritime law, and the same was also decided by the divine Augustus.

The passage evoking him is included in the *Synopsis Minor* without any changes from Maecianus' original text from *D.* 14.2.9, where the *princeps* is indicated as the figure who would first introduce the law of the Rhodians in Rome, following and old practice. This is precisely where the foundational value of the detail resided for the unknown author of the *prooimion* and his aim of taking advantage of the celebrated past.

Conclusions

It seems clear that our fragment was destined to remain rather confusing for the contemporary scholar. In fact, we would like to insist that both the original placement and its difficult exegesis constitute a work in progress that continues to create remarkable challenges to the full understanding of the text. These issues do not exclude the possibility that the fragment itself has been seen in a completely different light by the Byzantine tradition, which was more fortunate given the fact that it was originally written in Greek. The Byzantines were not interested on Eudaimon's incident and its subsequent, enigmatic verdict by Antoninus Pius, but they basically took from that text what was interesting for them: the reconnaissance of the law of the Rhodians as a source of universal value. In that sense, it could be used when not in concurrence with the law of the Romans, or when it received the emperor's blessing. The importance of the fragment *D.*14.2.9 is attested by *B.* 53.1.1, which collected the results of the doctrine following Justinian's great compilation, the *Corpus Iuris Civilis*.

Michael Attaleiates, in his *Ponema Nomikon*, directly extracted from the *Basilika*, reproduced the definition of the *Digesta*, which was preserved at the end of one of the two versions of the *prooimion* of the *Nomos Rhodion Nautikos*. This collection was composed in exactly the same period and in the same cultural environment as the *Basilika*, that is to say, after the re-establishment of the University of Constantinople thanks to the decision taken by Constantine IX Monomachos in 1046. The areas of application of the *Lex Rhodia*, as defined in *D.* 14.2.9, were extensively re-elaborated in *Synopsis Minor* N.15, in which the anonymous author of the collection tried to explain the relationship between customary law and imperial legislation. That time their connection was built on the concept of a 'residual' use of the *Lex Rhodia*, a notion that could be also found in the *prooimion* of the *Nomos Rhodion Nautikos*. Finally, Constantine Harmenopoulos in *Hexabiblos* 2.11.1 would preserve only the first part of the fragment *D.*14.29, endorsing the general rule without further explanation.

The tradition of the fragment *D.*14.2.9 sketched in this contribution yields results that are quite emblematic concerning the Byzantine conception of law, finding identification in a structure brought back from the past but kept alive by a continuous evolution. In that way, the emperor represented the point of union between the two worlds. All these elements justify why the fragment *D.*14.2.9 is still so relevant, because it connects the customary law of the *Lex Rhodia* with the will of the emperor itself. That notion was used by Gothofredus (*De imperio maris etc.*) and Hugo Grotius who with the work *Mare liberum seu De iure quod Batavis competit ad Indicana commercia dissertatio* (Leiden

1609) aimed at demonstrating the right of the Dutch crown to trade towards the East India. With that work, Grotius was leading an ideological battle in favour of the universality of sea law. Later on, John Selden stood up in defence of England and of the right of a sovereign state, through his treatise *Mare clausum seu de imperio maris*, (Leiden 1635).[64] However, all this is evidently the start of a completely different story.

Notes

1. The bibliography is extensive. Beside Kreller 1921; De Martino 1937; Osuchowski 1950 and Wieacker 1953; De Robertis 1953; then, Atkinson 1974; Manfredini 1983 (also id. 1984); Purpura 1985: 301–31 (preceded by Purpura 1976, both in *Studi romanistici in tema di diritto commerciale marittimo*, Messina 1996: 31–89 and 9–27; moreover, more recently, Purpura 2002, but also Purpura 1995; Marotta 1988: 73–80, 200–10; and, finally, Merola 2007.

2. *De imperio maris et de iure naufragii colligendi legeque Rhodia etc.*, Genevae, Sumpt. Ioannis ant. et Samuelis de Tournes, 1654: 43–60. On the medieval tradition we simply quote Zeno 1934: 17–22 (and Zeno 1946: 22–9); we would like to remember Goldschmidt 1888, too, a work mentioned by Max Weber, the year following its publication, in *Zum Geschichte der handelsgesellschaften im Mittelalter nach südeuropäische Quellen* (Stuttgart: Enke, 1889), as evidence of the importance of this matter. More recently, Zalewski 2016: 173–91 and Mataix Ferrandiz 2017.

3. De Martino 1937: 339–41, 345–6; moreover, Schulz 1946: 255. Strongly disapproving was Osuchowski 1950 who indicated that there was no connection between the *Lex Rhodia* and the institution of jettison (*iactus*) by confronting *D.* 14.2.1 (Paul. 2 *Sent.*, L. 1959) and *PS*. 2.7.1.

4. Icaria, the name of an island facing the central coast of Anatolia, could be mistaken for the region of Caria, which included a part of those coasts and where there was the city of Caunus (from which the well-known customs law comes from).

5. For example, Lenz 1994: 36

6. Atkinson 1974: 58–9. This has been the opinion expressed by Gothofredus, who thought that 'the law of the sea' was the subject of the verb κρινέσθω. Therefore, the emperor would have applied the *Lex Rhodia* not considering the publicans neither the *direptio ex naufragio*, which was already ruled via Roman law; Manfredini 1983: 377–8.

7. De Laet 1949: 205; more recently, Merola 2009 (but also id. 2016a and 2016b, exactly concerning the transmission during Augustus' reign from the publicans to the local communities concerning the tax collection on trade imports). Anyway, see Spagnuolo Vigorita and Mercogliano 1992: 99–102, together with Günther 2008: 14–20.

8. Krüger 1930.

9. Concerning the Roman legal system, relevant places are: *D.* 47.9.1pr. (Ulp. 56 *ad Ed.*, L. 1130), on the edict of the *praetor urbanus*; *D.* 47.9.3.8 (Ulp. 56 *ad Ed.*, L. 1334), on a *senatus consultum* by Claudius: Buongiorno 2010: 370–71; *D.* 47.9.5 (Gaius 21 *ad Ed. Prov.*, L. 337), on the edict of the *praetor peregrinus*; *D.* 47.9.7 (Call. 2 *Quaest.*, L. 107), on an edict by Hadrian which prohibited to steal from a wreckage together with another decision of the senate: Gerkens 1997: 156–7, but starting from *D.* 47.9.4.1, 152–6, then Marotta 1988: 333–5 and Zanon 1998: 140–2, both on the assignments *praefectus orae maritimae*; *D.* 47.9.4.1 (Paul. 54 *ad Ed.*, L. 678), on a rescript by Antoninus Pius which criminalized the case: Muciaccia 1977 and Muciaccia 1980 and moreover Molnar 1981; *C.* 11.6.1, short section of a constitution

always by the same emperor on the property of the shipment of the wreckage which would remain something belonging to the early owner: Solazzi 1939 and Pinzone 1982a, besides Pinzone 1982b, both on the shipwreck of the emperor in 214. On the edict of the praetor corresponding to *D*. 47.9 and on the *actio in quadruplum* given in case of the *rapina*, characterized, in comparison with the *furtum*, characterized by including the element of *vis* (force), which could be interpreted in a manner more or less extensive, Balzarini 1969: 383–9 and Vacca 1972: 102–6; moreover, now, Galeotti 2020: 202–8.

10. De Martino 1938.

11. On the matter of the distribution of the damage in case of shipwreck according to the reflexion of the jurisprudence, a problem strongly connected with the world of the sea trade of Rome, besides Osuchowski 1950 and before Huvelin 1929: 184–95, Wagner 1967 and Pókecz Kovács 1998; moreover, Thomas 1974; then, Honsell 1993 and Rheichard 1993; much more recently, Aubert 2007: mainly 166–7 and Krampe 2019 (together with other his works quoted in the bibliography of the article).

12. Scherillo 1950: 209–15 and especially 214–15; De Robertis 1953: 155 n. 4, 159 n. 19; the idea in Krüger 1930 and partially in De Martino 1937: 348 remained isolated: it supposed that the text would derive from an official act of the chancellery which preserved the imperial decision together with the name of the jurist who had inspired it, as that one which hypothesized that it would be a petition originally in Greek caused by the presence of an intermediary in the court (Atkinson 1974: 67 and 72, something similar can be appreciated in *D*. 48.7.7; Call. 5 *De Cognit.*; L. 37).

13. Martini 2005; Migliardi Zingale 2009; Tuccillo 2013.

14. De Martino 1937: 341–7; De Francisci 1929: 361 (and id. 1938, 493); against this kind of view, De Robertis 1953: 159.

15. De Robertis 1953: 159–60, 158 n. 12; Atkinson 1974: 57–8.

16. Manfredini 1983: 392–4; Purpura 1985: 312; *contra*, Merola 2007: 267–71.

17. The punctuation suggested by Theodor Mommsen and Paul Krüger is the following: the point after τῆς θαλάσσης and the comma after τῷ ναυτικῷ; Atkinson 1974: 48–9.

18. De Robertis 1953: 168–70 (together with De Robertis 1942: 263–9). Only Gothofredus thought that the emperor would have been another one and, in particular, Marcus Aurelius (*De dominio maris* cit. 33); moreover, Glück, von 1813: 25 n. 33. Anyway, Rougé 1969 and for further references Purpura 1985: 311 n. 82, but also Manfredini 1983: 376 n. 4.

19. Concerning the orality of the imperial answer, it is possible to think about a case of ἀπόκριμα otherwise of *interlocutio de plano* (during the ceremony of homage) or *in transitu* (in the course of travel): see Marotta 1988: 25–31 (but also Marotta, 2016: 99 n. 1).

20. Immediately after the *Divi Fratres* – *C*. 11.6.1, on which Pinzone 1982a: 80–91; moreover, Marcou 1995 and Ruggiero 2009: 425–7 – resolved the matter in case of missed declaration, called *professio*, of the shipment and of the *commissum*, which realized its sequestration, according to *D*. 39.4.16.8 (Marc. *Sing. de Delat.*, L. 13; more in general, Klingenberg 1977): *Si propter necessitatem adversae tempestatis expositum onus fuerit, non debere hoc commisso vindicari divi fratres rescripserunt*; Manfredini 1983: 391, but *contra* Purpura 1985: 309–11; moreover, always about the identification with the emperor, again ibid. 329–31.

21. De Robertis 1953: 164–8 and Marotta 1988: 74–7 on the expression κύριον εἶναι, which has, also in other contexts, a significance able to give the idea of a juridical authority: Hegadorn and Worp 1980; more specifically, Triantaphillopoulos 1964: 905–6 on κύριος τοῦ κόσμου; finally, Cumont 1940.

22. De Robertis 1953: 160–7, 171, quoting, for example, Volterra 1936 and Luzzatto 1946.

23. De Francisci 1967: 217–18, where the legal value of the *Lex Rhodia* is put in connection with the imperial power which had given it the official legitimation.

24. De Francisci 1948: 403–8, who makes an interesting reference to *D*. 27.1.6.2 (Mod. 2 *Excusat.*, L. 60), in which the mention τῷ κόσμῳ, referred exactly to Antoninus Pius and seems to refer to the emperor as universal ruler.

25. For some more recent references, Gofas 1995; Chevreau 2005; Schanbacher 2006; Merola 2007: 269–72; Žiha 2018. Finally, Gaurier 2004, in particular 145–223 on the famous comment given by Cuiacius. Also, Urbanik 2019: 331–5, starting from *D*. 1.3.32 (Iul. 84 *Dig.*, L. 819), on how the problem concerns the emperor's admission of the application of a foreign custom into the legal system. Another perspective is provided by, Galeotti 2020: 214–18, 242–7.

26. Atkinson 1974: 82–7; Biscardi 1983: 15–16.

27. Ziebarth 1929; Vélissaropoulos 1980; Rougé 1966.

28. Atkinson 1974: 73–7. Specific indications in Cic. *Leg Man.* 54 (together with *Part. or.* 34.118–123, *Inv. rhet.* 1.30.47, 2.32.98; moreover, [Sall.] *Ep. ad Caes.* 2.7.12); Polyb. 4.47.1; Str. 14.2.5. After a long time, Tert. *Adv. Marc.* 3.6: *Scilicet nauclero illi non quidem Rhodia lex, se Pontica caverat, errare Ioudaeos in Christum suum non potuisse*; on the apologist, who was born in the harbour city of Sinope on the Black Sea, Atkinson 1974 quotes *D*. 1.3.27 (Tert. 1 *Quaest.*, L. 5), where – *quia antiquiores leges ad posteriores trahi usitatum est* – there is a reference to legislations or old individual norms which would have been foreign to the Roman legal system (52–3; on the identification of the jurist with the father of the church, Martini 1975; 1997 and 2003). Finally, Isid. *Etym.* 5.17, cf. 2.10.

29. Arangio-Ruiz 1936: 384 n. 81: Kreller 1921 is quoted accordingly both on what concerns the customary and also Mediterranean origin of the legislation after ascribed to the Rhodians and the Hellenistic custom concerning ship damage, which was imported with some adjustments to the Roman legal system. In addition, De Martino 1938: 180–1.

30. Moschetti 1966: 177–84. Augustus got to govern thanks to his victory in the naval battle of Actium on 2 September of 31 BCE, establishing a new legal order for Egypt (Mélèze Modrzejewski 2014: 249–58); however, at the beginning of the *Res Gestae* 25 he reminds that *mare pacavi a praedonibus*. This may explain the link between the emperor who had received the petition and issued the rescript, that is to say Antoninus Pius, with Augustus himself. Moreover, the lines 92–3 of the custom law of Caunus appears as a legal source reflecting the will of the emperor, beside the *senatus consultum*. See also: Merola (Tricase 2016c) (together with Ferrary 2001). After all, κύριος had a Hellenistic origin and was in perfect syntony with the ideology of the *princeps* as organizer of the world through the law deriving from his charismatic power: on this matter, again De Francisci 1948: 204–12 (and 205 n. 4 on the religious meaning of the term).

31. The treaty between Rome and the Rhodians was signed in 164 BCE: Berthold 1984: 195–8; Schmitt 1957: 151–9; about the previous historical background, see Gruen 1975; Rice 1991; Gabrielsen 1997.

32. Purpura 1985: 318–24, where, together with the figure of the emperor as an *insula* (319–23), the political ideology expressed by Aelius Aristides is well considered: Oliver 1953; all this would find a complete realization in the universal vision of the Severian dynasty: now Corbo 2013 and much more recently Besson 2020; Marotta 1988: 77–9 together with Marotta 2016: 99–103, seem to point out (contradicting the previous group of scholars) that to κόσμος would be equivalent to οἰκουμένη, and therefore, referring to the actual inhabited land.

33. Scheltema and Van der Wal 1974: xi.

34. Scheltema and Van der Wal 1974: vii–xi.

35. Perentidis 1984: 266–72.
36. Perentidis 1984: 244–53 (Φ 29: Manuel I Comnenus' *neara* of 1166–1345) and Perentidis 1986: B 47, 1281; Angold 1978.
37. He originally hailed from the city of Attaleia (modern Antalya) but studied law in Constantinople. He became senator under Constantine X Doukas and was appointed (κειτὴς τοῦ στρατοπέδου) 'judge of the army' by Romanus IV Diogenes: see Haldon 2002. After the defeat of Manzikert (1071) he composed (precisely in 1073) the *Ponema Nomikon*, dedicated to Michael VII Doukas, while his historiographic work (see Kaldellis and Krallis 2012; on the relation with Michael Psellus, Ljubarskij 1995 and mainly Krallis 2006) would be dedicated to Nikephoros III Botaneiates. The *Diataxis*, written in 1077, is a simple will in favour of a cloister and a hospice: Gautier 1981. The *Ponema Nomikon*, on which also Schminck 1993, is in Zepos 1931c: 411–97 (from Sgoutas, 1861 = Zachariae von Lingenthal 1973; Leunclavius 1596: 1–79). We refer to Krallis 2012 and 2019.
38. Svoronos 1964; Apostolopoulos 1978.
39. Perentidis 1984: 252–72.
40. Perentidis 1994.
41. Troianos 2015: 256 n. 33.
42. Perentidis 1984: 257–72, 264 on *Pon.Nom.* 32.10 = *Syn.Min.* N.22.
43. Perentidis 1984: 270.
44. Van der Wal 1981: 153.
45. Troje 1971: 56 n. 24; Vanek 2007: 16–25.
46. Zepos 1931b: 324.
47. Kresten and Hunger 1969: 32–8.
48. Pardessus 1828: 196–7.
49. Perentidis 1984: 239–41.
50. Schminck 1992; Perentidis 1984: 246: the city cannot be Nicaea as claimed by Zachariae von Lingenthal in its *Delineatio*.
51. Even if, τέμνεται καὶ δικάζεται could be an annotation made by Leunclavius himself (Perentidis, 1984: 240).
52. Papastathis 1975.
53. Fögen 1986; *Codex Vaticanus* gr. 851 and Codex Parisinus gr. 1355 (among the sources there is not the *Synopsis Minor*, but there is for sure the Attaleiates' *Ponema*; 267–72.); Fögen 1981.
54. Hunger 1964: 15–45; also, Matino 2012: 81–5, together with Minale 2015; concerning this literature also Aerts et al. 2001 and before, Schmink 1959 and Van Bochove 1997; moreover, Pitsakis 2000; about a text which could be very interesting for our matter, again Schmink 1998; finally, Mazal 1974.
55. Above, concerning the text, Ashburner 1909: 39–41 (= Zepos 1931a: 93–4), but now Rodolakēs 2007: 115–17, Troianos 2015: 107–09 and Humphreys 2014: 179–93 together with table 13 of the *Appendix* and Humphreys 2017: 24–6, 113–28; moreover, Letsios 1996: 70–80; finally, again Rodolakēs 2007: 93–114.
56. Rodolakēs 2007: 100–10 (where also a consideration about the recall made at his time by Ashburner – 1909: lxxiv – to some places of the sea regulation of Trani in Apulia remounting to 1063; concerning this, Letsios 1996: 248–51 and before Marvulli 1963, together with Verger 1965). Anyway, I refer to this issue in Minale forthcoming.

57. Godefroy 1654: 48.
58. Amelotti 1958: 91–5; Amelotti 2011.
59. Ashburner 1909: lxxiv.
60. The confusion, mentioned by Ashburner 1909: lxxii, arises because both emperors had the names of Tiberius Claudius. In this case, even if the speech addressed to the sea people could recall Tac. *Ann.* 12.58 – *Reddita Rhodiis libertas, adempta saepe aut firmata, prout bellis externis meruerant aut domi seditione deliquerant* (…) – together with Suet. *Claud.* 25 and *Nero* 7, where the protagonist was indeed Claudius, referring to the year thirty-two of the *tribunicia potestas*, corresponding to 30–31 BCE, is correct for Tiberius: Kienast, Eck and Heil 2017: 72; moreover, always on the *tribunicia potestas*, which would contain the faculty to act with the senate, Fanizza 1981.
61. Claudius appears mentioned in the consulate of 53: the consuls of that year were also Quintus Aterius Antoninus and Decimus Junius Silanus Torquatus (Tac. *Ann.* 12.58, 13.34; Suet. *Tib.* 29.2 and moreover *CIL* VI 3340); Tortoriello 2004: 42–427.
62. According to a certain Western tradition, they held the role at Trajan's death; Ashburner 1909: lxxiii–lxxiv.
63. *NRN* 35; articles 43 and 44 concern the main mast, τὸ κατάρτιον, too; for some references to the classical Roman law: *D.* 14.2.3 (Pap. 19 *Resp.*): *Cum arbor aut aliud navis instrumentum removendi communis periculi causa deiectum est, contributio debetur. D.* 14.2.5.1 (Herm. 2 *Epit.*): *Arbore caesa, ut navis cum mercibus liberari possit, aequitas contributionis habebit locum. D.* 14.2.6 (Iul. 86 *Dig.*): *Navis adversa tempestate depressa ictu fulminis deustis armamentis et arbore et antemna Hipponem delata est ibique tumultuariis armamentis ad praesens comparatis Ostiam navigavit et onus integrum pertulit: quaesitum est, an hi, quorum onus fuit, nautae pro damno conferre debeant. Respondit non debere: hic enim sumptus instruendae magis navis, quam conservandarum mercium gratia factus est* (which is also in in *PS* 2.7.2: *Nave vel arbore vi tempestatis amissa vectores ad contributionem tenentur, nisi ipsis arborem salutis causa eruentibus navis salva sit*).
64. Tommasi 1997 together with Chiarella 2018; also, Izzo 2007.

BIBLIOGRAPHY

Abdelhamid, S. (2016), 'Against the throw-away-mentality: The reuse of amphoras in ancient maritime transport', in H. P. Hahn and H. Weiss (eds), *Mobility, Meaning and the Transformations of Things*, 91–106. Oxford.
Abel, F. M. (1933), 'Oronte et Lītāni', *Journal of the Palestine Oriental Society*, 13(3): 147–58.
Abulafia, D. (2011), *The Great Sea: A Human History of the Mediterranean*. London–New York.
Adams, G.W. (2007), *The Roman Emperor Gaius 'Galigula' and His Hellenistic Aspirations*. Boca Raton.
Aerts, W. J. et al. (2001), 'The Prooimion of the Eisagogé: Translation and Commentary', *Subseciva Groningana*, 7: 91–155.
Ahrens, S., H. R. Indgjerd, F. Kvalø, A. Simosi, E. Tagonidou and H. Vangstad H., eds, (forthcoming), *Southern Naxos Greek-Norwegian Underwater Survey*. Athens.
Ahrens, S., H. R. Indgjerd, F. Kvalø, E. Tagonidou and H. Vangstad (2017–18), 'Undervannsarkeologiske registreringer av skipsvrak og havner på Naxos', *Klassisk Forum*, 1–2: 53–62.
Ahrweiler, H. (1966), *Byzance et la mer. La marine de guerre. La politique et les institutions maritimes de Byzance aux VIIe-XVe s.* Paris.
Alexander, C. (2004), *The Bounty*, London–New York.
Alonso-Núñez, J. M. (2007), 'Piracy', in *Brill's New Pauly 11*, 284–85. Leiden.
Allen, J. R. (1887), *Early Christian symbolism in Great Britain and Ireland before the thirteenth century*. London.
Amelotti, M. (1958), 'L'epigrafe di Pergamo sugli ἀστυνόμοι e il problema della recezione di leggi straniere nell'ordinamento giuridico romano', *SDHI*, 24: 80–111.
Amelotti, M. (2001), 'Leggi greche in diritto romano', in E. Cantarella and G. Thür (eds), *Symposion 1997*, 225–34. Cologne–Weimar–Vienna.
Anderson, J. L. (1995), 'Piracy and World History: An Economic Perspective on Maritime Predation', *Journal of World History*, 6(2): 175–199.
Anderson, A. (2010), 'The Origin and Development of Seafaring: Towards a Global Approach', in A. Anderson (ed.), *The Global Origins and Development of Seafaring*, 3–16. Cambridge.
Ando, C. (2020), 'Public Law and Republican Empire in Rome, 200–27 BCE', in E. Cavanagh (ed.), *Empire and Legal Thought: Ideas and Institutions from Antiquity to Modernity*, 105–124. Leiden.
Andrés Santos, F. J. (2004), 'Aelio Marciano', in R. Domingo (ed.), *Juristas Universales I. Juristas antiguos*, 131–33. Madrid.
Andrich, L. (1904–11), 'Naufragio', *Digesto Italiano*, 15(2): 1303–55.
Angelopoulou, A. (2014), *Κορφάρι Των Αμυγδαλιών (Πάνορμος) Νάξου: Μια Οχυρωμένη Πρωτοκυκλαδική Ακρόπολη*. Athens.
Angold, N. (1978), 'The Date of the Synopsis Minor of the Basilics', *BMGS*, 4: 1–7.
Antonio, M. L. et al. (2019), 'Ancient Rome: A Genetic Crossroads of Europe and the Mediterranean', *Science*, 366: 708–14.
Apostolopoulos, D. (1978), *Τὸ Μέγα Νόμιμον. Συμβολή στην έρευνα του μεταβυζαντινού δημοσίου δικαίου*. Athens. PhD Diss.
Appadurai, A. (2014), *The Social Life of Things. Commodities in Cultural Perspective*. Cambridge.

Bibliography

Arangio-Ruiz, V. (1936), 'Societas re contracta e communio incidens', in [n.e.] *Studi in onore di Salvatore Riccobono* IV, 357–95. Palermo.

Archi, G. G. (1986), 'Sulla cosiddetta massimazione delle costituzioni imperiali', *SDHI*, 52: 161–94.

Armstrong, P. (2006), 'Rural settlement in Lycia in the eighth century: new evidence', in K. Dörtlük and T. Kayha (eds), *Proceedings of the III Symposium on Lycia*, 19–31. Antalya.

Armstrong, P. (2009), 'Trade in the East Mediterranean in the 8th Century', in M. M. Mango (ed.) *Byzantine Trade 4th–12th Centuries: The Archaeology of Local, Regional and International Exchange*, 157–78. Oxford.

Arnaud, P. (2005), *Les routes de la navigation antique: Itinéraires en Méditerranée*. Paris.

Arnaud, P. (2011), 'Ancient sailing-routes and trade patterns: the impact of human factors', in A. Wilson and D. Robinson (eds), *Maritime Archaeology and Ancient Trade in the Mediterranean*, 61–80. Oxford.

Arnaud, P. (2016), 'L'antiquité Classique et la Piraterie', in G. Buti and P. Hrodej (eds), *Histoire des pirates et des corsaires*, 21–74. Paris.

Arnaud, P. (2017a), 'Playing Dominoes with the *Stadiasmus Maris Magni*. The Description of Syria: Sources, Compilation, Historical Topography', in A. Külzer and M. Popovic (eds), *Space, Landscapes and Settlements in Byzantium*, 15–50. Novi Sad.

Arnaud, P. (2017b), 'Un illustre inconnu: Le Stadiasme de la Grande Mer', *CRAI*, 2: 701–27.

Arthur, P. (1990), 'Anfore dell'alto adriatico e il problema del "Samos Cistern Type"', *Aquileia Nostra*, 61: 282–95.

Arthur, P. (2012), 'From Italy to the Aegean and back – notes on the archaeology of Byzantine maritime trade', in S. Gelichi and R. Hodges (eds), *From one Sea to Another. Trading Places in the European and Mediterranean Early Middle Ages*, 337–51. Turnhout.

Arthur, P. (2018), 'Byzantine "Globular amphorae" and the early Middle Ages: Attempting to shed light on a dark-age enigma', *Archeologia Medievale*, 45: 281–87.

Ashburner, W. (1909), *The Rhodian Sea-Law*. Oxford.

Atkinson, K. M. T. (1974), 'Rome and the Rhodian Sea-Law', *Iura*, 25: 46–98.

Aubert, J. J. (2007), 'Dealing with the Abyss: The Nature and Purpose of the Rhodian Sea-Law on Jettison (*Lex Rhodia de iactu*, D 14.2) and the Making of Justinian's *Digest*', in J. W. Cairns and P. J. Du Plessis (eds), *Beyond Dogmatics: Law and Society in the Roman World*, 157–72. Edinburgh.

Aurigemma, S. (1960), *Italia in africa: scoperte archeologiche (1911–43): Tripolitania, vol.1. Monumenti d'arte decorativa. Parte prima: i mosaici*. Rome.

Autret, C., A. Kızılarslanoğlu and N. Rauh (2016), 'New Developments with Amphora Research in Western Cilicia', *ANMED Anadolu Akdenizi Arkeoloji Haberleri* 14: 333–37.

Avidov, A. (1997), 'Were the Cilicians a nation of pirates?', *MHR*, 12: 5–55.

Balmelle, C. and J.-P. Darmon (2017), *La mosaïque dans les Gaules romaines*. Paris.

Balzarini, M. (1969), *Ricerche in tema di danno violento e rapina nel diritto romano*. Padua.

Bakirtzis, C. (1995), 'The role of Cyprus in the grain supply of Constantinople in the Early Christian period', in V. Karageorghis and D. Michaelides (eds), *Cyprus and the Sea*, 247–52. Nicosia.

Bakirtzis, C. (2020), 'Sea Routes and Cape Drepanon: Excavations at Agios Georgios tis Pegeias, Paphos, Cyprus', in L. Nasrallah, C. Bakirtzis and A. Luijendijk (eds), *From Roman to Early Christian Cyprus*, 25–32. Tübingen.

Ballet, P. (1995), 'Relations céramiques entre l'Egypte et Chypre à l'epoque gréco-romaine et byzantine', in H. Meyza and J. Młynarczyk (eds), *Hellenistic and Roman Pottery in the Eastern Mediterranean*, 11–25. Warsaw.

Barkai, O. (2009), 'The Tantura F Shipwreck', in R. Bockius (ed.), *Between the Seas: Transfer and Exchange in Nautical Technology*, 33–9. Mainz.

Barkai, O. and Y. Kahanov (2016), 'The Tantura F shipwreck: Hull remains and finds – final report', *IJNA*, 45(1): 6–28.
Barkai, O., Y. Kahanov and M. Avissar (2010), 'The Tantura F Shipwreck. The Ceramic Material', *Levant*, 42: 88–101.
Barry, F. (2014), 'The "Mouth of Truth" and the Forum Boarium: Oceanus, Hercules, and Hadrian', *The Art Bulletin*, 93(1): 7–37.
Bass, G. (1991), 'Evidence of Trade from Bronze Age Shipwrecks', in N. H. Gale (ed.), *Bronze Age Trade in the Mediterranean*, 69–82. Jonsered.
Beaulieu, M. C. (2016), *The Sea in the Greek Imagination*. Philadelphia.
Becatti, G. (1961), *Scavi di Ostia IV: Mosaici e pavimenti marmorei*. Rome.
Bederman, D. J. (2001), *International Law in Antiquity*. Cambridge.
Benton, L. (2011), 'Toward a New Legal History of Piracy: Maritime Legalities and the Myth of Universal Jurisdiction', *International Journal of Maritime History*, 23(1): 225–40.
Beresford, J. (2012), *The Ancient Sailing Season*. Leiden.
Berg, J. R. (2013), '"Breasts of the North" and Other Apocalyptic Imagery in the *Cosmographia* of Aethicus Ister', in V. Wieser et al. (eds), *Abendländische Apokalyptik*, 563–76. Berlin.
Berthold, R. M. (1984), *Rhodes in the Hellenistic Age*. Ithaca, NY.
Besson, A. (2020), *Constitutio Antoniniana. L'universalisation de la citoyenneté romaine au 3e siècle*. Basel.
Bevan, A. (2014), 'Mediterranean Containerization', *Current Anthropology*, 55(4): 387–418.
Bianchi Fossati Vanzetti, M. (1995), *Pauli Sententiae. Testo e interpretatio*. Padova.
Bintliff, J. L. (2013), 'The Contribution of Regional Surface Survey to Byzantine Landscape History in Greece', in J. Poblome (ed.), *Exempli Gratia. Sagalassos, Marc Waelkens and Interdisciplinary Archaeology*, 127–39. Leuven.
Biscardi, A. (1983), 'Continuità della tradizione ed esigenze di rinnovamento nella compilazione bizantina del "Nomos Rhodion Nautikos"', in [n.e.] *Atti del 1. Congresso di diritto marittimo. La legge del mare in Italia dall'evo antico alle moderne codificazioni*, 15–26. Bari.
Blakely, S. (2018), 'Maritime risk and ritual responses: sailing with the gods in the Ancient Mediterranean', in P. De Souza and P. Arnaud (eds), *The Sea in History. The Ancient World*, 362–79. Woodbridge.
Blázquez, J.-M. (1993), *Mosaicos romanos de España*. Madrid.
Bligh, W. (2005) [1792], *A Voyage to the South Sea, for the Purpose of Conveying the Bread-Fruit Tree to the West Indies, Including an Account of the Mutiny on Board the Ship*, reprinted by Project Gutenberg e-book #15411.
Bloch, E. (1939), 'Inedita Ostiensia I', *Epigraphica*, 1: 37–41.
Blumenhagen, D. (1981), 'Containerization and hinterland trade', *Maritime Policy & Management*, 8(3): 197–206.
Bober, P. (1951), 'Cernunnos: Origin and Transformation of a Celtic Divinity', *AJA*, 55(1): 13–51.
Boetto, G. (2012), 'Les épaves comme sources pour l'étude de la navigation et des routes commerciales: un approche méthodologique', in S. Keay (ed.), *Rome, Portus and the Mediterranean*, 153–73. London.
Boin, D. R. (2013), *Ostia in Late Antiquity*. New York.
Bonifay, M. (2004), *Études sur la céramique romaine tardive d'Afrique*. Oxford.
Bonifay, M. and A. Tchernia (2012), 'Les réseaux de la céramique africaine (Ier – Ve siècles)', in S. Keay (ed.), *Rome, Portus and the Mediterranean*, 315–33. London.
Borbonus, D. (2020), 'Organized Collective Burial in the Port Cities of Roman Italy', in N. Bargfeldt, and J. Hjarl Petersen (eds), *Reflections: Harbour City Deathscapes in Roman Italy and Beyond*, 15–38. Rome.
Borgia, E. (2020), 'Foreigners from the Eastern Mediterranean at Ostia, Portus and Puteoli in the Imperial Period: A Reconsideration of the Matter through an Analysis of Funerary Inscriptions',

Bibliography

in N. Bargfeldt, and J. Hjarl Petersen (eds), *Reflections: Harbour City Deathscapes in Roman Italy and Beyond*, 39–51. Rome.

Börm, H. (2021), 'Procopius and the East' in M. Meier and F. Montinaro (eds), *Brill's Companion to Procopius*. Leiden.

Bosak-Schroeder, C. (2020), *Other Natures. Environmental Encounters with Ancient Greek Ethnography*. Princeton.

Bost, J.-P. et al. (1992), *L'épave Cabrera III (Majorque): échanges commerciaux et circuits monétaires au milieu du IIIe s. a. J-C*. Paris.

Bouras, C. (2016), 'The geography of connections: a harbour network in the Aegean Sea during the Roman Imperial period?', in K. Hoghammer, B. Alroth and A. Lindhagen (eds), *Ancient Ports. The geography of connections*, 201–24. Uppsala.

Bournias, L. C. (2014), 'Roman and Early Byzantine Lamps from the Island of Naxos in the Cyclades', in N. Poulou-Papadimitriou et al. (eds), *LRCW 4 Late Roman Coarse Wares, Cooking Wares and Amphorae in the Mediterranean: Archaeology and Archaeometry*, 787–98. Oxford.

Bowden, W. (2007), 'Nicopolis – The Ideology of the Late Antique City', in K. L. Zakhos (ed.), *ΝΙΚΟΠΟΛΙΣ Β', τόμος Ι*, 135–49. Preveza.

Boyd, M. J., N. Brodie and J. Wright, (forthcoming), 'Survey methods and procedures', in C. Renfrew et al. (eds), *Keros Island Survey. The sanctuary on Keros and the origins of Aegean ritual practice*. Cambridge.

Braudel, F. (1996), *The Mediterranean and Mediterranean World in the Age of Philip II*. Los Angeles.

Braun, B. (2004), 'Nature and Culture: On the Career of a False Problem', in J. S. Duncan, N. C. Johnson and R. H. Schein (eds), *A Companion to Cultural Geography*, 151–79. Malden.

Braund, D. (1993), *Piracy under the principate and the ideology of imperial eradication*. London.

Bravo, B. (1980), 'Sulân. Représailles et Justice Privée contre des étrangers dans les Cités Grecques', *ANSP*, 3: 675–987.

Bravo, B. (1981), 'Androlepsia. La Prise d'Hommes comme Vengeance d'un Meurtre commis dans une Cité étrangère', in M. Modrzejewski and D. Liebs (eds), *Symposion 1977*, 133–56. Cologne.

Bresson, A. (2016), *The Making of the Ancient Greek Economy: Institutions, Markets, and Growth in the City-states*. Princeton.

Broekaert, W. (2009), 'Tied down, wings cut? The relation between the State and the *navicularii* during the Later Roman Empire', in B. Antela-Bernárdez and T. Ñaco del Hoyo (eds), *Transforming Historical Landscapes in the Ancient Empires*, 169–73. Oxford.

Broodbank, C. (2000), *An Island Archaeology of the Early Cyclades*. Cambridge, NY.

Brooke, M. (1987), '*Interpretatio Christiana*: Imitation and Polemic in Late Antique Epic', in M. Whitby, P. Hardie and M. Whitby (eds), *Homo Viator: Classical Essays for John Bramble*, 285–96. Bristol.

Brubaker, L. (2004), 'The Elephant and the Ark: Cultural and Material Interchange across the Mediterranean in the Eighth and Ninth Centuries', *DOP*, 58: 175–95.

Brughmans, T. and J. Poblome (2016), 'Roman bazaar or market economy? Explaining tableware distributions through computational modelling', *Antiquity*, 90: 393–408.

Brughmans, T. and J. Poblome (2017), 'The case for computational modelling of the Roman economy: a reply to Van Oyen', *Antiquity*, 91: 1364–6.

Bruno, B. (2009), *Roman and Byzantine Malta. Trade and Economy*. La Valletta.

Bruno, B. and N. Cutajar (2013), 'Imported Amphoras as Indicators of Economic Activity in Early Medieval Malta', in E. Zanini, P. Pergola and D. Michaelides (eds), *The Insular System of Byzantine Mediterranean. Archaeology and History*, 15–29. Oxford.

Bruno, B. and N. Cutajar (2018), 'Malta between the ninth and tenth century. Two early medieval contexts', *Archeologia Medievale*, 45: 111–22.

Bibliography

Bruun, C. (1992), 'Water as a Cruel Element in the Roman World', in T. Viljamaa, A. Timonen and C. Krötzl (eds), *Crudelitas. The Politics of Cruelty in the Ancient and Medieval World*, 74–80. Krems.

Bruun, C. (2016), 'Tracing Familial Mobility: Female and Child Migrants in the Roman West', in L. de Ligt and L. E. Tacoma (eds), *Migration and Mobility in the Early Roman Empire*, 176–204. Leiden.

Bruun, C. (2017), 'La mentalità marinara di Ostia, città portuale, nella documentazione epigrafica e iconografica', in L. Chioffi, M. Kajava and S. Örmä (eds), *Il mediterraneo e la storia II. Naviganti, popoli e culture ad Ischia e in altri luoghi della costa tirrenica*, 215–27. Rome.

Bruun, C. (2020), 'A Group of Soldiers from Ostia (or So It Seems) Serving in Rome's Urban Cohorts', in K. Mustakallio, M. Silver and S. Örmä (eds), *'Mehr Licht', More Light, Più Luce. Studia in honorem Arja Karivieri*, 149–57. Turku.

Buongiorno, B. (2010), *Senatus consulta Claudianis temporibus facta. Una palingenesi delle deliberazioni senatorie dell'età di Claudio*. Naples.

Burns, T. S. (1994), *Barbarians within the Gates of Rome*. Bloomington.

Buxton, R. (2016), 'Mount Etna in the Greco-Roman *imaginaire*: Culture and Liquid Fire', in J. McInerney and I. Sluiter (eds), *Valuing Landscape in Classical Antiquity*, 25–45. Leiden.

Cadinu, M. (2013), 'Elementi di derivazione islamica nell'architettura e nell'urbanistica della Sardegna medievale. I segni di una presenza stabile', in R. Martorelli (ed.), *Settecento-Millecento. Storia, Archeologia e Arte nei 'secoli bui' del Mediterraneo dalle fonti scritte, archeologiche ed artistiche alla ricostruzione della vicenda storica*, 387–426. Cagliari.

Cadinu, M. (2017), 'Urban planning and new towns in medieval Sardinia', in M. Hobart (ed.), *A Companion to Sardinian History, 500-1500*, 497–551. Leiden.

Caldwell, C. H. (2021), 'Vegetius' naval appendix and the Battle of the Hellespont (324 CE)', in J. T. Chlup and C. Whately (eds), *Greek and Roman Military Manuals. Genre and History*, 216–27. London.

Camardo, D. and M. Notomista (2013), 'Il "Ninfeo" della Casa di Nettuno ed Anfitrite di Ercolano (V, 7–6). Nuovi dati archeologici dai recenti lavori di restauro', *Vesuviana*, 4: 157–98.

Cameron, A. and J. Long (1993), *Barbarians and Politics at the Court of Arcadius*. Berkeley.

Caraher, W. R., D. Nakassis and D. K. Pettegrew (2006), 'Siteless Survey and Intensive Data Collection in an Artifact-rich Environment: Case Studies from the Eastern Corinthia, Greece', *J. Mediterr. Archaeol.*, 19(1): 7–43.

Carile, A. and S. Cosentino (2004), *Storia della Marineria Bizantina*. Bologna.

Cassayre, A. (2010), *La justice dans les cités grecques. De la formation des royaumes hellénistiques au legs d'Attale*. Rennes.

Cassola, F. (1968), *I gruppi politici nel III secolo a.C.* Trieste.

Casson, L. (1971), *Ships and Seamanship in the Ancient World*. Princeton.

Casson, L. (1994), *Ships and Seafaring in Ancient Times*. London.

Catalano, P. (1964), 'Cic. *De off.* 3.108 e il così detto diritto internazionale antico', in *Synteleia Arangio-Ruiz*, 373–83. Naples.

Cataldi, S. (1983), *Symbolai e relazioni tra le città greche nel V sec. a.C.* Pisa.

Çaykent, Ö. and L. Zavagno, L. (2014), *Islands of the Eastern Mediterranean: A History of Cross-Cultural Encounters*. London–New York.

Carter, T., D. Contreras, S. Doyle, D. D. Mihailović, T. Moutsiou and N. Skarpelis (2014), 'The Stélida Naxos archaeological project: New data on the middle Palaeolithic and Mesolithic Cyclades', *Antiquity Project Gallery*, 88 (341).

Cébeillac-Gervasoni, M., M. L. Caldelli and F. Zevi (2010), *Epigrafia Latina: Ostia. Cento iscrizioni in contesto*. Rome.

Cecarelli, P. (2013), *Ancient Greek Letter Writing: A Cultural History (600 BC– 150 BC)*. Oxford.

Chatzilazarou, D. (2018), 'An Aegean Coastal Settlement in the End of Late Antiquity: The Case of Schinoussa near Naxos', in J. Crow and D. Hill (eds), *Naxos and the Byzantine Aegean. Insular Responses to Regional Change*, 195–222. Athens.

Bibliography

Chevreau, E. (2005), 'La *lex Rhodia de iactu*: un exemple de la réception d'une institution étrangère dans le droit romain', *RHD,* 73: 67-79.
Chiarella, P. (2018), 'Ugo Grozio, il mare: patrimonio dell'umanità', *Il diritto marittimo,* 4: 808-22.
Chic García, G. (2013), 'Violencia legal y no legal en el marco del estrecho de Gibraltar', in A. Álvarez-Ossorio Rivas, E. Ferrer Albelda and E. García Vargas (eds), *Piratería y seguridad Marítima en el Mediterráneo Antiguo,* 15-29. Seville.
Chrysos, E. (1981), 'Συμβολή στην Ιστορία της Ηπείρου κατά την πρωτοβυζαντινή εποχή (Δ'-ΣΤ' αι.)', *ΗΠΕΙΡΩΤΙΚΑ ΧΡΟΝΙΚΑ,* 23: 9-111.
Clarke, J. (2014), 'The Struggle for Control of the Landscape in Book 1 of Rutilius Namatianus', *Arethusa,* 41: 89-106.
Clarke, K. (1999), *Between Geography and History: Hellenistic Constructions of the Roman World.* Oxford.
Collar, A. (2013), *Religious networks in the Roman Empire: The spread of new ideas.* Cambridge.
Collins, M. (2018), *St George and the Dragons: The Making of English Identity.* Stroud.
Condos, T. (1997), *Star Myths of the Greeks and Romans.* Grand Rapids.
Connolly, S. (2010), *Lives behind the Laws: The World of the Codex Hermogenianus.* Bloomington-Indianapolis.
Constantakopoulou, C. (2007), *The Dance of the Islands: Insularity, Networks, the Athenian Empire and the Aegean World.* Oxford.
Constantakopoulou, C. (2017), *Aegean Interactions. Delos and Its Networks in the Third Century.* Oxford.
Corbo, C. (2013), *Constitutio Antoniniana: ius philosophia religio.* Naples.
Corcoran, S. (2013), 'The Gregorianus and Hermogenianus assembled and shattered', *MEFRA,* 125(2): 1-24.
Coriat, J. P. (1997), *Le Prince législateur.* Rome.
Cosentino, S. (2008), 'Constans II and the Byzantine Navy', *BZ,* 100(2): 577-603.
Cosentino, S. (2013), 'Mentality, Technology and Commerce: Shipping amongst Mediterranean islands in Late Antiquity and Beyond', in E. Zanini, P. Pergola and D. Michaelides (eds), *The Insular System of Byzantine Mediterranean. Archaeology and History,* 65-76. Oxford.
Cosentino, S. (2018), 'Insularity, economy and social landscape in the early Byzantine period', *Rivista di Studi Bizantini e Neo-Ellenici,* 55: 89-104.
Craik, E. (1980), *The Dorian Aegean.* London.
Crow, J. and D. Hill, eds (2018), *Naxos and the Byzantine Aegean. Insular Responses to Regional Change.* Athens.
Crowe, M. J. (1990), *Theories of the World from Antiquity to the Copernican Revolution.* Mineola.
Cuiacius, I. (1758), 'Ad tres póstumos libros codicis Justiniani commentarii', in *Opera omnia,* X. Naples.
Culham, P. (2018), 'The Roman Empire and the seas', in P. De Souza and P. Arnaud (eds), *The Sea in History. The Ancient World,* 283-93. Woodbridge.
Cumont, F. (1940), 'Traian "kosmokrator"', *REA,* 42: 408-11.
Cunliffe, B. (2008), *Europe Between the Oceans, Themes and Variations: 9000 BC – AD 1000.* New Haven-London.
Cutler, A. (2001), 'Gifts and Gift Exchange as Aspects of the Byzantine, Arab, and Related Economies', *DOP,* 55: 247-78.
Dagron, G. and J. Rougé (1982), 'Trois horoscopes de voyages en mer (5ᵉ siècle après J.-C.)', *RÉB,* 40: 117-33.
D'Amico, E. (2017), 'Approaches and Perspectives on the Origins of Venice', *MAAR,* 62: 209-30.
Darley, R., J. Jarrett and L. Zavagno (2019), 'Editorial', *Al-Masāq,* 31: 129-39.
Darling, L. T. (2012), 'The Mediterranean as a Borderland', *Review of Middle East Studies,* 46(1): 54-63.

Dawes, E. and N. H. Baynes (1948), *Three Byzantine Saints: Contemporary Biographies of St. Daniel the Stylite, St. Theodore of Sykeon and St. John the Almsgiver*. London.

Day, J. (1985), *God's conflict with the dragon and the sea: Echoes of a Canaanite myth in the Old Testament*. Cambridge.

Decker, M. (2016), *The Byzantine Dark Ages*. London.

De Francisci, P. (1929), *Storia del diritto romano* II.1. Rome–Milan.

De Francisci, P. (1948), *Arcana Imperii* III.1. Milan.

De Francisci, P. (1967), 'Per la storia della legislazione imperiale durante il principato', *BIDR*, 9: 187–226.

De Laet, S. J. (1949), *Portorium. Étude sur l'organisation douanière chez les Romains, surtout à l'époque du Haut-Empire*. Bruges.

Delahaye, H. (1925), 'Life of Constantine the Jew', in *Acta Sanctorum (AASS), Novembris IV*, 638. Turnhout.

Delaporte, L. (1923), *Catalogue des cylindres, cachets et pierres gravées de style oriental, II – acquisitions*. Paris.

Delbarre-Bärtschi, S. (2014), *Les mosaïques romaines en Suisse*. Basel.

De Ligt, L. and L. E. Tacoma (2016), 'Approaching Migration in the Early Roman Empire', in L. de Ligt and L. E. Tacoma (eds), *Migration and Mobility in the Early Roman Empire*, 1–22. Leiden.

Dellaporta, A., C. Diamanti, M. Vogkli, C. Sakellakou and S. Tseva, (forthcoming), 'Later Pottery', in C. Renfrew et al. (eds), *Keros Island Survey. The sanctuary on Keros and the origins of Aegean ritual practice*. Cambridge.

Dell'Oro, A. (1960), *I libri de officio nella giurisprudenza romana*. Milan.

Delogu, P. (2012), 'Questioni di Mare e Costa', in S. Gelichi and R. Hodges (eds), *From one Sea to Another. Trading Places in the European and Mediterranean Early Middle Ages*, 459–66. Turnhout.

De Martino, F. (1937) 'Lex Rhodia. Note di Diritto Romano Marittimo I', *RDN*, 3: 335–49.

De Martino, F. (1938), 'Lex Rhodia. Note di Diritto Romano Marittimo II and III', *RDN*, 4: 3–38, 180–212.

De Matteis, L. M. (2004), *Mosaici di Cos. Dagli scavi delle missioni italiane e tedesche (1900–1945)*. Athens.

Demesticha, S. (2013), 'Amphora Typologies, Distribution, and Trade Patterns: The Case of the Cypriot LR1 Amphorae', in M. L. Lawall and J. Lund (eds), *The Transport Amphorae and Trade of Cyprus*, 169–78. Aarhus.

De Robertis, F. (1942), 'Dal potere personale alla competenza dell'ufficio', *SDHI*, 8: 255–308.

De Robertis, F. (1953), 'Lex Rhodia. Critica e anticritica su D. 14.2.9', [n.e.] in *Studi in onore di Vincenzo Arangio-Ruiz nel 45. anno del suo insegnamento* III, 155–73. Naples.

De Salvo, L. (1992), *Economia privata e pubblici servizi nell'impero romano: i corpora naviculariorum*. Messina.

De Souza, P. (1999), *Piracy in the Greco-Roman World*. Cambridge.

De Souza, P. (2008), 'Rome's Contribution to the Development of Piracy', *MAAR*, Suppl. 6: 71–96.

Devecka, M. (2019), 'From Rome to the Moon: Rutilius Namatianus and the Late Antique Game of Knowledge', in T. Biggs and J. Blum (eds), *The Epic Journey in Greek and Roman Literature*, 243–62. Cambridge.

De Vos, A. and M. De Vos (1982), *Pompei, Ercolano, Stabia*. Rome–Bari.

Diamanti, C. (2010), *Local Production and Import of Amphoras at Halasarna of Kos Island (5th–7th c.)*. Athens.

Diamanti, C. (2016), 'The Late Roman Amphora workshops of Paros island in the Aegean Sea: Recent results', *Rei Cretariae*, 44: 691–8.

Dillon, M. and Garland, L. (2010), *Ancient Greece: Social and Historical Documents from Archaic Times to the Death of Alexander the Great*. New York.

Bibliography

Dossey, L. (2010), *Peasant and Empire in Christian North Africa*. Berkeley.
Drucker, P. (1965), *Cultures of the North Pacific Coast*. New York.
Drummond, W. (1826), *Origines; or, Remarks on the origin of several empires, states, and cities*. London.
Ducruet, C. and T. Notteboom (2012), 'The worldwide maritime network of container shipping: spatial structure and regional dynamics', *Global Networks*, 12(3): 395–423.
Duffy, E. (2012), 'Introduction to the 2012 Edition', in Jacobus de Voragine, *The Golden Legend*, xi–xx. Princeton.
Dunbabin, K. (1999), *Mosaics of the Greek and Roman World*. Cambridge.
Dunbabin, K. (1978), *The Mosaics of Roman North Africa: Studies in Iconography and Patronage*. Oxford.
Dunsch, B. (2015), 'Why Do We Violate Strange Seas and Sacred Waters?', in M. Grzechnik and H. Hurskainen (eds), *The Sea as Bridge and Boundary in Greek and Roman Poetry*, 17–42. Cologne–Weimar–Vienna.
Durliat, J. (1990), *De la ville antique à la ville Byzantine*. Rome.
Eck, W. (2016), 'Ordo Senatorius und Mobilität: Auswirkungen und Konsequnzen im Imperium Romanum', in E. Lo Cascio and M. J. Groen-Vallinga (eds), *The Impact of Mobility and Migration in the Roman Empire*, 100–15. Leiden.
Eckardt, H., ed. (2010), *Roman Diasporas. Archaeological approaches to mobility and diversity in the Roman Empire*. Portsmouth, RI.
Egea, M. E. G. (1997), 'Piratas o estadistas: la política exterior del reino vándalo durante el reinado de Genserico', *Polis*, 9: 107–29.
Eger, A. (2015), *The Islamic-Byzantine Frontier: Interaction and Exchange Among Muslim and Christian Communities*. London.
El Safadi, C. and F. Sturt (2019), 'The Warped Sea of Sailing: Maritime Topographies of Space and Time for the Bronze Age Eastern Mediterranean', *JAS*, 103: 1–15.
Engels, D. (2016), '"The Rule of the Sea is indeed a Great Matter." Mediterranean Identities and the Idea of Thalassocracy', *Latomus*, 75: 289–313.
Eraslan, Ş. (2012), 'Antik Dönem Sanatında Okeanos Figürleri / Oceanus Figures in Antique Art', *Sanat Dergisi-Sayı*, 22: 157–66.
Eraslan, Ş. (2015), 'Iconographic Differences of Oceanus in the Mosaic Art', in G. Trovabene (ed.), *Paris, XII Colloquio AIEMA*, 195–200. Paris.
Eraslan, Ş. (2015), 'Oceanus, Tethys and Thalassa in the Light of Antioch and Zeugma Mosaics', *The Journal of International Social Research*, 37(8): 454–62.
Erdkamp, P. (2016), 'Seasonal Labour and Rural-Urban Migration in Roman Italy', in L. de Ligt and L. E. Tacoma (eds), *Migration and Mobility in the Early Roman Empire*, 33–49. Leiden.
Fairchild Ruggles, D. (2004), 'Mothers of a Hybrid Dynasty: Race, Genealogy, and Acculturation in al-Andalus', *Journal of Medieval and Early Modern Studies*, 34: 65–94.
Fanizza, L. (1981), 'Senato e principe in età tiberiana: i profili costituzionali', *Labeo*, 27: 36–53.
Farace, V. (2015), *Agia Varvara in Cipro e le relazioni artistiche fra Bisanzio e l'Islam fra ottavo e nono secolo*. Venice. MA Thesis.
Fear, A. T. (2010), *Orosius: Seven Books of History against the Pagans*. Liverpool.
Fébvre, L. (1922), *La Terre et l'évolution humaine*. Paris.
Fejfer, J. and H. Mathiesen (1995), 'The Site of Ayos Kononas', in J. Fejfer (ed.), *Ancient Akamas*, vol. 1: *Settlement and Environment*, 73–86. Aarhus.
Ferg, E. (2020), *Geography, Religion, Gods, and Saints in the Eastern Mediterranean*. London.
Ferrarini, S. (1963), 'Note sul concetto di naufragio', *RDN*, 1: 98–102.
Ferrary, J.-L. (2001), 'À propos des pouvoirs d'Auguste', *CGG*, 12: 101–54.
Fickett-Wilbar, D. (2003), 'Cernunnos: Looking a Different Way', *Proceedings of the Harvard Celtic Colloquium*, 23: 80–111.

Fischer, A. (2014), 'Rewriting History: Fredegar's Perspectives on the Mediterranean', in A. Fischer and I. Wood (eds), *Western Perspectives on the Mediterranean*, 55–75. London.

Fögen, M. T. (1981), 'Die Scholien zur Hexabiblos im Codex vetustissimus Vaticanus Ottobonianus gr. 440', in D. Simon (ed.), *Fontes Minores* 4: 256–345. Frankfurt.

Fögen, M. T. (1986), 'Hexabiblos aucta. Eine Kompilation der spätbyzantinischen Rechtswissenschaft', in [n.e.] *Fontes Minores* 7: 259–333. Frankfurt.

Fois, P. (2011), 'Il ruolo della Sardegna nella Conquista Islamica dell'occidente (VIII secolo)', *Rivista dell'Istituto di Storia dell'Europa Mediterranea*, 7: 5–26.

Fois, P. (2016), 'Omayyadi e Bizantini in Sardegna: concezioni e realtà di una lunga guerra (706–752/3)', in M. M. Aldón and M. Massaiu (eds), *Entre Oriente y Occidente. Textos y espacios medievales*, 51–72. Cordoba.

Fois, P., P. Giorgio Spanu and R. Zucca (2013), 'Le città della Sardegna centro-occidentale fra VIII e XI Secolo', in R. Martorelli (ed.), *Settecento-Millecento. Storia, archeologia e arte nei secoli bui del Mediterraneo*, 249–70. Cagliari.

Foss, C. (1994), 'The Lycian Coast in the Byzantine Age', *DOP*, 48: 1–52.

Foucher, L. (1963), *La maison de la procession dionysiaque à El Jem*. Paris.

Foucher, L. (1975), 'Notes sur l'iconographie du Dieu Océan', *Caesarodunum*, 10: 639–74.

Frakes, R. (2011), *Compiling the* Collatio Legum Mosaicarum et Romanarum *in Late Antiquity*. Oxford.

Freu, Chr. (2009), 'Dockers et portefaix du monde romain: réflexions à partir de *CTh* XIV, 22, 1 concernant le corpus des *saccarii* du Portus romanus', in J. J. Aubert and P. Blanchard (eds), *Droit, religion et société dans le Code Théodosien*, 303–26. Geneva.

Frezza, P. (1949), '*Ius gentium*' *Nuova Rivista di diritto commerciale, diritto dell'economia, diritto sociale*, 2(1–4): 26–51.

Frier, B. et al. (2016), *The Codex of Justinian: A New Annotated Translation, with Parallel Latin and Greek Text*. Cambridge.

Fuhrmann, C. J. (2012), *Policing the Roman Empire: Soldiers, Administration, and Public Order*. Oxford.

Gabrieli, R. S., M. P. C. Jackson and A. Kaldeli, A. (2007), 'Stumbling into the Darkness: Trade and Life in Post-Roman Cyprus', in M. Bonifay and J.-C. Tréglia (eds), *LRCW 2 Late Roman Coarse Wares, Cooking Wares and Amphorae in the Mediterranean: Archaeology and Archaeometry*, 791–801. Oxford.

Gabrielsen, V. (1997), *The Naval Aristocracy of Hellenistic Rhodes*. Aarhus.

Gabrielsen, V. (2001), 'Economic activity, maritime trade and piracy in the Hellenistic Aegean', *REA*, 103(1–2): 219–40.

Gal, D., H. Saaroni and D. Cvikel (2021), 'A new method for examining maritime mobility of direct crossings with contrary prevailing winds in the Mediterranean during antiquity' *JAS*, 129: 1–15.

Galeotti, S. (2020), *Mare monstrum. Mare nostrum. Note in tema di pericula maris e trasporto marittimo nella riflessione della giurisprudenza romana*. Naples.

Gall, T. L. and J. Hobby (2009), *Worldmark Encyclopedia of Cultures and Daily Life, IV*. Farmington Hills.

Garlan, Y. (1999), *Guerre et économie en Grèce ancienne*. Paris.

Garnsey, P., K. Hopkins and C.R. Whittaker, eds (1983), *Trade in the Ancient Economy*. Berkeley–Los Angeles.

Gasparri, C., ed. (2013), *Palazzo Massimo alle Terme: le collezioni*. Milan.

Gautier, P. (1981), 'La diataxis de Michel Attaliate', *Revue des études byzantines*, 39: 5–143.

Gauvrier, D. (2004), *Le droit maritime romain*. Rennes.

Gerkens, J.-F. (1997), '*Aeque perituris . . .*'. *Une approche de la causalité dépassante en droit romain classique*. Liège.

Bibliography

Ghedini F. and M. Novello (2005), 'Mare realistico e mare mitologico nella produzione musiva dell'Africa Proconsolare: alcuni esempi', in [n.e.] *Aequora, πόντος, jam, mare... Mare, uomini e merci nel Mediterraneo antico*, 182–94. Rome.

Ginalis, A. (2014), *Byzantine Ports. Central Greece as a link between the Mediterranean and the Black Sea, I*. Oxford. PhD Diss.

Ginalis, A. (2017), 'The Pelion Peninsula Byzantine Port Networks along Inhospitable Coastlines', in T. Papacostas and M. Parani (eds), *Discipuli dona ferentes: Glimpses of Byzantium in Honour of Marlia Mundell Mango*, 3–36. Turnhout.

Gkoutzioukostas A. and X. Moniaros (2009), *Περιφερειακή διοίκηση αναδιοργάνωση της Βυζαντινής αυτοκρατορίας από τον Ιουστινιανό Α' (527–565)*. Thessaloniki.

Glassman, R. M. (2017), *The Origin of Democracy in Tribes, City-States and Nation-States*. New York.

Glück, von, C. F. (1813), *Ausführliche Erläuterung der Pandekten* XIV. Erlangen.

Godefroy, J. (1654), *De imperio maris et de iure naufragii colligendi legeque Rhodia etc*. Geneva.

Gofas, D. C. (1995), 'Lex Rhodia de iactu' in M. H. Nordquist and N. Moore (eds), *Entry into Forces of the Law of the Sea Convention*, 29–46. The Hague.

Goldschmidt, L. (1888), *Lex Rhodia und Agermanament*, in *Zeitschrift für das gesammte Handelsrecht*, 35: 37–90, 321–95.

Goldsworthy, A. (2003), *The Fall of Carthage*. London.

Good, J. (2009), *The Cult of Saint George in Medieval England*. Woodbridge.

Gordon, J. M. and A. Kouremenos (2020), 'Introduction. Mediterranean Archaeologies of Insularity in the Age of Globalization', in A. Kouremenos and J. M. Gordon (eds), *Mediterranean Archaeologies of Insularity in the Age of Globalization*, 1–26. Oxford.

Grainger, J. D. (1991), *Hellenistic Phoenicia*. Oxford.

Green, A. R. W. (2003), *The Storm-god in the Ancient Near East*. Winona Lake.

Green, S. J. (2000), 'Multiple Interpretation of the Opening and Closing of the Temple of Janus: A Misunderstanding of Ovid *Fasti* 1.281', *Mnemosyne*, 53(3): 302–9.

Grotius, H. (2009), R. Feentra and J. Vervliet (eds), *Mare Liberum 1609–2009*. Leiden.

Gruen, E. S. (1975), 'Rome and Rhodes in the Second Century B.C.: A Historiographical Inquiry', *CQ*, 25: 58–81.

Gruen, E. S. (1986), *The Hellenistic World and the Coming of Rome*. Berkeley.

Guiley, R. (2001), *The Encyclopedia of Saints*. New York.

Guimier-Sorbets, A.-M. (2019), *Mosaïques d'Alexandrie. Pavements d'Égypte grecque et romaine*. Alexandria.

Günther, S. (2008), *Vectigalia nervos esse rei publicae. Die indirekten Steuern in der römischen Kaiserzeit von Augustus bis Diokletian*. Wiesbaden.

Gürkan, E. S. (2018), 'Between Connectivity and Isolation: Insularity and Flow of Information in the Sixteenth-Century Mediterranean', in G. D. Pagratis (ed.), *War, State and Society in the Ionian Sea (late 14th–early 19th century)*, 25–58. Athens.

Haddad, H. S. (1969), '"Georgic" Cults and the Saints of the Levant', *Numen*, 16(1): 21–39.

Hadjikyriacou, A. (2017), 'Envisioning Insularity in the Ottoman World', *Interdisciplinary Journal of Middle East Studies*, 18: vii–xix.

Hagedorn, D. and K. A. Worp (1980), 'Von ΚΥΡΙΟΣ zu ΔΕΣΠΟΤΗΣ. Eine Bemerkung zur Kaisertitulatur in 3./4. Jhdt.', *ZPE*, 39: 165–77.

Haldon, J. (2002), 'The Krites tou Stratopedou: A New Office for a New Situation?', *Travaux et Mémoires*, 14: 279–86.

Haldon, J. (2016), *The Empire That Would Not Die. The Paradox of Eastern Roman Survival, 640–740*. Princeton.

Harpster, M. (2019), 'Sicily: A Frontier in the Centre of the Sea?', *Al-Masaq*, 31(2): 1–13.

Harries, J. (2007), *Law and Crime in the Roman World*. Cambridge.

Harries, J. (2009), *Law and Empire in Late Antiquity*. Cambridge.

Harris, W. (1994), *Heraclitus: The Complete Fragments, Translation and Commentary, and The Greek Text*. Middlebury.
Harris, W. V. (2006), 'The Mediterranean and Ancient History', in W. W. Harris (ed.), *Rethinking the Mediterranean*, 1–42. Oxford.
Harris, W. V. (2011), *Rome's Imperial Economy: Twelve Essays*. Oxford.
Hartman, S. (2017), 'Introduction: Naturalizing Culture and Countering Nature in Discourses of the Environment', in S. Hartman (ed.), *Contesting Environmental Imaginaries. Nature and Counternature in a Time of Global Change*, 1–10. Brill.
Heckel, W. and L. A. Tritle (2009), *Alexander the Great: A New History*. Hoboken.
Heher, D., J. Preiser-Kapeller et al. (2017), 'Vom Lokalen zum Globalen. Maritime Netzwerke des Austauschs, der Versorgung und Mobilität an den byzantinischen Balkanküsten und in der frühmittelalterlichen Welt', in S. Kalmrig and L. Werther (eds), *Häfen im 1. Millennium AD: Standortbedingungen, Entwicklungsmodelle und ökonomische Vernetzung*, 193–224. Mainz.
Heikell, R. (1998), *Mediterranean Cruising Handbook*. St. Ives.
Helm, R. (1929), *Hippolytus Werke. IV: die Chronik. Die Griechischen Christlichen Schriftsteller der ersten drei Jahrhunderte*. Leipzig.
Helttula, A., T. Gestrin, M. Kahlos, R. Pentti-Tuomisto, P. Tuomisto, R. Vainio and R. Valjus, eds (2007), *Le iscrizioni sepolcrali latine nell'Isola Sacra*. Rome.
Henig, M. (1995), *Religion in Roman Britain*. London.
Herman, G. (1987), *Ritualised Friendship and the Greek City*. Cambridge.
Herren, M. W. (2011), *The Cosmography of Aethicus Ister. Edition, translation, and commentary*. Turnhout.
Herzfeld, M. (2006), 'Practical Mediterraneanism: Excuses for Everything, from Epistemology to Eating', in W. V. Harris (ed.), *Rethinking the Mediterranean*, 45–63. Oxford.
Heslin, K. (2011), 'Dolia shipwrecks and the wine trade in the Roman Mediterranean', in D. Robinson and A. Wilson (eds), *Marine Archaeology and Ancient Trade in the Mediterranean*, 157–68. Oxford.
Hill, D. J. A., R. Håkon and K. Ødegard (2017), 'Kastro Apalirou, Naxos, a Seventh Century Urban Foundation', in E. Rizos (ed.), *New Cities in Late Antiquity: Documents and Archaeology*, 281–92. Turnhout.
Hodder, I. (2012), *Entangled: An Archaeology of the Relationships between Humans and Things*. Malden, MA.
Hodges, R. and D. Whitehouse (1983), *Mohammed, Charlemagne, and the Origins of Europe: Archaeology and the Pirenne Thesis*. Ithaca.
Hohlfelder, R. L., and R. L. Vann (2000), 'Cabotage at Aperlae in ancient Lycia', *IJNA*, 29(1): 126–35.
Hohlfelder, R. L. (2005), 'Aperlae in Lycia: Ancient Maritime Life beyond the Great Harbors', *Classics Ireland*, 12: 13–30.
Hollis, D. and J. König, eds (2021), *Mountain Dialogues from Antiquity to Modernity*. London.
Honoré, T. (1962), 'The Severan Lawyers. A Preliminary Survey', *SDHI*, 28: 162–232.
Honsell, H. (1993), '*Ut omnium contributione sarciatur quod pro omnibus datum est*. Die Kontribution nach der *lex Rhodia de iactu*', in M. Josef, W. Schermaier and W. Steiner (eds), *Ars boni et aequi. Festschrift für Wolfgang Waldstein*, 141–50. Stuttgart.
Horden, P. and N. Purcell (2000), *The Corrupting Sea: A Study of Mediterranean History*. Oxford-Malden, MA.
Hornung, S. (2011), *Luxus auf dem Lande: die römische Palastvilla von Bad Kreuznach*. Bad Kreuznach.
Humphreys, M. T. G. (2014), *Law, Power, and Imperial Ideology in the Iconoclast Era, c. 680–850*. Oxford.
Humphreys, M. T. G., ed. (2017), *The Laws of the Isaurian Era. The Ecloga and its Appendices*. Liverpool.

Bibliography

Hunger, H. (1964), *Prooimion. Elemente der byzantinischen Kaiseridee in den Arengen der Urkunden*. Vienna.
Huvelin, P. (1929), *Études d'histoire du droit commercial romain. Histoire externe, droit maritime*. Paris.
Huxley, G. (1976), 'A Porphyrogenitan Portulan', *GRBS,* 17: 295–300.
Indgjerd, H. R. (2020), *Settlement and Contact on Late Roman and Early Medieval South Naxos, Keros and Kato Kouphonisi*. St Andrews. PhD Diss.
Indgjerd, H. R., and C. Diamanti, (forthcoming), 'Archaeometric Analyses of 5th–8th c. Ceramic Assemblages from the Central Cyclades', in M. A. Cau, J. M. Macias and A. Ribera (eds), *LRCW 7. Late Roman Coarse Wares, Cooking Wares and Amphorae in the Mediterranean*. Oxford.
Irby, G. L. (2021), *Conceptions of the Water World in Greco-Roman Antiquity*. London.
Izdebski, A. (2013), *A Rural Economy in Transition: Asia Minor from Late Antiquity into the Early Middle Ages*. Warsaw.
Izzo, F. ed. (2007), *H. Grotius, Mare liberum*. Naples.
Jeffreys, E. and J. Pryor (2006), *The Age of the Δρομων, the Byzantine navy ca. 500–1204*. Leiden.
Jézègou, M.-P. (2008), 'L'épave Ouest-Embiez 1: proposition d'un modèle de réexportation de produits verriers et du vin à la charnière des IIe/IIIe siècles après J.-C.', in J. Pérez Ballester and G. Pascual (eds), *Comercio, redistribución y fondeaderos. La navegación a vela en el Mediterráneo*, 451–60. Valencia.
Jidejian, N. (1992), *The Story of Lebanon in Pictures*. Beirut.
Johnson, J. F. (2005), *Saint Michael the Archangel in Medieval English Legend*. Woodbridge.
Johnstone, P. (1974), *The Archaeology of Ships*. London.
Kaegi, W. (1968), *Byzantium and Decline of the Roman Empire*. Princeton.
Kajava, M. (1999), 'Murenae, Oysters and Gilt-Heads: Fish for Name, Table, and Show in Ancient Rome', *Acta Classica Universitatis Scientiarum Debrecensis,* 34–5: 253–68.
Kaldellis, A. (2019), *Romanland: Ethnicity and Empire in Byzantium*. Cambridge, MA.
Kaldellis, A. and D. Krallis, eds, (2012), *The History. Michael Attaleiates*. Cambridge, MA.
Kapitän, G. (1969), 'The Church Wreck off Marzamemi', *Archaeology,* 22: 122–33.
Kardulias, P. N. (2020), 'Afterword', in A. Kouremenos and J. K. Gordon (eds), *Mediterranean Archaeologies of Insularity in the Age of Globalization*, 275–80. Oxford.
Karivieri, A. (1996), *The Athenian Lamp Industry in Late Antiquity*. Helsinki.
Karivieri, A., ed. (2020), *Life and Death in a Multicultural Harbour City: Ostia Antica from the Republic through Late Antiquity*. Rome.
Karivieri, A. (2020a), 'Living in Apartment Blocks and *domus*, Lighting in Homes and Public Spaces', in A. Karivieri (ed.) 2020, 123–7.
Karivieri, A. (2020b), 'Ostia as Centre of Production', in A. Karivieri (ed.) 2020, 209–18.
Karivieri, A. (2020c), 'Theatre and Pantomime, Gladiatorial Games and *venationes* – Animal Hunts', in A. Karivieri (ed.) 2020, 295–303.
Karivieri, A. (2020d), 'New Trends in Late Antique Religions, Beliefs and Ideas: Christianity, Judaism, Philosophy and Magic in Ostia', in A. Karivieri (ed.) 2020, 371–85.
Katzev, M. (1990), 'An Analysis of the Experimental Voyages of the Kyrenia II', in H. Tzalas (ed.), *Tropis II*, 245–56. Athens.
Kaygusuz, I. (1984), 'Funerary Epigram of Karzene (Paphlagonia): A Girl Raped by the Goths?', *EA,* 4: 61–2.
Keay, S. (2012), 'Introduction', in S. Keay (ed.), *Rome, Portus and the Mediterranean*, 1–21. London.
Keay, S. (2020), 'The Portus Romae', in A. Karivieri (ed.) 2020, 41–8.
Kempe, M. (2009), 'Beyond the Law. The Image of Piracy in the Legal Writings of Hugo Grotius', in H. Blom (ed.), *Property, Piracy and Punishment: Hugo Grotius on War and Booty in De Iure Praedae: Concepts and Contexts*, 379–95. Leiden.
Kienast, D., W. Eck and M. Heil (2017), *Römische Kaisertabelle. Grundzüge einer römischen Kaiserchronologie*. Darmstadt.

Kiourtzian, G. (2000), *Recueil des inscriptions grecques chrétiennes des Cyclades: de la fin du IIIe au VIIe siècle après J.-C.* Paris.
Kiraz, G. (2009), *The Acts of Saint George and the Story of His Father from the Syriac and Garshuni Versions.* Berlin.
Klami, H. T. (1984), 'Iulius Paulus. Comments on a Roman lawyer's career in the III century', in *Sodalitas* IV, 1829–1841. Naples.
Klingenberg, G. (1977), *Commissum. Der Verfall nichtdeklarierter Sache im römischen Zollrecht.* Graz.
Knapp, A. B. (1997), 'Mediterranean Maritime Landscapes: Transport, Trade and Society on Late Bronze Cyprus', in S. Swiny et al. (eds), *Res maritimae: Cyprus and the Eastern Mediterranean from prehistory to Late Antiquity,* 153–62. Atlanta.
Kokkorou-Alevras, G., D. Grigoropoulos, C. Diamanti and M. Koutsoumpou (2016), 'Maritime Connections of Halasarna on Cos from Prehistory to Late Antiquity: A View Based on the Pottery and Other Finds', in K. Höghammar, B. Alroth and A. Lindhagen (eds), *Ancient Ports. The geography of connections,* 167–200. Uppsala.
Kopaka, K. (2008), 'What is an island? Concepts, meanings and polysemies of insular *topoi* in Greek sources', *European Journal of Archaeology,* 11: 179–97.
Krallis, D. (2006), 'Attaleiates as a Reader of Psellos', in C. Barber and D. Jenkins (eds), *Reading Michael Psellos,* 167–91. Leiden.
Krallis, D. (2012), *Michael Attaleiates and the Politics of Imperial Decline in Eleventh-century Byzantium.* Tempe, AZ.
Krallis, D. (2019), *Serving Byzantium's Emperors. The Courtly Life and Career of Michael Attaleiates.* London.
Krampe, C. (2019), '*Lex Rhodia de iactu: navis quae perit* (D. 14.2.4.1)' in E. Chevreau, C. Masi Doria and J. M. Rainer (eds), *Liber amicorum. Mélanges en l'honneur de Jean-Pierre Coriat,* 443–9. Paris.
Kreller, H. (1921), '*Lex Rhodia.* Untersuchungen zur Quellengeschichte des römischen Seerechts', *ZHR,* 85: 258–367.
Kresten, O. and H. Hunger (1969), *Katalog der griechischen Handschriften der Österreichischen Nationalbibliotek. II. Codices juridici. Codices medici.* Vienna.
Krüger, H. (1930), 'Roms Juristen und ihre Werke', in [n.e.] *Studi in onore di Pietro Bonfante nel 40. anno d'insegnamento* II, 301–37. Milan.
Kulikowski, M. (2007), *Rome's Gothic Wars: From the Third Century to Alaric.* Cambridge.
Labruna, L. (1971), *Vim fieri veto: alle radici di una ideologia.* Naples.
Labruna, L. (1972), 'Les racines de l'idéologie répressive de la violence dans l'histoire du droit romain', *Index,* 3: 525–38.
Labruna, L. (1986), *Tutela del possesso fondiario e ideologia repressiva della violenza nella Roma repubblicana.* Naples.
Lambert, W. G. (2013), *Babylonian Creation Myths.* Winona Lake.
Lambertini, R. (1980), *Plagium.* Milan.
Lambrinoudakis, V et al. (2003), 'Naxos – Das Heiligtum von Gyroula bei Sangri: Eine neugefundene, drei Jahrtausende alte Kultstätte der Demeter', *Antike Welt,* 33: 387–406.
Lampinen, A. J. (2015), 'A Helping Hand from the Divine. Notes on the Triumphalist Iconography of the Early Theodosians', *Acta Byzantina Fennica,* 4: 9–38.
Langdon, S. (1989), 'The Return of the Horse-Leader', *AJA,* 93(2): 185–201.
Laiou, A. and C. Morrisson (2007), *The Byzantine Economy.* Cambridge.
Lapidge, M. (2006), 'The career of Archbishop Theodore', in M. Lapidge (ed.), *Archbishop Theodore: Commemorative Studies on his Life and Influence,* 1–29. Cambridge.
Larsson Lovén, L. (2020), 'People at Work in Ostia', in A. Karivieri (ed.) 2020, 225–30.
Laurence, R. (2020), 'Ostia between Rome and the World', in A. Karivieri (ed.) 2020, 57–63.
Lazzarini, M. L. (1980), 'Due iscrizioni greche di Ostia', in *Miscellanea* (Tituli 2), 193–8. Rome.

Bibliography

Lazzarini, M. L. (1996), 'L'incremento del patrimonio epigrafico greco ostiense dopo *Roman Ostia*', in A. Claridge and A. Gallina Zevi (eds), *'Roman Ostia' Revisited: Archaeological and Historical Papers in Memory of Russell Meiggs*, 243–7. London.

Le Bohec, Y. (2018), 'La marine de guerre romaine de 284 à 363', in P. De Souza and P. Arnaud (eds), *The Sea in History. The Ancient World*, 484–95. Woodbridge.

Leidwanger, J. (2013a), 'Amphorae and Underwater Survey: Making Sense of Late Roman Trade from Scattered Sherds and Shipwrecks', in M. Lawall and J. Lund (eds), *The Transport Amphorae and Trade of Cyprus*, 179–90. Aarhus.

Leidwanger, J. (2013b), 'Opportunistic Ports and Spaces of Exchange in Late Roman Cyprus', *J. Marit. Archaeol.*, 8(2): 221–43.

Leidwanger, J. (2013c), 'Between local and long-distance: a Roman shipwreck at Fig Tree Bay off SE Cyprus', *JRA*, 26: 191–208.

Leidwanger, J. (2018), 'New investigations of the 6th-c. A.D. "church wreck" at Marzamemi, Sicily', *JRA*, 31: 339–56.

Leidwanger, L. (2020), *Roman Seas. A Maritime Archaeology of Eastern Mediterranean Economies.* Oxford.

Leidwanger, J., E. S. Greene and N. Tuna (2015), 'A Late Antique Ceramic Assemblage at Burgaz, Datça Peninsula, South-West Turkey, and the 'Normality of the Mixed Cargo' in the Ancient Mediterranean', *IJNA*, 44(2): 300–11.

Lenel, O. (1889), *Palingenesia Iuris Civilis.* Leipzig.

Lenel, O. (1927), *Das Edictum Perpetuum.* Leipzig.

Lenz, H. M. (1994), *Privilegia fisci.* Pfaffenweiler.

Letsios, D. (1996), *Nomos Rhodiōn Nautikos – Das Seegesetz der Rhodier. Untersuchungen zu Seerecht und Handelsschiffahrt in Byzanz.* Rhodes.

Leunclavius, J. (1596), *Jus Graeco-Romanum* II. Frankfurt.

Lewis, D. (1994), *We, The Navigators, the ancient art of landfinding in the Pacific.* 2nd edn, Honolulu.

Licordari, A. (2020), 'The Population of Ostia: Composition and Working Activities: an Analysis of Inscriptions', in A. Karivieri (ed.) 2020, 165–71.

Lilie, R.-J. (2005), 'The Byzantine-Arab Borderland from seventh to ninth century', in F. Curta (ed.), *Borders, Barriers, and Ethnogenesis. Frontiers in Late Antiquity and the Middle Ages*, 13–21. Turnhout.

Lindstedt, I. (forthcoming), 'Religious warfare and martyrdom in Arabic graffiti (70s–110s AH/690s–730s CE)', in F. Donner and R. Hasselbach-Andee (eds), *Scripts and Scripture: Writing and Religion in Arabia, 500–700 CE.* Chicago.

Lintott, A. (1999), *Violence in Republican Rome.* Oxford.

Liverani, M. (1993), *Akkad, the First World Empire: Structure, Ideology, Traditions.* Leiden.

Ljubarskij, J. N. (1995), 'Miguel Ataliates y Miguel Pselo (Ensayo de una breve comparacion)', *Erytheia*, 6: 85–95.

Lo Cascio, E. (2016), 'The Impact of Migration on the Demographic Profile of the City of Rome: A Reassessment', in L. de Ligt and L. E. Tacoma (eds), *Migration and Mobility in the Early Roman Empire*, 23–32. Leiden.

Loreto, L. (2001), *Il bellum iustum e i suoi equivoci. Cicerone ed una componente della rappresentazione romana del 'völkerrecht' antico.* Naples.

Lounghis, T. (2010), *Byzantium in the Eastern Mediterranean: Safeguarding East Roman Identity (407-1204).* Nicosia.

Lounghis, T. C. (2018), 'The Byzantine War Navy and the West, Fifth to Twelfth Centuries', in G. Theotokis and A. Yıldız (eds), *A Military History of the Mediterranean Sea. Aspects of War, Diplomacy, and Military Elites*, 21–43. Leiden.

Luccarelli, M. and S. Bergman (2015), *Spaces in-between. Cultural and Political Perspectives on Environmental Discourse.* Leiden.

Lütbow, U.V. (1976), 'Das Seedarlehen des Callimachus', in *Festschrift für Max Kaser zum 70 geburtstag*, 329–49. Munich.
Luzzatto, G. I. (1946), 'Ricerche sull'applicazione delle costituzioni imperiali nelle provincie', in G. G. Archi (ed.), *Scritti di diritto romano in onore di Contardo Ferrini*, 265–93. Milan.
Lynch, R. J. (2016), 'Cyprus and Its Legal and Historiographical Significance in Early Islamic History', *JAOS*, 136: 535–50.
Ma, Q. (2020), 'Islands and the world from an anthropological perspective', *Int. J. Anthropol.*, 4: 2–17.
MacDowell, D. M. (1963), *Athenian Homicide Law in the Age of the Orators*. Manchester.
MacGibbon, J., trans. (1982), *Nouveau Cours de Navigation des Glénans*. Boston.
Maiorano, M. and L. Paroli (2013), *La Basilica Portuense. Scavi 1991–2007*. Rome.
Malamat, A. (1965), 'Campaigns to the Mediterranean by Iahdunlim and Other Early Mesopotamian Rulers', in H. G. Güterbock and T. Jacobsen (eds), *Studies in Honor of Benno Landsberger on his Seventy-fifth Birthday*, 365–74. Chicago.
Malamat, A. (1994), 'Das heilige Meer', in I. Kottsieper, J. van Oorschoot, D. Rümheld and H. M. Wahl (eds), *Wer ist wie Du, Herr, unter den Göttern? Studien zur Theologie und Religionspeschichte Israels für Otto Kaiser zum 70. Geburtstag*, 65–74. Göttingen.
Malamut, É. (1988), *Les îles de l'Empire byzantin. VIIIe–XIIe siècles*. Paris.
Malamut, É. (2001), 'Les îles de la mer Égée entre l'Antiquité et Byzance', in P. Brun (ed.), *Les îles de l'Égée dans l'Antiquité. REA*, 103: 25–48.
Mallan, C. and C. Davenport (2015), 'Dexippus and the Gothic Invasions: Interpreting the New Vienna Fragment (*Codex Vindobonensis Hist. gr.* 73, ff. 192^v–193^r)', *JRS*, 105: 203–26.
Maloney, E. and E. Chapman (1983), *Piloting, Seamanship and Small Boat Handling*, 56th edn. New York.
Manfredini, A. D. (1983), 'Il naufragio di Eudemone', *SDHI*, 49: 375–94.
Manfredini, A. D. (1984), 'Una questione in materia di naufragio', in [n.e.] *Sodalitas. Scritti in onore di Antonio Guarino* V, 2209–25. Naples.
Manfredini, A. D. (1986), 'Les naviculaires et le naufrage', *RIDA*, 33: 135–48.
Mango, C. and R. Scott (1997), *The Chronicles of Theophanes Confessor*. Oxford.
Mantovani, D. (2018), *Les Juristes écrivains de la Rome antique. Les œuvres des juristes comme literature*. Paris.
Marchaj, C. (1985), *Sailing Theory and Practice*. London.
Marchaj, C. (2000), *Aero-Hydrodynamics of Sailing*. London.
Marcou, G. (1995), 'Nomos Rhodion Nautikos e la scoperta a Rodi di una colonna di marmo con l'iscrizione di Paolo (D. 14, 2)', in E. Turco Bulgherini (ed.), *Studi in onore di Lefebvre D'Ovidio* I, 609–39. Milan.
Marlier, S. and P. Sibella (2002), 'La Griglia, a dolia wreck of the 1st Century BC from Corsica, France', *IJNA*, 31(2): 161–71.
Marotta, V. (1988), *Multa de iura sanxit. Aspetti della politica del diritto di Antonino Pio*. Milan.
Marotta, V. (2016), *Esercizio e trasmissione del potere imperiale (secoli I–IV d.C.). Studi di diritto pubblico romano*. Torino.
Martelli, E. (2013), *Sulle spalle dei saccarii. Le rappresentazioni di facchini e il trasporto di derrate nel porto di Ostia in epoca imperial*. Oxford.
Martin, G. and J. Grusková (2014a), '"Dexippus Vindobonensis" (?) Ein neues Handschriftenfragment zum sog. Herulereinfall der Jahre 267/268', *Wien. Stud.*, 127: 101–20.
Martin, G. and J. Grusková (2014b), '"Scythica Vindobonensia" by Dexippus (?): New Fragments on Decius' Gothic Wars', *GRBS*, 54: 728–54.
Martini, R. (1975), 'Tertulliano giurista e Tertulliano padre della Chiesa', *SDHI*, 41: 79–124.
Martini, R. (1997), 'Ancora su Tertulliano', *BIDR*, 100: 117–26.
Martini, R. (2005), 'D. 43.10.1: ex astunomikou monobiblou tou Papinianou', in [n.e.] *Atti dell'Accademia Romanistica Costantiniana* 15: 243–51. Naples.

Bibliography

Marvulli, N. (1963), 'Nómos Rhodíon Nautikós e Ordinamenta et consuetudo maris edita per consules civitatis Trani', *Archivio Storico Pugliese,* 16: 42–64.

Maschi, C. A. (1976), 'La conclusione della giurisprudenza classica all'età dei severi. Iulius Paulus', *ANRW,* 15(2): 667–707.

Mataix Ferrándiz, E. (2017), 'Will the circle be unbroken? Continuity and change of the *Lex Rhodia*'s jettison principles in Roman and Medieval Mediterranean rulings', *Al-Masaq,* 29(1): 41–59.

Mataix Ferrándiz, E. (2019), '"*De incendio ruina naufragio rate nave expugnata.*" Origins, context and legal treatment of shipwrecking in Roman law', *RIDA,* 66: 153–95.

Matino, G. (2012), *Lex et scientia iuris. Aspetti della letteratura giuridica in lingua greca.* Naples.

Matthews, J. (1993), 'The Making of the Text', in J. Harries and I. Wood (eds), *The Theodosian Code. Studies in the Imperial Law of Late Antiquity,* 19–44. London.

Mawani, R. (2018), *Across Oceans of Law. The Komagata Maru and jurisdiction in the Time of Empire.* Durham, NC.

Mazal, O. (1974), *Die Prooimien der byzantinischen Patriarchenurkunden.* Vienna.

McCann, A. C. and J. P. Oleson, eds (2004), *Deep-water shipwrecks off Skerki Bank, the 1994 Survey.* Portsmouth.

McCormick, M. (1995), 'Byzantium and the West, 700–900s', in R. McKitterick (ed.), *New Cambridge Medieval History, vol. II c. 700–900,* 349–83. Cambridge.

McCormick, M. (1986), *Eternal Victory: Triumphal rulership in Late Antiquity, Byzantium and the Early Medieval West.* Cambridge.

McCormick, M. (2001), *Origins of the European Economy: Communications and Commerce AD 300–900.* Cambridge.

McCormick, M. (2012), 'Movements and Markets in the First Millennium. Information, Containers, and Shipwrecks', in C. Morrisson (ed.), *Trade and Markets in Byzantium,* 51–98. Washington.

Megaw, A. H. S. (1950), 'Three vaulted basilicas in Cyprus', *JHS,* 66: 48–56.

Meier, M. (2020), 'The Justinianic Plague: An Inconsequential Pandemic? A Reply', *Medizinhistorisches Journal,* 55(2): 172–99.

Meiggs, R. (1973), *Roman Ostia.* Oxford.

Mélèze Modrzejewski, J. (2014), *Loi et coutume dans l'Égypte grecque et romaine.* Warsaw.

Melotti, M. (2020), 'St Hippolytus and the Martyrs of Ostia. The Sea and the Construction of a New Christian Landscape', in A. Karivieri (ed.) 2020, 387–97.

Mentxaka, R. (1988), 'Stellionatus', *BIDR,* 30: 277–335.

Merola, G. D. (2007), 'Una lex collegii marittima? A proposito di D. 14.2.9', in E. Lo Cascio and G. D. Merola (eds), *Forme di aggregazione nel mondo romano,* 259–72. Bari.

Merola, G. D. (2009), 'Roma ebbe una politica doganale? Portoria e commerci nell'impero romano', in A. Storchi and G. D. Merola (eds), *Interventi imperiali in campo economico e sociale: da Augusto al Tardoantico,* 55–78. Bari.

Merola, G. D. (2016a), 'Augusto, le imposte, le province', *Maia,* 68: 321–33.

Merola, G. D. (2016b), 'La revisione augustea della lex portus Asiae', in B. Takmer, E. N. Akdoğu Arca and N. Gökalp Özdil (eds), *Vir doctus anatolicus. Studies in Memory of Sencer Şahin,* 627–34. Istanbul.

Merola, G. D. (2016c), 'Su Augusto e il potere normativo del princeps' in I. Piro (ed.), *Scritti per Alessandro Corbino* 5: 69–84. Tricase.

Merrills, A. H. (2005), *History and Geography in Late Antiquity.* Cambridge.

Merrills, A. H. (2013), 'Geography and memory in Isidore's *Etymologies*', in K. D. Lilley (ed.), *Mapping Medieval Geographies. Geographical Encounters in the Latin West and Beyond, 300–1600,* 45–64. Cambridge.

Merrills, A. H. (2018), 'Rome and the Vandals', in P. De Souza and P. Arnaud (eds), *The Sea in History. The Ancient World,* 494–510. Woodbridge.

Metcalf, D. (2014), 'The North–South Divide in Byzantine Cyprus: Some Evidence from lead Seals and Coins', in C. Stewart, T. W. Davis and A. M. Weyl Carr (eds), *Cyprus and the Balance of Empires: Art and Archaeology from Justinian I to the Coeur de Lion*, 57–68. Boston.

Meyboom, P. G. P. (1977), 'I mosaici pompeiani con figure di pesci', *Mededelingen van het Nederlands Instituut te Rome*, 39: 49–93.

Michaelides, D. (2001), 'The Ambo of Basilica A at Cape Drepanon', in J. Herrin, M. Mullett and C. Otten-Froux (eds), *Mosaic: Festschrift for A.H.S. Megaw*, 43–56. London.

Migliardi Zingale, L. (2009), 'Ancora sugli *astynomoi* in D. 43.10.1', [n.e.] in *Studi in onore di Remo Martini* II, 801–19. Milan.

Millar, F. (1969), 'P. Herennius Dexippus: The Greek World and the Third-Century Invasions', *JRS*, 59: 12–29.

Minale, V. M. (2015), 'Diritto romano e ideologia politica bizantina dagli Isauri ai macedoni: prima dei Basilici', *Index*, 43: 537–54.

Minale, V. M. (forthcoming), 'L'attività del senato nella cultura giuridica dell'ultima età macedonica: per un'interpretazione del prooimion del Nomos Rhodion Nautikos', in P. Buongiorno and M. Miglietta (eds), *Byzantinische Quellen für das Studium der senatus consulta*. Stuttgart.

Moatti, C. (2004), *La mobilité des personnes en Méditerranée de l'Antiquité à l'époque moderne*. Rome.

Moatti, C. (2006), 'Translation, Migration, and Communication in the Roman Empire: Three Aspects of Movement in History', *CA*, 25(1): 109–40.

Moatti, C. (2013), 'Immigration and cosmopolitanization', in P. Erdkamp (ed.), *The Cambridge Companion to Ancient Rome*, 77–92. Cambridge.

Moitrieux, G. (2014), 'Témoignages sous influence: Les images des divinités gallo-romaines', *Latomus*, 73(1): 149–62.

Molè, M. (1971), 'Una vexata *quaestio* in tema di furto', in *Studi Volterra 3*, 69–87. Milan.

Moll, B. (2005), 'L'Imperi Romà d'Orient a Menorca: el Testimoni Numismatic', *Gaceta Numismatica*, 157: 5–44.

Momigliano, A. (1942), 'Terra Marique', *JRS*, 32: 53–64.

Morabito, P. M. (2011), 'Saint George and the Dragon: Cult, Culture, and the Foundation of the City', *Contagion: Journal of Violence, Mimesis and Culture*, 18: 135–53.

Mordechai, L. and M. Eisenberg (2019), 'Rejecting Catastrophe: The Case of the Justinianic Plague', *P&P*, 244(1): 3–50.

Moschetti, C. M. (1966), *Gubernare navem, gubernare rem publicam. Contributo allo studio del diritto marittimo e del diritto pubblico romano*. Milan.

Moschetti, C. M. (1977), 'Naufragio', *ED*, 27: 547–58.

Moschetti, C. M. (1983), 'Pirateria', *ED*, 33: 873–910.

Molnar, I. (1981), 'Vis maior', *Iura*, 32: 73–105.

Moss, J. R. (1973), 'The effects of the policies of Aëtius on the history of Western Europe', *Historia*, 22: 723–8.

Muciaccia, G. (1977), 'L'elemento fortuito nel diritto romano e comune', *AG*, 193: 63–81.

Muciaccia, G. (1980), 'L'uso del termine "casus" nel diritto penale romano', in [n.e.] *Atti del II Seminario Gardesano*, 335–55. Milan.

Munitz, J. A. (2006), *Anastasii Sinaitae Quaestiones et responsiones*. Turnhout.

Müller, K. (1855), *Geographi Graeci Minores. Volume I*. Paris.

Murray, W. (1987), 'Do Modern Winds Equal Ancient Winds?', *MHR*, 2(2): 139–67.

Mustakallio, K. and A. Karivieri (2020), 'Contacts over the Sea: Evidence from Mosaics Decorating the Piazzale delle Corporazioni and the Terme delle Province', in A. Karivieri (ed.) 2020, 73–82.

Mustakallio, K. (forthcoming), 'Cultural Borrowing, Appropriation, or Forgery in a Multicultural Context – Ostian Artefacts with an Egyptian touch', in C. Krötzl, K. Mustakallio and M. Tamminen (eds), *Negotiation, Collaboration and Conflict in Ancient and Medieval Communities*. London–New York.

Bibliography

Nawotka, K. (2017), *The Alexander Romance by Ps.-Callisthenes. A Historical Commentary*. Leiden.
Nesselrath, H.-G. (2005), "Where the Lord of the Sea Grants Passage to Sailors through the Deep-Blue Mere No More': The Greeks and the Western Seas', *G&R*, 52: 153–71.
Nicolet, C. (1991), *Space, geography, and politics in the early Roman Empire*. Ann Arbor.
Noy, D. (2000), *Foreigners at Rome: Citizens and Strangers*. London.
Noy, D. (2020), '*Electa mihi domus est Ostia felix*: The Burial and Commemoration of Migrants at Ostia and Portus', in N. Bargfeldt and J. Hjarl Petersen (eds), *Reflections: Harbour City Deathscapes in Roman Italy and Beyond*, 53–62. Rome.
Nutton, V. (1969), 'Five Inscriptions of Doctors', *PBSR*, 37: 96–9.
Oberhelman, S. M. (2008), *Dreambooks in Byzantium. Six Oneirocritica in Translation, with Commentary and Introduction*. Farnham.
Olcott, W. T. (1911), *Star Lore: Myths, Legends, and Facts*. Dover.
Oliver, A. (2001), 'A Glass Opus Sectile Panel from Corinth', *Hesperia*, 70(3): 349–63.
Oliver, J. H. (1953), 'The Ruling Power: A Study of the Roman Empire in the Second Century through the Roman Oration of Aelius Aristides', *TAPA*, 43(4): 869–1003.
Olson, A. (2020), *Environment and Society in Byzantium, 650–1150. Between the Oak and the Olive*. London.
Opai, A., and A. Tsaravopoulos (2011), 'Amphorae of Dressel 24 Similis type in the central Aegean area (Chios-Erythrai-Kyme)', *ABSA*, 106(1): 275–323.
Ormerod, H. A. (1997), *Piracy in the ancient world: An essay in Mediterranean history*. Baltimore.
Osuchowski, W. (1950), 'Appunti sul problema del "iactus" in diritto romano', *Iura*, 1: 292–300.
Palazzolo, N. (1980), 'Le modalità di trasmissione dei provvedimenti imperiali nelle province (II–III sec. d.C.)', *Iura*, 28: 40–94.
Palmer, A. (1993), *The Seventh Century in the West-Syrian Chronicles*. Liverpool.
Palmer, C. (2009), 'Windward Sailing Capabilities of Ancient Vessels', *IJNA*, 38(2): 314–30.
Palumbo Stracca, B. M. (1997), 'Hybris barbarica e sophrosyne greca: l'epitafio per Domitilla', *Romanobarbarica*, 14: 15–32.
Papacostas, T. (2001), 'The Economy of Late Antique Cyprus', in S. Kingsley and M. Decker (eds), *Economy and Exchange in the East Mediterranean during Late Antiquity*, 107–28. Oxford.
Parker, A. J. (1992), *Ancient Shipwreck of the Mediterranean and the Roman Provinces*. Oxford.
Parker, A. J. (1992), 'Cargoes, containers and stowage: the ancient Mediterranean', *IJNA*, 21(2): 89–100.
Parlasca, K. (1959), *Die römischen Mosaiken in Deutschland*. Berlin.
Papathanassopoulos, G., and D. Schilardi (1981), 'An underwater survey of Paros, Greece: 1979. Preliminary report', *IJNA*, 10(2): 133–44.
Paulian, A. (1979), 'Le Dieu Océan en Espagne: un thème de l'art hispano-romain', *MCV*, 15: 115–33.
Perentidis, S. (1984), 'Recherches sur le texte de la Synopsis minor', in D. Simon (ed.), *Fontes Minores* 6, 219–73. Frankfurt.
Perentidis, S. (1986), 'L'empereur né le jour de Pâques. Michel IX Paléologue et la date de la Synopsis minor', in D. Simon (ed.), *Fontes Minores* 7, 253–7. Frankfurt.
Perentidis, S. (1994), *Théodose Zygomalas et sa Paraphrase de la Synopsis minor*. Athina.
Pérez Martín, I. (2016), 'Chronography and Geography in Tenth-Century Constantinople: the Manuscript of the *Stadiasmos* (Madrid, BN, MSS/4701)', *Geographia Antiqua*, 25: 79–97.
Pettegrew, D. K. (2007), 'The Busy Countryside of Late Roman Corinth: Interpreting Ceramic Data Produced by Regional Archaeological Surveys', *Hesperia*, 76(4): 743–84.
Pharr, C. (1952), *The Theodosian code and novels: and the Sirmondian constitutions*. Princeton.
Philaniotou, O. (2003), 'Συγκρότημα ελαιοτριβείων στον Πύργο του Χειμάρρου στη Νάξο', in A. Polymerou-Kamilaki, P. I. Kamilakis and L. Karapidaki (eds), *Ελιά και το Λάδι στον Χώρο και τον Χρόνο*, 73–83. Athens.

Picard, C. (2018), *Sea of the Caliphs. The Mediterranean in the Medieval Islamic World*, tr. N. Elliott. Cambridge, MA.
Pieri, D. (2005), *Le commerce du vin oriental à l'époque byzantine (IVe-VII s. ap. J.-C.). Le témoignage des amphores en Gaule*, Institut Français d'Archéologie du Proche-Orient. Beirut.
Pinna, F. (2010), 'Le Testimonianze archeologiche relative ai rapporti fra Arabi e la Sardegna nel Medioevo', *Rivista dell'Istituto di Storia dell'Europa Mediterranea* 4: 11-37.
Pinzone, A. (1982a), 'Naufragi, fisco e trasporti marittimi nell'età di Caracalla (su CI. 11, 6, 1)', *Quaderni Catanesi*, 7: 69-109.
Pinzone, A. (1982b), 'Mario Massimo e la Vita di Caracalla', *Bollettino di studi latini*, 12: 240-6.
Pirenne, H. (1936), *Mohammed and Charlemagne*. New York.
Pitsakis, K. G. (2000), 'Η ιστορία της Ρώμης και του Ρωμαικού Δικαίου στα βυζαντινά και μεταβυζαντινά νομικά εγχειρίδια', in [n.e.] *Τιμαί Ιωάννου Τριανταφυλλοπούλου. Τελετή επιδόσεως τιμητικού τόμου*, 399-436. Athens.
Pitts, M. and M. J. Versluys (2014), *Globalisation and the Roman World World History, Connectivity and Material Culture*. Cambridge.
Pókecz Kovács, A. (1998), 'Les problèmes du "iactus" et de la "contributio" dans la pratique de la *lex Rhodia*', in S. Lakos, D. M. Peter and B. Szabo (eds), *A bonis discere. Festagabe für Janos Zlinszky*, 171-88. Miskolc.
Policante, A. (2015), *The Pirate Myth. Genealogies of an Imperial Concept*. London.
Pollera, A. (1991), 'Annonam adtemptare et vexare vel maxime darddanarii solent'. D. 47.11.6: note sulla repressione dei crimini annonari', *Index*, 19: 405-31
Polzer, M. E. (2008), 'Toggles and Sails in the Ancient World: Rigging Elements Recovered from the Tantura B Shipwreck, Israel', *IJNA*, 37(2): 225-52.
Presuhn, É. (1878), *Les Décorations Murales de Pompéi*. Leipzig.
Price, S. (2012), 'Religious Mobility in the Roman Empire', *JRS*, 102: 1-19.
Prigent, V. (2012), 'Chypre entre Islam et Byzance', in J. Durand and D. Giovannoni (eds), *Chypre entre Byzance et l'Occident (IVème-XVIème) siècle*, 79-93. Paris.
Pritchett, W. (1991), *The Greek State at War. Part 5*. Berkeley.
Procopiou, E. (2018), 'New Evidence for Early Byzantine Ecclesiastical Architecture of Cyprus', in M. Hoerster, D. Nicolaou and S. Rogge (eds), *Church Building in Cyprus (Fourth to Seventh Centuries). A mirror of Intercultural Contacts in the Eastern Mediterranean*, 73-98. Münster-New York.
Prowse, T. (2016), 'Isotopes and Mobility in the Ancient Roman World', in L. de Ligt and L. E. Tacoma (eds), *Migration and Mobility in the Early Roman Empire*, 205-33. Leiden.
Pryor, J. H. (1988), *Geography, Technology, and War: Studies in the Maritime History of the Mediterranean, 649-1571*. Cambridge.
Pryor, J. H. (2004), 'The *Stadiodromikon* of the *De Cerimoniis* of Constantine VII, Byzantine warships, and the Cretan expedition of 949', in J. Chrystomidès, C. Dendrinos and J. Harris, (eds), *The Greek Islands and the Sea*, 77-108. Camberley.
Pulak, C. (2005), 'Discovering a Royal Ship from the Age of King Tut: Uluburun, Turkey', in G. F. Bass (ed.), *Beneath the Seven Seas: Adventures with the Institute of Nautical Archaeology*, 34-47. London.
Pulak, C. (2010), 'Uluburun Shipwreck', in E. R. Cline (ed.), *The Oxford Handbook of the Bronze Age Aegean*, 862-76. New York.
Pungetti, G. (2012), 'Islands, culture, landscape and seascape', *Journal of Marine and Island Cultures*, 1(2): 51-4.
Purcell, N. (2013), 'On the significance of East and West in today's "Hellenistic" history: reflections on symmetrical worlds, reflecting through world symmetries', in J. Prag and J. Crawley Quinn (eds), *The Hellenistic West. Rethinking the Ancient Mediterranean*, 367-91. Cambridge.
Purcell, N. (2018), 'Taxing the Sea', in P. De Souza and P. Arnaud (eds), *The Sea in History. The Ancient World*, 319-34. Woodbridge.

Bibliography

Purpura, G. (1976), 'Relitti di navi e diritti del fisco. Una congettura sulla *lex Rhodia*', *AUPA*, 36: 69–87.
Purpura, G. (1985a), 'Il regolamento doganale di Cauno e la *lex Rhodia* in D. 14, 2, 9', *AUPA*, 38: 273–331.
Purpura, G. (1985b), 'Polizia (dir.rom)', *ED* 24: 101–11.
Purpura, G. (1986), 'Rinvenimenti sottomarini nella Sicilia Occidentale', *Archeologia subacquea*, 3: 139–60.
Purpura, G. (1995), 'Il naufragio nel diritto romano: problemi giuridici e testimonianze archeologiche' *AUPA*, 43: 463–76.
Purpura, G. (2002), '*Ius naufragii*, sylai e *lex Rhodia*. Genesi delle consuetudini marittime mediterranea', *AUPA*, 47: 273–92.
Pryor, J. and E. Jeffreys (2006), *The Age of the Δρόμων: The Byzantine Navy ca. 500–1204*. Leiden.
Rainbird, P. (2000), *Archaeology of Islands*. Oxford.
Raptis, K. and O. M. Bakirtzis (2008), 'Agios Georgios, Pegeia – Cape Drepanon: Integrating an Excavation Site into an Archaeological Landscape', in G. Papantoniou (ed.), *Proceedings of the 5th Annual Meeting of Young Researchers on Cypriot Archaeology*, 87–95. Oxford.
Rauh, N. (2003), *Merchants, Sailors, and Pirates in the Roman World*. Stroud.
Rauh, N., C. Autret and J. Lund (2013), 'Amphora Design and Marketing in Antiquity', in M. Frass (ed.), *Kauf, Konsum und Märkte. Wirtschaftswelten im Fokus – Von der römischen Antike bis zur Gegenwart*, 145–81. Wiesbaden.
Reames, S. L. (1985), *The Legenda Aurea: A Reexamination of Its Paradoxical History*. Madison.
Reddé, M. (1986), *Mare Nostrum. Les infrastructures, le dispositif et l'histoire de la marine militaire sous l'empire romain*. Rome.
Redford, D. B. (1992), *Egypt, Canaan, and Israel in Ancient Times*. Princeton.
Reese, D. S. (2002), 'Fish: Evidence from Specimens, Mosaics, Wall Paintings, and Roman Authors', in W. F. Jashemski and F. G. Meyer (eds), *The Natural History of Pompeii*, 274–291. Cambridge.
Reitz-Joosse, B. (2016), 'Land at Peace and Sea at War: Landscape and the Memory of Actium in Greek Epigrams and Propertius' *Elegies*', in J. McInerney and I. Sluiter (eds), *Valuing Landscape in Classical Antiquity*, 276–96. Leiden.
Renfrew, C. (2013), 'Keros and the Development of the Project', in C. Renfrew, O. Philaniotou, N. Brodie, G. Gavalas and M. J. Boyd (eds), *The Settlement at Dhaskalio*, 3–18. Cambridge.
Renfrew, C. et al., (forthcoming[a]), 'The Southeast Naxos Survey: The sanctuary at Keros and terrestrial and maritime networks of the Aegean Early Bronze Age', in E. Marmaras et al. (eds), *3rd International Cycladological Conference: The Cyclades through time: Space–People*. Syros.
Renfrew, C., et al., eds (forthcoming[b]), *Keros Island Survey. The sanctuary on Keros and the origins of Aegean ritual practice*. Cambridge.
Reynolds, P. (2018), 'Amphorae in Beirut from the Umayyads to the Crusaders: A guide to trends in local and imported products', *Archeologia Medievale*, 45: 91–110.
Rheichard, I. (1993), *Die Frage des Drittschadensersatzes im klassischen römischen Recht*. Cologne–Weimar–Vienna.
Rice, E. E. (1991), 'The Rhodian Navy in the Hellenistic Age', in W. R. Roberts and J. Sweetman (eds), *New Interpretations in Naval History*, 29–50. Annapolis, MD.
Rice, C. (2016), 'Shipwreck cargoes in the western Mediterranean and the organization of Roman maritime trade', *JRA*, 29: 165–92.
Rice Holmes, T. (1909), 'Could Ancient Ships Work to Windward?', *CQ*, 3(1): 26–39.
Riches, S. (2000), *St. George: Hero, Martyr and Myth*. Cheltenham.
Rickman, G. (1980), *The Corn Supply of Ancient Rome*. Oxford.
Riley, J. A. (1979), 'The coarse pottery from Berenice', in J. A. Lloyd (eds), *Excavations at Sidi Krebish, Bengazi. (Berenice) II*, 91–467. Tripoli.
Rodolakēs, G. E. (2007), Ἀπὸ τὸν Νόμο Ῥοδίων στὸ 53ο Βιβλίο τῶν Βασιλικῶν. Athens.

Bibliography

Roller, D. W. (2006), *Through the Pillars of Herakles: Graeco-Roman Exploration of the Atlantic*. London.

Roller, D. W. (2010), *Eratosthenes' Geography. Fragments collected and translated, with commentary and additional material*. Princeton-Oxford.

Rollinger, R. (2012), 'From Sargon of Agade and the Assyrian Kings to Khusrau I and Beyond: on the Persistence of Ancient Near Eastern Traditions', in G. B. Lanfranchi, D. M. Bonacossa, C. Pappi and S. Ponchia (eds), *Leggo! Studies Presented to Frederick Mario Fales on the Occasion of His 65th Birthday*, 725–43. Wiesbaden.

Rollinger, R. (2019), 'Herennius Dexippus und die Tradition der Perserkriege im Imperium Romanum', *Historische Zeitschrift*, 308: 297–331.

Romm, J. S. (1992), *The Edges of the Earth in Ancient Thought*. Princeton.

Ross, D. J. A. (1967), *Alexander and the Faithless Lady: A Submarine Adventure*. London.

Rougé, J. (1966), 'Le droit de naufrage et ses limitations en Méditerranée avant l'établissement de la domination de Rome', in R. Chevallier (ed.), *Mélanges d'archéologie et d'histoire offerts à André Piganiol* III, 1467–79. Paris

Rougé, J. (1969), 'Ὁ θειότατος Αὔγουστος', *Revue de philologie, de littérature et d'histoire anciennes*, 43: 83–92.

Roussos, K. Z. (2017), *Reconstructing the Settled Landscape of the Cyclades. The islands of Paros and Naxos during the Late Antique and Early Byzantine centuries*. Leiden.

Rubin, Z. (1986), 'The Mediterranean and the Dilemma of the Roman Empire in Late Antiquity', *MHR*, 1: 13–62.

Ruggeri, V. (1998), 'An archaeological survey in the gulf of Keramos and on the northern shore of the peninsula of Halicarnassos', *Araştırma Sonuçları Toplantısı*, 15(1): 201–17.

Ruggeri, V. (2001), 'La Licia Bizantina', *Pegaso*, 1: 147–74.

Ruggiero, I. (2009), 'Immagini di ius receptum nelle Pauli Sententiae', in *Studi in onore di Remo Martini* III, 425–71. Milan.

Ruggiero, I. (2017), *Ricerche sulle Pauli Sententiae*. Milan.

Rumpf, A. (1939), *Die Meerwesen auf den antiken Sarkophagreliefs*. Berlin.

Sacco, G. (1984), *Iscrizioni greche d'Italia, Porto*. Rome.

Said, E. W. (1978), *Orientalism*. New York.

Salomies, O. (2002), 'People in Ostia: Some Onomastic Observations and Comparisons with Rome', in C. Bruun and A. Gallina Zevi (eds), *Ostia e Portus nelle loro relazioni con Roma*, 135–59. Rome.

Salomies, O. (2020), 'Prominent Families of Ostia', in A. Karivieri (ed.) 2020, 159–64.

Salomon, F. et al. (2018), 'Geoarchaeology of the Roman port-city of Ostia: Fluvio-coastal mobility, urban development, and resilience', *Earth-Science Reviews*, 177: 265–83.

Santamaria, C. (1984), 'L'épave "H" de la Chrétienne à Saint-Raphaël (Var)'. *Archaeonautica*, 4: 9–52.

Schanbacher, D. (2006), 'Zur Rezeption und Entwicklung des rhodischen Seewurfrechts in Rom' in B. R. Kern et al. (eds), *Humaniora–Medizin–Recht–Geschichte. Festschrift für Adolf Laufs zum 70. Geburtstag*, 257–73. Berlin-Heidelberg.

Scheidel, W. (2013), 'The shape of the Roman world', *Princeton/Stanford Working Papers in Classics*, 1–27.

Scheidel, W. (2015), 'ORBIS: the Stanford geospatial network model of the Roman World', *Princeton/Stanford. Working Papers in Classics*, 1–27.

Scheidel, W. and E. Meeks (2019), *ORBIS: The Stanford Geospatial Network Model of the Roman World*. http://orbis.stanford.edu.

Scheltema, H. J., and N. Van der Wal, ed. (1974), *Basilicorum libri LX* A.7. Groningen.

Scherillo, G. (1950), 'Note critiche su opere della giurisprudenza', *Iura*, 1: 204–22.

Schmink, A. (1959), 'Quellenstudien zum Prooimion der Epanagoge', *BZ*, 52: 68–81.

Bibliography

Schmink, A. (1988), 'Das Prooimion der Bearbeitung der Nomokanons in 14. Titeln durch Michael und Theodoros', in L. Burgmann (ed.), *Fontes Minores* 10, 357–86. Frankfurt.
Schminck, A. (1992), *Thessalonizensische Jurisprudenz in der Palaiologenzeit* (Thessaloniki) [unpublished].
Schminck, A. (1993), 'Ein rechtshistorische "Traktat" in Cod. Mosq. gr. 475', in L. Burgmann, L. (ed.), *Fontes Minores* 9, 81–96. Frankfurt.
Schmitt, H. H. (1957), *Rom und Rhodos. Geschichte ihrer politischer Beziehungen seit ersten Beruhrung bis zum Aufgehen des Inselstaates im römischen Weltreich*. Munich.
Schmuhl, Y. and B. Steidl (2008), 'Welterbe Limes. Roms Grenze am Main. Die Steindenkmäler', *Mitteilungen der Freunde der Bayerischen Vor- und Frühgeschichte*, 121: 3–47.
Schulz, F. (1946), *History of Roman Legal Science*. Oxford.
Sessa, K. (2019), 'The New Environmental Fall of Rome: A Methodological Consideration', *Journal of Late Antiquity*, 12(1): 211–55.
Sgoutas, L. (1861), Ποίημα Νόμικον', Θέμις, 8: 47–155.
Shaw, B. D. (1997), 'Bandit highlands and lowland peace: the mountains of Isauria–Cilicia', *Journal of the Economic and Social History of the Orient*, 33: 199–233.
Shepard, J. (2014), 'Bunkers, Open Cities and Boats in Byzantine Diplomacy', in D. Dzino and K. Perry (eds), *Byzantium, Its Neighbours and Its Cultures*, 3–33. Brisbane.
Sirks, A. J. B. (1992), *Food for Rome: The Legal Structure of the Transportation and Processing of Supplies for the Imperial Distributions in Rome and Constantinople*. Amsterdam.
Sirks, A. J. B. (1998), 'Archives used with or by *corpora*, working for the Annona of Rome and Constantinople', in C. Moatti (ed.), *La mémoire perdue. Recherches sur l'administration romaine*, 325–43. Rome.
Sirks, B. (2002), 'Sailing in the Off-season with Reduced Financial Risk', in J. J. Aubert and B. Sirks (eds), *Speculum Iuris: Roman Law as a Reflection of Economic and Social Life*, 134–50. Ann Arbor.
Smith, M. S. (1994), *The Ugaritic Ba'al Cycle: Volume I: Introduction with Text, Translation and Commentary of KTU 1.1–1.2*. Leiden.
Snively, C. S. (2007), 'Late Antique Nicopolis', in K. L. Zakhos (ed.), *ΝΙΚΟΠΟΛΙΣ Β', τόμος Ι*, 739–49. Preveza.
Solazzi, S. (1939), 'Su CI 11,6 *de naufragiis*', *RDN*, 5: 253–65.
Solin, H. (2020), 'The Wall Inscriptions of Ostia', in A. Karivieri (ed.) 2020, 319–32.
Spagnuolo Vigorita, T. and F. Mercogliano (1992), 'Tributi (diritto romano)', *ED* 45: 85–105.
Spanu, P. G. and R. Zucca (2004), *I Sigilli Bizantini della ΣΑΡΔΗΝΙΑ*. Rome.
Spiro, M. (1978), *Critical corpus of the mosaic pavements on the Greek mainland, fourth/sixth centuries, with architectural surveys*. New York.
Starr, C. G. (1989), *The Influence of Sea Power on Ancient History*. Oxford.
Steinbeck, J. (1976), *The Acts of King Arthur and His Noble Knights: From the Winchester Manuscripts of Thomas Malory and Other Sources*. New York.
Stewart, H. (1977), *Indian Fishing, Early Methods on the Northwest Coast*. Seattle.
Stisi, V. and A. Means (forthcoming), '1st Millennium Pottery', in C. Renfrew et al. (eds), *Keros Island Survey. The sanctuary on Keros and the origins of Aegean ritual practice*. Cambridge.
Stone, D. L. (2014), 'Africa in the Roman Empire: Connectivity, the economy, and artificial port structures', *AJA*, 118(4): 565–600.
Stoneman, R. (2012), *The Book of Alexander the Great. A Life of the Conqueror*. London.
Straumann, B. (2015), *Roman Law in the State of Nature: The Classical Foundations of Hugo Grotius' Natural Law*. Cambridge.
Suski, R. (2017), 'Dexippus and the Repelling of the Gothic Invasion in the years 267–268', *Eos*, 104: 303–16.
Svoronos, N. G. (1964) *Synopsis major des Basiliques et ses Appendices. Recherches sur la tradition juridique à Byzance*. Paris.

Sweetman, R. J. (2016), 'Networks: Exile and Tourism in the Roman Cyclades', in J. F. D. Frakes, M. Egri and S. E. Alcock (eds), *Beyond Boundaries: Connecting Visual Cultures in the Provinces of Ancient Rome*, 46–61. Los Angeles.
Tacoma, L. E. (2015), 'Roman Elite Mobility under the Principate', in N. Fisher and H. van Wees (eds), *'Aristocracy' in Antiquity. Redefining Greek and Roman Elites*, 125–46. Swansea.
Tacoma, L. E. (2016a), *Moving Romans. Migration to Rome in the Principate*. Oxford.
Tacoma, L. E. (2016b), 'Bones, Stones, and Monica. Isola Sacra Revisited', in E. Lo Cascio, L. E. Tacoma and M. J. Groen-Vallinga (eds), *The Impact of Mobility and Migration in the Roman Empire*, 132–54. Leiden.
Tacoma, L. E. and E. Lo Cascio (2016), 'Writing Migration', in E. Lo Cascio, L. E. Tacoma and M. J. Groen-Vallinga (eds), *The Impact of Mobility and Migration in the Roman Empire*, 1–24. Leiden.
Talbot, C. H. (1954), *The Anglo-Saxon Missionaries in Germany: Being the Lives of SS. Willibrord, Boniface, Sturm, Leoba and Lebuin together with the Hodoeporicon of St. Willibald and a Selection from the Correspondence of St. Boniface*. London.
Tammuz, O. (2006), 'Mare Clausum? Sailing Seasons in the Mediterranean in Early Antiquity', *Mediterranean History Journal*, 20: 145–62.
Tarwacka, A. (2009), *Romans and Pirates: Legal Perspective*. Warsaw.
Tarwacka, A. (2018), 'Some Remarks on Piracy in Roman law', *Annuaires de droit maritime et oceanique*, 36: 295–309.
Taylor, R. (2000), 'Watching the Skies: Janus, Auspication, and the Shrine in the Roman Forum', *MAAR*, 45: 1–40.
Teall, J. L. (1959), 'The Grain Supply of the Byzantine Empire, 330–1025', *DOP*, 13: 87–139.
Theodoropoulos, P. (2020), 'The Migration of Syrian and Palestinian Populations in the 7th Century: Movement of Individuals and Groups in the Mediterranean', in J. Preiser-Kapeller et al. (eds), *Migration Histories of the Medieval Afroeurasian Transition Zone*, 261–87. Leiden.
Thomas, J. A. C. (1974), 'Juridical Aspects of Carriage by Sea and Warehousing in Roman Law', *Recueils de la Société Jean Bodin pour l'Histoire Comparative des Institutions*, 32: 117–60.
Throckmorton, P. (1972), 'Romans on the sea', in G. F. Bass (ed.), *A History of Seafaring based on Underwater Archaeology*, 65–86. London.
Thylander, H. (1951–2), *Inscriptions du port d'Ostie*. Lund.
Thommen, L. (2012), *An Environmental History of Ancient Greece and Rome*. Cambridge.
Tilly, C. (1978), 'Migration in Modern European History', in W. W. McNeill and R. S. Adams (eds), *Human migration: patterns and policies*, 48–72. Bloomington–London.
Tobler, T. and A. Molinier (1880), *Bernard, Itinerarium. Itinera hierosolymitana et descriptiones terrae sanctae 1.2*. Geneva.
Tommasi, C. (1997), 'La "libertà dei mari". Ugo Grozio e gli sviluppi della talassocrazia olandese nel primo Seicento', *Scienza e Politica* 9: 35–53.
Töyräänvuori, J. (2016), 'The Symbolic Ambiguity of the Mediterranean Sea in Ancient Semitic Mythology', in A. Berner, J.-M. Henke, A. Lichtenberger, B. Morstadt and A. Riedel (eds), *Das Mittelmeer und der Tod: Mediterrane Mobilität und Sepulkralkultur*, 435–46. Paderborn.
Töyräänvuori, J. (2018), *Sea and the Combat Myth: North West Semitic Political Mythology in the Hebrew Bible*. Münster.
Töyräänvuori, J. (2021), 'Wings, Weapons, and the Horned Tiara: Iconographic Representation of the Deity of the Mediterranean Sea in the Bronze Age', *AABNER*, 1: 89–127.
Treadgold, W. (1997), *A History of Byzantine State and Society*. Stanford.
Triantaphillopoulos, J. (1964), 'Varia graeco-romana', in *Synteleia Arangio-Ruiz* II. 903–8. Naples.
Troianos, S. (2015), *Le fonti del diritto bizantino*. Torino.
Troje, H. E. (1971), *'Graeca leguntur'. Die Aneignung des byzantinischen Rechts und die Entstehung eines humanistischen Corpus iuris civilis in der Jurisprudenz des 16. Jahrhunderts*. Cologne–Vienna.

Bibliography

Tuccillo, F. (2013), 'Brevi note sull'Ἀστυνομικὸς μονόβιβλος', in C. Cascione, C. Masi Doria and G. D. Merola (eds), *Modelli di un multiculturalismo giuridico. Il bilinguismo nel mondo antico. Diritto, prassi, insegnamento* I, 323–38. Naples.

Tuori, K. (2006), 'Hadrian's Perpetual Edict: Ancient Sources and Modern Ideals in the Making of a Historical Tradition', *JLH*, 27(3): 219–37.

Tuori, K. (2016), *The Emperor of Law: The Emergence of Roman Imperial Adjudication*. Oxford.

Tzavella, E. (2013), 'The Byzantine Chapel and its Finds', in C. Renfrew et al. (eds), *The settlement at Dhaskalio*, 87–91. Cambridge.

Tzavella, E. (2016), 'Dhaskalio Keros: An Unknown Early Byzantine Church, Its Ceramic Finds, and Small-Scale Navigation in the Central Aegean', in B. Krsmanović, L. Milanović and B. Pavlović (eds), *Proceedings of the 23rd International Congress of Byzantine Studies*, 333–7. Belgrade.

Tzavella, E. (2018), 'Dhaskalio, Keros: An unknown Early Byzantine church', in J. Crow and D. Hill (eds), *Naxos and the Byzantine Aegean. Insular Responses to Regional Change*, 177–94. Athens.

Urbanik, J. (2019), 'Jósef inter gentes. On Status and Law between Centre and Periphery', *JJP*, 49: 289–345.

Vacca, L. (1972), *Ricerche in tema di 'actio vi bonorum raptorum'*. Milan.

Valérien, D. (2014), 'The Medieval Mediterranean', in P. Horden and S. Kinoshita (eds), *A Companion to Mediterranean History*, 77–90. London.

Vallejo Girvés, M. (2012), *Hispania y Byzancio: Una relación desconocida*. Madrid.

Van Bochove, T. E. (1997), 'Οὐ κελεύομεν· συνεκεφαλαιώσαμεν καὶ ῥᾳδίαν ἔντευξιν παρέσχομεν. Some Remarks with Respect to the Nature of the Preface to the Basilica', in [n.e.] *Analecta Atheniensia ad ius byzantinum spectantia* I, 155–68. Athens.

Van der Wal, N. (1981), 'La version florentine de la collection des 168 novelles', *RHD*, 49: 149–58.

Van Doorninck, F. (1972), 'Byzantium, mistress of the sea: 330–641', in G. F. Bass (ed.), *A History of Seafaring based on underwater archaeology*, 133–58. London.

Vanek, K. (2007), *Ars corrigendi in der frühen Neuzeit. Studien zur Geschichte der Textkritik*. Berlin.

Van der Ploeg, G. (2017), 'African and Ostian Connections: The Case-study of Lucius Caecilius Aemilianus', *Ancient Society*, 47: 221–36.

Van der Ploeg, G. (2020a), 'Wine Trade and Commercial Connections in Ostia Antica', in K. Mustakallio et al. (eds), *'Mehr Licht', More Light; Più Luce. Studia in honorem Arja Karivieri*, 177–84. Turku.

Van der Ploeg, G. (2020b), 'Shipowners and *Curatores* in Ostia', in A. Karivieri (ed.) 2020, 181–6.

Van Dommelen, P. (1999), 'Island in History', *JMA*, 12(2): 246–51.

Van Haeperen, F., ed. (2019), *Regio I: Ostie, Porto (Fana, templa, delubra. Corpus dei luoghi di culto dell'Italia antica*. Rome.

Van Nuffelen, P. (2012), *Orosius and the Rhetoric of History*. Oxford.

Van Oyen, A. (2017), 'Agents and commodities: a response to Brughmans and Poblome (2016) on modelling the Roman economy', *Antiquity*, 91: 1356–63.

Varinlioğlu, G. (2019), '"Imagine there is no (is)land": Conceptualizing Byzantine Islands in Southern Asia Minor', in K. Durak and I. Jevtić (eds), *Identity and the other in Byzantium*, 93–111. Istanbul.

Varvaro, M. (2006), 'Note sugli archivi imperiali nell'età del principato', *AUPA*, 51: 381–431.

Veikou, M. (2012), 'Byzantine Histories, Settlement Stories: Kastra, "Isles of Refuge", and "Unspecified Settlements" as In-between or Third Spaces', in T. Kioussopoulou (ed.), *Οι βυζαντινές πόλεις, 8ος– 15ος αιώνας, Προοπτικές της έρευνας και νέες ερμηνευτικές προσεγγίσεις*, 159–206. Rethymno.

Veikou, M. and I. Nilsson (2018), 'Ports and Harbours as Heterotopic Entities in Byzantine Literary Texts', in C. von Carnap-Bornheim et al. (eds), *Harbours as Objects of Interdisciplinary Research – Archaeology+History+Geosciences*, 265–77. Mainz.

Velissaropoulos-Karakostas, J. (1977), 'Les *symbola* d'affaires. Remarques sur les tablettes archaïques de l'île de Corfou', in *Symposion 1977*, 71–83. Cologne.

Vélissariopoulos, J. (1980), *Les nauclères grecs. Recherches sur le institutions maritimes en Grèce et dans l'Orient hellénisé*. Geneva–Paris.

Verger, A. (1965), 'Nómos Rhodiôn Naytikós, in *Novissimo Digesto Italiano* XI', 316–20. Torino.

Villinger, P. (1603), *Bilgerfahrt und Beschreibung der Hierusolomitanischen Rei in das heylig Land, unnd deren Provintzen Palestina*. Konstanz.

Vionis, A. K. (2013), 'Reading Art and Material Culture: Greeks, Slavs and Arabs in the Byzantine Aegean', in B. Crostini and S. La Porta (eds), *Negotiating Co-Existence: Communities, Culture and Convivencia in Byzantine Society*, 103–27. Trier.

Vionis, A. K. (2016), *Naxos between Late Antiquity and the early Middle Ages: decline or stability?*, in B. Krsmanović et al. (eds), *Proceedings of the 23rd International Congress of Byzantine Studies: Round Tables: Belgrade, 22–27 August, 2016*, 329–32. Belgrade.

Vionis, A. K. (2018), 'Settled and Sacred Landscape of Cyprus: Church and Landscape in the Xeros Valley during the Early Byzantine Period', in M. Hoerster, D. Nicolaou and S. Rogge (eds), *Church Building in Cyprus (Fourth to Seventh Centuries). A Mirror of Intercultural Contacts in the Eastern Mediterranean*, 45–70. Münster.

Vlassopoulos, K. and I. K. Xydopoulos (2015), 'Introduction: the study of violence and community in ancient Greece', in K. Vlassopoulos, I. K. Xydopoulos and E. Tounta (eds), *Violence and Community: Law, Space and Identity in the Ancient Eastern Mediterranean World*, 1–27. London.

Volterra, E. (1936), 'L'efficacia delle costituzioni imperiali emanate per la provincia', in [n.e.] *Studi di storia e diritto in onore di Enrico Besta* I, 449–77. Milan.

Volterra, E. (1971), 'Il problema del testo delle costituzioni imperiali', in [n.e.] *La critica del testo. Atti del Secondo Congresso Internazionale della Società Italiana di Storia del Diritto*, 821–1097. Florence.

Voute, P. (1972), 'Notes sur l'iconographie d'Océan. À propos d'une fontaine à mosaïques découverte à Nole (Campanie)', *MEFRA*, 84(1): 639–73.

Vroom, J. (2012), 'From one coast to another: early Medieval ceramics in the Southern Adriatic region', in S. Gelichi and R. Hodges (eds), *From one Sea to Another. Trading Places in the European and Mediterranean Early Middle Ages*, 353–91. Turnhout.

Vroom, J. (2016), 'Ceramics', in P. Niewöhner (ed.), *The Archaeology of Byzantine Anatolia. From the End of Late Antiquity until the coming of the Turks*, 176–93. Oxford.

Wade, J. (2018), 'The eternal spirit of Thalassa: The transmission of classical maritime symbolism into Byzantine cultural identity', *Journal of the Australian Early Medieval Association*, 14: 51–69.

Wagner, H. (1967), 'Die *Lex Rhodia de iactu*', *RIDA*, 44: 357–80.

Walter, C. (2003), *The Warrior Saints in Byzantine Art and Tradition*. London.

Warnking, P. (2015), *Der römische Seehandel - Rahmenbedingungen, Transportwege, Wirtschaftlichkeit*. Rahden–Westfalen.

West, M. L. (1997), *The East Face of Helicon: West Asiatic Elements in Greek Poetry and Myth*. Oxford.

Westgate, R. (2000), 'Pavimenta atque emblemata vermiculata: Regional Styles in Hellenistic Mosaic and the First Mosaics at Pompeii', *AJA*, 104(2): 255–75.

Whitby, M. and M. Roberts (2018), 'Epic Poetry', in S. McGill and E. J. Watts (eds), *A Companion to Late Antique Literature*, 221–40. Oxford.

Whitewright, J. (2007), 'How Fast is Fast? Technology, trade and speed under sail in the Roman Red Sea', in J. Starkey, P. Starkey and T. Wilkinson (eds), *Nautical Resources and Cultural Connections of the Red Sea*, 77–88. Oxford.

Whitewright, J. (2008), *Maritime Technological Change in the Ancient Mediterranean: The Invention of the Lateen Sail*. Southampton. PhD Diss.

Bibliography

Whitewright, J. (2009), 'The Mediterranean Lateen Sail in Late Antiquity'. *IJNA*, 38(1): 97–104.
Whitewright, J. (2011), 'The Potential Performance of Ancient Mediterranean Sailing Rigs'. *IJNA*, 40(1): 2–17.
Whitewright, J. (2018), 'Sailing and Sailing Rigs in the Ancient Mediterranean: implications of continuity, variation and change in propulsion technology'. *IJNA*, 47(1): 28–44.
Whittaker, C. R. (2004), *Rome and Its Frontiers: The Dynamics of Empire*. London.
Wickham, C. (2004), 'The Mediterranean around 800: On the Brink of the Second Trade Cycle', *DOP*, 58: 161–74.
Wickham, C. (2005), *Framing the Early Middle Ages*. Oxford.
Wickham, C. (2018), 'Some concluding observations', *Archeologia Medievale*, 45: 289–92.
Wieacker, F. (1953), 'Iactus in tributum nave salva venit (D. 14,2,4,pr.). Exegesen zur *Lex Rhodia* de iactu', in *Studi in memoria di Emilio Albertario* I, 515–32. Milan.
Wilkes, J. (1992), *The Illyrians*. Chichester.
Williams, M. F. (2004), *The making of Christian communities in Late Antiquity and the Middle Ages*. London.
Williams-Forte, E. (1983), 'The Snake and the Tree in the Iconography and Texts of Syria During the Bronze Age', in L. Gorelick and E. Williams-Forte (eds), *Ancient Seals and the Bible*, 18–43. Malibu.
Wilson, A. (2011), 'Developments in Mediterranean shipping and maritime trade from the Hellenistic period to AD 1000', in D. Robinson and A. Wilson (eds), *Marine Archaeology and Ancient Trade in the Mediterranean*, 33–60. Oxford.
Wilson, A., K. Schörle and C. Rice (2012), 'Roman ports and Mediterranean connectivity', in S. Keay (ed.), *Rome, Portus and the Mediterranean*, 367–91. London.
Woolf, G. (2016a), 'Moving Peoples in the Early Roman Empire', in E. Lo Cascio and L. E. Tacoma, (eds), *The Impact of Mobility and Migration in the Roman Empire*, 25–41. Leiden.
Woolf, G. (2016b), 'Movers and Stayers', in L. De Ligt and L. E. Tacoma (eds), *Migration and Mobility in the Early Roman Empire. Studies in Global Social History*, 438–61. Leiden.
Yacoub, M. (1995), *Splendeurs de Mosaïques de Tunisie*. Tunis.
Yacoub, M. (2016), *Carrés Couleurs: Mosaïques Romaines De Tunisie*. Tunis.
Zachariae von Lingenthal, K. E. (1973), 'Ποίημα Νόμικον', in *Kleine Schriften zür römischen und byzantinischen Rechtsgeschichte* I, 356–464. Leipzig.
Zalewski, B. (2016), 'Creative Interpretation of *lex Rhodia de iactu* in the Legal Doctrine of *ius commune*', *Krytyka Prawa*, 8: 173–91.
Zamperini, A. (2013), *Le grottesche. Il sogno della pittura nella decorazione parietale*. San Giovanni Lupatoto. Verona.
Zanon, G. (1998), *Le strutture accusatorie della cognitio extra ordinem nel principato*. Padova.
Zapheiropoulou, M.-K. (2006), *Emblemata vermiculata. Hellenistische und spätrepublikanische Bildmosaiken*. Paderborn.
Zarmakoupi, M. (2015), 'Hellenistic & Roman Delos: the city & its emporion', *Archaeological Reports*, 61: 115–32.
Zavagno, L. (2011–12), 'At the Edge of two Empires. The Economy of Cyprus between Late Antiquity and the early Middle Ages', *DOP*, 65(6): 121–55.
Zavagno, L. (2013), 'Two Hegemonies, One Island: Cyprus as a "Middle Ground" between the Byzantines and the Arabs (650–850 A.D)', *Reti Medievali Rivista*, 14: 3–32.
Zavagno, L. (2018), '"Islands in the Stream": For a new history of the large islands of the Byzantine Mediterranean', *MHR*, 33(2): 152–3.
Zavagno, L. (2019), 'Going to the Extremes: The Balearics and Cyprus in the Early Medieval Byzantine Insular System', *Al-Masāq*, 31(2): 155–7.
Zavagno, L. and B. Kızılduman (2018), 'A countryside in transition: the Galinoporni-Kaleburnu plain in the passage from Late Antiquity to the Early Middle Ages (ca. 600–850)', *Památky archeologické*, 109: 233–51.

Zeno, R. (1934), 'Influenze romane e bizantine nella formazione del diritto marittimo medievale', in *Atti delle manifestazioni culturali pro Tabula d'Amalpha* I, 1–33. Naples.
Zeno, R. (1946), *Storia del diritto marittimo italiano nel Mediterraneo*. Milan.
Zepos, J. and P. Zepos, eds (1931a), *Jus Graecoromanum* II. Athens.
Zepos, J. and P. Zepos, eds (1931b), *Jus Graecoromanum* VI. Athens.
Zepos, J. and P. Zepos, eds (1931c), *Jus Graecoromanum* VII. Athens.
Zerjadtke, M. (2020), 'Thematische Einführung. Der Problemkomplex "Topos" und seine Facetten', in M. Zerjadtke (ed.), *Der ethnographische Topos in der Alten Geschichte*, 11–26. Stuttgart.
Ziebarth, E. (1929), *Beiträge zur Geschichte des Seeraubs und Seehandels im alten Griechenland*. Hamburg.
Žiha, N. (2018), 'On Reception of Greek Maritime Norms, or How to Find a Perfect Place for a Foreign Principle in the Roman Legal System', in A. Katančević, M. Vukotić, S. Vandenbogaerde and V. M. Minale (eds), *History of Legal Sources. The Changing Structure of Law*, 213–22. Belgrade.
Zuccotti, F. (1992), 'Symbolon e stipulatio', in F. Pastori (ed.), *Testimonium amicitiae*, 305–439. Milan.

INDEX

Achelous, Acheloös (river) 34
Achilles Tatius 153
Actium (battle of) 49, 51, 178 n.30, 200
Acts of the Seventh Ecumenical Council 121
Adonis 19, 20, 22
Adriatic Sea 44, 76, 182, 205
Aegean Sea viii, 7, 24 n.31, 53, 54, 57, 62, 90, 92, 96–109, 117, 126 n.21, 161, 182, 184–7, 189, 198–200, 202, 204–5
Aelia Uluzibbira (mod. Sidi Bou Ali) 80
Aelius Aristides 50, 52, 178 n.32, 198
Aelius Samius Isocrates, P. (sophist) 74
Aesculapius 74
Africa (province, region) 14, 32, 35–8, 40–2, 48 n.105, 54–7, 60–1, 72–4, 76–7, 80, 82, 99–100, 106, 114, 117, 147 n.92, 157, 160
African Red Slip Ware 96, 99, 106
Agapetus (rhetorician) 60
Akko (Palestine) 57, 66
Al-Balādhurī, Aḥmad ad ibn Yaḥyā ibn Jabir (historian) 66
Aleppo 15
Alexander the Great 1–2, 8 n.1, n.4, 13, 16, 18–19, 23 n.23, 24 n.34–5, 57
Alexandria 23, 27–8, 38, 58, 73–4, 76, 78, 83, 87 n.132, 117–19, 150, 158
Algeria 37
Ambracian Gulf 49
Ammianus Marcellinus 59
Amorgos 108
Amphitrite 37
Amphorae 79, 92, 95–102, 105, 109–10, 115, 118, 121, 123–4, 160
Anastasius (emperor) 56
Anastasius the Sinaite 121, 125
Anchialus (city) 53
anchorages, opportunistic ports 58, 66, 79, 90, 92, 95–6, 99, 105, 108, 116, 118, 162
Andromeda 18
Anicii (gens) 72, 74
Annaeus Atticus, C. 76
annona 110, 115, 117–18, 120, 124, 140, 142, 147 n.82, 148 n.101, 168
Antioch 20–1, 33, 46 n.49, 52, 73
'*antipatheia' topos* 27–8, 38–9, 41–2, 45, 48
Antoninus Pius 136, 148, 167–9, 175–6, 178, 180
Antoninus Placentinus 118

Aperlae (Lycia) 105, 119
Aphrodite 18, 20, 58
Apollo 34, 74
Aquileia 62
Arabs 57–9, 63, 66 n.84, 115, 118, 121–5, 136, 153
Aramaic cults 83
Arcadius (emperor) 51
Archontes 122
Aristotle 1, 24 n.27, 27, 39, 42, 44 n.8, 150, 161
Armenia 42
Arrian (*Anabasis*) 16
Aşağı Mazı (Caria) 119
Ashkelon 14, 19
Asia Minor 48 n.105, 98–100, 104, 107, 117, 150, 158, 160–1, 165 n.78
Assyria, Neo–Assyrian empire 15, 23 n.23
Athens 20, 53–4, 73, 99–100, 158, 160–1, 172
Atlantic (Ocean) 29, 49
Augustine (ecclesiastical writer, saint) 22 n.6, 74, 85 n.36, n.38–40, 137
Augustus (emperor) 25 n.39, 51, 64 n.5, 75–6, 135, 145 n.39, 167–9, 173–4, 176 n.7, 178 n.30
Aulus Gellius 49, 64

Baal (god) 14, 20, 22–3, 25
Babylonia 13, 15, 16, 24
Bad Kreuznach (town in Germany) 31, 34–6, 8–9
Bad Vilbel (town in Germany) 40, 47
Baetica (province) 72, 79, 160
Balearic Islands 54, 123, 160
Basilika (collection) 169–70, 175
Berytus (mod. Beirut) 23, 120
Bible, Biblical 24, 63, 126, 128
Bithynia 74, 78
Black Sea, Pontus Euxinus xiii, 53, 65, 108, 178
Bosporus 53
Britain, Britannia 18, 33, 36, 43, 49, 75
Bronze Age 14–17, 71, 88, 96, 98, 160, 162
Byzantine (East) Rome, Byzantine Era 6, 9 n.30, 20, 49, 58, 61, 64 n.8, 67 n.94, n.105, 68 n.125, 88, 90, 92, 95–6, 101–2, 105–7, 109–10, 114–25, 126 n.21, 162, 167, 169–70, 173–5

cabotage 101–2, 105–6, 108–9, 115, 117, 149, 159, 162
Caligula 13, 18, 19, 25 n.37, n.39, 51, 64 n.7, n.20–1

Index

Caliphate (Rashidun or Umayyad) xiii, 57, 116–17, 120, 124
Caracalla 136, 139–40, 145–7
Caria 117, 119, 161, 163, 176
Carthage, Carthaginians 13, 18, 24, 54–6, 60, 77, 80, 100, 115, 117, 143, 160
Cassius Dio 18, 65, 84, 144–5
Cernunnos (divinity) 34, 36–7, 43, 46
Christ(ianity), Christianization 13–14, 19–21, 25 n.47, 26, 36–7, 43, 46 n.52, 60–1, 63, 72, 74–5, 83–4, 93, 118–19, 123
Cicero 27, 44 n.11, 49, 63 n.4, 64 n.10, n.19, 134, 144 n.16, n.19–20, n.26, 146 n.70, 158, 164 n.55, 165 n.70, 178 n.28
Cilicia, Cilician 58, 98, 100, 107, 110, 112, 119, 145, 148
Codex Gregorianus 140
Codex Hermogenianus 140
Codex Iustinianus 137, 139, 140, 142, 146 n.67, 147 n.76, n.93, 148 n.102, n.104, 165 n.72, 176 n.9, 177 n.20
Codex Theodosianus 65, 137, 140, 146, 147 n.84, n.88, n.91, n.95–6, 148 n.97, n.102–4, 165 n.72
connectivity, networks 4–5, 7, 59, 71–3, 76, 78–9, 88, 97–8, 101–2, 104–7, 109, 114–16, 118–19, 121, 124–5, 149, 154
conquest (also of the sea) 1–3, 13–18, 21, 24, 55, 59, 66, 114–15, 117–18, 136, 153
  see also triumph, triumphalism
Constans II (emperor) 56, 118, 120
Constantine I (emperor) 20, 22, 51, 74, 138
Constantine VII Porphyrogenitus (emperor) 62
Constantine IX Monomachus (emperor) 175
Constantine X Doukas (emperor) 179
Constantine Harmenopoulos, *Hexabiblos* 170, 172–3, 175
Constantinople 22 n.3, 31, 32, 51, 53, 55–6, 66 n.87, 78, 82, 100, 103, 108–9, 114–15, 117–20, 122, 124, 175, 179 n.37
Constantius Chlorus (emperor) 51–2
Corinth 82, 99, 108–9, 153
corruption (idea of) 52, 60, 141
Crete 57–8, 61, 100, 103, 108, 145 n.45, 160
Cyclades 5, 8, 61, 88, 90, 92, 99–100, 102–9, 159, 167
Cyprus 53, 57–8, 61, 66 n.84, 73, 90, 98, 100–3, 115–25, 128 n.101, 154, 158, 164 n.60

danger, *see* risk
Delos 7, 62, 104–6, 109, 156, 158, 161, 164 n.51
Demosthenes 143 n.8–9, 160, 165 n.69–70
Dexippus, *see* Herennius Dexippus (historian)
Dhaskalio (Keros) 88, 91, 96
Digesta 6, 9 n.20, 134–5, 137, 135, 139, 141, 143 n.2, n.5, 144 n.28–30, 145 n.50, 146 n.63, n.69–71, n.73, 147 n.75, n.77, n.79, 148 n.97, n.99, n.101, n.106, 165 n.70, 167–73, 175, 176 n.3, n.9, 177 n.12, n.20, 178 n.24–5, n.28, 180 n.63
Diocletian (emperor) 14, 137
Diodorus Siculus 15, 23, 148
Domus dei Dioscuri (Ostia) 72
Dordogne (river) 41
dromon 57
Dura Europos (near mod. Al-Salihiyah) 83

Egrilii (*gens*) 73
Egypt, Egyptian xiii, 14, 19, 24 n.29, 57–8, 75, 78, 83, 99, 117–18, 121, 123–4, 149, 152–4, 160, 168, 178 n.30
Egyptian cults 75, 83
elites 4, 49, 50, 53, 71–2, 84, 116, 120, 122–3
Emporia 78–9, 101, 105
environment(al)
  contested 3, 50, 59, 62
  impact of human societies 14, 36, 41–2, 53, 59–60, 68, 71, 115, 142
  interactions 2, 4–5, 63, 88, 90, 114–16, 120–2, 124, 126, 139
  lived, experienced 3, 6–8, 36, 56, 149
  metaphors 2–3, 35, 50–2, 58–63, 67
  perceptions, imagined 1–4, 16, 26, 31–2, 36–7, 43–4, 50–7, 59, 61–3, 169
Ephesus (near mod. Selçuk) 74, 93, 99, 100, 107–8, 158
Euboea 105
Eudaimon of Nicomedia 167–70, 175
euploiai inscriptions 92–3, 108
Eusebius of Caesarea 20
Eusebius Scholasticus 51, 64
Exarchate of Ravenna, *see* Ravenna
Expositio totius mundi et gentium 52, 64 n.31, 67 n.90, 116, 126 n.30

Fabii (*gens*) 73
Flavius Fravitta (*magister militum*) 51
folklore, folk wisdom 39, 54, 159
Fortuna (personification) 74
Fortunatianus (rhetorician) 139, 147
freedmen, *liberti* 74–5
fresh water 16, 22, 29, 41–2, 47 n.90, 81, 149, 154

Gades (mod. Cádiz) 79, 160
Gaia 29
Gaïnas (*magister militum*) 51, 55
Gaius (jurist) 9, 138, 144 n.28, 146 n.62–3, 147 n.75, 176 n.9
Galen (medical writer, doctor) 74, 85 n.33
Gallienus (emperor) 53
Gargilius Iulianus, Q. (*qui et* Semelius) 80
Garni (Armenia) 42
Gaul, Gaulish 36, 40–2, 48 n.107, 76–8, 145 n.46

Index

Geiseric (ruler) 55–6, 60–1
Germania, Germany 26–7, 31, 34–5, 39–43, 46, 51, 84, 145
Germanicus (Elder, Younger) 18, 25 n.39
Goths, Gothic 53, 56, 61, 63, 65–6, 82, 136
graffiti 75, 80, 122, 152–3
Gratian (emperor) 140
Greece (region) 31, 54, 58, 62, 65, 99, 107
Green Man (personification, character) 29–32, 43
Gregoriopolis (Ostia) 81
Grotius, Hugo 143, 145, 175–6

Hadrian (emperor) 135, 173–4, 176 n.9
Hamilcar Barca 13, 18, 24
Hannibal Barca 18, 26
harbours, ports 3, 52, 71–7, 79–83, 85, 90–2, 95, 98, 105–9, 116–19, 157–61, 164, 168, 178
Hellenistic era 2, 14–17, 20, 22, 23 n.25, 36, 49, 88, 92, 95–6, 103–8, 118–19, 159, 169, 173, 178 n.29–30
Heracles, Hercules 20, 25, 31, 48
Heraclius (emperor) 114
Herculaneum 29–30
Herennius Dexippus (historian) 53–4, 65 n.47, n.51
Heruli 53
Hesiod, *Theogony* 15, 29, 45 n.22
Hesperides 29, 42
Hippolytus (mythical figure) 103
Historia Augusta 54, 67 n.90, 145 n.56–7
Homer 8, 9 n.36, 63, 92, 117, 143 n.9
Horace 27, 44 n.3, n.7, 145 n.39
hostels 72, 75, 77
hybrid beasts, *see* monster, sea monster
Hyginus 9, 15, 23

Ibiza 160
Icaria 167, 176 n.4
IKEA 26
Illyrian Wars 49
Index Florentinus 167
infrastructure 5, 81, 90, 92, 95, 105–6
innovation 1, 7, 9, 149
inscriptions, epigraphy 13, 15–16, 23 n.21, n.23, 34–5, 38, 51, 64 n.25, 65 n.49, 67, 71–80, 82, 84 n.19, n.23, n.30, n.32, 85 n.52, n.62, n.65–6, n.69, 86 n.90–1, n.106, n.108, 87 n.124, n.131, 92–3, 100, 107, 118, 121, 123, 134, 136, 143 n.8, n.15, n.144 n.24, 145 n.39, n.56, 161, 165 n.75, n.78, 167, 180 n.61
Ionian Islands 62
Ios 108
Isauria 59
Isidore of Seville 57, 62, 67, 178
islands

as environments 5, 7–8, 20, 55, 58, 61, 67, 98, 100–8, 114–17, 120–5
as threshold environments 115
resilience 5, 81, 106–7, 115, 120–1, 123, 125
small islands 5, 62, 88–90, 95–6, 98, 105–9, 118
Isola Sacra of Ostia 28, 76, 78–82
Istrus, Istria (city) 53
Italia, Italy, Italian 31, 38, 72, 78, 96, 160
Italica (city) 72
Italica (person) 72, 74

Jacobus de Varagine, *Legenda Aurea* 14, 22–3 n.7
Janus (divinity) 114
Jerome (ecclesiastical writer, saint) 74–5
Jews, Judaism 65, 75, 83, 93
John the Baptist 43
Josephus (historian) 18, 24 n.34, 65 n.37, 145 n.47, 160, 165 n.71
Joppa (Jaffa/Yafo) 18
Judaea 18, 145 n.47
Jupiter 49, 74
Jupiter Dolichenus 83
Justinian, Justinianic 21, 54–6, 60–1, 67, 114–15, 117, 126, 139–40, 169, 175
Justinianic Plague 115, 126
Juvenal 44, 77, 86

Karpas Peninsula (Cyprus) 119
Karpathos 62
Kastro Apalirou (Naxos) 88, 101
Kato Kouphonisi 89, 90–1, 95–6, 98–100, 104, 108
Keros 88–90, 95–6, 98, 100, 104, 108, 110
Khosrow (Sassanid ruler) 13, 20–2
knowledge, epistemic templates 3, 5, 7, 39, 49, 53, 55, 145 n.55, 159
Kos 98, 105, 107, 112, 164
Kythnos 156, 164

Laestrygonians 9, 49
lamp(s) 99–101
lamprey 41–2, 44, 47–8
Late Antique Little Ice Age (LALIA) 115, 126 n.15
Lateran basilica 74
Lateranus (consul) 77
Latium 71
legitimation, legitimacy 15, 19, 21, 23, 49, 120, 134, 178
Leo I (emperor) 56
Leptis Magna 14
Levantine 14–15, 17, 19–20, 22–3, 57, 121, 123, 158
Lex Rhodia 6, 167–76, 178
liburna 51
Libya 37, 48, 99
Licinius (emperor) 20, 22 n.3, 51
Lixus (Morocco) 42

211

Index

lobster, crustacean 3, 27–30, 32–3, 37–9, 41, 45 n.15, 46 n.52, n.60, 48 n.93, n.97
Lombards 68, 82
Lucius Verus (emperor) 173
Lugal–Zaggesi (Akkadian king) 23 n.17, n.21
Lusitania (province) 79, 160
Lusius Rufus, Q. 78
Lycia 65, 105, 117, 119, 127

Ma'arrat al-Nu'man (Syria) 42
Macedonia, Macedonian 1, 16, 24, 57, 124, 173
Malta 75, 114–15, 120, 123–4
Marcian (jurist) 136, 145, 148
Marcus Aurelius 54, 72, 177
mare nostrum 49, 50, 59, 124, 143
Martin I (pope) 108–9
Megara 161
Melqart 20, 24 n.31
Mercury (divinity) 34
Mesopotamia 13–16, 21, 23 n.17, n.19, 57, 83
Michael, archangel 13, 20, 22 n.3
Michael Attaleiates, *Ponema Nomikon* 170, 173, 175
Michael VII Doukas (emperor) 171, 179 n.37
Middle Ages 13, 14, 19, 22 n.7, 31, 43, 47 n.80, 74, 81, 88–90, 95, 101–2, 105, 107, 114–15, 120, 124–5, 126 n.15, 176 n.2
migration 4, 71–3, 75–7, 79–83, 121
Mildenhall Treasure 31, 47 n.68
Milos 92, 106
Minoan(s) xiv, 152–3
Misenum 78, 80
Mithras, *mithraeum, -a* 83
mobility, travel 2–5, 7, 26, 43, 52, 54, 62, 71–5, 77–83, 84 n.5, 92, 101–3, 107–9, 115, 118–19, 121–3, 125, 150, 152, 154, 158–9, 174, 177 n.19
Mogontiacum (mod. Mainz) 35
molluscs 37, 39
Monica (saint) 74
monster, sea monster 1, 14–15, 17–18, 26, 31, 40–1
Monte Testaccio 102
Montréal-du-Gers 36
mosaics 26–48, 61, 64 n.9, 72, 75–7, 119, 153
Moses 24 n.34, 48
morals 52, 59, 63, 117, 135
moray eel 27–9, 37–42, 44 n.7–8, n.10, 45 n.15, 46 n.61, 47 n.82, n.90, 48 n.93, n.97–8
Mount Casius (Kasios) 14
Muʿāwiyah (caliph) 57–8, 66 n.87
Murecine Tablets 160
murena, see moray eel
mythology 2–3, 13–22, 26–7, 29–31, 37, 40, 42, 46 n.60, 50, 174

Naoussa Bay (Paros) 97, 101, 156
naturalistic depictions 27–8, 38

nature (social construct) 2, 8 n.5, 15, 50, 53, 58–61, 63, 92, 140, 169
navicularii 76–7, 85 n.58, 140
navigation, sailing, shipping 4–7, 8 n.12, 35, 49–52, 54, 57, 60–3, 64 n.11, 75, 77–8, 80, 90, 92, 96, 100, 102–10, 115–21, 124–5, 134–5, 140, 149–62, 163 n.19–22, n.28, n.31, 164 n.47, n.60, 169–71, 180 n.63
Naxos 5, 89–90, 92–3, 95, 97–101, 103–4, 107–10
Near East xiii–xiv, 15, 24 n.28–9, 82
Neolithic era xiii, 81, 89
Neptune 30, 36–7, 43, 44 n.4, 47 n.70, 49, 74
Nereids 30–1, 72
Nereus 173–4
Nero (emperor) 30, 173–4, 180 n.60
Nicomedia (mod. İzmit) 74, 78, 137, 167–8
Niketas (*archon kai druggarios*) 124
Nikopolis (Epirus Vetus) 31, 66 n.60
Nomos Rhodion Nautikos, see Rhodian sea law
Nonnus of Panopolis 20
North Africa xiii, 14, 32, 35–8, 40–2, 48 n.105, 54–7, 60–1, 72–4, 76–7, 80, 82, 96, 99–100, 106, 114, 117, 160
North African Keay 61 and 62 (ceramic) 96, 99
North Sea 145
Northern Italy 58, 62
Novellae (compilation) 66 n.68, 171
numinosity of the sea 49–50
Nur-Dagan (Hittite king) 15
nymphaeum, -a 3, 26, 30–1, 47 n.83

Oceanus (a person) 74
Oceanus (personification, divinity) 26, 29–44, 45 n.28, n.31, n.41–2, 46 n.44, n.46, n.49–50, n.52, n.61, n.67–8, 47 n.70, n.82–3, 48 n.99–100, n.103, n.107–9
octopus, cephalopods 27–8, 38–41, 48 n.93, n.97
Odyssey, see Homer
Olbia 53
Oppian, *Halieutica* 39, 45 n.14, 47 n.80
Orbe (town in Switzerland) 30
ORBIS (online project, model) 102–3, 107–8
orbis terrarum (concept) 51–2
Orientalism 22
Orontes (river) 33
Orosius 57, 60, 65 n.45, 67 n.101, n.103, n.106
Ostia 4, 28, 30, 33, 39–40, 44 n.4, 46 n.68, 71–83, 84 n.19, 85 n.58, 87 n.110, n.132, 160, 168, 180 n.63
Ovid 9 n.35, 15
oysters, shellfish 27, 39

Pacific 149, 156, 163 n.10
Palestine (region) 57, 75, 99–100, 121
Palmyrene deities 83
Pammachius 74

Index

Pamphylian Sea/Gulf of Antalya 2, 16, 18, 24 n.34
Pan 31, 37
Pannonia (province) 76
Panormos (Naxos) 89, 92, 94–100, 104, 108–10
Paphos (Cyprus) 118, 121, 164
Papinian (jurist) 168
Paros 7, 95, 97–8, 101, 106, 108, 112 n.58, 156, 158, 164 n.51
Patras 82, 99
Paul (jurist), *Pauli Sententiae* 136, 138–9, 144 n.30, n.36, 146 n.70, 147 n.75, 176 n.3, n.9
Paulina (person) 74
Pausanias 18, 65 n.49
peace, pacification 4, 6, 14, 21, 51, 58, 67 n.117, 114–15, 121, 133, 135, 145 n.39, 178 n.30
Peloponnese 104–5
peregrini 72, 76
Pergamon, the Great Altar of 29
periploi 7, 103
Persia
    Achaemenid 13, 16, 23 n.24, 24 n.34–5, 54
    Sassanid 13, 20–2, 57–8
personifications 3, 14–6, 29–31, 36–7, 42–4, 50, 74, 116
Pertinax (emperor) 173–4
Petra (Jordan) 42
Phileatine Lake, Derkos/Delkos (mod. Derkoz Gölü) 53
Phocaean Fine Ware 118
Piazzale delle Corporazioni 76–7
pilgrimage, pilgrims 74, 115–16, 118–19, 121, 125
piracy 6, 36, 49–50, 52–4, 59, 64 n.19, 65 n.36, n.39, n.56, 66 n.66, 115, 134–6, 137, 142, 143 n.11, 144 n.18–19, 145 n.39, n.43, n.47, 163 n.11
Piraeus 158–60, 164 n.60
Pliny the Elder 23 n.24, 41, 44 n.8, 45 n.14, 64 n.5, n.11, 143 n.5, 145 n.39
Pliny the Younger 72, 84 n.7, n.9
Polybius 18, 24 n.33, 64 n.6, 143 n.5, n.8–9, n.15, 178 n.28
Pompeii 27, 29, 30–1, 45 n.17, 152, 160
Pompeius, Sextus 145 n.39
Pompey, Cn.Pompeius Magnus 49–50, 52, 145 n.47
Populonia 28
Porphyrogennetan *Excerpta* 54, 65 n.51–2, n.55, 66 n.64
Porta Laurentina 80
Porta Romana 81
Portus 4, 71–83, 85 n.46, 86 n.83
Poseidon 16, 19–20, 23 n.25
power-projection, propaganda, political mythologies 4, 6, 15–16, 19–21, 23 n.21, n.25, 25 n.39, 49, 52–5, 61, 114, 116–17, 120–3, 133–5, 142, 178 n.23, n.32

praefectus
    annonae 140, 168; *see also annona*
    Aegypti 168
    orae maritimae 176 n.9
    praetorian prefect 72, 140
    urbi 72–3
Praeneste (mod. Palestrina) 27, 72
Priscus of Panium (historian) 56, 66 n.64, n.70
Proconnesian marble 118
Procopius 20–1, 55–6, 61, 66 n.70, n.72–3, 67 n.115, n.117
Prudentius 83–4, 87 n.134, 98 n.134
(Pseudo-)Callisthenes 1
(Pseudo-)Hyginus 9 n.35, 15, 23 n.14
Pseudo-Methodius 58
publican, *publicani* 139, 147 n.82–3, 167, 176 n.6–7
Punic Wars 49, 56, 66 n.71, 142
Pupienus (emperor) 35
Puteoli 78, 82, 150
Pylades, M. Aurelius (pantomime artist) 75

Quaestura exercitus (administration) 108–9, 117
Quodvultdeus of Carthage (bishop) 60

Ravenna 43, 48 n.108, 61
Red Sea 18, 24 n.34, 155, 164 n.40
Republican period, Roman 27, 49–50, 55, 60, 73, 134–5, 142
rhetoric 4, 50–3, 55, 59, 65 n.39, 67 n.110, 139, 169
Rhine 40, 51
Rhodes 53, 57–8, 98, 104–6, 108–9, 158, 161, 169
Rhodian sea law 167, 169–75, 178 n.29, n.31, 180 n.63
risk, danger 1–4, 7, 36, 42, 50–1, 53–6, 59–63, 92, 96, 117, 141, 146 n.58, 168, 174
Romanitas 40
Romano-Celtic 34, 36
Rome (city) 55, 61, 71–83, 102, 108, 117, 147 n.92, 160, 174
Rubrii (*gens*) 74
Rutilius Namatianus 61, 67 n.111, n.114

sacrifice, offering 16, 21
San Vitale (Ravenna) 61
Santa Aurea Basilica (Ostia) 74
Santorini, Thera 100, 108, 153
sailing rig 78, 106, 149–57, 163 n.21, 164 n.45, n.53
Saint George (saint) 2, 13–14, 19–20, 22, 25 n.47
Saint-Émilion (Gironde) 41
Saint Menas (saint) 118
Saint Peter's Basilica 74
Saint-Romain-en-Gal (Rhône) 40, 47 n.85
salmon 27
Salus (personification) 74
Samos 99–100

213

Index

Samos Cistern type (ceramics) 96, 99
Sardinia (island), Sardinia et Corsica (province) 76–7, 82, 114–16, 120–3, 125, 128 n.101
Sargon of Agade (Akkade) 13, 15, 17, 23 n.17, n.19, n.21
Saxons 136, 145 n.58
Sbeitla (Tunisia) 41
Schinoussa 88
Scythians 53–4, 65 n.47
Scythopolis (Palestine) 75
seafaring, *see* navigation
seafloor 1–2, 90, 95, 97
Sea of Marmara 58, 107
seasons, seasonality 4–5, 7, 8 n.12, 22, 24 n.29, 50, 71, 75, 90, 149–50, 154, 158–9, 163 n.8
Seleucia Pieria 21, 52
senate, senators 72–4, 140, 174, 176 n.9, 178 n.30, 179 n.37, 180 n.60
Seneca 44 n.8, 48 n.93, 77, 86 n.73
Septimius Severus (emperor) 32, 77, 83, 145 n.53–4, 173
Serapis 83
Severan period 77, 141, 145
Sextii (*gens*) 73
sexualized imagery 53, 58
shellfish, *see* oysters, shellfish
ships 1, 3, 6–7, 25 n.37, 42, 52–4, 56–7, 59–60, 62, 75–6, 78–80, 82, 92, 95–7, 100, 105, 107–9, 119, 121, 135, 138–41, 144 n.18, 145 n.47, 149–62, 163 n.8, n.17, n.19, 164 n.45, 168, 178 n.29
shipwrecking 6, 133–42, 143 n.5
shipwrecks
   Barthélemy B 79
   Cabrera III 79, 145 n.41
   Cavalière 79
   Culip IV 79
   Dramont E 162
   Embiez Ouest 78
   Fig Tree Bay 119, 121
   Ius naufragii 133–5, 137, 139–42, 176 n.2
   Kyrenia, Kyrenia II (replica) 155, 158, 161, 164 n.60
   Madrague de Giens 78, 152
   Marzamemi 'Church wreck' 118
   Serçe Limanı 102
   Skerki Bank wrecks 160, 165 n.68
   Tantura 121
   Uluburun 160, 162, 165 n.66
   Yassiada (Yassi Ada) 102, 152, 162
Sicilia, Sicily 27, 38, 44 n.10, 56, 58, 61, 100, 114, 117–18, 120, 122, 160
Sidon (city) 23, 152
Sidonius Apollinaris 55, 66 n.71
Silenus 31
Sinis (Sardinia) 122
slave, slavery 41, 58, 62, 71, 74–5, 77, 79, 82, 115, 125, 135
Slavs 62–3, 173
Smyrna (mod. Izmir) 107
Spain, Hispania 42, 48 n.98, 72, 160
Stadiasmus of the Great Sea 92, 102–7, 116, 126 n.27
stars, constellations 7, 16–17, 24 n.28–9, 29
Statilius, T. (doctor) 74
seals, sigillography 17, 115, 122–4, 152, 174
Stoechades 61
storm(s) 7, 14–17, 19–22, 59–61, 67 n.102, 92, 135, 146 n.58, 169
Strabo 2, 8 n.7, 16, 18, 64 n.5, 144 n.23, 145 n.39, 148 n.110, 178 n.28
Suetonius 18–19, 25 n.37, 51, 64 n.20–2, 145 n.39, 160, 165 n.71, 180 n.60–1
Switzerland 27, 31
Sykhada (Cyprus) 119
Symmachus 72, 83, 84 n.16
Synopsis Minor (compilation) 170–3, 175, 179 n.42, n.53
Syracuse 56, 120
Syria 14–20, 23 n.25, 33, 42, 58–9, 73, 75, 83, 119, 121
Syriac 19
Syros 92–3, 156

Tacitus 26, 44 n.3, 64 n.7, 145 n.45–7, 160, 165 n.71, 180 n.60–1
Tantura (Palestine) 121
Tarraco (mod. Tarragona) 39, 41, 47 n.78, 82
taxation 58, 106, 120–4, 139, 149, 161, 167, 176 n.7
technology 1–2, 7, 54, 78, 109, 149, 152–3, 162
terra marique formula 36, 49, 51, 55, 144 n.26
Tethys (divinity) 42
Thalassocracy 64 n.5, n.16, 55, 60, 66 n.71, 115, 126 n.14
Tharros (Sardinia) 123
Thasos 161
Theodore of Tarsus (archbishop of Canterbury) 58, 66 n.86
Theodoric the Great 43, 56
Theodosius I (emperor) 51, 140
Theodosius II (emperor) 55, 66 n.69, 160
Theophanes (chronicler) 55, 66 n.62, n.69–70, 122
Theophrastus (philosopher) 150
Thessalonica 108, 172
Thrace 56, 73, 76
Thuburbo Maius 30
Tiber (river) 4, 71, 76, 80–1, 83
Tiberius (emperor) 25 n.39, 165 n.71, 173–4, 180 n.60
Tomis (city) 53
topography 8, 59, 90, 92, 95, 116, 154
topos, topoi 2, 4, 27, 41, 48 n.93, 50, 58, 60–1, 67
Torba (Caria) 119

Toscana 61
trade, merchants xiii, 6–7, 36–7, 49, 52–4, 61–2, 71, 76–9, 80, 82–3, 87 n.110, 88–90, 97–8, 100–2, 105–9, 115, 117, 119,122–5, 134–5, 141, 148 n.99, n.101, 149, 152–3,159–62, 168, 173, 175, 176 n.1, n.7, 177 n.11, 180 n.63
Trajan (emperor) 72–3, 79, 173–4, 180 n.62
Trebatius 49–50
Triton(s) 30, 37
triumph, triumphalism 1–4, 13–18, 21–2, 23 n.19, n.21, 24 n.35, 44 n.4, 49–51, 55, 57, 59, 61, 63, 83, 114, 136, 142, 178 n.30
Tunisia (country), Tunis (city) 26, 30, 32, 37–8, 44 n.5, 47 n.83, 99, 106, 124
Tyre (city), Tyrians 20, 24 n.35, 57, 158–9
Tyrrhenian Sea 123–4, 160

Ugarit 14–15, 19, 25 n.47
Ulpian (jurist) 135–6, 139, 141, 143 n.5, 144 n.28–9, 36, 146 n.69, n.71, n.73, 147 n.75, n.77, n.79, 148 n.97, n.99, n.101, 176 n.9
Umayyads xiii, 57, 61, 116, 120, 122–3, 125
universalism 29, 50–1, 55, 170, 173, 175–6, 178 n.24, 178 n.32
Uranus 29
Urbanus, M. Munatius Sulla 35

Valentinian (emperor) 140
Valerius Faltonius 72
Valerius Serenus, C. 83
Valerius Veturius, *civis Afer* 82
Vandals 54–6, 59–61, 63, 65 n.54, 66 n.71, 82, 87 n.121, 114, 117, 126 n.38, 136

Vegetius 59
Velleius Paterculus 50, 64 n.5, n.18
Venerianus (naval commander) 54
Venice 62
Venus 29, 37, 72
Verulamium (mod. St Albans) 33–6, 46 n.49–50
Vespasian (emperor) 173–4
Victor Vitensis (bishop) 60
'*Vienna Dexippus*' 53–4
Villa di Baccano 32–3
Virgil 29, 45 n.24
Visigoths 82, 136
Vitalian (*magister militum*) 52
Volusianus (Augustine's correspondent) 74
Volusianus (*vir clarissimus*) 72
Volusius Maecianus (jurist) 167–71, 175

warehouse 77–8, 81, 110, 124
warfare, naval 49–52, 54–9, 61, 63, 65 n.34, n.50, 66 n.74, 114–15, 121, 123, 126 n.13, 178 n.30
wealth, profit 1, 6, 36–7, 58, 72, 116–17, 119, 124, 141, 147 n.78, 148 n.101, 161
Willibald of Wessex 121
wind(s) 7, 24 n.33, 56, 59, 92, 95–6, 149–59, 161–2, 163 n.20, 164 n.45, n.49, n.51 n.60

Xerxes 23

Yamm (Levantine sea god) 15, 17
Ygeinos (*pansophos*) 74

Zeus 15, 19–20, 22 n.3, 25 n.47
Zosimus (historian) 53, 64 n.27, 65 n.43–4, 74, 145 n.56–7

www.ingramcontent.com/pod-product-compliance
Lightning Source LLC
Chambersburg PA
CBHW062218300426
44115CB00012BA/2118